W9-BSZ-184

Vesco

VESCO

Robert A. Hutchison

PRAEGER PUBLISHERS
New York • Washington

Published in the United States of America in 1974
by Praeger Publishers, Inc.
111 Fourth Avenue, New York, N.Y. 10003

Library of Congress Cataloging in Publication Data

Hutchison, Robert A   1938–
  Vesco.

  1. Vesco, Robert.
HV6766.V48H87   364.1′63′0924   [B]   73-8399
ISBN 0-275-19860-X

Printed in the United States of America

Contents

A section of photographs follows page 184.

Vesco

1

The Biggest Swindle

Presenting Robert Vesco, a financial wizard who decided at an early age to become rich, famous, and one of the most powerful men alive ⌣ How he stumbled upon Investors Overseas Services (IOS) ⌣ Reference is made to some of his stepping stones, including several Nixons, a curlicue to Watergate, and an array of pocket politicians from many lands

Robert Lee Vesco, the son of a Detroit auto worker, always wanted to be rich and famous and one of the most powerful men alive. He certainly became wealthy by looting Investors Overseas Services, the world's largest offshore mutual fund complex, of $500 million. As an international wheeler-dealer, and later a fugitive from justice, he achieved fame—although notoriety is a better word. However the power he craved eluded him entirely.

In a few short years Vesco, or "Big Bobby" as the hefty, beady-eyed financier was sometimes called by his dedicated staff of co-conspirators, rose from obscurity as the founder and president of a Fairfield, New Jersey, manufacturer of pneumatic valves and specialized machinery to become the largest international swindler of our time. In addition to plundering IOS, he:

- attempted to bribe, and then threaten, President Richard Nixon
- tried—with some success—to put the governments of Costa Rica and the Bahamas in his pocket
- became the subject of more extradition requests from more countries than anyone else in recent history
- once in command of such an impressive sum as $500 million, was barred from operating in the major financial centers of the Western world, which he had so ardently hoped to dominate

I

Despite the trappings of great wealth, the illusions of influence and power, and the means of mobility—including a personal Boeing 707 and a $1.5 million seagoing yacht—by mid-1973 Vesco was a virtual prisoner in two well-guarded retreats in the Bahama Islands and Costa Rica.

Vesco, an egocentric whiz kid with a talent for deception and intrigue, started his business career at sixteen as an auto mechanic, later becoming a junior draftsman and working his way up to sales engineer of aluminum products before hitting the road to personal fortune at twenty-four as a nickle-and-diming entrepreneur. He was a great success. With a mind like a calculator and the sharp eye of a financial opportunist, it wasn't long before he burst into the world of million-dollar checks, thousand-dollar-a-plate dinners at political fund-raising events, and rendezvous with heads of state, bigtime Mafia *capos,* and ranking Cabinet ministers.

Vesco mastered the art of debt financing early in his career, producing as his springboard to high finance a highy leveraged, little-known conglomerate by the name of International Controls Corporation, with headquarters alongside a small private airport at Fairfield, New Jersey. After little more than three years of conglomerateering, Vesco had produced a rickety, cash-tight combine that owned a country wide grab bag collection of two dozen manufacturing concerns whose sales had risen from $1.3 million to a peak of $101 million annually.

As the architect of International Control's impressive growth, Vesco was held in awe by a small clique of operators in and around Wall Street. But Vesco, who was proud of his financial agility, wanted international recognition. He chaffed under the heavy regulation of the U.S. capital markets by agencies like the Securities and Exchange Commission (SEC) and naturally drifted toward the regulatory vacuum of the offshore world. A sudden crisis at IOS, the huge Swiss-based mutual fund empire founded by the Brooklyn-bred financier Bernie Cornfeld, provided Vesco with the perfect opportunity.

IOS, in an incredibly short fifteen-year lifespan, had elbowed its way up the growth ladder to occupy a place among the major financial institutions of the world. The IOS group of companies had developed into a labyrinthine network of more than 250 corporate entities tied through clever legal structuring to a semi-amorphous parent holding company that was registered eventually as a nonresident Canadian corporation. But, except for a few surface comparisons, similarities between IOS and other large public corporations were non-existent. For even though IOS gave the impression that it was managed like most other multinationals and was subject to the same operating restrictions, the group's management structure was largely illusory when it came to the use and control of corporate power. And this was a structural flaw that Vesco knew how to exploit.

Cornfeld, Vesco quickly realized, was not an ordinary businessman but essentially a merchandiser of dreams. And dreams are fine in rising markets, but once the wave has crested and the markets begin to slide loyalties are almost instantly repegged to more material standards.

Cornfeld would ask the same questions, only more subtly phrased, of associates and clients. "What are your financial objectives in life?" IOS salesmen were trained to ask prospective investors. "A house? A college education for your kids? A yacht on the Mediterranean or a villa in Spain? By placing money each month in an IOS Investment Program you can achieve your financial goals," the prospect was told.

Cornfeld would ask the same questions, only more subtly phrased, of his salesmen. By selling well they earned the right to acquire IOS stock. "The way that this stock keeps doubling you can't afford not to exercise your option," Cornfeld was fond of saying. And behind every IOS operation was a pyramiding get-rich notion that was all-consuming.

Effective power inside the organization was concentrated in Cornfeld's hands and in the hands of two other individuals he had brought with him to the top of the IOS beanhill—Edward Cowett, the general counsel, who became IOS's president and self-described chief operating officer, and Allen Cantor, the sales chief. This triumvirate shared a common vision of what IOS was really all about. They translated their vision into projects for development and gave the orders that were necessary for IOS's day-to-day operations.

Perhaps the best example of how this vision worked was given to four hundred of the company's top sales captains in August 1969 in Geneva. A giant $110 million public offering of IOS common stock, the largest equity underwriting in European history, was only six weeks away. The importance of this underwriting was explained by the triumvirate to the almost breathless sales managers, who would afterward return to their respective sales areas around the world and spread the good word about the IOS stock to the people working under them in the IOS sales structure.

The first speaker on the rostrum was trim and silky Cornfeld, full of charm and charisma. His keynote address to the conference, held in the ballroom of Geneva's largest hotel, set the theme for the free-ranging euphoria that was to characterize IOS operations for the next half-year or so until disaster finally struck.

"In the process of growing," Cornfeld told the managers, "our company has become extremely profitable, and you, as stockholders, have shared in this wealth. More than one hundred members of the firm have become millionaires and many more will reach this goal in the few years ahead."

The sales people loved Bernie. Always on such occasions he was electric, emotive, highly attractive in his element. They cheered and applauded him, gave him a standing ovation, and later, as he walked down the aisle to leave the flag-decked ballroom, rushed over to shake his hand and pat him on the back of his mod-style suit. When Cornfeld told them they would become rich, they believed him.

For weeks prior to the conference, the middle member of the triumvirate, Ed Cowett, had been working out the details of the extremely complicated underwriting. Cool and confident Cowett, then not yet forty, with pointed black beard and round professorial glasses, looked like Mephistopheles and was one of the sharpest securities lawyers around. It was really Cowett, working in Cornfeld's shadow, who developed the offshore concept to its highest degree of perfection.

Cowett explained to the managers, "There are very few companies in the world that will make the kind of money that we will make this year, next year, and in the years to come. By permitting people from the outside world to share in, and benefit from, that profitability [through floating off 11 million IOS common shares to the public], we will be assisting our own growth and our own ability to realize greater profitability in the future."

"IOS is reaching for the moon," was a popular saying at the time. "Our sales are going sky high!" To prove it the company had just completed the most successful six-week sales contest in its history, the IOS Space Explorers Contest, with 15,000 Astroplanners taking part. "Set all systems on go, and aim high. The sky's the limit!" was the launching spiel for the 1969 summer contest, which produced a record face amount of $450 million in sales.

In case anyone really had doubts that the sky was IOS's limit they should have been washed away after listening to Allen Cantor, the third and youngest member of the triumvirate. After twelve years in the business, Cantor even spoke like Bernie, using many of the same stock phrases Cornfeld used and many of the same mannerisms. He also had grown a beard like Bernie, only Cantor's was bushier and flecked with gray. But Cantor, unlike Cornfeld, had difficulty making top-level decisions; he rarely signed a document unless Cowett's signature was already on it. Thought of as a pillar of conservatism by his colleagues, Cantor delivered a talk about the future growth of IOS that was perhaps the most delusionary of all.

"Is it impossible," he asked rhetorically, "that perhaps in ten years from now we will be managing assets of $100 billion?" The reply, of course, was not entirely unexpected. "To the generation that put men on the moon, all things are possible—and history is waiting for someone to do them first."

Cantor brought the conference to a historic close with one last statement of faith, which made all previous ones seem like Boy Scout pledges: "As Bernie said, and as I have said, in the process each and every person here can become a millionaire."

Then, as if that statement were not already incredible enough, he rephrased it in an even more reckless fashion. *"We will all become millionaires, that is for sure,"* Cantor assured the managers. "But what is just as sure is that the enjoyment and the personal growth of becoming a millionaire will far exceed the value of a million dollars. Best of luck, and thank you!"

Not ten years later, as Allen Cantor suggested, but just ten months later—in April 1970—events at IOS took a significant new turning, and the roles of the three bearded wisemen were drastically altered. The company's common stock had come out the previous autumn in an unparalleled rush of speculation. From then on it flopped steadily backward, dropping from a high of $19 until it sunk below the $10 issuing price the following spring, leading to a palace coup d'état that tumbled the triumvirate from power.

Associates and employees who had listened to Cornfeld, Cowett, and Cantor and had purchased large quantities of company paper, often on credit, found themselves financially wiped out. Accounting by-plays of questionable orthodoxy, unauthorized loans, imprudent investments, stock option plan cheating, private offshore trusts, and dubious tax avoidance schemes all had contributed to the collapse.

It was curious to note in the great IOS debacle that followed only two people really understood the nature of the company's problems. One was Bernie Cornfeld, who had lost the confidence of his board of directors and of the financial community at large. The other was Robert Vesco, who spotted in ailing IOS an exceptional opportunity.

When word of the budding crisis in Geneva first reached Vesco that April, he was puzzling over how to raise $2 million to service his company's elaborate debt structure. Although artfully kept hidden from the public, the situation at International Controls had become "very marginal as to whether the company would survive," one of Vesco's directors later admitted. Vesco, however, had programmed away enough reserves and deferred credits so that International Controls's perilous condition would not show up in the financial statements for another year or two. In the meantime he planned to keep the ball rolling with another big acquisition, and the unregulated IOS, even if in some sort of difficulty, offered him an almost perfect takeover target. He immediately began a three-month analysis of the Cornfeld empire, which led to his direct involvement in the ensuing debacle.

When Vesco finally appeared before the IOS board of directors in August 1970 with a strange "rescue" offer, the Geneva boardmen were spellbound by his cool, direct approach. They accepted him for what he purported to be, the "savior" of IOS.

While the directors voted to accept in principle Vesco's offer of assistance, Cornfeld, ousted from the chairmanship of IOS, sat brooding at his Villa Elma lakeside residence less than a mile away. Someone suggested that Vesco should pay Cornfeld a visit. After all, Bernie was IOS's largest shareholder, owning 15 per cent of the preferred stock. And Bernie was threatening a major proxy fight to regain control of his baby. That in itself was about the biggest liability any potential investor in the company faced.

So Vesco called on Cornfeld. He was even invited back to dinner, and Cornfeld, predictably, said Vesco had lousy table manners.

Using more Cornfeldian terms on the day that the IOS founder was locked out of corporate headquarters, Bernie screamed, "That hoodlum Vesco isn't going to touch this company." And he promptly moved to enjoin International Controls from closing its proposed loan agreement with IOS.

Cornfeld, almost in the same breath, explained that he was under-taking his fight to protect the shareholders and fundholders from the threat of a rapacious interloper. And when Cornfeld pronounced that there would be "no deal with Vesco!" it had the same emotional ring behind it as Winston Churchill's stammering, "There will be no peace with Hitler!"

IOS was on the thin rim of disaster. The investments of almost 1 million clients were at stake. Yet everything about the drama was unreal, *Die Götterdämmerung* transformed into a cheap comic operetta. The most incredible point of all, however, was that the authorities in those jurisdictions where a handle existed over IOS—notably Canada and Switzerland—allowed it to continue. And so, in this crazily staged atmosphere, with the world financial press filling some of the best seats in the house, the corporate rape of IOS soon began in earnest.

Vesco, by then well on his way to international infamy as a liar and a cheat, knew exactly how to exploit the mayhem that reigned at IOS, outmaneuvering Cornfeld to place himself in a dominating position in company councils. Then through a further use of deception, a dazzling deployment of two-way mirrors and slick bookkeeping procedures that baffled even the most experienced accountants, and some very tricky financial footwork, he was soon busily at work diverting IOS's assets into what he presumed were legally impenetrable waters—a Sargasso Sea of shell companies, dummy banks, and secret numbered accounts.

In January 1971, before his grand looting scheme was fully operational, Vesco attended a meeting in Geneva of senior IOS sales executives to consider the "challenges and opportunities of the future." Vesco's bluntness in discussing corporate affairs, which some mistook for frankness, still gave him limited credibility in the eyes of many ranking IOS officials.

When asked by one of the hopeful participants at that meeting how he and his team of management "experts" intended to end the wave of bad press reports about the company and its intensifying problems, Vesco responded in characteristic fashion, first pausing to reflect a moment, then commenting in a deep, cadenced drawl that sounded very much like a parody of an airlines captain, "Well—err—um—we have a saying that you can't win a pissing contest with a skunk."

Roars of laughter rolled forth from the thirty-three sales managers, described in the IOS staff newspaper of that week as "truly a fine bunch of men, certainly among the finest," and everybody thought that Bob Vesco was a prince of a fellow. However, their laughter was short-lived. Within a few months the last units of the once mighty IOS sales force were disbanded; the company would never again sell another mutual fund program.

Three years later what remained of IOS was in the hands of court-appointed liquidators. Once the most powerful force in offshore finance, IOS had crumbled into ruins, the victim of Vesco's $500 million corporate rip-off. That was self-help of impressive dimensions, earning Vesco the sobriquet "the Bootstrap Kid." But the impressive thing was not just the money involved, it was the names: Republican names, and Nixon names. This was not, as Nicholas Von Hoffman pointed out in the *Washington Post,* "one of those deals where the Nixon people can claim they just happened to meet the Bootstrap Kid at a cocktail party but they didn't know anything about it. They took part in it. They were on the payroll." [1]

By then Vesco had severed all connections with International Controls and IOS; they had become serious liabilities for him. An attempt to shed his American citizenship was not quite so successful. Declared a fugitive from U.S. justice, and with warrants out for his arrest in Europe as well, he spent millions seeking refuge in any South American country that would have him.

Although better as a manipulator of the abstract, and particularly the

[1] Nicholas Von Hoffman, "Taking Stock of the New American Puritanism," *Washington Post,* March 2, 1973.

more abstruse elements of a balance sheet, Vesco enjoyed wielding influence. And once he became an international financier, naturally he
sought the best influence money could buy. With $200,000 diverted
from an IOS dividend company he made an undeclared contribution to
Richard Nixon's Committee to Re-elect the President in April 1972.
It was, in fact, the largest cash donation received by CREEP. Vesco's
hot-money gift, illegally concealed by the Nixon re-election campaign
under the 1971 Federal Election Campaign Act, was an undisguised
attempt to block a continuing SEC probe into his fraudulent activities.

Ironically, it was this relatively minor item, representing less than
one-half of 1 per cent of the total assets he was accused of plundering,
that brought Vesco his greatest notoriety. Accepted without qualms,
Vesco's secret $200,000 went in CREEP's "currency fund," which bank-
rolled the Republicans' political espionage efforts.

The Vesco contribution, which later he attempted to portray as
"extortion money," became quickly identified as a curlicue to Watergate.
It carried the stench of high corruption and—although belatedly returned—was all the more sordid because it demonstrated just how
easily a determined seeker of influence on the fringe of organized
crime could misuse the American political system to place himself and
others beyond the reach of the law.

The reverberations were great. For the first time since the Teapot
Dome oil-rights scandal of the Harding Administration fifty years before,
two former U.S. Cabinet officers—Attorney General John N. Mitchell
and Commerce Secretary Maurice H. Stans, the leaders of President
Nixon's re-election drive—were indicted by a federal grand jury in New
York on charges of attempting to impede justice, conspiracy, and
criminal perjury.

After a tense forty-eight-day trial, both Mitchell and Stans were
acquitted in April 1974. But it was really Vesco, the exotic exile, who
was on trial in that New York courtroom.

Vesco, his name by then on the front pages of newspapers around the
world, was described by one of the jurors, Clarence Brown, a letter
carrier from Ossining, New York, as "the real culprit . . . using these
people. [He] seemed to want to get something going."

This is the tale of that "something" Vesco wanted to get going. It is
the extraordinary tale of one man's genius for deceit and how his efforts
to achieve that something—the broad fame, great wealth, and power
far beyond the reach of ordinary men—were financed at the expense of
more than 200,000 investors whose savings he transferred into an array
of shell companies created to siphon money out of the IOS group and
into his own pocket.

It is also the tale of how, in concocting his grand looting scheme, he attempted to convey the impression of wanting to assist the authorities while using every hidden ploy available to sabotage their work. It seemed hardly incidental that in planning the looting of IOS Vesco sought to link not only the highest officials of the Nixon Administration but also members of the Nixon family to a cheap conspiracy to defeat justice. In reaching the summit of international roguery, Vesco's web of influence also stretched to the presidential palaces of Spain, Costa Rica, and three other Latin republics; the office of the Prime Minister of the Bahama Islands; the Prince of the Netherlands; and official ministries in a half-dozen other lands around the world.

Vesco flaunted the fact that he was virtually exempt from prosecution because national securities laws, he discovered, cannot be enforced internationally. He based his "success" on the contemptuous reasoning that if he moved fast enough no country could apply its securities regulations. Vesco was riding the crest of a jet-age trend that was transforming even the most regional exchange into an internationally accessible market place. When considered on the face of his achievements, hardly a more eloquent argument existed for the creation of an international securities commission to coordinate and supplement the efforts of national agencies in cases that overflow into several sovereign jurisdictions. After all, he made fact of theory.

2

The Deal-Maker

How a poor boy from Detroit became a wheeling-dealing entrepreneur as the first step in his climb to international notoriety

Robert Vesco had three goals in life when at sixteen he left high school and started work in an East Detroit car repair shop. His first objective, he said, was "to get the hell out of Detroit" and go east where he had been told vast reserves of venture capital were waiting for bright young men like himself to come along and tap. His second goal was to be president of a company—any company. His third was to become a millionaire.

His father, Donald Vesco, American-born of poor Italian immigrant parents, had labored most of his life as an assembly line worker, and later foreman, at the Chrysler plant in Detroit. Young Vesco resented this not so much for what the long hours of hard work meant to his father but for the fact that "every kid wants to have a new car and this and that," and his father couldn't provide it for him.[1]

Standoffish and introverted as a youth, Vesco later said he felt discriminated against because his name ended in a vowel. The only tangible evidence of discrimination, however, came after he moved east to Connecticut when he was refused membership in a somewhat pretentious Darien country club, which he attributed to his Italian background. His mother, née Barbara Sasek, was Yugoslav by birth. He had an older sister who looked after the home when his mother took an office job to help make ends meet.

The Vescos lived on the edge of a factory district in a distinctly working-class neighborhood of predominantly Italian, Jewish, and Negro

[1] Munro Schwebel tapes, No. 2, p. 12. (Author's transcripts provided through private sources.)

families. In this environment Vesco developed the instincts of a junior "operator"; he was twice arrested by the Detroit police, once for loitering in a place of illegal business and the other for driving a stolen car. But in both cases the charges against him were not pressed.

At school he gravitated toward math and calculus. He was accepted at Cass Technical High, one of Detroit's finer high schools, even though it was out of his district. "He and his father would hit the books every night at a table in the kitchen. Sometimes they'd still be poring over them, his father and the boy, at two and three in the morning," a next-door neighbor recalled.[2]

Vesco liked student life at Cass Tech all right, but he didn't last there beyond his sophomore year. Financial pressures forced him to take his first job at sixteen as an apprentice repairman with the Holly Body Shop in Saint Claire Shores. It was knuckle-skinning work.

"We took in cars that were wrecks and we put new fenders on, painted them—that was during the day. At night and on weekends I worked as a driver. Including the moonlighting, I made $50 a week." [3]

Vesco's reminiscences of his early career were for the benefit of Munro Schwebel, a fancy New York public relations promoter with long sideburns, a rounded paunch, and expensive taste in wine, women, and food. Vesco hoped that Schwebel—who had once gypped another of his clients, offshore financier Cornfeld, out of a cool hundred thousand dollars in a race horse tax write-off deal—could gain him some sweet-smelling nationwide recognition as an intrepid financier back in the late 1960s. But Schwebel died suddenly of a heart attack.

Vesco explained how he took one more crack at high school the following year but dropped out of Detroit's Denby High in early 1953, soon after marrying Patricia J. Melzer, a small, plain-faced girl with dark hair, originally from Bad Axe, Michigan. She was sixteen and he was seventeen. Their first son, Daniel, was born later that year.

By then Vesco had gone back to work, this time as a blueprint operator and trainee draftsman at the old Packard Motor Car Company, where he stayed ten months. While with Packard, he said, he took night courses three times a week at Wayne State University as "part of my own internal improvement program to get an engineering background." [4] However, the registrar's office at Wayne State had no record of his attendance.

In May 1954, eighteen-year-old Vesco read a want ad for a junior engineer. The employer was Detroit's Bohn Aluminum & Brass Corporation. Even though not qualified for the position, he applied and got the

[2] *New York Post,* June 12, 1973.
[3] Schwebel tapes, No. 1, pp. 2–3.
[4] *Ibid.,* p. 4.

job. "There was no doubt that there was a questionable lack of background . . . but I thought that after getting in I could perform," he said. And he did just that, demonstrating an early trait that remained with him throughout much of his career. "Bob always performs. He keeps his commitments," said several of his early associates. Some, of course, changed their opinion after watching him shift around IOS's millions twenty years later.

Vesco stayed with Bohn over a year, progressing to the point where he was "physically designing tools and then from there . . . into estimating costs." [5]

The hours he spent at the Bohn plant were long—up to ten and twelve hours a day—apparently necessary when you have to learn as much as Vesco needed to know. And he was earning a flat salary—no overtime —of only $55 a week.

"It was at that point that I decided I wanted to be president of a company. . . . It was very much of a planned thing. What I did was look around and whereas the presidents of other companies were typically engineering or manufacturing type people I felt they should be more marketing and sales oriented. So I quit Bohn and went to work at Reynolds Metals Company" as a project engineer in sales. [6]

Big things happened to Vesco at Reynolds. His salary more than doubled when he joined the company in November 1956, but the $505.50 a month he took home hardly paid the bills. It restricted his wardrobe to a sports jacket and one pair of slacks—he couldn't afford a suit. He was just under twenty—not old enough to buy his customers a drink—although he worked hard at appearing older than he actually was. He grew a mustache to add years to his appearance and started lying about his age.

During the year and a half he remained at Reynolds he struck up a lasting friendship with a more experienced salesman ten years his senior, Richard Evans Clay, who was to become a trusted member of Vesco's inner group during the looting of IOS. A tall, smooth-talking native Virginian raised in Kentucky, he and Vesco immediately put their minds together to concoct an early exploit that became famous in the campaign history of The Bootstrap Kid.

When Bob Vesco first walked into the Reynolds plant the company was concentrating on developing new applications for aluminum in the automotive industry. This was significant because it provided grist for the homespun legend that was fabricated during the middle years of Vesco's success. Vesco claimed he put his engineering talents to work

[5] *Ibid.*, p. 6.
[6] *Ibid.*, p. 9.

on the problem of selling more aluminum to the automobile companies and designed the first aluminum grill ever used by Oldsmobile. It went into service, still according to Vesco, on the 1958 Oldsmobile. A spokesman at Oldsmobile told a reporter that aluminum grills were introduced on production models only in 1966. "But [Vesco] may have worked on an experimental model years ago," the spokesman conceded.[7]

"The idea was to get more pounds of aluminum per car . . . and we found a good way to do that," Vesco explained. Steel grills used to come in separate sections, but Vesco, according to the legend, designed one that was extruded as a single piece of aluminum so that when damaged "you had to pull the whole damn thing out to put in a whole new one, and it ran you three times as much money."

Vesco said he received a measure of recognition for this contribution to the company's future earnings in the form of "a beautiful letter from A. J. Reynolds and a check for $500."

"A special bonus of $500, and Bobby responded by quitting," Clay added.

"I had already made up my mind to leave," Vesco said. "At that point I was looking around and I still wanted to be president. I was looking around at people who were becoming presidents of companies. I was looking more at the financially oriented type of person now that I had the sales engineering background. The next thing to do was to get into something like a staff function . . . so that I could get experience as a general manager running something and being directly responsible for it and [at the same time] getting exposed to the financial community as such." [8]

Following his master plan for self-advancement, in 1957 Vesco shifted to Olin Mathieson Chemical Corporation's regional office in Detroit as an extrusion engineer. Clay tagged along with him. Vesco's starting salary was $750 monthly. Shortly after making the move he was promoted to the post of administrative assistant in the engineering division and transferred to the head office in New York City—exactly what he had counted on. One of his earliest goals was thus achieved.

Vesco stayed with Olin Mathieson—later the Olin Corporation—three years, longer than with any other employer. One of his supervisors at Olin said that Vesco was a "brilliant engineer" but that he possessed certain "irritating personality quirks" and an ego "too large for his age." Physically, Vesco was a colorless person with a tendency toward spreading flaccidity. He stood six-feet-one, weighed about 200 pounds, and had dark, greased-down hair, heavy eyebrows, and small,

---

[7] *New York Post,* June 12, 1973.
[8] Schwebel tapes, No. 1, p. 12.

avaricious eyes that conveyed the impression of eternal wariness. He did not stare at people but coldly peered through them, and his speech was often brutally direct.

He had moved his family east and rented a small frame house in Rowayton, Connecticut, but now he wanted out. He thought $10,560 a year was not fair pay. In fact he felt his superiors at Olin had exploited his services, which by then extended to interdepartmental consulting, and he was indignant because at twenty-four they wouldn't promote him to an executive role.

"Of course, all my ex-bosses and people in less authoritative spots were making two to three times that," he confided with a touch of bitterness.[9] So he decided to strike out on his own as a manufacturers' representative. The reason for his termination was labeled incompatibility.

"I rented a house in New Jersey, where it was a lot cheaper."

"Where?" he was asked.

"In Denville. I borrowed some money from a bank in New York—$2,000 or something like that. It carried me for a few months. I had a 1957 Plymouth. I used to hop in the car Monday morning and come back Saturday night after trying to sell and buy things."

"Was your office your home?"

"No, my car. My car and the telephone booth.

"Fortunately, after not too many months I did make a few measly good put-togethers. I made a deal with a company by the name of Eagle Aluminum Products. Eagle had a plant in Dover, New Jersey. It had a press which was sitting dormant. So I made a deal with them that I would get selling for that press if they would put a crew on, and we would split the profits. I would sell at whatever price I chose and they would figure the cost of making the product. So they hired three or four guys to run the press and I trotted out and got business for it. And as a result made quite a few dollars."[10]

Thus began the first business venture of Robert Lee Vesco as a somewhat-in-debt boy financier and lately discharged extrusion engineer from Olin.

The precocious Vesco, then not yet twenty-five, said he had been contemplating the shift to his new entrepreneurial status for several months and quickly zeroed in on the idle press at Eagle Aluminum Products. Ingeniously, he got a portion of the profits in return for filling up some of Eagle's excess capacity, then took a share of some of Eagle's customers' profits by giving them credit when it was a questionable risk to do so. His stock in trade included storm windows, garage doors, aluminum awnings, aluminum siding, and like products.

[9] *Ibid.,* p. 21.
[10] *Ibid.,* p. 22.

"It was a struggle, but I was my own boss," he told friends years later. He had some calling cards printed up that said he was the president of a company called Aluminum Services Incorporated. ASI was his own creation—little more than a desk in the corner of the front office at the Eagle plant in Dover. It had the same telephone number as Eagle and shared the same secretary.

"I got a few other guys who moonlighted on sales. I had to pay them a commission, but then I had the terrible problem of accounts receivable, because I was in effect selling the product for my own account. And in the course of this some of my receivables went bad. So I took stock instead in the companies that couldn't pay. It was my first taste as an equity owner—generally in losing concerns."

Being a stockholder, even in such obviously shaky enterprises, was more exciting than being a trade creditor, Vesco discovered. It was more of a gamble, and Vesco, an ardent poker player, liked to gamble.

"I could see that if things were successful the value of the stock would go up one heck of a lot faster than the commissions I could make, which were going quite good at that time, I might add."

A meticulous person who made each business decision with the deliberation of a chess player—he boasted of having been a junior chess champion in Detroit, a claim that, like so many others, was never confirmed—he worked according to a carefully prepared master plan. The plan was flexible, with fallback positions, alternate moves, and updated objectives constantly under review.

More and more of his time gradually was spent dealing with the financial and organizational problems of the companies in which he had an equity stake. Eventually he left Aluminum Services and its limited horizons to his friends at Eagle and turned all his efforts to acting as a smalltime country doctor for smalltime ailing corporations.

There are a few key people in Robert Vesco's career without whose help his rise to international prominence would hardly have been possible. Malcolm Evans McAlpin, a patrician-looking brokerage company executive and former chairman of a small Delaware company named All American Engineering, was one of them.

McAlpin, a resident of Morristown, the county seat located ten miles south of Denville in the New Jersey hills, represented the top of the Eastern upper crust for the hungry Detroit hustler. Vesco, who had learned almost everything he knew about social graces in a machine shop, realized some refinement of style was needed if he were to rub shoulders with the financial barons of this world. He was impressed by McAlpin's excellent contacts and smooth sense of business etiquette. So

Vesco set about deliberately to befriend McAlpin, hoping no doubt that some of this practiced suburbanite's suavity would rub off on him.

Perhaps because McAlpin was twenty-eight years older than Vesco a relationship born of mutual fascination eventually developed between the two men. McAlpin presented a welcome father image for the grasping entrepreneur. After all, he knew the lore of Wall Street, had a seat on the exchange, and could introduce his Denville neighbor to many of the fabled Wall Street names that had become essential to young Vesco in his new calling. What's more, McAlpin was one of the few people the impetuous Vesco deferred to on questions of boardroom conduct. Early in their relationship, for instance, McAlpin counseled Vesco never to take a drink at business luncheons. "Let the others drink," he advised. "That's how some of the best deals are made." Vesco always followed this advice.

"Mac," one of his friend recalled, "was a pretty fancy guy. A graduate of Princeton with a splendid home out in the country, swimming pool and tennis court. He drove a Mercedes and always was looking for a quick buck. Mac was very sold on Vesco. He told me to jump if I could get a piece of the action because he said I'd make a lot of money."

McAlpin was in many respects a very "fancy guy." His cars were easily spotted on the winding country roads around Morristown by their distinctive New Jersey license plates—MAC-1, MAC-2, MAC-3, and so on—a gimmick that Vesco soon adopted for his own cars. He impressed guests at his brick home atop a wooded hillock northeast of Morristown by showing them around the grounds, which once had been a winter campsite for George Washington's army.

All American Engineering, Incorporated, was headquartered in Wilmington, Delaware and listed on the American Stock Exchange but never really developed; it plodded along on minor government contracts. "We started looking for small acquisitions and mergers to build it up. In the early 'sixties a friend told me to go out to Caldwell, New Jersey, and have a look at Captive Seal Corporation," McAlpin said in a 1973 interview.

Captive Seal was a tiny, money-losing operation based in Caldwell, some twelve miles east of Morristown. Founded in 1957, it manufactured high-pressure valves, regulators, and switches for use in missile and rocket projects for NASA and the U.S. Navy though "manufactured" is a big word for its operation. Captive Seal had eight people working in a shed out back assembling its miniature valves.

Captive Seal's majority stockholders were asking $2 million in cash for the company, and All American was prepared to offer half a million in AAE stock. "There was just no way that we could see the company being worth that much, so we let it drop," McAlpin said.

However, the person McAlpin discovered running Captive Seal "was this Mr. Vesco, a very charming, bright, and presentable young man." Vesco went down to Wilmington with McAlpin and made a presentation to the All American board. Confidentially he told McAlpin he thought the Captive Seal owners were asking too much for their troubled little company. The All American directors agreed, but they were so impressed with Vesco—then only twenty-seven—that they attempted to steal him away from Captive Seal.

Vesco said he was grateful for the job offer but decided to stick it out with Captive Seal and build the company into a public corporation, adding that maybe one day their two companies could do a deal together.

As a result of his efforts to keep Captive Seal afloat, Vesco had met, and impressed, a sometime financial adviser to the Rothschilds, Dr. Benjamin R. Payne. A New York based promoter, Payne was able to introduce Vesco to a number of European sources of capital, among them Geneva banker Georges Karlweis, righthand man of Baron Edmund de Rothschild. Karlweis was managing director of Banque Privée, a small but active Geneva merchant bank owned by Baron de Rothschild. As it happened Banque Privée held a 50% interest in a small US-based venture capital company that provided the initial funding for Captive Seal. Now the venture capital firm decided to wind up the Caldwell operation as a hopeless case. But Vesco at last saw his opportunity to become president of an operating concern, one he could use as a vehicle corporation for his later high-wire performances.

In the summer of 1965 Vesco approached Captive Seal's silent partners with an offer to purchase all outstanding Captive Seal stock, thereby saving the bank the expense of a winding-up operation. The agreed-upon price of $50,000, payable in five yearly promissory notes, was a far cry from the $2 million previously demanded. Vesco concluded the transaction and next went to see McAlpin to invite him to join the board. "Vesco maintained that he had paid somewhere between $100,000 and $200,000," McAlpin reported.

Vesco was still a very plausible young man, so no one doubted his word as long as the story he told seemed reasonable. Certainly he had just pulled off one of the minor coups of his career by acquiring Captive Seal entirely by use of credit, but this he told no one.

Although not yet apparent, Vesco's practice of deception was rapidly developing. His early use of dupery he might have defended as harmless, as in the case of the line he fed McAlpin, but it demonstrated a fatal flaw in his personality that would mushroom to ugly proportions.

Now that he had launched himself into the acquisition game, Vesco could hardly step back. He had formed the month before a New Jersey company which he grandly named International Controls Corporation, into which he poured all Captive Seal's assets and about $137,000 in liabilities.[13]

The third company upon which Vesco's future empire was founded, and the one that interested him the most, was a nearly defunct Florida concern known as Cryogenics Incorporated. This strange creation, founded six years before, had run into depressing financial problems and was heavily in debt with aggregate losses of about $450,000. Nevertheless, it was a public company, and that was important; its million shares of over-the-counter stock were held by about 800 shareholders. Vesco was interested in acquiring the inexpensive shell of a company that was publicly registered for stock trading purposes. He could therefore use this shell as the vehicle to transform his planned International Controls mini-conglomerate into a public corporation without obtaining authorization to issue securities or going through the complex SEC stock registration and filing requirements. Basically, it was a time-saving convenience for someone like Vesco who was in a terrible hurry. Cryogenics was then put on the shelf until he was ready to bring his three companies together in happy corporate union.

In preparation for that move, Vesco appointed himself president of Cryogenics in December 1965. He had borrowed 51 per cent of Cryogenics's outstanding stock from Western Business Assistance Corporation, a small venture capital firm located in San Francisco. WBAC was only too glad to oblige the innovative architect of intricate financial structures, since WBAC's directors were certain that Cryogenics was nearly bankrupt.

The man behind this easy shifting of Cryogenics stock was a vice-president of WBAC, Richard W. Pershing, who was convinced he had met in Vesco the money genius of the twentieth century. Pershing was soon to become president of Hale Brothers Associates, Incorporated, another San Francisco investment company and the largest shareholder in Broadway-Hale Stores. Hale Brothers had two partners on the boards of Bank of America and Western Bancorporation, respectively the largest bank in the world and the eighth largest bank holding company in the world—important contacts for a rising conglomerate-builder like Vesco.

Vesco also impressed Wilbert Snipes, a Morristown banker who became tremendously important to the New Jersey deal-maker when it came time to carve up the IOS empire. Snipes, then vice-president of the Trust Company of Morris County, must have thought he was in the presence of a real comer. Vesco described for the banker his plans

[13] International Controls Corp. Preliminary Prospectus Dated November 28, 1967, p. 7.

to merge Captive Seal with Cryogenics to produce what he constantly described as his fantastic "money-making machine." Vesco wasn't kidding. With slippery financial reporting he set out to manufacture pneumatic valves and instant income.

Vesco was delighted with Snipes. He angled, schemed, and then decided to work his deception on the Morristown banker. "I took a long shot," he confided afterward. "I popped into [Snipes's] office one day and said, 'I want to bid on this big government contract and I don't have enough money. We think we have the know-how to make it, design it, and everything else if we get you to finance us.'" [14]

Snipes said that was fine. The Trust Company of Morris County loaned International Controls $50,000, half of which Vesco used to purchase a raggle-taggle manufacturer of minor precision products ranging from air turbine dentist drills to five-foot torsion bars for military trucks in Cherry Hill, New Jersey. But more important, said Vesco, "the loan sort of broke the ice" and gave International Controls its first commercial credit rating. The company then claimed a tiny net worth of $320,000 but was growing fast.

Vesco kept on juggling with his cash-tight troika until one week before Christmas 1966, when he called a special meeting of Cryogenics shareholders at the Roosevelt Hotel in New York. Prior to the meeting he had formally concluded the merger of Captive Seal into his International Controls shell. Now he proposed the merger of International Controls, financially the stronger corporation, into the nearly defunct Cryogenics. Vesco's plan for this corporate consolidation was overwhelmingly approved. He exchanged a small percentage of his stock in International Controls, his privately held company, for all the stock of the publicly traded Cryogenics and ended up by owning 59 per cent of the combined operation. As part of the agreement Cryogenics, the surviving corporation, changed its name to International Controls Corporation.

Hence, Vesco explained, "we became a public company through the back door." [15] He named himself president of the newly constituted vest-pocket conglomerate and hired a prestigious firm of certified public accountants, Lybrand, Ross Brothers & Montgomery, to audit the accounts. By the end of the year International Controls declared sales of $1.3 million and its first tiny profit of $62,000.[16]

The stock was then trading over the counter in the two-dollar range, not bad for a company that had twenty employees, and was a struggling one-plant operation with 7,800 square feet of floor space. Total net

[14] Schwebel tapes, No. 2, p. 22.
[15] *Ibid.*, p. 20.
[16] International Controls Corp. 1968 Annual Report, Mr. Vesco's letter to shareholders.

worth had jumped to $700,000 [17] with some creative accounting, and Vesco promised that within five years sales would top $100 million.

Vesco had brought with him into the merged corporation at least three of his future stars. One was Dick Clay, the former automotive sales manager at Olin's aluminum division, who now became Vesco's vice-president for marketing. There was also Ralph P. Dodd, the plant manager at Captive Seal, who was named vice-president of production and planning. Another important member of the inner management clique was Mrs. Shirley Bailey, a trim little lady about ten years older than Vesco who had been the corporate secretary at Captive Seal. She now became Vesco's personal assistant, a sort of executive secretary *par excellence*.

Vesco doubled the International Controls board of directors, bringing aboard Dick Pershing, the seed capital specialist; Will Snipes, the Morristown banker; and Carl W. Anderson, a partner in the ill-fated New York brokerage firm of Orvis Brothers & Company.

One of the deciding factors that gave impetus to his shoestring conglomerate was a private placement of International Controls stock which he arranged on his own despite the fact that all odds were against its success.

"At that point we had kind of a master plan. Like when I bought Captive Seal it had eight people, but it didn't have any machines. It was just an assembly operation. So . . . in order to merge some little companies together we had to get some capital. And Ruth Axe [president of the $25 million Axe Science Corporation mutual fund] put in $200,000 in the form of a private placement. That was really the money that made it possible to finally get off the hook. It gave us the operating capital. It was really the key financing."

"Why did she do it?" Vesco was asked.

"Well, she fell in love, I guess," he responded unabashedly.

"I talked to her two or three times by myself. In fact, her attorneys told her not to do it. But she did it anyway. She actually—she tried to hire me. Well, I guess I did intrigue her with my financial agility. I guess that's really why she put the money in," he explained.[18]

Axe Science Corporation received 120,000 shares of International Controls at what must have seemed like bargain prices, for with Vesco at the helm it became a very hot number and the shares soon began to climb in value; everything seemed to be running, for a change, at a profit.

With the Axe cash in hand, Vesco went after Century-Special Corpo-

[17] Century-Special Corp. Notice of Special Meeting, audited statement of June 30, 1967, p. 13.
[18] Schwebel tapes, No. 2, p. 23.

ration of Brooklyn, acquiring it for stock. Century-Special had $4 million in sales—four times International Controls's turnover—and two plants producing machine parts for the aircraft industry and electro-mechanical components for computers and photocopiers. The earnings picture was uneven but Vesco needed the $200,000 in cash Century-Special held in the treasury.

The acquisition of Century-Special, International Controls's second production facility, helped boost net earnings for 1967 to $543,000 on sales of $6.8 million.[19]

The company had already outgrown the old Captive Seal premises and was searching for a new headquarters location. Thus in October 1967 the budding Vesco conglomerate purchased Fairfield Aviation Corporation, which operated under lease a 600-acre private airport in Fairfield, New Jersey next to Caldwell. In addition to maintaining a small fleet of aircraft, Fairfield Aviation provided air-taxi and charter services, operated a flight school, and acted as the local Cessna dealer. Vesco liked the image projected by his acquisition of a private airfield and started taking flying lessons. He also worked on plans for construction of a leased two-story office building at 200 Fairfield Road on the northern rim of the airfield to house his growing general staff.

International Controls after two years of hectic existence was now poised for really explosive growth that would see its sales rocket to more than $67 million in the coming year. But the company was in chronic need of cash. With all its bank accounts combined, International Controls could scrape together only $576,000 at the end of 1967. Remarkable as it may seem, one year later the Fairfield combine was operating twenty-seven plants across the country, employing approximately 5,800 persons. Achieving this incredible feat with other people's money meant that Bob Vesco had to break just about every rule in the acquisition handbook.

Bent on implacable growth at any price, in the summer of 1968 Vesco engaged in one of the dirtiest takeover battles ever when he sought to force the merger of Electronic Specialty, a West Coast company much larger than International Controls, with his bounding Fairfield concern. Electronic Specialty eventually succumbed to the Vesco onslaught, although the merger ended up costing more than twice what it should have. But in Vesco's view both his dirty tactics and the exorbitant price were justified, for his capture of Electronic Specialty provided him with the broader power base he needed to launch him on his quest for world-girding influence and fame.

[19] International Controls Corp. 1968 Annual Report, Mr. Vesco's Letter to Shareholders.

3

Electronic Specialty

*Vesco engineers one of the dirtiest takeover battles of the con-
glomerate era, thereby boosting sales of his International Controls
from $6.8 million to $67 million in a single year*

Vesco's technique for harnessing investor cupidity was to merge
small companies in "glamour" industries, change the methods of accounting whenever it suited him, and sustain an image of earnings
growth. This was relatively simple in the bull market of the 1960s. It
enabled him to float to paper millions on a wave of optimism and
gullibility.

In 1968 that wave reached its crest. It was the Year of the Conglomerate—a year when a record number of corporate mergers and
acquisitions took place in the United States, more than 4,000 of them
in all, almost double the total of the preceding year and ten times the
number recorded in 1950. The takeover battles that resulted were often
bitterly divisive and demoralizing to the business community. Some of
America's richest and most respected companies became vulnerable
to sudden capture by a new and daring kind of business operator. Ap-
prehension and even fear replaced the old self-assurance in the board-
rooms and executive suites of the prime target companies.

Of particular concern were the accounting practices used by some
merger-minded managements to influence favorably the per-share earnings of their companies and the widespread floating of debt securities to
finance their often outlandish acquisitions. Furthermore, it was no
longer a question of taking over another company to achieve deeper
market penetration or greater product extension—nothing so harmonious
as that. The merger madness produced such unlikely combinations as
meat packing and insurance, shipbuilding and frozen foods, and—in

the case of International Controls—rocket casings, cryosumps, wheel hubs, computer software components, furniture castings, and aircraft flap tracks.

Few people understood the intricate financial structures used in conglomerate construction better than Bob Vesco. And whiz-kid Vesco was definitely on the merger trail. International Controls, he announced, had jumped upon the "bandwagon of extreme diversification."

After completing two acquisitions in 1967, International Controls considerably raised its sights in 1968, the year of its most explosive growth, and set out to pick up eight more companies. This was immediately reflected in the 1967 earnings figures, which were restated upward from 31 cents a share—six times 1966 earnings—to 74 cents a share, including "extraordinary items." [1] This last-mentioned catchall was a device Vesco used for improving the appearance of neat stepladder progression in International Controls's per-share earnings. The pattern was marred, however, by the heavy acquisition expenses incurred in 1968, causing the Fairfield combine to show a net loss for the year of $1.07 per share.[2] But Vesco accepted this as the price to be paid for promoting his vest-pocket conglomerate to pint-sized giant—listed 688th by sales in *Fortune*'s directory of the 1,000 largest U.S. industrial corporations—within the incredibly short span of four years.

The first enterprise on his 1968 shopping list was Kenyon Electronics, Incorporated, a small Jersey City manufacturer of specialty transformers. Kenyon came into the fold for $800,000 in cash and 15,625 shares. The cash aspect of the transaction was academically intriguing since International Controls's balance sheet showed that, only days before the acquisition appeared on the books, Vesco's "money-making machine" held a mere half-million dollars in liquid bank deposits. But Vesco pulled a rabbit out of the hat by arranging with International Controls director Wilbert Snipes to borrow $750,000 from Trust Company National Bank, formerly Trust Company of Morris County, of which Snipes was senior vice-president.[3]

Vesco's strategic sense of timing—always managing to come up with the right amount of cash at the right time—was one of the great mysteries of his meteoric rise to prominence. Sometimes his source of funding was clearly disclosed, while on other occasions the financing he received remained clouded in relative obscurity.

Certainly there was no great mystery when in early January 1968, as the Kenyon deal was still under consideration, he turned for the first time to an offshore source of capital. Through Georges Karlweis of

---

[1] International Controls Corp. Form S-1 filing, November 13, 1970, pp. 13–14.
[2] *Ibid.*, p. 13.
[3] International Controls Corp. proxy statement, June 13, 1969, p. 29.

Banque Privée in Geneva he contacted IOS director C. Henry Buhl III.

Buhl, IOS's senior investment officer, had heard glowing reports about Vesco from Edmund de Rothschild, owner of Banque Privée and a cousin of the Paris and London Rothschilds. "Vesco had been up to Edmund's house for dinner, and Edmund found him very bright," Buhl said.

At that point Edmund de Rothschild and Georges Karlweis had every reason to think highly of their client, the junior financier. As an early backer of International Controls, Banque Privée, according to Buhl, had made a million dollars on Vesco's stock.

"Edmund kept on telling me I should meet this guy. Finally one day Vesco walked into my office and started telling me about this little company he had called International Controls," Buhl later recalled.

After a few meetings, Vesco persuaded IOS's senior investment officer to purchase 50,000 unregistered shares of International Controls treasury stock. The price tag was $600,000. Vesco said he needed the money to help finance International Control's acquisition program, which sounded reasonable to Buhl. The private placement was routed through IIT—an International Investment Trust, a Luxembourg-registered mutual fund founded by IOS in 1960.

Some weeks later IIT acquired a second block of 50,000 International Controls shares, apparently from Vesco's personal holdings. The fund bought it near the top of the price curve, paying an inflated $968,000 for its next nibble of the tight little International Controls operation. Buhl, who became fast friends with Vesco, later said he knew nothing of the second transaction. But, as his 1973 testimony on Vesco's business dealings would reveal, Buhl had a notoriously bad memory.

Meanwhile, with help from Dick Pershing, the San Francisco venture capital specialist who sat on the International Controls board, Vesco drew up an expanded list of possible target companies for his 1968 acquisition program. The program was to be financed with the sale of stock to IIT and three other securities flotations by which Vesco succeeded in raising a total of $40 million in six months. The sum was outrageously high for a company that had started the year with a net worth of $2 million, but even so it did not suffice, and Vesco had to run to the Bank of America for supplementary financing to the tune of $17.74 million.

High on Vesco's acquisition list appeared one firm traded on the Big Board that was *ten times* larger than International Controls. For the moment, however, this particular candidate remained mysteriously identified as "Company A," which in itself was indicative of a certain evolution. As Vesco's empire expanded, his manner became increasingly secretive. This obsession with the hidden and obscure began to affect his personality, gradually transforming him into quite a different individual from the "most attractive, most able, most interesting young man with an unlimited capacity for work" whom Malcolm McAlpin first met at the old Captive Seal offices in Caldwell.

"In the beginning he was very open and easy to work with. Then communications with him became increasingly difficult. He was always away or closeted in meetings and you couldn't reach him. It got worse and worse. His ambitions and designs eventually became overpowering," McAlpin said.

Vesco purposely kept his directors only partially informed of his real intentions, his sources of financing, even the reasons for his frequent trips to Europe at the company's expense and the people he contacted there. It became part of his *modus operandi* to unveil just that portion of the current game plan directly relating to each of his associates, so that only he himself and a restricted inner circle had a full overview of the game board at any given time.

The company's first big offering came in February 1968—an exotic mixture of paper termed "ICC units," which included debentures combined with warrants to buy additional shares at a stated price sometime in the future, and common stock. This novel investment package was constructed in such a way that it allowed International Controls to twice reap returns.

Initially, International Controls netted $6.2 million through the sale of the units. The second return came five months later because of a provision written into the debenture part of the offering. Under the original terms, buyers of the debentures were given warrants to acquire a total of 200,000 additional shares of common stock. But they could not exercise the warrants for at least one year unless the company first redeemed the debentures. Then, if the debentures were repurchased by the company, the holders had only thirty days to exercise the warrants. After that, they would expire.

As the players in Vesco's game of Senior Monopoly swept around the board at breathtaking speed, it became important to achieve a listing for the company's stock on a major exchange, and so in May 1968, Vesco succeeded in having International Controls cleared for listing on the American Stock Exchange. The stock opened strong at 29⅝. Unusually heavy trading immediately pushed it upward, and it ended a hectic second quarter at an all-time high of 50⅞—better than double the stated price at which the ICC unitholders were permitted to exercise their warrants.

"The ICC stock was by then inflated out of sight, and it did look like everything was going to the moon," McAlpin said.

International Controls naturally opted to call in the debenture part of the units, forcing the warrant-holders to exercise their option, thereby infusing ICC with additional cash. Understandably the warrant holders, given the right to buy the stock at half the market price, jumped at the opportunity to convert their warrants into common stock. They paid the company an additional $4.83 million for a second slice of common stock—enough to pay off the debentures with interest and leave more than $2 million of new cash in the treasury. Everybody was happy.

In June the thirty-two-year-old president of International Controls pulled off a third coup by concluding a private placement that brought in $4.6 million more. The stock went to two companies—Vizcaya Compania Naviera S.A. and Hellenic Shipping & Industries Company, Limited—owned by Greek shipping magnate Leonidas Goulandris. The placement was arranged through the Lausanne office of Orvis Brothers. Orvis, a marginal brokerage house plagued by financial problems—it went out of business in the 1970 bear market crash— also had handled the International Controls unit offering. The firm's senior partner, Carl W. Anderson, an International Controls director, personally held 64,300 shares of International Controls common stock. It was a nicely incestuous relationship.

Vesco, who came to Lausanne for the closing of the Goulandris private placement, told the local Orvis manager, "Don't worry, Henri, whatever happens your interest will be looked after." Vesco was extremely grateful, and said so, for Vizcaya and Hellenic were the manager's personal clients. But when it came to paying a one percent commission—$46,000—Vesco reneged, claiming that Orvis Brothers in New York already collected some $200,000 in underwriting fees [4] from International Controls, which in his view was sufficient to cover whatever was owed to the Lausanne manager. As Vesco had recently purchased a limited partnership in Orvis, nobody cared to argue the point, and the manager was never paid.

New ground was next pioneered in July when Vesco decided, again on the strength of the planned acquisition program, to borrow $25 million from European investors. Underwriters of the $25 million issue were Butlers Bank Limited, a small Bahamian bank that was to go out of business four years later, and the ill-fated Orvis Brothers— hardly an impressive group.

Vesco met Allan Butler, chairman of Butlers Bank in Nassau, through IOS investment manager Henry Buhl, and quickly he adopted the smooth, good-looking Harvard graduate as his offshore banker. Butler was very obliging, arranging back-to-back loans, or loans secured by

[4] International Controls Corp. proxy statement, June 13, 1969, p. 36.

other loans, which allowed Vesco to sidestep the necessity of disclosing certain inappropriate dealings.

Vesco personally worked out many of the tricky tax and legal details of the bond offering and then went off to Europe to sell almost the entire issue within two weeks, surprising even Dick Pershing. "I think it was almost a miracle, but Bob hung in there and did it," Pershing told Scott Schmedel of the *Wall Street Journal*.[5]

Miracle or not, the July 1968 Eurobond offering was scarcely a stunning affair. Fortunately, though, Vesco had a friend at IOS in Geneva.

By this time much of the luster had worn off Vesco's image in the eyes of his Banque Privée backers. He was still considered very bright, to be sure, but Banque Privée's managing director, Georges Karlweis, thought Vesco was moving too fast. And finance, according to Karlweis, is like driving a car: If you go off the road at 100 mph you are bound to wind up in trouble, perhaps even fatally so.

But Henry Buhl apparently liked the International Controls Euroissue, even though Karlweis claimed that anyone who read the offering prospectus and still invested in the bonds was clearly a fool. International Controls was so hard-pressed for cash that it was impossible to meet the 5½ per cent annual interest payments on the bonds out of its current earnings. Obviously this was not a situation to please conservative bankers. Nevertheless, Buhl saw to it that IOS's IIT fund stepped in and saved the underwriting from flopping.

At Buhl's instigation IIT purchased 25 per cent of the underwriting. Although International Controls announced that the bonds would be listed on the Luxembourg Stock Exchange, they never were. No market developed for them, which meant that IIT was left holding a bagful of dubious paper.

In this instance Vesco's gratitude for Buhl's help assumed a different color than it had with the Orvis manager in Lausanne. Buhl was offered a handsome commission but wisely declined. Instead Vesco directed a donation of $11,000 to Buhl's alma mater, the Brooks School, in North Andover, Massachusetts, with instructions that it be paid into the Buhl Faculty House Fund; $28,000 went to Carnegie Hall International, a charitable foundation for eminent music lovers; and $40,000 went to the A. E. Smith Foundation, a New York charity of which Buhl's mother, Mrs. Thomas J. Morrison, was one of the principal patrons. Buhl was very happy. So was Vesco. After all, his charity had served a double purpose; charitable donations are tax deductible; but also he had made the contributions in International Controls stock,

[5] *Wall Street Journal*, August 31, 1970.

obtained through the ICC units offering, to avoid a Securities Exchange Act of 1934 provision whereby short-swing profits by insiders are recoverable by the company.

With the Eurobond offering completed, Vesco next swept the controversial Texas businessman S. Mort Zimmerman off his feet. Zimmerman, who pleaded guilty in 1972 to mail and securities fraud in an unrelated case in Miami and received five years' probation, was chairman of Intercontinental Industries, Incorporated, of Dallas, which had a division in Garland, Texas, that made bomb and missile motor casings.[6] The Garland plant was a real money spinner as long as the Vietnam war remained in high gear, since it supplied the air force with a sizable percentage of its ordinance requirements in medium and heavyweight bombs. The air force dropped no less than 7.4 million tons of explosives during nine years of war in Indochina, so the bomb business was very good.

Vesco offered Zimmerman $11 million in cash and stock for the bomb plant. The property, Intercontinental Manufacturing Company, was to be delivered "promptly" after presentation of a signed auditor's report. Zimmerman agreed to sell but later sued Vesco for not fulfilling one of the provisions of the contract. Vesco finally settled out of court, giving Zimmerman an additional 275,000 shares of International Controls.

By mid-June 1968, just prior to the deal with Zimmerman, Vesco had narrowed the list of prime targets for his biggest merger to one candidate—the unnamed Company A—even though his directors favored a merger with a small and more compatible company. However, International Controls director Dick Pershing had already met with Bank of America people to determine whether the bank would extend the necessary credit, which, together with its own cash, would enable International Controls to make a tender offer for the stock of Company A. Although Pershing referred to the target only as Company A, it later emerged that Company A was in fact Electronic Specialty Company (ELS), a Pasadena-based leader in processing high-temperature and high-strength materials for the air transport, aerospace, nuclear, and conventional power industries. Electronic Specialty had annual sales of $67 million, compared to $6.8 million for International Controls.

As a manufacturer of a wide range of electronic and aerospace components, though at a more sophisticated level than International Controls, it qualified as a "glamour" operation. Founded in 1944, it

[6] The president of another Intercontinental subsidiary, Valley Die Cast Corp. of Detroit, was Michael ("Big Mike") Polizzi, cited in congressional hearings as a prominent member of the Detroit Mafia.

had maintained an excellent growth record; it had twelve operating divisions and a net worth of $31 million.

Vesco went after his new quarry with vigor, and the battle that ensued was ferocious. "It was one of the terrible takeover fights of our times," said Mel Rosen, deputy director of IOS's investment department and a confirmed Vesco follower. "This Vesco is one of the keenest and cleverest financial men of our times," he announced to his colleagues at IOS.

But the grubbiness of the tactics Vesco employed entangled him in a round of lawsuits, which drew the SEC's attention and left the president of International Controls with a tarnished image. He became known in investment banking circles as a shady customer, acquisitively aggressive and very hard-hitting—in short a man to be wary of.

As originally planned the takeover of Electronic Specialty carried a price tag of $19.5 million. But the battle was so hot and heavy it ended up costing International Controls a minimum of $50 million. "That was the beginning of the end," McAlpin noted regretfully.

Vesco's first step was to visit the Rockefeller Brothers offices in New York to discuss their sizable interest in Electronic Specialty. One of Rockefeller Brothers's officers, Charles Smith, was also a director of Electronic Specialty and a close friend of the ELS founder and chairman, William H. Burgess. Vesco asked Smith to arrange an immediate meeting with Burgess to discuss the proposed merger.

Concurrently, Vesco instructed Butlers Bank to purchase in its name but for an International Controls account up to 100,000 shares of ELS at prices of less than $40 a share. Due to the short notice, Butlers had time to acquire only 43,500 shares—about 2.5 per cent of ELS's outstanding stock—before the meeting with Burgess took place later that same week.

Burgess, when contacted by Smith, was not happy about talking with Vesco but had little choice. Smith told Burgess that if he refused to meet the Fairfield delegation he "would soon read some adverse news" in the press.[7]

"It was obviously a threat," said Burgess later, confirming that Smith had made the approach. He added, "From what I knew of Vesco— and I had taken a prior look at International Controls—I concluded that I was not interested in getting involved with him."

Nevertheless, the meeting went forward. Vesco flew out to California and, accompanied by Dick Pershing, spent the entire day of Friday, July 26, discussing with Burgess and C. Ray Harmon, Electronic Specialty's president, International Controls's operations and plans. Vesco also informed Burgess for the first time that International Con-

[7] 296 Federal Supplement, p. 464.

trols had acquired a large block of ELS stock. However, every time Burgess inquired how much stock International Controls held, Vesco avoided answering the question. In fact, he intentionally misled Burgess by implying, without actually saying so, that International Controls owned substantially more than 100,000 shares.

"These are negotiating tactics and we did not say anything untrue. But we didn't answer the question either," Vesco replied when questioned by the SEC a few weeks later.

Negotiations continued the following week in New York, ending in a standoff, with a fair amount of animosity on both sides.

The clash between Vesco and Burgess was heightened by their widely different social attitudes. Vesco considered the chairman of Electronic Specialty a snob, the perfect image of dilettante management. Burgess looked upon Vesco as a corporate interloper, certainly no damned good for Electronic Specialty, and dangerous for America too!

"Top management was more interested in playing golf and chasing girls. There was no harm in chasing girls, but you can do that on your own time. And going off on safaris down in Africa. But this was their idea of being bigtime management, so to speak," Vesco said privately of Burgess.[8]

Vesco has always held a naturally arrogant attitude toward the press unless he thought selected media representatives could help him promote his backhanded schemes. The following week information of the intended ELS takeover was leaked to the *Wall Street Journal*. It appeared in the widely read column "Heard on the Street" of July 31, five days after the West Coast meeting with Burgess:

The stock of Electronic Specialty, which jumped about 50% in price since mid-April, continued its upward movement yesterday.

The issue spurted 1¼ to 40⅜ on a turnover of 25,000 shares. Its high for the year is 42¼; its low 25⅜.

Wall Streeters attribute much of the stock's sharp rise to rumors of a possible takeover attempt. There were reports yesterday that a tender for control of the concern might be forthcoming within a week at between $45 and $50 a share.

The company behind the bid was rumored to be International Controls, a junior conglomerate with interests in fluid power, computers and aerospace fields. Its stock was off ⅜ yesterday to 39⅛.

According to brokerage house reports, International Controls, whose 1967 volume was less than a tenth of Electronic Specialty . . . has already taken a stock position in the concern. This position was said to be about 5% of Electronic Specialty's roughly 2 million shares outstanding.

[8] Schwebel tapes, No. 2, p. 30.

Vesco gloated. He called Burgess, purportedly for the purpose of underlining their common interest in allaying rumors of a takeover. Nevertheless, again as part of his "negotiating tactics" that later were honed for use against IOS, he allowed Burgess to believe that the *Wall Street Journal* article was accurate in reporting that International Controls held about 5 per cent, or approximately 100,000 shares, of ELS's stock.

Burgess's final response to Vesco's wooing was given at their next meeting in New York on Saturday, August 3. He informed Vesco that Electronic Specialty was not interested in a merger on any terms and that indeed his company intended to proceed with long negotiated plans to merge with Carpenter Steel Company (later Carpenter Technology Corporation) of Reading, Pennsylvania. As a result of their weekend discussions, Electronic Specialty agreed to purchase from International Controls up to 50,000 shares of ELS stock at $42 per share. However, this agreement was never honored; Vesco's sincerity in accepting it must be seriously questioned, since that same day he proceeded to draft the outline of a proposed tender offer to purchase 1 million ELS shares.

Just before the market opened on Monday, August 5, the Dow Jones broad tape reported that agreement had been reached to merge Electronic Specialty and Carpenter Steel into a new corporation of which William Burgess would be chairman. Thirteen minutes later there followed a confirmation by Vesco that International Controls had broken off its merger talks with Electronic Specialty. The matter seemed ended.

But in reality Vesco had no such intention. In spite of his statement to the Dow Jones news service that "the discussions were broken off by International Controls," he went right on drafting details of a tender offer with his investment bankers, Smith Barney & Company, including the proposed price, the number of shares to be acquired, and the size of the dealer-manager fee.

Then Vesco did a curious thing. On Tuesday, August 6, toward the end of the day, he placed an order with Orvis Brothers to *sell* 10,000 ELS shares at no less than $35. The order was carried out after 3 P.M., permitting only 5,400 to be sold. But the order was never reinstated, because Smith Barney and International Control's attorneys, Hogan & Hartson, upon learning of the maneuver, became extremely concerned. They advised Vesco that further sales might be considered a culpable manipulation of the market if International Controls intended thereafter to make a formal tender offer.

Vesco desisted from making further sales of ELS stock but by no means remained idle. He broke off discussions with Electronic Specialty for the repurchase of 50,000 ELS shares by refusing to supply data concerning the original purchase of the stock, including the exact number of shares held by International Controls and the price paid. Thus the oral agreement concluded two weeks earlier collapsed. Each side charged the other with bad faith.

Smith Barney had consistently counseled Vesco against attempting to gain control of ELS in a manner that would be judged hostile by its management. On Friday, August 16, the blue-chip New York investment bankers declined to act as dealer-manager when it became evident Vesco had made up his mind to go ahead anyway, even though at this point he did not have the approval of his own board. Vesco now turned to Orvis Brothers, who eagerly accepted the dealer-managership. The same day International Controls filed its required Schedule 13-D with the SEC disclosing its tender plans and motivations. ELS closed in the market at $34.

Next day, Saturday, he swung the International Controls board over to the idea of a hostile tender. In opposition to ELS management, Vesco was going ahead with his offer to buy the controlling interest in the company. His argument was that the market had clearly indicated ELS stockholders were not favorable to the Carpenter Steel merger proposal. The board reluctantly consented, and preparations feverishly went ahead over the weekend. On Monday, August 19, the full terms of the surprise offer were published in advertisements appearing in the *Wall Street Journal,* the *New York Times,* the *Los Angeles Times,* and the *San Francisco Chronicle.*

The final conditions of offer called for the purchase of 500,000 shares (25 per cent, later extended without limitation) of Electronic Specialty's stock at $39, five points above the last market closing price, and payment of $1,236 per $1,000 debenture. Electronic Specialty's management was stunned. Burgess, who had thought the threat had passed, now telegraphed shareholders, then issued a statement to the press, and later he wrote shareholders advising them not to accept the offer.

On Thursday and Friday of the same week Vesco was called upon to testify before the SEC about the possibility of fraud and misrepresentation. As a result of his talks with the Commission staff, International Controls amended its original filing with the SEC to make its intentions more clear.

Meanwhile, lawyers for Burgess brought action in the U. S. District Court for the Southern District of New York seeking a temporary restraining order against International Controls pending a full-scale hearing of Electronic Specialty charges that "International Controls Corp. and certain unknown persons engaged in a fraudulent scheme to acquire control of Electronic Specialty Co." and that "International

Controls sold and caused other persons to sell ELS common stock in an attempt to deflate the market price."

The motion for a preliminary injunction against International Controls was heard before Judge Edward C. McLean in mid-September. After three days of hearings, Judge McLean held that, first, the written tender offer was misleading and contained false statements concerning International Controls's actual intentions; second, the plaintiff had standing to sue; and third, Burgess would probably succeed at trial in establishing that a violation of securities laws had occurred. Despite all this, the judge refused the relief requested on grounds that "to grant a preliminary injunction here might do the stockholders more harm than good." [9]

"If the plaintiffs succeed at trial, they should be able to obtain relief against the voting by International Controls of its newly acquired stock," Judge McLean stated in his decision. And so the injunction was refused, and the case was set down for immediate trial.

By this time Burgess had committed a fatal error. The previous day he had advised shareholders that if the injunction were denied it seemed likely that ICC would gain voting control. In conceding defeat prematurely, he announced he would sell out and resign, leaving the company to Vesco. Consequently he said that management withdrew its former "recommendation that you do not tender your shares" since it was "unable to predict what will happen if the company is taken over by International Controls Corp."

Hence when the judge refused Burgess's motion to block Vesco's offer, half a million common shares and over $1 million in debentures flooded into the Chemical Bank, agents for the tender offer, including 129,810 shares from Burgess (he retained 1,000). This meant that at the end of the offer a total of 1,038,946 shares and $5,210,000 principal amount of debentures had been received—far more than Vesco had bargained for—giving International Controls 55 per cent of the ELS stock.

Although the last-minute tidal wave of tendered shares and debentures almost bankrupted International Controls, Vesco was triumphant.

In October 1968 the main case went to trial in the U.S. District Court for the Southern District of New York before Judge Morris E. Lasker. The hearings lasted several days, with Electronic Specialty and Burgess requesting that International Controls be required to divest itself of the stock.

Judge Lasker handed down his decision in December granting summary judgment against International Controls but denying an order for divestiture of the stock.

[9] 296 Federal Supplement (1968), p. 469.

In his remarkable decision, Judge Lasker found that "ICC's course of conduct does not measure up to the standards" of the antifraud provisions of the Securities Exchange Act. "ICC, through Vesco, made misleading statements on several key occasions, in private discussions with Electronic Specialty and in public releases, claiming that it had no intention of proceeding to a tender offer, when it in fact did."

However, the court believed that "the requested relief is impractical, inappropriate and punitive in nature. So far as is known, no court has ever utilized its powers under the Securities Act to cause divestiture of stock obtained in violation of the Act"—a notion that some laymen might find difficult to understand. Nevertheless, there it was. One might well have asked what use, then, is the law in protecting corporations and stockholders from raiders like Vesco. The lawbreaker received a slap on the wrist, was told not to do it again, but was allowed to keep the spoils.

As could be imagined, the judgment satisfied no one. Vesco was found guilty but not punished. Burgess was told he had reason, but too bad—the damage was already done, so let it be. Both sides appealed. The appellate court, one month later, held that the record did not establish International Controls's intent to mislead both the target corporation and the public. The three-judge panel dismissed the action, with one of the three judges dissenting in part. Vesco was vindicated. Or was he?

At a special meeting of Electronic Specialty shareholders in Pasadena one week later—at the end of January 1969—International Controls placed six of its nominees on the ELS board. Burgess and Harmon resigned and Vesco was named chairman, president, and chief executive officer. The one holdover from former management was Elmer A. Sticco, ELS's executive vice-president.

Not everyone in the Fairfield camp was as pleased as Vesco. During the next six months two of his directors resigned from the International Controls board: Warren E. Dunn, a Denville attorney; and Richard Pershing, who became president of Hale Brothers Associates in San Fancisco. Carl Anderson, the senior partner of Orvis Brothers, left the board in September 1970. They were replaced by Frank G. Beatty, a former partner of International Controls's auditors, Lybrand, Ross Brothers & Montgomery; Elmer Sticco of ELS; Merle Thorpe, Jr., of the Washington law firm Hogan & Hartson; and Stanley Hiller, Jr., a private investment counselor and financial adviser who now became chairman of Vesco's board of directors. Hiller, then president of Hiller Aircraft Company, was introduced to Vesco by Malcolm McAlpin.

In the big selloff of ELS stock that followed, International Controls was left with a paper loss of $17.4 million; furthermore, the company had saddled itself with a debt burden that its normal operating income would have great difficulty in covering. The interest requirements on the $25 million Euroconvertibles, floated so confidently seven months before, ran to $1.4 million a year. It also had borrowed $17.74 million from Bank of America, which cost another $1.6 million in annual interest charges.

To put the figures in perspective, the paper loss on the Electronic Specialty stock was roughly 1.8 times International Controls's total assets at the date of its last audited report, and interest requirements were five times 1967 earnings. Worse, the battle had been so disruptive of management that the company was operating at a loss. As an added insult, the Goulandris family in Lausanne, after paying almost $34 a share for their 137,000 shares in June 1968, seven months later found they had a paper loss of just over $1 million. For the first time in his short career, rather than making money for his investors, the young Fairfield financier had "bombed them out of their skulls."

As a final footnote to the Electronic Specialty adventure, on August 1, 1969, Dick Clay issued a press release announcing that International Controls had completed the acquisition of ELS's common stock and was merging ICC Sub Corporation—a wholly owned subsidiary of International Controls—into Electronic Specialty. "As a result of the merger, International Controls owns 100 percent of Electronic Specialty's common stock, and, accordingly, ELS common stock will no longer be publicly traded."

The acquisition program completed, International Controls posted sales for 1969 of $100,679,000 and a net worth of $41.7 million. Vesco had reached an important step on his ladder. He had predicted that tiny International Controls, when it was first formed, would achieve sales of $100 million within five years. He had accomplished it within four. "Now we are in a phase of digesting monsters," he said. "We've reached a plateau. Now we have to show the managerial capabilities. And as part of this we have to do some refinancing." [10]

Vesco was concerned that the public didn't understand his disparate collection of companies but clearly had grasped the fact that International Controls really was "top heavy on debt." At this point he began paring off some of the unprofitable entities to trim costs and raise cash. One of the first to go was a third-level airline with the promising name of Golden West. International Controls had acquired this goose five months before for the equivalent of more than $1.5 million in stock.

[10] Schwebel tapes, No. 2, p. 27.

"The concept was [to create] a national air commuter service. But the price tag was just too great. . . . It was a big mistake which we should have never done," he said.[11]

At the end of 1968 International Controls sold Golden West for a meager $100,000 and, in its rush to divest itself of the "ultimate plan to have a network of third-level airlines under the ICC name," recorded a $1.4 million loss on the deal. When combined with the monster legal fees resulting from the Electronic Specialty fray, the over-all net loss for 1968 was a less than golden $3,174,311.

Vesco was nonplussed. After achieving his first major goal in corporate life—sales of $100 million—he realigned his principal objectives. "Now that I'm at the top," he said, "my personal goals still are— Well, maybe I didn't define my original goals quite adequately. The reason I wanted to get there was to show that, well, I could run a company better than someone else could. But now objectively I've got to build up [International Controls] to possibly a billion-dollar company. It's running efficiently; it's got adequate financial capabilities."

"Why a billion?" he was asked.

"Well, because it's more than a million. Then, when I get to a billion I probably will want to get to a hundred billion," Vesco calmly announced.[12]

To construct with his financial nuts and bolts nothing less than the largest company in the world had become, then, The Bootstrap Kid's ultimate goal.

[11] *Ibid.*, p. 28.
[12] *Ibid.*, p. 9.

4

Executive Growth Fund:
The Fund That Flopped

An international guide to the offshore jungle and how the Finagling Financier decides to set up his own unregulated mutual fund, which flops — Introducing several of Vesco's future star performers in the Looting of IOS, men of rare fiduciary talents

Vesco's progress in the world of $100 million balance sheets could be measured by his changing life-style. Affluence didn't burst upon his closely knit family; it came slowly in a neat stepladder fashion that paralleled the earnings progression of International Controls.

The seven-room dwelling in Denville had become cramped with the arrival of Bobby, Jr., the Vescos' fourth and last child, but not until three years later did they find a property that suited them in the neighboring township of Boonton, less than ten miles away and only thirty miles west of New York. So in 1967 the modest $27,000 Denville home was sold for $35,000 and the family moved a step upward into the more affluent Rockaway Valley area of Boonton.

The Vescos purchased a spacious ranch house on a four-and-a-half-acre site along Old Denville Road for $52,000 from a local liquor store owner. It was not far from the Rockaway River Country Club, which the family had joined and where Vesco occasionally played golf, but badly, never breaking one hundred.

Old Denville Road was a narrow, curving lane heavily lined with trees, hedges, and $80,000 homes on the south bank of the Rockaway River. The house the Vescos acquired was secluded behind a row of spruce trees in a wooded dell that sloped gently down to the river.

During the next six years Bob Vesco remained as elusive to his neighbors in Boonton Township as he later was to federal investigators who pursued him halfway around the world. Gradually he added on to the estate until he had accumulated close to eighty acres and three other houses. One of the houses, a small bungalow situated on one and a half acres along the western boundary of the estate, had been owned by an International Controls employee named Scott whom Vesco had transferred out to California. As part of the transfer package, Vesco had International Controls buy the property, which he then incorporated into his expanding estate, installing his parents in the Scott bungalow rent-free. Vesco's intention was to transfer ownership of the Scott property at cost to one of his family holding companies, but he never got around to it. It was an eminent example of his using corporate assets to finance his personal deals.

Numerous improvements were made to the new Vesco estate. The entrance was marked by two squat stone gateposts, and a circular driveway led down to a paved parking lot beside the main house. Vesco added an extra wing onto the house and made other lavish alterations at a cost of $500,000. He built a swimming pool for the kids, tennis courts, a one-acre artificial pond, and a $75,000 riding stable with box stalls for eighteen horses.

One item that riled the neighborhood was his application in 1971 to build a helipad. The township council, under heavy pressure from the local citizenry, opposed the project, but Harry Sears, Vesco's Boonton lawyer, won approval for the helipad from the state Transportation Department in Trenton. Sears, who also represented the township council, had the state issue a license before the council members got around to ruling helicopter depots illegal.

The children were enrolled in the private Wilson School in nearby Mountain Lakes. Vesco donated a specially equipped wing for the school so that Bobby, Jr., who had been born with a coordination disability and required special help, could attend. His generosity also extended to a plot of land adjoining the school, which he had International Controls purchase and set aside as a future residence for the headmaster.

From Old Denville Road it was a comfortable fifteen-minute drive to the newly completed Fairfield headquarters of International Controls. His office was a large **L**-shaped room with a big conference table in the lounge area. A framed picture of young Vesco seated on a banquet dais within shoulder-tapping distance of Lyndon Johnson and Richard Nixon adorned his desk. Behind the desk was a door to a bathroom, sauna, and private gym. On occasion he impressed visitors by asking them to step outside a moment so he could take a confidential call from John N. Mitchell, then the U.S. Attorney General.

He had become a bigtime operator in a smalltime setting. Vesco began to give the impression that International Controls was too small for him. He had grown restless and was seriously looking around for a better vehicle to take him to the heights of power and influence. Real power, he decided, could not be gained by manufacturing pneumatic valves but resided with the control and movement of capital. He began to devise ways of combining the merchant side of his business with creative financing, and indeed in conversations with friends visualized himself as a "merchant financier."

Vesco began to look around for possible openings into the world of high finance, where he was convinced he could make better use of his unusual financial agility. His initial contact with Henry Buhl and IOS's IIT fund had been so promising that he began to study closely the unregulated offshore investment arena.

Cornfeld's formula for raising offshore capital was so successful that his IOS Ltd. and its foreign-registered mutual funds spawned a multitude of copycat creations, which grew at an astonishing rate into a full-fledged "offshore" industry. Totally unhampered by national controls, wide open to the most brazen forms of financial chicanery, the offshore investment industry became a paradise for swindlers, bucket-shop operators, and whiz-kid financiers of every stripe. It generated fantastic wealth for the promoters but mostly staggering losses for the investors.

This kaleidoscopic world had assumed a carnival atmophere by 1968; there were estimated to be 165 truly offshore funds in existence by then, with combined assets of $3.6 billion, and mighty IOS was larger than all other groups combined, controlling more than 50 per cent of the total offshore fund assets under management.[1]

These funds obtained their offshore status by incorporating in such distant tax havens as the Virgin Islands, Bermuda, the Netherlands Antilles, Liberia, and the Cayman Islands—not to mention the two offshore capitals, Panama and Nassau in the Bahamas. The fund operators were careful to conduct little or no business at their home bases, which generally were nothing more than a mail drop. They were unlikely, therefore, to be prosecuted in such places for offenses committed abroad.

This meant that a fund incorporated in Panama but mismanaged from a villa overlooking Lake Lugano in Switzerland by a Greek principal and sold through a Liechtenstein distributor to Brazilian and Scandinavian investors was unlikely to receive much attention in a Panamanian court of law. Because the new breed of international funds

[1] Mutual Fund Industry Review, prepared by the IOS Sales Management Department, March 9, 1970.

were incorporated outside of the major markets in which they were sold, they were not, initially, subject to national regulation. That was the essence of "offshoreness."

Once offshore operators fully cottoned to the beauty of the beast that IOS embodied, they devised all sorts of hybrid animals that invested in a wide variety of merchandise from whisky futures to high-risk commodity contracts. Some funds specialized in bank stocks or real estate, others in shipping, holiday resorts, and even mythical insurance companies—a far cry from the original concept of security through diversification and professional management, which had made mutual funds a trusted investment medium for millions of Americans.

The imaginative offshore operators christened their vehicles with such descriptive names as the Pyramid Fund, InFund, First Liberty Fund, the Midas Fund and the extremely short-lived Israel Development Fund N.V., administered by Shalom Limited ("Shalom, Shalom . . . send your money to P.O. Box 188, Geneva Airport," went their unintentionally humorous ads).

Nevertheless, there was enough magic attached to the word "offshore" that it did attract some serious institutions. These included Britain's largest bank, Barclays, with nine offshore trusts; Bank of New York, which, in addition to its $80 million NAMF (Netherlands Antilles Mutual Fund), took a 25 per cent equity participation in the Nassau-registered Securities Management Company Limited, a carbon copy of IOS with administrative headquarters in Geneva and assets under management of about $150 million.

Others much less respectable flocked into the arena. Among them was one Allen Jones Lefferdink, a Nebraska-born certified life underwriter and crony of Elliot Roosevelt, younger brother of IOS's James Roosevelt. Lefferdink decided to move offshore in the mid-1960s after his fly-by-night combine of fourteen loan and insurance companies, banks, and real estate concerns headquartered in Boulder, Colorado, suddenly dissolved into bankruptcy. Although Lefferdink was acquitted on several counts of securities, mail, and wire fraud, he found the going had become too tough in the closely regulated U.S. markets and elected to set up his new World Investments and Insurance Limited in Hamilton, Bermuda.

In 1965 he founded his own version of IOS's Fund of Funds, which he modestly named Mutual Funds of America Limited, a nonresident Canadian corporation. He then proceeded with the money it brought in to invest in the fund's custodian, sponsor, distributor, and manager all rolled into one—which by lucky chance was his own World Investments and Insurance Limited. Business was so brisk that Mutual

Funds of America pulled in more than $2 million in two years, encouraging Lefferdink to set up three other funds—Universal Bank Stock Fund, World Insurance Stock Fund, and World Real Estate Stock Fund—all registered in Panama.

With money collected by Universal he established two banks, Atlantic Trust Bank on the island of Guernsey and Atlantic Trust Bank S.A. in Panama, with branches in Saint Maarten and Grand Cayman in the Caribbean. Depositors were offered free life insurance by Lefferdink's World Insurance Limited plus 10 per cent annual interest on two-year certificates of deposit and 6 per cent on ordinary checking accounts.

Lefferdink concentrated on the affairs of his Atlantic Trust Bank, moving $3.5 million of its deposits through a stateside correspondent bank into a series of obscure receptacles. The money and the receptacles promptly disappeared. Part of the cash was thought to have been invested in a tiny Brussels-based hedge fund appropriately named the Fortune Fund. Once in control of the Fortune Fund, he transferred its offices to Luxembourg and proceeded to siphon off $600,000, replacing the money with shares of his other funds.

Lefferdink meanwhile had shifted headquarters and was operating his farflung empire from the quintessential base for offshore adventures, a $225,000 yacht called *Sea Wolf*. He advertised lavishly in leading international newspapers and magazines for salesmen, inviting prospective recruits to "join us aboard the *Sea Wolf* to discuss your future with an unusual sales organization. We pay the world's highest commissions!"

The ads contained a picture of ex-naval lieutenant Lefferdink upon the *Sea Wolf*'s poop deck gazing out to sea, in search of new investment horizons, no doubt. When at last he disappeared from sight, all that he left behind was a slew of empty corporate shells and a few bewildered salesmen to take the rap. Several were arrested; others lost everything they owned to Lefferdink, who was last believed to be in hiding in Mexico City. His bag: an estimated $15 million.

Another international drifter was Walter Voss, the Dutch-born founder of elusive Intercambio International Bancario of Panama. Balding, wild-eyed Voss's escapades with a London stripper named Lady Cadillac delighted the British press, but the whereabouts of more than $10 million he was said to have lifted from unsuspecting investors in Europe has remained an unsolved mystery.

Perhaps the most outrageous of the offshore crew was an American mortgage trickster named Jerome D. Hoffman, a native of Saint Louis. Ten months after being permanently barred from the securities business in New York State for milking more than $1 million from U.S.,

Canadian, and Puerto Rican businessmen on phony promises of obtaining mortgage money for them, the engaging Hoffman set out to emulate Bernie Cornfeld's success in offshore waters.

Hoffman, a little man with a high-pitched laugh, began his offshore cruise in early 1969 when he was thirty-eight, incorporating his International Investors Group in Liberia. IIG became the mother company of two sleazy promotions known as Real Estate Fund of America (REFA) and Fund of the Seven Seas (FOSS). The two funds were incorporated in Bermuda and maladministered from London, where Hoffman maintained offices under the name of International Investors Group (London) Services Limited.

Hoffman talked Britain's Reginald Maudling, then deputy leader of the Conservative Party and later a Home Secretary in Edward Heath's Cabinet, into becoming president of IIG. Maudling was not the only prominent individual to join forces with this practiced fraudsman. Robert F. Wagner, three-term Democratic Mayor of New York City, became chairman of REFA and its ugly sister FOSS.

Hoffman's antics rocked the sinking offshore industry in 1970, no doubt quickening the final plunge. His specialty was "twisting" clients out of the IOS funds into one of his own doomed creations. In that way he collected an estimated $12 million, most of which went down the drain in the form of unconscionably high overhead expenses, advertising costs, and commissions to IIG management to support Hoffman's high living before the two IIG funds finally collapsed.

Hoffman bailed out of London in a hurry in November 1970, moving to Rome for a month, where he announced the suspension of operations just before the Italian police swooped in. The ever alert Hoffman was one step ahead of them. He had packed his files into the company's Mercedes and disappeared, popping up in Athens for a time, then in Zurich, where he was negotiating to buy a bank, and next in New York, where some months later he was indicted for fraud in connection with his earlier mortgage activities. He pleaded guilty and in 1972 was sentenced to two years' imprisonment. Ten months later he was paroled from the Marion Penitentiary in Illinois.

Unfortunately, there were dozens more like Hoffman who thought they had discovered the golden fleece. The slickest and largest operation after IOS was Gramco, a joint invention of two unlikely young "financiers" from Miami, a onetime White House student intern, Keith Barish, and a Cuban refugee, Rafael Navarro. Their USIF real estate fund collected $250 million in three years.

Gramco's best-known director was Pierre Salinger, John F. Kennedy's press secretary. Its gimmick was "liquid real estate." At its height Gramco's USIF claimed to be "the world's biggest buyer of U.S. real estate," and it probably was. But the piano wire that tied together this intricately structured collection of meridional holding companies snapped apart in October 1970. USIF was forced to suspend redemptions, and two years later the fund was reorganized under court supervision as a closed-end Bahamian trust with assets of $193 million. Its portfolio included 250 major pieces of U.S. property, representing a cross-section of some of the nation's best real estate.

Barish's financial triumph started in January 1967 when he was twenty-four. Navarro had been a "high-ranking diplomat at the United Nations" at twenty-one when Castro pulled the rug out from under him. A priceless piece of Gramco advertising copy that appeared in a twenty-one page *Time* magazine insert during the summer of 1970 proclaimed:

> Barish has the aura of a man with a mission who dreams of larger goals than merely making a lot of money. He wants to put money to work for people, and he glows when he talks about it. ". . . I like to think that we are engaged in responsive capitalism, a system that uses money for social good, for creating jobs, to prevent economic injustice, and in the long run make the world a better place in which to live."

Less than four months later the balloon went up. Barish and Navarro calmly walked away from the debris having extracted through Gramco Management a modest $40 million in commissions, or roughly 17 per cent of all the money invested by Gramco's trusting clients. That was responsive capitalism of majestic dimensions!

Two years later Barish and Navarro were hit with a gigantic class action. A couple of aroused clients had joined together and were seeking $40 million in damages, plus punitive consideration and recovery of legal costs. The suit, filed in Philadelphia, alleged that Gramco Management, incorporated in the Bahamas and controlled by Gramco International S.A., a privately held Panamanian concern, had charged USIF excessive commissions.

But the booby prize for downright chicanery went to Allied Fund for Capital Appreciation (AFCA), which advertised under the slogan "Watch it Grow!" AFCA was a Panamanian trust launched offshore in October 1969, just as the long U.S. market advance was ending. It hoodwinked investors into parting with a sum sometimes alleged to have been as high as $35 million, although in reality half that amount probably was closer to the mark.

Little is known about the origin of AFCA except that initially it was 50 per cent owned by its silent "investment adviser," Harry Neil Kelly, Jr., who served from October 1962 to November 1964 in a U.S. penitentiary for a fraud conviction involving a securities firm. Kelly avoided all reference to his two-year employment gap except when pressed, at which time he would reluctantly confide that he had been on assignment abroad for the CIA. His business partner, AFCA president Clifford J. Bennett, a Canadian, became the focus of an international police search extending to a dozen countries. He was arrested on fraud charges in 1971 by the Royal Canadian Mounted Police at Yellowknife, in Canada's remote Northwest Territories, and sentenced to five years' imprisonment.

AFCA's custodian of securities and cash was listed as the Midwest National Trust Company of Panama City. But upon investigation it was discovered that no such company existed. Instead a shadow custodian was found under the name Midwest National Banking Corporation, also of Panama City. The only assets controlled by this Midwest, however, turned out to be a one-room office with desk, typewriter, automatic phone-answering device, and an unplugged telex machine. There was, quite assuredly, no trace of the $35 million.

There were others too numerous to mention, all variations on the same unrestricted, unregulated offshore theme most concisely captured by a series of advertisements in the international editions of *Time* and *Newsweek*: "The International Real Estate Investment Fund offers maximum capital growth return and maximum security through diversification, with unequalled ease of liquidity." Maximum Return and Guaranteed Security plus Ease of Liquidity were three essential ingredients of the offshore pipedream, to which should be added a large measure of greed. Nobody has yet discovered the magic formula for liquid real estate. But in the case of InterCapital, sponsor of the above-quoted ad, apparently 1,200 suckers believed the impossible and entrusted no less than $4.6 million to the firm's president, the American promoter George R. Cassidy. Three years later, in 1971, the fund was forced into liquidation. In its short existence, two-thirds of the assets had dwindled away.

A resident of Nassau, George Cassidy was a graduate of one of the best offshore academies—New Providence Securities, the Bahamian company that managed the high-flying Capital Growth Fund. The New Providence–Capital Growth complex was controlled by a portly Texas cattleman, Clovis William McAlpin (no relation to Malcolm McAlpin), one of the offshore greats after Bob Vesco and Bernie Cornfeld.

Clovis's older brother, Gordon Taylor McAlpin, told a Costa Rican labor court in 1972 that Cassidy had been "systematically robbed" by the younger McAlpin.

"Cassidy was a lawyer and a man of fine business ability," said Gordon, apparently in all seriousness. "When Clovis was struggling [in the early 1960s] to get New Providence Securities and Capital Growth Fund into a position that at least would pay enough for him and his family to eat regularly, George Cassidy bought New Providence stock from Clovis which made it possible for Clovis to continue his efforts," Gordon McAlpin told the court.[2]

In 1967 Cassidy suffered a business setback in Nassau and had to sell his 40 per cent interest in New Providence, representing about 400,000 shares, to raise some urgently needed capital. The elder McAlpin arranged for the sale of 100,000 shares to an officer of Hayden, Stone & Company, the New York brokerage house, which did a lot of business with Capital Growth, for $80,000. He and a friend took another 100,000 shares, also for $80,000. Then, according to Gordon McAlpin, Clovis stepped in like a vulture and picked up all but 50,000 of the remaining 200,000 shares at a dollar apiece, knowing full well he had another buyer for them "at something like $8 or $10 per share."

A year later a disillusioned forty-two-year-old Cassidy resigned his directorship with New Providence and decided to try his own hand at offshore navigation, with disasterous results. McAlpin meanwhile moved on to much greater conquests. He had temporarily shifted his operations base to Zurich, and then to London, before becoming the first off-shore operator to discover Costa Rica as a safe haven when the going got sticky.

Capital Growth Fund had risen to a peak of perhaps $90 million in assets when the Big Bear ambled over the horizon in early 1970. The fund quickly collapsed under the influence of reverse leverage to about $20 million. Many of the 16,000 investors sustained huge losses—but they had in the interim provided a lush livelihood for McAlpin.

As money started to roll into the Capital Growth coffers in the late 1960s, McAlpin at last could afford to pay decent salaries for professional people to look after the fund's affairs. Thus in 1967 he hired a leading New York chartist away from Gerald Tsai's Manhattan Fund. Eugene Chamides, who became Capital Growth's vice-president of investments, had been an adviser to Tsai at Fidelity Capital Fund during its best performance days, then worked with him on the setting up of the $500 million Manhattan Fund. Under Chamides, Capital Growth's share value almost doubled from $9.60 to $18 in one year. But Chamides became concerned when McAlpin started charging the fund a 1 per cent securities handling fee, which Chamides considered unfair to the clients.

Already on board the New Providence cruise ship at the time was assistant treasurer Ulrich Jacob Strickler, a Swiss accountant from the

[2] Costa Rican Third Labor Court, San José, transcript of reply from G. T. McAlpin to a statement before the court by C. W. McAlpin on March 7, 1972.

nearby town of Herrliberg on Lake Zurich's northern shore. Strickler, a tall, silent man with deep-set eyes, long sideburns, and a subservient manner, became McAlpin's major domo, organizing work permit needs for close to 100 staffers by then legally or illegally working for Mc-Alpin at the Zurich offices. In addition to his native German, Strickler spoke fluent English, French, and Spanish and accurately took shorthand in all four. His typical response when asked to perform the impossible was, "Yes sir, will be done."

Mr. Will-Be-Done, as he became known, had spent a year in Ephrata, a small textile town in southeastern Pennsylvania, learning English from the Pennsylvania Dutch, and eight years in Peru working for a Swiss insurance company. His dream was to save enough money to buy a hotel, which he and his schoolteacher wife, Eva, could run.

McAlpin's sales director was S. Paul Palmer, a former Hayden Stone fund sales manager. Hayden Stone had retained the plaid-stamp innovators, The E. F. McDonald Company, to design and run a series of sales contests for Hayden Stone associates. The person E. F. Mc-Donald sent over to work out the details was a shifty little man with a percolating sense of humor named Gilbert R. J. Straub. Shortly after joining Capital Growth in early 1968, Palmer called upon the services of Straub to stimulate sales for the McAlpin crew.

"He was great on premiums," one Capital Growth executive recalled of Straub. "He always had some gimmick that cost a fortune and was as useless as a halo in hell."

At one conference in Rome to interest German bankers in the merits of Capital Growth, Straub handed out miniature gold bars as souvenirs. The bars were only gold-painted but had the weight and appearance of small ingots. McAlpin loved it. The bankers were polite. However, not much business resulted.

The courtly McAlpin, then in his late fifties, soft-spoken with a leisurely Texan drawl, an almost perfect department-store Santa Claus with his white, wavy hair and twinkling blue-gray eyes, had but one basic rule in business: "Never learn a foreign language."

He hardly spent any time in Zurich, because the Swiss were hesitant to give him a work permit, and they gently began to ease the McAlpin operation out of the country.

London became the next port of call on the Capital Growth cruise. McAlpin bought a $200,000 home in Surrey, ordered a chauffeur-driven Rolls Royce, and prepared posh new London offices in the fashionable Mayfair district. When he wasn't in London he was cruising the Caribbean aboard his $430,000 yacht.

McAlpin appropriately named his sport-fishing cruiser the *Give-Up*.

According to Gordon, brother Clovis was receiving $600,000 a year in illegal kickbacks on brokerage commissions from broker-dealers who dealt with Capital Growth. Gordon said he knew about this because Clovis had promised to cut him in for 10 per cent of the give-up income if he would help manage the fund's blossoming investments in Costa Rica.

The offshore antics of McAlpin became too much for the professional ethics of Chamides, and one day, when things were going from bad to worse in Zurich, the disgruntled vice-president of investments walked into S. Paul Palmer's office and announced, "Boy, I'm so fed up I'm ready to start my own fund."

Chamides found an instant echo. Straub was also in Palmer's office, apparently discussing a similar reflection. "Hold it. Don't do anything yet. We've got just the man for you. Sit still until we get him here," Straub responded, much to Chamides's mystification.

Straub's man was none other than a little-known New Jersey entrepreneur, Robert Lee Vesco, who was then engaged in the takeover battle of his life, the fight for Electronic Specialty. Vesco's hankering to own an offshore mutual fund was founded on the correct assumption that risk capital was more easily assembled offshore than onshore during the cash-tight end of the conglomerate era.

Dozens of American corporations, many of them financially hard pressed and some quite definitely on their last legs—Four Seasons Nursing Homes, Commonwealth United, King Resources Company, and Penn Central among them—had crossed the Atlantic to prospect the loosely regulated European capital markets and had come home with the breadbasket temporarily replenished. Between 1965 and 1970, U.S. companies tapped the Eurodollar arena for close to $6 billion.[3] Now, if Vesco could control just a little corner of that arena he would by all reason be a powerful man. The thought surely had crossed his mind.

Vesco appeared on the unrestrained offshore scene during its twilight hours, just as fences started going up in Europe to keep financial freebooters like Lefferdink, Hoffman, Voss, McAlpin, and others from further plundering unprotected national markets. The West Germans were the first to come out with stringent new regulations governing foreign mutual fund operations, followed by the Swiss and Luxembourgois, requiring offshore funds to submit to strict registration requirements before being allowed to sell their shares to the public. Vesco's coming to Zurich in the industry's last dusky moments of glory was due

[3] William J. Casey, chairman of the SEC, addressing the First International Meeting on Stock Exchanges, March 15, 1972, in Milan, Italy.

largely to the conspiratorial efforts of Straub, a man of many qualities but about the last person in the world one would want to have in a fiduciary position.

Straub had joined Capital Growth as director of marketing in August 1968. He was a good organizer, a soft-shoe artist who liked to remain behind the scenes. McAlpin paid him $20,000 a year with no contract.

Straub said he always knew he would end up working for Bobby Vesco (he pronounced it "Babby"). Like Vesco, he was an aviation enthusiast and flew his own Cessna. In the early 1960s the two had some business dealings together in the Bahamas, where Straub had been president of a closet-sized organization known as Bank Securities Limited. They were involved in a land development project on Eleuthera Island, east of Nassau, where it was said Straub had title to some land surrounding a World War II PT boat base, near a small hotel in the center of the slender, 104-mile-long island. The only problem with the Eleuthera land development scheme was that someone else also claimed title to the land.

Straub's major asset was that he knew an awful lot of fast-moving and influential people. He introduced Vesco to New York attorney Howard F. Cerny, who became a key man in many of their subsequent ventures. Cerny, a former assistant district attorney for Queens in 1966 and 1967, had moved swiftly upward in the legal profession to the point where he maintained expensive offices on Park Avenue and once claimed to represent President Nixon's two brothers, Edward and Donald. Cerny had a security mania, was in fact an expert on electronic eavesdropping, and has been described as more a super-private-detective than a high-class lawyer. With these qualifications he was called upon to counsel Vesco on his offshore operations.

A few weeks after Straub's pronouncement that he had an angel who wanted to finance an offshore fund, Vesco took a short detour on one of his flying visits to see Henry Buhl at IOS in Geneva and arrived in Zurich with Carl Anderson of Orvis Brothers. They discussed the setting up of a hedge fund with Straub and Chamides as the key officers. The idea was to find $5 million in pump-priming cash, then build the fund up to a hoped-for $100 million in assets, at which time no new subscriptions would be accepted. The entire operational range of the proposed creation was to be bound by the Standard & Poor's 500 Composite.

Vesco thought it sounded like a good idea. Yes, indeed, he would be able to put together the $5 million from private sources—mainly wealthy European investors like the Goulandris family.

Vesco returned to New Jersey, and the Capital Growth bankers conference at the Rome Hilton followed a few weeks later. S. Paul Palmer knew John King, the Denver natural resources tycoon, and invited him to address the bankers on the "Great American Outlook." Straub said he could line up F. Donald Nixon for the keynote speech, but a last-minute change of plans prevented the President's brother from attending. However, Howard Cerny came—at McAlpin's expense—to follow up on the plans for the new fund.

The Rome conference resulted in a preliminary agreement on how to proceed with incorporation of the fund, its management company, and a Zurich service company for sales and administration. Cerny tentatively was made president of the fund management company; Straub was appointed executive vice-president; and Chamides was made senior vice-president. They called it Executive Growth Fund.

Confirmation came from Vesco two weeks later in New York. Straub and Chamides flew over for a frantic meeting with "Babby" at his suite in the Waldorf Astoria. There were about twelve persons present, including a New Jersey judge, Howard Cerny, Wilbert Snipes, Harry Sears, and Carl Anderson, all eating turkey sandwiches and watching Vesco get dressed in a rented suit of tails for his big night in the ballroom downstairs—the 1968 Alfred E. Smith Memorial Dinner.

The verbal commitment was that Vesco, in partnership with Anderson, would pay in the necessary capital—$500,000—to set up shop and find the first $5 million to start the fund's portfolio. He reviewed the list of brokerage houses that would be called upon to service the fund. He crossed off Bache and Bear, Sterns—both had gotten bagged by Vesco—and substituted Orvis Brothers and Shearson Hammill. He asked, finally, that people on the Street not be told he was behind the fund—at least not until it had grown to respectable size. "Because of my political affiliations, if it were known at this time it might present some difficulties," he was said to have suggested, causing speculation as to what new maneuvers he might have been planning.

"That $10,000 chicken dinner at the Waldorf turned out to be rather a fowl affair," it was later remarked. The reference was intended for the fund that flopped. Vesco, though, was late taking his place on the dais just behind Johnson and Nixon, which later caused him to quip on occasion, "I keep Presidents waiting." IOS directors Jimmy Roosevelt and Henry Buhl, whose mother helped organize the annual Al Smith banquets, were there to keep him company.

Straub and Chamides returned to Zurich and apprised McAlpin of their resignations from Capital Growth Fund. Strickler came over as well to serve as managing director of the new fund service company. The initial incorporating arrangements were made through Georges

Philippe, managing director of Bank Cantrade, a small Zurich bank that later played a major role in Vesco's capture of IOS.

Philippe, a typically cool and reserved Swiss banker with a mask for a face, was tremendously impressed by Vesco and helped set up The Executive Financial A.G., central holding company of The Executive group, in the Swiss tax-shelter canton of Zug. A management company was formed in Luxembourg, where the fund was incorporated. Banque Commercial S.A. in Luxembourg, Irving Trust Company in New York, and Bank Leu in Zurich were appointed the fund's custodians. The initial forty-five-day offering period began on April 14, 1969. A second fund, The Executive Fund, with a minimum investment requirement of $100,000, was planned but never got off the drawing board.

Straub meanwhile was told by Vesco to take over-all charge of the project, and with Strickler he set about looking for a cheap Swiss bank to purchase. Here again S. Mort Zimmerman appeared on the scene. He happened to know of a small Swiss bank that was going for a song.

Zimmerman was by no means a total stranger to the banking world. Through one of his Dallas holding companies he owned four banks and controlled the ill-fated State Fire & Casualty Company of Texas, whose April 1969 collapse with an $8 million hole in the balance sheet earned him a five-year probationary sentence for fraud.

Vesco and Cerny opened negotiations to buy the bank Zimmerman had led them to in Geneva. Its name was Exchange and Investment Bank. Straub and Strickler had been down from Zurich to look over the establishment and came back with the report that it was "bootiful." It had extra work permits, money to manage, and a mutual fund already set up with $7 million in it. What could have been better?

Exchange and Investment Bank may have been "bootiful," but it had serious problems with the Swiss Banking Commission and the U.S. Attorney's office in New York. Robert Morgenthau, then U.S. Attorney for the Southern District of New York, had discovered that Exchange and Investment Bank was in fact a laundromat for Meyer Lansky's gambling interests. The owners of record turned out to be two New York brassiere manufacturers. They were said to be fronting for Ben Siegelbaum, a Mob "money-man"; Ed Levinson, a veteran Las Vegas gambler who fronted for Lansky in the ownership of several casinos; and Lou Poller, who was backed to the hilt by Teamster Brotherhood funds. Poller was a former president of the Miami National Bank. According to Morgenthau, more than $2 million a month skimmed from the operations of the Flamingo Hotel and Casino in Las Vegas went through Miami National Bank to Exchange and Investment Bank in Geneva and came back to the States again through a variety of channels.

Furthermore, Exchange and Investment Bank had been cited the year before as being involved in a conspiracy to defraud Chase Manhattan of $2 million. It was not the most savory of establishments.

But the appointments were first class. Located in a modern downtown Geneva office building, the bank looked like a typical Fifth Avenue operation with a huge circular vault door in the window, thick red carpeting, and a long rosewood counter. Only one thing was missing—clients.

The managing director, Henri-Albert Jaques, was a little concerned because he didn't know who owned 60 per cent of his bank. Otherwise, the business was straightforward and ran smoothly, he said. "We do between $3 million and $4 million weekly in brokerage business with orders coming in from Nassau and Miami," he reported to one of Vesco's emissaries.

Negotiations for the Geneva bank's purchase were coordinated by Howard Cerny. When informed that a posh bank without any apparent clients seemed somewhat fishy, he snapped back, "Don't worry about a thing. We already know all about this. I've reported it to the FBI."

And, indeed, the deal went no farther. However, with Berne drafting new regulations for foreign mutual fund operations in Switzerland it became imperative to have a representative Swiss bank that would accept responsibility for Executive Growth's registration with the Federal Banking Commission. The search for a bank continued, and in December 1969, with an additional $175,000 investment from Vesco, Executive Financial purchased a small Lucerne-based bank with cobwebs in the windows called Standard Commerz Bank. To give the bank the required 51 per cent Swiss ownership, 49 per cent of the stock was held by Executive Financial, 49 per cent by Ulrich Strickler, who became the managing director, and 2 per cent by the former owner.

Executive Growth Fund never reached $500,000 in assets. The stock market had turned bearish and the $5 million Vesco promised from European friends never arrived. "The market broke forty or fifty points about that time. That was the reason the fund didn't go," he said.

Vesco told the *Wall Street Journal* he owned only a minority interest in the Executive Growth venture and had "absolutely nothing" to do with its operations.[4] This was not what he told Malcolm McAlpin. "Bob asked me to look in at his office in Zurich to see if we could work out something with his mutual fund operation," McAlpin said.

Straub sent a limousine to the airport to meet McAlpin, who was on his way home from a holiday in Greece. Straub was all charm, McAlpin remembered, but the office was in turmoil. Chamides had resigned,

4 *Wall Street Journal,* September 3, 1971.

and the fund was stagnating without professional management. McAlpin decided there was little he could do to help and returned to New York. Straub who subsequently was named president of Executive Growth Management S.A. and Executive Financial A.G., spent a lot of his time setting up appointments for Vesco with IOS's Henry Buhl. He hired a chauffeur and purchased a Mercedes and a Jaguar. At its peak in late 1969 the Executive group had fifteen people on the payroll.

Straub designed a $27,000 ad campaign to get sales rolling. It produced more than 1,000 responses, but all the letters were stuffed into a desk drawer and never answered. Straub's operating ability was somewhat restricted by the fact that the Swiss authorities had refused to grant him a work permit. He was so petrified about being uncovered as a wetback in Zurich that every time the postman rang the doorbell he hid in a back room, one associate recalled.

Vesco kept on sending money over on an erratic schedule of $40,000 or so every few months to meet the mounting office expenses. "They're pissing money down a hole over there," he was heard to remark in Fairfield. Finally, when it was all added up, Vesco had invested something like $400,000 and Anderson an additional $160,000 with little to show in return.

During the next two years Vesco played down or denied altogether his connection with an offshore mutual fund that flopped. After coming out at $10 a share, by the end of 1969 Executive Growth was floundering around $5 a share. The fund hobbled along until late May 1970, as Vesco was structuring his play for IOS, when a desperate Straub telexed New York pleading for funds. The operation, he said, was literally on the verge of bankruptcy. It was time to bail out.

Straub and Strickler found a buyer for the Executive group of companies in the person of yet another graduate of the Capital Growth academy. He was Harry H. Crow, formerly of Little Rock, who was then living in London. Crow paid $60,000 for the management and sales companies that operated Executive Growth Fund, which meant that Vesco's loss on the operation was close to half a million dollars.

Vesco told Scott Schmedel of the *Wall Street Journal* that he didn't remember much about his association with Executive Growth Fund. In any event, he said, it was "insignificant" and "irrelevant" to his later role in IOS. "Personal investments are personal business," Vesco said, "and they aren't relevant." [5]

Vesco also denied to the SEC, in sworn testimony given in April 1971, that he had any participation in a foreign financial group prior to his involvement with IOS.

"Had you ever had any banking or brokerage affiliation with a fi-

[5] *Ibid.*

nancial institution in Switzerland before [opening a personal account with Bank Cantrade in Zurich about one year ago]?" he was asked by a member of the Commission staff.

"Before the Cantrade account? No," Vesco replied.

"So Cantrade was the first affiliation you've had. Is that correct?"

"The first and only." [6]

But, when questioned by shareholders at an IOS annual general meeting about his qualifications to run a troubled financial services combine the size of IOS—at the time the myth was being propagated that Vesco was the "savior" of IOS—Vesco replied, "My background has been primarily financial, although I studied somewhat to be an engineer at one point in time. International Controls has grown primarily through its financial expertise. . . . Beyond that I had significant involvements in . . . brokerage business on Wall Street. . . . I've also been on the boards of various banks, have indeed owned one myself along with having owned a very small offshore mutual fund personally." [7] He didn't identify the mutual fund, but he insisted it wasn't Executive Growth.

Perhaps it was out of concern not to trouble his "political affiliations," as he had suggested earlier, which was stretching gullibility pretty thin, but the whys and wherefores of Vesco's attempts to deny past ownership of a fund complex that flopped remained obscure. Rejection of any association with failure seemed more likely.

All the same, the experience Vesco gained in his unsuccessful Executive Growth operation would be invaluable to him during the summer of 1970, when he came to make his move for control of crisis-bound IOS.

[6] Vesco testimony before the SEC, April 1971, p. 54.
[7] IOS Ltd. Transcript of Annual Meeting, Toronto, June 30, 1971, p. 35.

5

A Haven for Black Money

How, twelve years before Vesco's first dabblings in international finance, Bernie Cornfeld enlisted the help of a "Blue Sky" legal expert to build the perfect offshore fund ~ The coming of the Moneycatcher and the big territory grab ~ From running a mutineers' gantlet on the Congo River to bicycling through South America on the IOS hot money route

Bernie Cornfeld, like Robert Vesco, understood the cupidity, and innocence, of people who wanted to get rich quick. Cornfeld was among the first to realize that investor dynamics had changed significantly during the decade of reconstruction following World War II. Not only in Europe but around the world a new affluence had placed unprecedented wealth in the hands of unsophisticates who could easily be "sold" on investing their money with less traditional institutions domiciled in such havens as Tangiers or Panama. The sales pitch employed stressed capital appreciation rather than capital preservation and, as an enticing extra, complete client anonymity, which translated into an absence of income tax controls.

Born in Istanbul on August 17, 1927, to emigrant parents of modest means, Cornfeld had spent the first years of his life in Vienna, where his mother, Sophie, a nurse from Odessa, had attended business school before World War I. His father, a motion picture executive, was Rumanian, which gave the future offshore financier a decidedly international outlook from the day he was born.

At the height of the Depression, one year after the Vienna Kreditanstalt collapse, the Cornfelds moved to America. Soon afterwards his parents separated. Little Beno, as Sophie called her son, grew up in Brooklyn with a maddening stutter and a glint of repressed mischief in his pale green eyes.

After graduating from Brooklyn College he became a social worker in Philadelphia for a time, taught psychology for a term at Bryn Mawr, the exclusive liberal arts college for girls near Philadelphia, then returned to New York and began selling mutual funds. He found the work challenging, and it gave him the freedom he needed. He liked it better than social work, he said, because "in social work you find that most problems you deal with have an economic base. But by encouraging people to create savings through mutual funds you prevent most of these problems from occuring before they exist."

Cornfeld's imagination always had been one of the more lively things about him. This was firmly underlined in late 1955 when he arrived in Paris on a half-holiday, half-selling expedition. He soon met a couple of girls in the Left Bank bars and cafés he visited and decided that Europe really was the place to be. After testing his New York sales approach in the Paris area, successfully selling a few mutual fund programs to expatriate Americans, in early 1956 he placed a recruiting ad in the *International Herald Tribune* that spoke of an empire blessed by the sun rising over Montmartre. To the casual reader the tone of the ad might have sounded sober enough, but in typical Cornfeld fashion the language was a minor masterpiece of misrepresentation.

> INVESTMENT FIRM, distributing monthly investment programs in leading American Mutual Funds, is expanding its European operations. We are looking for American men and women who wish to make a career of the investment business. We offer an education in estate planning in our training program along with the opportunity of earning over $10,000 a year. If you have sales ability, a willingness to work hard and a sense of humor, contact us. Write: Box 28, 225 Herald.

The firm, of course, was baby IOS, actually still in an embryonic form since it had not officially been born. But even so, it was expanding from the living room of Cornfeld's two-room Paris studio, which he rented in the fashionable XVIe arrondissement. Whether it was the sense of humor, the willingness to work hard, or the earnings opportunity, the ad produced an unlikely collection of seventeen men and a woman who in the first year pulled hard together to bring in just over one million dollars in sales.[1]

Young Cornfeld, then twenty-nine, had talked New York investment manager Jack Dreyfus into giving him overseas distribution rights to a new product whose symbol was a shaggy lion standing in the middle of Wall Street. Known as the Dreyfus Fund, it became the first of the

[1] Sales figures, as is the custom in the mutual fund industry, always refer to the total "face amount" of the ten- or fifteen-year investment plans that are "contracted" to be made by the investor. Like so much else in this industry, it is an illusory figure.

U.S. growth funds. Cornfeld and his little band of salesmen, none of whom had any experience in the securities business, started by selling Dreyfus investment programs to American servicemen at NATO bases in France. As their contacts with Europeans gradually expanded, Cornfeld began to suspect that there might be millions of well-to-do people all over the world willing to invest in mutual funds, provided they were sold hard enough and offered a unique selling proposition—freedom from exchange controls and tax collectors' surveillance. To guarantee these two essentials, in 1958 Cornfeld decided to base his operations in Switzerland, where faceless Swiss bankers maintain a highly sophisticated parallel currency market and tax evasion is not a criminal offense.

There was one other reason for the move to Geneva. The French authorities had begun an early investigation of IOS to determine whether it was breaking France's strict currency controls—which it was—by shipping clients' undeclared dollars to New York as forage for the Lion of Wall Street. The hungry Lion then had assets totaling $36 million, but within eight years they were to surpass $2 billion, to a large extent due to the heroic efforts of the IOS sales force. Cornfeld's response to IOS's first run-in with government controls was to load the client files into the back of his secondhand Chrysler convertible and drive them to Switzerland.

Cornfeld might always have remained a moderately successful mutual fund salesman had he not met the nimble-minded Edward M. Cowett. Originally from Springfield, Massachusetts, where his father was a lawyer, Cowett was a *cum laude* graduate of Harvard Law School, class of '54. He spent two more years at Harvard as a research associate, then slid straight into the expanding mutual fund industry about the time Cornfeld was setting up his Investors Overseas Services in Paris.

A slightly built man with dark, piercing eyes, black slicked-back hair, and acrobatic poise, Cowett was then only twenty-six, three years Cornfeld's junior, but already an acknowledged expert on Blue Sky Law, which regulates the sale of securities within the various states.

Blue Sky laws derive their colorful name from shady operators who offer unsuspecting investors all sorts of promises as to the future performance of the stocks they peddle so that the client believes he has "the world with a fence around it and a blue sky overhead." Cowett's book on Blue Sky Law, which he co-authored with his distinguished professor at Harvard, Louis Loss, became the standard reference work.

The Blue Sky expert was an associate in the New York law firm that acted as counsel to the Dreyfus Fund when Cornfeld first encountered him. However, Cowett was soon specializing in sleazy promotional issues of the sort that Blue Sky laws are intended to guard against. Of course, no more qualified authority existed in the land. But his activities were not appreciated by his partners, who asked him to resign. Cornfeld, though, was quick to take him on as general counsel.

In April 1960 Cowett flew to Geneva for his first on-site inspection of the IOS operations. The IOS carousel was turning faster than ever, with annual sales of $20 million, but Cornfeld was having difficulty raising capital to finance the self-generating expansion of his sales force, then 150 strong. At that point he asked himself, Why not raise the necessary working capital from the very people who were benefiting most from the firm's success by selling them an equity participation?

The idea had the simple touch of genius to it. No sooner had Cowett arrived in Geneva than Bernie asked him to look into the matter with an eye to giving it some legal polish. The fact that IOS had not yet been incorporated hardly seemed to matter.

Cowett quickly came up with the basic design for the IOS Stock Option Plan. The number of shares any one associate could acquire was determined by the total face amount of investment programs he sold. The escalating options ranged upward to 20,000 shares and were cleverly calculated to cost the salesmen a little more than they generally could afford. But the vision of one day becoming rich like Cornfeld made them accept.

The IOS Stock Option Plan became the gilt on the gingerbread. The 20,000-share limit, furthermore, did not take into account the successive stock splits that cascaded one after another as IOS matured, which was how the early directors built up such truly prodigious holdings of company paper.

The formula used to determine the value of the stock was put together by Cowett in such a way as to practically guarantee the price would constantly rise at an awesome rate. While the myth was intact, it assured that the shareholders, all key people in the company, would remain loyal to the firm and continue to sell at an ever rising pitch.

After two years operating from a Swiss haven and within weeks of issuing the first stock options, Cornfeld, upon the advice of Cowett, got around to incorporating IOS Ltd., the corporate kingpin of his growing empire, as a *sociedad anonima* in Panama. This transformation of IOS from a sole proprietorship to a stock company with limited liability marked the beginning of offshoreness as a consciously promoted concept. Cowett spent the next decade constantly refining and improving the concept, but with that April 1960 move he laid the jurisprudential foundations for the outstanding success and unparalleled debacle that would follow.

Nine years later, in 1969, Cowett transferred IOS's registered offices to the financial backwater of Saint John, New Brunswick. By then he had observed that Canada offered classical offshore operations like IOS the same tax-free benefits as a banana republic. Furthermore, Canada's strong financial markets would facilitate the listing of IOS securities when the time was at hand. More important, though, both Cornfeld and Cowett were to learn that Canadian regulatory agencies exercised little influence over nonresident corporations that conducted their affairs elsewhere. In the process, Cowett had created at Cornfeld's peril a business that was uniquely ripe for manipulation.

With Cowett's legal quicksand for a firm foundation, IOS's spectacular development as a transnational financial institution was now constructed around the dual pillars of "black," or illegal, sales and the designing of slick international mutual funds whose operations, conveniently cloaked by strict foreign secrecy laws, defied regulation. Unfortunately, these two mainstays of IOS's growth contained the structural faults that ten years later would permit the offshore giant, after it was brought to its knees by a grueling crisis of confidence, to be plundered of its assets.

About the time the fearless deal-maker Bob Vesco was striking out on his own to become a millionaire, Cornfeld's senior salesmen—some of them earning as much as $80,000 a year by then—were returning from such out-of-the-way places as Afghanistan and the upper reaches of the Orinoco with wild stories of potential clients just waiting for the right kind of investment vehicle to come along and carry off their undeclared profits for safekeeping abroad. American mutual funds, because of their disclosure requirements, were not ideally suited for this type of work. After Cornfeld and Cowett had given the problem their careful consideration, it dawned on them that a truly "worldwide mutual fund" specially tailored to the requirements of the international investor might be an excellent vehicle for soaking up the loose flight capital that abounded in the farthest reaches of this newly affluent world.

An international banker from Geneva, Tibor Rosenbaum, claimed that he was the first person to suggest to Cornfeld the idea of founding "an international investment trust." Rosenbaum, later the Liberian Ambassador to Austria, was president of International Credit Bank in Geneva. He said that Cornfeld liked the sound of his idea for an international investment fund and suggested that IOS and ICB might successfully combine their resources in creating just that sort of product. This was not the way the project developed, however. Cornfeld immediately spoke with Cowett; the Blue Sky expert wasted no time in setting up a suitable vehicle in Luxembourg, where taxes on fund holdings were only $6 per $10,000 and regulatory controls did not then exist. When Rosenbaum returned to see Cornfeld some months later to discuss the project in greater depth, IOS's first dollar fund was already on the launching pad.

IIT, an International Investment Trust, was rushed into service in December 1960 with much back-slapping and self-congratulation. Keeping IIT on the rails, though, proved more of a problem than Cornfeld had bargained for. IOS, whatever insiders might have deluded themselves into thinking, was essentially a company of salesmen. Clearly, managing other people's money was to remain beyond IOS's capacities for some time to come.

Among the "unique advantages" listed by Cowett in IIT's first prospectus was an assurance to prospective clients that sagely stated, "Prudence requires that there should be certain basic restrictions to protect the investor, and these restrictions have been imposed on IIT Management."

While omitting to specify what these restrictions were, the flimsy eight-page document added that "management of IIT intends to invest *limited portions* of the Fund's capital in those special and local investment situations which, after a thorough examination, appear to involve a comparatively small risk factor and an unusually high profit potential."

Special situations became Cowett's specialty. By the end of 1961, the fund's first full year of operation, he had tiny IIT invested in eight special situations for a total value of $100,000.

In spite of the unsettled world situation following the Berlin crisis and the Bay of Pigs disaster, burgeoning IIT had moved into 1962 fully confident that a profitable year lay ahead. In fact, so well was IIT's $3.7 million portfolio diversified—a total of 113 positions in twenty countries—that in the headlong market crash that summer the fund tumbled in share value 30 per cent below issuing price. It was IOS's first brush with disaster. Cornfeld blamed the fund's performance gap on generally poor market conditions and the difficulty of finding competent investment advisers in Europe who were trained in U.S. management techniques.

However, the real story behind IIT's 1962 troubles was quite different. It involved Ed Cowett's court-martial before the IOS board of directors and the loss of his IOS and IIT directorships. Cowett had obviously felt that the "basic restrictions" referred to in the IIT prospectus did not apply to him. He had, from his New York office, acted as legal adviser to a succession of small companies which he then helped go public. His technique was to bring out stock issues in these companies with splendid offering circulars and then to push the price skyward on a cloud of enthusiasm.

On the side, Cowett, was also making a market in some of these stocks while ensuring that IIT took a position in them. Of course, if the market in his little fliers were maintained on margin—borrowed money—the profits stood to be even greater. As long as stock prices continued to rise there was no problem. But should they fall, with prudence thrown to the wind catastrophe never lags far behind.

And did the market fall! On Monday, May 28, 1962, it dropped like a stone. The Dow Jones Industrial Average dipped a staggering 34.95 points—its sharpest decline in thirty-three years. In that Blue Monday tumble and its aftermath Cowett was left holding large positions in a number of his wonder babies which overnight placed the Blue Sky expert nearly $1 million in debt, which meant that he had to give serious consideration to filing a petition in bankruptcy.

In an effort to marshal all available resources to bail himself out of this predicament, Cowett "borrowed" some IOS corporate funds on deposit at a major New York bank for his own personal use. He also negotiated the sale of his IOS stock—2,500 shares purchased from Cornfeld in 1960—in a transaction that IOS itself had intended to conclude. He sold the stock to New York fund manager John Templeton for $100,000. It was a cloudy deal, quite contrary to the terms of the IOS Stock Option Plan, which of course he was eminently familiar with since he had drafted them.

When his personal financial difficulties were uncovered, he was arraigned before the IOS board and asked to explain the possible unfavorable implications his various dealings might have for IOS and the fledgling IIT. Cowett, admitting that he had "exercised poor judgment," said he preferred not to talk about it and quietly handed in his resignation, thereby end-running a motion before the board calling for his ouster.

Fortunately for Cowett, Cornfeld stepped in and personally helped him out. With $50,000 in swing money loaned by Cornfeld, Cowett was able to stave off bankruptcy. The scandal blew over, but Cowett had to withdraw from his New York law firm, move to Geneva permanently, and go to work for Cornfeld on a full-time basis to pay off his debt. Bernie was delighted. He thought he had his legal eagle in a gilded cage, and a heavily mortgaged one at that.

Cornfeld meanwhile slipped one of his newest recruits, C. Henry Buhl III, into the vacant IIT Management presidency and gave him orders to nurse the pale IIT back to robust health. Before joining IOS in mid-1961, Buhl had been European manager of the New York brokerage house, later defunct, of McDonnell & Company. His starting salary at IOS was $100 a week—the highest the company had ever paid up to that time. But Cornfeld was impressed by Buhl's family background and asked Henry to put his many excellent banking contacts to use drumming up some institutional interest in the struggling IIT fund.

Once the IIT situation was again more or less under control, it had become evident to Cornfeld and his top lieutenants that new tools were needed if IOS was to make a significant breakthrough in the international market. Bernie's 500-man "piece corps" (for the piece of the capitalistic system that Cornfeld said they were selling) had already saturated most of the U.S. embassies and military bases in Europe, North Africa, and the Middle East, and his salesmen, for lack of better game, had begun stalking the indigenous populations. With IIT temporarily in disgrace the game was difficult. And although the Dreyfus Fund was certainly an excellent performer, it had serious disadvantages for investors who were not U.S. citizens. For one thing, dividends paid by Dreyfus were subject to American withholding tax. For another, should one of IOS's non-American investors die before liquidating his Dreyfus program there might be U.S. inheritance taxes to pay, and this could tie up a non-resident's money for several years.

In understanding and solving these problems, Ed Cowett was indispensable, and for this reason he remained available to the company as general counsel. Cowett pointed out to thte IOS board of directors that, while people are subject to death duties, corporations are not.

Cowett suggested that IOS form an investment program for its clients which would itself be incorporated outside U.S. jurisdiction. In this way, rather than having people directly own the shares of the mutual funds, the owner of record would become a company.

Thus, Cowett pointed out, when the holder of an IOS investment program died there would be no taxes due to any government by the mutual fund since a corporation, as the owner of record, is an entity that does not die. The directors, all of them outstanding salesmen but otherwise not particularly gifted in general business, liked Cowett's idea. A Company called IOS Investment Program Limited was duly created in the Bahamas, where there is no taxation. The new company became the common trust holder of mutual fund shares purchased by IOS clients.

The tax-saving features of the IOS Investment Program were first-class, but without products to sell it remained only an empty shell. Obviously IOS had thought of this, and work was under way to shape a second mutual fund that would solve the company's lack of management skills, since this newly envisaged fund would invest only in other professionally managed mutual funds.

There are two stories about how Cornfeld came up with the idea for a fund of funds. Whichever version is correct is of little consequence because the concept ended up making Cornfeld famous during the booming 1960s, his name a household word.

The more romantic version, and the one favored by IOS, claimed that the idea was dreamed up by Cornfeld, Cowett, and Jean Auer, IOS's first director of Canadian operations, during a winter's night sleigh ride atop Montreal's Mount Royal. After being struck by their brainwave, the three men immediately set about forming the idea into what seemed like a perfect investment vehicle with the intensity of a band of revolutionaries plotting social upheaval.

A more likely version of how The Fund of Funds came into existence is that it was plagiarized from the North American Investment Fund, a small offshore operation that a team of Miami businessmen were about to launch from a secure tax base in the Netherlands Antilles. Richard Hammerman, a Miami insurance underwriter, was interviewed by the North American group for a management position. The Miami promoters told Hammerman their idea for an investment company that any idiot could manage because it invested exclusively in well-run U.S. funds.

Hammerman told the Miami group he would think over their employment offer, then boarded a plane for Geneva to sound out Cornfeld. Bernie liked what he heard and asked Hammerman to stay around and head IOS's planned insurance division. Cornfeld's next step was to sit down with Ed Cowett and, using a Canadian multifund investment program prospectus for additional inspiration, structure their new investment company as a nonresident Province of Ontario corporation with registered offices in Toronto.

For a long while no one could decide what the new fund should be called. Cornfeld held out for the very noble and biblical-sounding The Fund of Funds Limited. Finally the others, who thought it corny, gave in. Bernie, as usual, got his way. But Bernie was also, as usual, right. The name clicked. The Fund of Funds had instant appeal. The product looked so dazzling when it first came out that IOS's sales volume immediately doubled.

The Fund of Funds was launched simultaneously with the IOS Investment Program in October 1962, just as the U.S. markets began to turn around, giving it the best of all possible performance boosts. Issued at $10 a share, it climbed in net asset value per share over the next six years to an all-time high of $27, with total assets soaring to $797 million.

The IOS sales force went wild with enthusiasm and immediately gave FOF all sorts of inventive names. The Dollar-Crested Moneycatcher, a rare bird at that, was one. The Crested Traveler was another. The appeal of this strange bird was that its early structure appeared to provide investors with double security, double diversification, and double management. On this basis it was widely sold and widely accepted, perhaps because the first Fund of Funds prospectus neglected to mention that shareholders had no voting rights. All voting shares were held by IOS Ltd. through one of its assignees, FOF Management Company. This meant that the management company could change the fund's structure at will, control its investments, and set all manner of policy decisions without consulting the public "Class A" shareholders.

The IOS Investment Program, under which IIT and FOF were now sold, had another feature that proved to be a worldbeater. In IOS jargon, this creature was known as a CAPINS, which stood for Capital Accumulation Program with Insurance.

Basically this meant that a client was able to purchase, as an optional extra, insurance coverage that guaranteed the completion of his investment program should he die before its term. This service was quite common in the U.S. fund industry, but since no American or European company would underwrite client risk in every one of the sixty-odd countries where IOS was then operating, the Geneva fundmen decided to found their own insurance company, which they named International Life Insurance Company S.A.

ILI, as this alphabetical addition to the IOS family became known, was incorporated in Luxembourg early in 1962, with Dick Hammerman as president. It was a meaningful event in IOS's history as it marked the company's first attempt to move out of the strictly mutual fund end of the business and into as many branches of the financial services field as possible.

The launching of the IOS Investment Program coincided with one of the greatest adventures in IOS history. The Big Territory Grab had a cast of Bernie Cornfeld's hundreds, a cash flow of millions. From it evolved the designs and decisions that would shape the IOS sales organization over the years ahead, in both geographical and managerial terms. While it contained many of the elements of IOS's startling success, it also held the seeds of its destruction. The Big Territory Grab ended up creating a top-heavy sales structure that was stimulated by an over-generous stock option plan into producing illusory volume, operated at a loss, and was dependant on high-risk, scandal-prone "black" business in illegal sales areas.

To keep track of the territory concessions and to rule on the overrides awarded to the pioneering IOS representatives who staked their claims to new sales areas the fastest, Allen Cantor was brought back to Geneva from Iran, where he had built up a successful clandestine operation that was raking in several millions a month. Cantor was installed on the top floor of the corporate headquarters at 119 rue de Lausanne in a tiny office next to Bernie's and promoted to chief sales administrator.

Cantor, a onetime Brooklyn Law School student, had forsaken his law degree to go to work for Cornfeld back in 1958. He had spent the summer traveling in Europe that year and decided he wanted to stay, so he attended an IOS training session, becoming a junior salesman. Cowett actually took credit for spotting Cantor, once the law school dropout began making a mark for himself in the sales field, as a "man with top management stuff." After the 1970 crisis of confidence, however, Cowett reversed this appraisal, stating that Cantor was one of the architects of IOS's downfall. Cowett fingered Cantor as the one responsible for putting in place the inefficient IOS sales structure, which eventually grew so burdensome that it ate up earnings faster than the Blue Sky expert could gear up new profit centers.

Promotion in the field structure was based on an individual's ability to sell. The more a salesman sold, or the more the group he supervised produced in business volume, the higher he climbed in the field hierarchy. The higher a manager rose on the promotions list, the more overriding commissions he received and the wealthier he became. Then, just as important, greater sales volume tied in with personal promotion equaled a more generous stock option allotment, and the more stock a salesman held the greater his voice became in company councils.

Fierce rivalry inevitably broke out among the major producers as they fought to bring newly discovered territories into their respective spheres of influence. Override-hungry regional managers stood like generals before huge wall maps of the world planning their global strategy, skirmishing if necessary with rival IOS managers to extend or maintain their control over marginal, less productive areas. This rather strange and capricious system, supposedly based upon modern management concepts, more closely resembled something feudal in design. The major fiefdoms were divided among the strongest overlords.

Early on in the game two IOS recruits foresaw most of what was to come and decided that teamwork was the best way of achieving fast and effective sales dominance. From sharing an apartment in Paris they built one of the most cavalier partnerships in the topsy-turvy world of offshore finance.

Don Q. Shaprow and George Landau started their IOS careers in 1959 and were sent to Africa to hunt down new business. Shaprow rose quickly in the organization, obtaining a personal sales volume of $5 million by the time he was elected to the IOS board of directors in 1962. Balding, with cheeks full of marbles, and generally good-humored, Shaprow had sold only two things before finding shelter under Cornfeld's roof: light bulbs in his father's hardware store back in Buffalo, New York, and cars to GIs in Europe.

George Landau was another kettle of fish. Even before graduating from IOS's five-day training course he had sold his first $60,000 in Dreyfus business. He went on with Shaprow in Africa to chalk up $4.5 million in personal volume over the next three years. Born in Poland in 1932, Landau spent the war years as a refugee in Iran, emigrating afterward to the United States. A science graduate from the University of Rochester in upstate New York, he worked as a salesman with the Nuclear Power Division of Westinghouse before joining IOS.

Landau and Shaprow devised a common strategy based on high personal volume, which put them in a dominating position in the IOS structure in very quick order. Sharing their commissions as they went, they proceeded to tear apart Africa, wherever possible recruiting new salesmen to work under them by promising a secure future and a slice of the action for those who qualified for an IOS stock option.

One IOS salesman who followed the Landau-Shaprow trail through parts of West Africa was warned by the U.S. Embassy in Monrovia, capital of Liberia, not to use the same sharp tactics employed by his two supervisors, as the embassy would be unable to offer assistance if he got into trouble. And trouble, he soon found out, was plentiful.

On a service visit to Lamco (Liberian American Mining Company) camps out in the bush, our itinerant investment counselor said he found a string of people complaining that they had been oversold by that "very nice Mr. Landau of yours." The personnel manager at one camp claimed he had told Landau he only had $3,000 to invest. Landau, instead of selling the mark a modest, fully paid program, turned around and signed him up to a ten-year $18,000 capital accumulation program in the Dreyfus Fund, using the $3,000 as the first two years' down payment.

For Landau, the benefits of such a sale were evident since it meant he would be credited with six times the volume and four times the commission. On the other hand, the client, mistakenly convinced he had a fully paid investment, was eventually declared delinquent for not continuing his payments. Finally a check for roughly $1,300 was returned to him in the mail—all that remained of his initial investment after deduction of the sales and administrative charges.

Shaprow and Landau, meanwhile, had decided that they needed a foothold in Europe. Since many of their clients in Africa were of Dutch origin they moved into the Netherlands, and from there they staked their claim to all Dutch-speaking areas of the world. With these new territories added to their roster at headquarters, no other IOS associate was allowed to sell in the Netherlands, and later the other Benelux countries, without the express authorization of Shaprow or Landau, and without paying them an override on any contracted business.

Hence the Netherlands became the center of an empire never dreamed of by William of Orange. Sales crews were dispatched from Amsterdam to Africa, the Caribbean, and even farther afield to the Dutch East Indies of olden times. By 1966 the Landau-Shaprow territories, known under the code Europe VI–Africa I, were producing $5 million monthly in sales volume. By 1969, just before the crash, their total had jumped to $14 million monthly.

Under these conditions good times and bad times were all the same for the Landau-Shaprow machine. In fact bad times, politically speaking, were generally better, as they meant a rush of flight capital in IOS's direction. Thus, during the Congo crisis of the early 1960s the former Belgian colony became one of the most lucrative Landau areas. There were little contretemps now and then, but nothing serious.

One IOS carpetbagger, Douglas MacKinnon, was captured by the Congolese rebels and held hostage in Matadi's Palace Hotel. From the window he saw one Belgian get his brains bashed in by an Armée Nationale Congolaise mutineer, and he heard vivid reports from others of women being raped and children who were savagely beaten.

MacKinnon and the other European prisoners at the hotel escaped one night in the dark and were taken aboard a Belgian freighter. They spent two days and two nights on the Congo River, running without pilot or lights, before they passed through the islands at the mouth of the Congo and made it out to sea. When MacKinnon touched ground again he sent an epic telegram to Cornfeld in Geneva describing the incredible mayhem of those terrible days and recounting his lucky escape.

When the telegram was read out to Cornfeld, according to Mac-Kinnon, the IOS founder gave this reply: "That's all very well and fine. But did he sell anything?"

Another rich Landau-Shaprow territory was Nigeria, where general manager Joe Sands was in command. Throughout the entire two-year Diafran conflict Sands, who was wanted in Rhodesia on charges of fraud resulting from his sales efforts there, had twelve IOS reps operating across the country. So well known were some of them to the local authorities that they were given greater freedom of movement than most U.N. and other foreign aid personnel helping General Yakubu Gowon get the country back together. While the Russians and British poured assistance into strife-torn Nigeria, Sands and his corpsmen were busy shipping some of it up to Geneva for investment in the IOS dollar funds.

The rise of IOS as an offshore power that transcended national jurisdictions and rivaled smaller governments in its sweep of influence was directly related to the infusion of hot money into the dollar funds. The IOS Investment Program, finally, was not—as Cornfeld and his associates so often proclaimed—the custodial bookkeeper of investments belonging to close to one million small and intermediate fundholders, portrayed for the most part as law-abiding folk eager to share in the profits of IOS-styled People's Capitalism. It became, rather, a device for sheltering international flight capital.

IOS's army of sales executives broke their backs smuggling currency worth hundreds of millions of dollars from countries with restrictive exchange controls and stringent revenue reporting requirements. These illegal activities were notorious and resulted in prohibitions against IOS's continued operations in many parts of the world.

Nowhere was this hot money trade more highly developed than in Latin America. There IOS sales managers had found a most astute way to remove funds from developing economies and clandestinely transfer them into investment accounts in Geneva.

Under this "added service," a client would entrust at least $50,000—the minimum amount accepted for such transactions—to an IOS rep, who would have it smuggled out of the country by special courier. Once the money arrived in Geneva it would be deposited with International Credit Bank and then "loaned" back to its owner at 6 per cent annual interest. IOS salesmen carried special forms for such "loan requests." The "loan" proceeds, naturally, were invested in The Fund of Funds or IIT. The "loan" was collateralized by the fund shares. The "loans" were extended on a one-year renewable basis and could be canceled on thirty days' notice.

The "loan" could then be shown on the Latin American's books as being required for foreign representation fees, promotion abroad, European travel, or whatever. Since the contracting of a loan through a foreign bank was above board, the client was legally entitled to send money out of the country to cover interest and eventual repayment of principal.

The money for the phony loans was picked up on a more or less regular basis by Sylvain Ferdman, an officer of International Credit Bank. Using his frequent trips on what euphemistically became referred to as the "Ferdman bicycle circuit," he served all twenty Latin American countries where IOS did business. The money was bagged to Geneva in a suitcase and deposited at International Credit Bank. If ever the bag were opened at Geneva airport by customs inspectors, Ferdman might have been offered the services of a Swiss security guard to escort him to the bank. There is no restriction on the entry or exit of capital from Switzerland.

By employing such quasi-legal methods the lucky IOS client was able to export double the amount of capital he wished held secretly abroad. Once the "loan" was "repaid," as far as the authorities were concerned the client maintained no foreign exchange outside the country, since on his accounting ledger everything had been squared away. Squared away was right—in an undeclared Fund of Funds or IIT investment program. It was a variation of the Mafia skimming technique, but attractively packaged for everyday citizens in search of illicit profits.

Ferdman had been Cowett's roommate at Harvard, where no doubt some of their later activities together loosely had been kicked about, as college students tend to do when discussing their future plans. Ferdman became extremely practiced at bagging hot money, and his talents were not limited to the South American run. A porky, ebullient naturalized Swiss who worked for Tibor Rosenbaum as an "economic adviser," he was soon sought by a federal grand jury sitting in New York to give testimony concerning his role as a courier of Mafia funds between the United States and secret bank accounts in the Bahamas and Switzerland. Once the wind had blown over these proceedings, all Ferdman would say about his travels was, "When you're a young man sometimes you do things you later regard as having been foolish."

Suitcases of black money skimmed off the top of Mob-controlled rackets and gambling were carried from Miami and other Eastern Seaboard cities via two routes to Geneva—one direct by commercial airlines, the other through the Bahamas—where the hot cash was inducted into the international banking system and transferred through normal channels to Swiss banks and trusts. In this manner an estimated two million to three million dollars a week made its way to Geneva during the high period of IOS's growth.

Cornfeld thought that very little Mafia money went into the IOS funds. But he didn't exclude the possibility that the Mafia had used IOS as a laundromat for some of its hot money. "There were hundreds of transactions each day and it just wasn't possible to know about each one of them," he said.[2]

"There were the occasional million-dollar investments—even some of more than a million dollars—that we received, and those, of course, I knew about. Most of them came from the Middle East."

Then he added, "You know, it wasn't the kind of situation where we would receive instructions to open this or that account for a Mr. Lucky Luciano. Things just didn't happen that way.

"Anyway," he concluded after a moment's reflection, "most Swiss banks were doing exactly the same thing [as ICB], only their couriers never got caught. It was unfortunate that Sylvain was followed and found out. He was unlucky."

There were variations of the loan trick, and by no means was it geographically limited to Latin American investors. Nothing was

[2] In July 1969, IOS's peak month, there were more than 2,000 individual client transactions processed each working day at the IOS computer center in Nyon, Switzerland.

sacred. In some instances diplomatic pouches were used to run the cash, particularly on the route between Athens and Rome. From Rome the money filtered northward and crossed the Swiss frontier at Chiasso in southeastern Switzerland, where a number of banks seemed to exist largely on IOS transit business. Another favored device was the so-called ZIL account for smuggling dollars out of Brazil. This method was somewhat circuitous, as first the money went to Israel in the form of a charitable donation—the Brazilian authorities permitted the export of capital for charitable causes—and from Tel Aviv the cash contribution went by bank transfer into a floating account at Geneva that was labeled the ZIL account. Every time an investment application form marked ZIL was processed in Geneva the money was withdrawn from the floating account and placed in the specified Funds of Funds or IIT program.

Travel agency gimmicks also were devised, but the volume of business soon outstripped these rather ingenious ploys, which centered on the prepayment of travel arrangements in a soft-currency country, canceling them and requesting reimbursement in a hard-currency area. For a time IOS even considered going into the travel business, purchasing a small travel agency in New York, but it abandoned its plans when airlines and other suppliers got an inkling of what was going on.

From the moment IOS was able efficiently to demonstrate to middle-class investors that one did not have to be a member of the Mafia to salt away black money in a numbered bank account, the company's sales boomed—from $294 million in annual face amount in 1964 to $3 billion in 1969. A straight operation could never have made it so big so fast. The IOS mutual funds in very short order had become the largest pool of unregulated investment dollars in the world.

IOSers always assumed that a certain percentage of the assets under management in the mutual funds—totaling $2.3 billion when the 1970 crash occurred—would remain locked into the funds no matter what happened. This mattress of motionless cash became known around IOS as "Mug's Money." It was the focus of a great deal of speculation. The people who had invested the Mug's Money were not in a position to redeem it—at last not for a while—because it ran the risk of being identified as the proceeds of white-collar or organized crime.

Nobody really knew what percentage of the total IOS fund assets actually constituted Mug's Money, but members of middle management made frequent estimates, which placed it in the range of $150 million to $250 million—a lot of dead cash by anyone's standards. Such an inert cache was bound to attract plunderers. Which, of course, it did.

6

Ambassador at Large

A $100 million tax fraud is uncovered in Brazil, and Jimmy Roosevelt becomes IOS's ambassador of the free enterprise system, beginning a "dubious association," which Cornfeld uses to sell even more mutual funds — The Swiss chafe at being used as a haven for financial piracy, and Cornfeld reacts by sponsoring an international peace conference

The bagging of hot cash, however, did not always run smoothly. Armistice Day 1966, for example, was one of the darkest days in IOS history. During the night police in seven Brazilian cities, coordinated by the Army Intelligence Service, closed in on IOS's undercover offices, arrested at least thirteen top salesmen, and seized the files of more than 10,000 clients.

The raid was so well organized that, contrary to custom in Brazil, surprise was total and the results were devastating. The impact on morale at headquarters in Geneva may be inferred from the fact that until then Brazil had been IOS's largest market, with sales in 1966 running at a rate of $50 million per annum in face amount.

The head of Brazil's Internal Revenue Service charged IOS with illegally exporting over an eight-year period some $100 million in hard cash. The money was alleged to have been carried to Geneva by couriers and invested in The Fund of Funds, IIT, and other IOS products. It was, newspapers around the world reported, the largest tax swindle in Brazilian history.

An IOS statement, issued shortly after the news broke, blandly denied the "wild allegations" that the company was "directly" involved in the "income tax investigation" going on down there. Ed Cowett, who was in New York attending to matters related to the SEC's attempt to gain access to IOS's client files,[1] told newsmen who reached him at his suite at the Saint Regis Hotel that the company "did relatively little business in Brazil." In terms of later volume, the $4 million a month that IOS had been extracting from Brazil was relatively little, but by 1966 standards it represented a gold mine. Ed Cowett was playing it cool. When asked about the illegal removal of currency from the country, he replied, "We don't take payment in cruzeiros."

The Brazilian investigating magistrate appointed to the case had news for Cowett. "IOS has for a long time been aware of the illegality of its operations in Brazil," he told reporters. To back up his statement he charged IOS with nine major counts of tax and currency fraud, which under Brazilian law could have cost the company a maximum of $10 million in penalties and fines.

The senior IOS director in Brazil, a Shanghai-born Dane and an ex–Hong Kong shipping agent named John Jessen, was hauled from his home in Recife, the Venice of Brazil, at six in the evening by police and flown by military transport to Rio, where he was locked up for a week in the overcrowded Central Prison during the worst heat wave of the summer until IOS finally won his release.

Jessen was joined in jail by his number two man, Fred Börlin, a high-living Swiss noted for his expensive cars, fast girl friends, and frequent parties, Herbert Haupt von Buchenrode, later head of IOS operations in Vienna, and an alleged ex-army colonel from Israel, Jacob Tzur. Tzur eventually became IOS's director of client services, but unfortunately his career ended on a negative note in the summer of 1972 when he was arrested by the Geneva police. Charged with embezzling $115,000 from the investment account of a wealthy Arab doctor, although he steadfastly maintained his innocence, Tzur was sentenced to four years' imprisonment.

When Jessen, Börlin, von Buchenrode, Tzur, and the others started screaming for help from the depths of their ill-ventilated prison cell, IOS responded by sending a tough intelligence operator by the name of Jerry Berkin, for many years employed by U.S. military intelligence, down to Rio with instructions to do all in his power to spring the salesmen from prison.

"I'll just play it by ear," Berkin said before leaving the seventh-floor executive offices in Geneva. "It sounds like another typical IOS job to me."

[1] In December 1965 the SEC demanded that IOS produce a complete list of its American clients and details of their transactions with the company; if a breakdown of American clients were not available, the SEC demanded a list of all IOS's clients around the world. IOS refused to comply with the SEC demand, claiming it was bound by Swiss banking secrecy, and brought a court action seeking to enjoin the SEC from continuing its investigation.

The men were quietly released and slipped out of the country, never to return. Berkin, in recognition of his talents, later was asked to form an internal security force for IOS that numbered more than one hundred strong. But that was hardly where the Brazilian scandal ended. Long lists of IOS clients, their account numbers, and amounts invested began appearing in the local papers. The names thus revealed included wealthy industrialists, landowners, several parliamentary figures, a supreme court justice, and a number of highly placed army officers.

As a result of the tremendous publicity surrounding IOS's problems in Brazil, the company started having trouble in other Latin American countries. In Bogotá, IOS general manager Tom Branham was thrown in jail once the Colombian authorities realized what business he was in. In Bolivia, Paraguay, and Peru IOS was accused of seriously depleting the local hard currency reserves. A threatened scandal in Chile was skillfully covered up after pressure was applied in Washington and Santiago.

Among Brazil, the SEC, and the other IOS hot spots the atmosphere on the seventh floor at 119 rue de Lausanne was becoming extremely unpleasant when, one day in late November 1966, Cornfeld complained over the telephone to Cowett in New York that their plans for hiring IOS's very own trouble-shooting ambassador seemed to be dragging.

"Gee, Ed, I wish Jimmy would hurry up and make his announcement. We sure could use some good press around here," said an unusually depressed Cornfeld.

"I'll see what I can do," Cowett promised.

Earlier that summer IOS had started courting Jimmy Roosevelt, oldest son of Franklin Delano Roosevelt, with promises of a $100,000 salary if he would become an IOS director. Roosevelt was then U.S. Ambassador to the United Nations Economic and Social Council. He tentatively accepted a seat on the board of The Fund of Funds but reserved his decision on the remainder of the Cornfeld offer until he had given it more consideration. IOS, to be sure, lost no time in telling the world about Roosevelt's choice of mutual funds. And as the news spread it was predictably greeted with cries of conflict of interest.

The *New York Times* called it a show of "poor taste and judgment." In an editorial headed "Dubious Association," the *Times* blasted Roosevelt, stating that he had "every right as a citizen to put the prestige of his great family name and his own distinguished career in Congress on the line in the service of this company. But not the prestige of the United States of America, which he represents before the councils of the world."

The tough editorial didn't stop there. It went so far as to proclaim it was "clearly a matter of national embarrassment for an ambassador to be a director of a company involved in litigation against the government of which he is part." [2]

Even to Roosevelt it became clear that he had put the wrong foot forward, and upon returning to New York later that week he publicly back-tracked, renouncing his appointment to the FOF board while he served out the remainder of his term as second-ranking U.S. delegate to the United Nations.

Cowett did succeed, however, in prompting Jimmy to speed up his resignation from the U.N. post, and once again Roosevelt's decision, coming as it did in the midst of the Brazilian scandal, caused considerable public comment.

Cornfeld was relieved to welcome Jimmy aboard and proudly announced that Roosevelt would be given an "ongoing role as an ambassador of the free enterprise system."

"Nothing could be more fitting," Cornfeld said, "than a member of the family that has figured so prominently in the development of the American economy assuming a key role in the industry that encompasses the free enterprise system's most salient message—ownership in industry on the part of all people—through the firm that is the most actively bringing this concept to the entire world."

While Cornfeld was ecstatic with pride for having notched up more points for the fraternity, a lot of other people thought it was not so terribly fitting. No matter, though, for this time Roosevelt sallied forth unembarrassed and unconcerned. One of the reasons he wished to leave the U.N., he told reporters at a press conference on December 14, 1966, at his East Side Manhattan town house, was that his $26,000 salary as ambassador did not nearly meet his expenses. After all, Roosevelt was a man who had been married three times (and was soon to be married a fourth) and who had six children to support.

Speaking into a forest of radio and television microphones placed on the desk his father had bought him (Woodrow Wilson had used it aboard the S.S. *Washington* en route to the Paris peace conference), Roosevelt explained how he would occupy his time as Cornfeld's roving diplomat. It was no dubious association, he told them, but one of the "most challenging assignments of my life."

"In the past several years I have become familiar with some of the economic problems faced by the developing . . . nations. I believe that private enterprise should play an extremely significant role in the development of economic growth and political stability of these nations," he said.

"Because of its international character and worldwide resources in personnel and investment expertise, IOS can make a significant contri-

2 *New York Times,* August 10, 1966.

bution in this area. It is for this reason that I am pleased to join IOS to play an active role in a vast and exciting new undertaking—the establishment of a series of national mutual funds organized on a local basis in various countries of the world. . . . It is to be expected that these funds will serve to lure back into the local investment sectors runaway or hoarded moneys and otherwise help develop economic confidence through the establishment of sound domestic financial vehicles for domestic and international investments," Roosevelt announced in his customary blustering manner.

"This," he added in closing, "is a capitalistic program—but capitalism with a social conscience. If we have the success we anticipate, this new program can have far-reaching results, not only in terms of its own impact, but in terms of the example it might set for similar programs on the private and governmental level. I find this to be an enormously exciting concept and one in which I am most eager to play an active role."

For the record it is interesting to compare Roosevelt's claim that "as many as a dozen of these [national funds] may be in operation within eighteen months to two years" with the results he achieved.

Over the next four years Roosevelt hired no fewer than five ambassadors, the head of at least one international organization, and an impressive battery of lawyers and economists, who jetted more mileage around the world than the U.N. Development Program staff could manage in two decades. It was one of IOS's highest-cost operations, and yet the results were less than impressive. Not a single national fund was created to assist those developing economies that had contributed so much to IOS's initial success. On the other hand a second generation of IOS funds did follow, specially tailored for the national markets of the United Kingdom, Italy, Germany, Sweden, and France—all highly industrialized countries.

One of the first problems that confronted Roosevelt as IOS's roving ambassador was the snowballing of bad publicity resulting from the company's aggressive selling methods in the so-called sensitive (i.e., illegal) areas. One particularly menacing side effect produced by this high-risk exposure in the hot-money markets struck deeply at the heart of the mutual fund giant in its home city of Geneva, almost causing early disaster.

The trouble started in Guatemala when the Swiss Embassy there put out a statement denying that the bumptious Cornfeld creation, still flying a Panamanian flag, was in any way a Swiss concern. This was evidently a difficult notion to put across to the Central Americans, because IOS salesmen and IOS sales literature made pointed reference to the stability of the Swiss franc, the tranquility of Swiss politics, and the secrecy offered by Swiss banks.

The Swiss legation at Guatemala City served all of Central America, so the notice issued by Ambassador Jean Humbert in December 1966 was widely circulated, once again bringing IOS's activities in that area of the world under concentrated fire. Ambassador Humbert went one step farther, however. He addressed a bristling memorandum to the foreign ministry in Berne complaining bitterly about the harm IOS was doing to Switzerland's image abroad. In Berne it was read, digested, and placed in the thickening dossier on IOS. Soon afterward a full-scale investigation of the company's operations from Geneva was under way.

Meanwhile newspapers in Guatemala, El Salvador, and Costa Rica published the text of an unusual circular from the Swiss commercial attaché bluntly declaring that IOS was a Panamanian imposter of a Swiss corporation. Furious over such high-level attempts to sabotage the company's flourishing sales efforts, one local associate wrote to Geneva demanding that Ambassador Humbert be properly reprimanded for making such "totally inaccurate statements." The misguided associate added in his letter a touch of mystery to heighten the drama and, he hoped, his chances of getting some response. "It would not surprise me," he said, "if all this was the work of our ex-collaborator, agent No. 6758." This was no James Bond adventure, but a chapter from the everyday life of an IOS career man in Costa Rica. "In any case," he stressed in his missive to the head office, "it will be necessary that you make strong representation to the federal government in Berne and make sure they remonstrate their ambassador for the diffusion of information that is damaging to a corporation of his country."

Unfortunately, this time around the procedure worked in reverse. A few weeks later the company received a letter of warning from the powerful Swiss Bankers Association in Basel. The SBA told IOS in clear and certain terms to modify its sales policies, which were deemed "prejudicial to the interests of Switzerland."

To underline how potentially damaging the IOS misrepresentations were, the SBA highlighted one case of a Paraguayan newspaper that carried the banner headline "Conspiracy Against the National Economy." The story accused IOS, which it mistook for a Swiss company, of doing Paraguay grave economic harm.

"The actions of your representatives deployed in many countries where the local authorities are seeking to limit the export of capital can, in the measure where your company is considered a Swiss enterprise, provoke considerable animosity against our country and the Swiss financial community," the SBA said.

With negative radiation building up in the Swiss press—one newspaper, the staid *Journal de Genève,* in a widely quoted lead article directed against IOS, asked, "Is Switzerland Becoming a Haven for Financial Piracy?"—the federal government moved into action with a degree of speed rarely shown by bureaucratic machinery anywhere in the world.

One of the first things the federal police discovered about IOS in early 1967 was that the company had work permits for only ninety-five foreigners while it employed more than 1,000 persons, many of them pretty young secretaries registered at the local university and with the Contrôle de l'Habitant as students. Outraged by IOS's scoff-law attitude, the authorities threatened to padlock the doors at 119 rue de Lausanne and begin a floor-by-floor search.

The dramatic intervention of the Swiss authorities caught Cornfeld totally off balance, for he had judged the company too big to budge, with too much money to spend and too many important friends to protect it. Nevertheless, to insure his interests were well represented he hired the country's leading criminal lawyer, rotund and witty Raymond Nicolet, in a move that automatically was interpreted as an admission of guilt. Jimmy Roosevelt also was asked to do his bit, visiting with the local council of ministers and personally assuring them that as long as he worked for IOS the company would respect the law and local custom. Of this he gave his word.

In addition to the direct intervention of the police, a commission of jurists was formed to revise the federal laws on mutual funds. The object was to prevent unregistered foreign interlopers, in the absence of any international control over offshore operators, from ever again abusing Swiss hospitality. The jurists spent the next four years drafting a new set of regulations, which finally was rushed into service in 1971, just as IOS came tumbling down.

It didn't take long before word was about that the entire IOS operation faced expulsion from Switzerland. To head off this catastrophic development, in early 1967 Cornfeld and his lawyers entered into immediate negotiations with the Geneva State Council while desperately seeking new headquarters space, employment quotas and concomitant tax treaties in London, Beirut, Monte Carlo, and Montreal. After much deliberation Ferney-Voltaire, a sleepy French border town less than a ten-minutes drive to the north of Cornfeld's Geneva nerve center, was chosen as the best bet for a partial relocation of the group's extensive administrative apparatus.

Already the Geneva Contrôl de l'Habitant had drawn up a list of 150 "unmentionables" who were expelled from the country as a warning to the seventh floor at 119 rue de Lausanne while negotiations continued with the State Council. Then, weeks later, the State Council issued an ultimatum giving IOS ninety days to put its house in Geneva in order or be totally shut down for business in Switzerland.

While these delicate talks were still under way, IOS addressed a confidential *aide memoire* to the Council members pointing out that the company was pouring money into the local economy at a rate of $20 million a year. For example, in the *aide memoire* it was projected that in 1966 IOS paid $1.7 million to the Swiss post office; $1.5 million in commissions to Swiss banks; $266,210 to Swissair, the national airlines; and $626,000 in cantonal taxes. Fines and bribes were calculated separately.

Simultaneously, Cornfeld and his top lieutenants engaged in a frantic race to have IOS's slate wiped clean in France. This campaign to remove from the record all earlier references to exchange control violations went right to the office of the Prime Minister and future President of the Republic, Georges Pompidou. Finally the green light was given by Olivier Guichard, a member of Pompidou's Cabinet, who assured IOS by letter that there would be no government opposition to the establishing of an administrative complex in the underdeveloped, underpopulated department of Ain, where Ferney-Voltaire was situated.

The last bit of excitement Ferney experienced was a little more than 200 years before. That was when François-Marie Arouet, master of the Age of Reason, moved into town. Voltaire, as he was better known, also moved from Geneva to escape from the interfering city fathers, and for more than twenty years he made Ferney a thriving little community. But once the "Patriarch of Ferney" died, the village sank back into lethargy and there remained till Bernie Cornfeld arrived.

After hurried talks with Roland Ruet, the local mayor, Cornfeld paid $320,000 to purchase a 120-acre site about five minutes' walk from Voltaire's chateau, and within the ninety-day grace period accorded by the Swiss a task force of laborers constructed five dark blue prefabricated buildings with enough working space for 500 employees.[2] Part of the deal signed with Mayor Ruet stated that within thirty months IOS would complete construction of a permanent office complex on the property it had purchased. By mid-1974 all that remained of that magnificent intention was a gaping two-million-dollar hole, half-filled with water—named Loch Landau by the last bitter employees in honor of ex-IOS director George Landau, who was IOS's administrative vice-president when the excavations began.

IOS's takeover of Ferney, almost doubling the town's population at one blow, traumatized the local citzenry. As moving vans transferred

[2] Later expanded to accommodate a work force of 1,400.

six tons of high-density client files across the border, Gallic tempers began to rise, creating an uncomfortable micropolitical situation that had to be carefully controlled.

Sixty-two per cent unmarried, one-quarter German, one-quarter English, the remainder from forty-two other nationalities, and with an average age of twenty-four, the first 500 IOS staff members who came to Ferney had vital recreation requirements, which the town was not equipped to provide. There were only five cafés, no movie theaters, no night spots until IOS built one exclusively for its staff, nor any sporting facilities.

Left to their own devices, the staff organized a succession of high escapades. Resulting from their practice of the oldest sport known to man, there erupted an epidemic of venereal disease that caused much fascination at the World Health Organization in Geneva, where it was discussed as a textbook example of modern recreational hazards in a rootless social environment.

While the Geneva press lost its decorum long enough to give the topic some light-hearted coverage, the next-to-last straw came for the Ferney natives when late one night an IOS jokester, probably after consuming a good quantity of the local wine, equipped himself with brush and can of paint and changed the "F" to "B" on the road signs leading into town so that they read "Berney-Voltaire" in honor of the IOS founder.

As reward for putting his Swiss house in order, the federal authorities permitted Cornfeld to keep his well-known Geneva address at 119 rue de Lausanne. But for this they extracted one further promise. IOS had to stop insinuating it was a Swiss company. On all sales literature, program certificates and letterheads the Geneva address was changed to read "executive branch offices" and the place of incorporation—Canada, Panama, the Bahamas, or wherever—had to be prominent.

The question of control—internal and external—was a constant pain in IOS's backside, as demonstrated by its successive run-ins, first with the French and later with the American and Swiss authorities. IOS worked hard at allaying fears of the professional and lay public about the apparent absence of controls. But the treatment employed was little more than cheap public relations gimmickry.

Post-Brazil, the downstairs lobby at 119 rue de Lausanne was redone in leather and velvet with ships' furniture and campaign pieces—interpreted by Cornfeld's decorator as a sign of security. When clients entered the heavy glass front doors they were greeted on the mezzanine deck by two long-legged receptionists in Pierre Cardin uniforms. The IOS girls would smile warmly and ask visitors to sign a control registry. Two guards smartly turned out in blue blazers with Fund of Funds buttons and IOS ties stood on either side of the girls. The guards were members of the newly created in-house security department. This private police force, referred to by Cornfeld as his Keystone Kops, was headed by Jerry Berkin. The guards gave the impression that control was omnipresent within the Cornfeld framework and that IOS was acting efficiently as its own policeman.

The situation became academically intriguing when one realized where power resided at IOS. What frightened most people was that in the absence of any external restraints Cornfeld and Cowett, and to a lesser extent Cantor, could do anything they pleased with the clout generated by $2 billion under management.

The company knew no financial controls and had a chaotic management structure. Financial reporting was primitive, IOS's computer system overloaded and full of bugs. Expansion without time for consolidation or the laying in of financial reserves had opened so many cracks in the organizational fabric that even the latest IBM 360 computer was unable to straighten things out. Too quickly papered over and forgotten in the rising inflow of management fees from the funds, these structural faults lay in waiting like skeletons in the closet.

Cornfeld turned down attempt after attempt to bring in professional consultants to set up viable management mechanisms for the company. Cornfeld knew it would serve no purpose, one corporate officer complained, because the experts would demand he give up his autocratic hold on executive power, and this he was not yet prepared to do.

"What do we need experts for anyway?" was his classic response. "After all, it's no mistake that we have gotten to the top of our industry without outside help. Nobody knows this business better than we do."

So everybody nodded their agreement with Bernie. In company councils his will stood out like a giant obelisk, virtually unassailable in its force of presentation and (lack of) rationale. With few exceptions, Cornfeld's lieutenants and sergeants-major were too weak, too indebted, or too incompetent to oppose his ways, and certainly none could compete with the legal cleverness of Cowett. It was as though Bernie and Ed had hand-picked them that way.

Basically, the SEC viewed fund holding companies as devices "for pyramiding control in the hands of an individual or group of individuals." When taken to Cornfeldian extremes this could become a problem of biblical-sounding complexity, namely, control of control—or which set of hands was really pulling the strings?

The thought that IOS, with its twenty mutual funds, could exert substantial leverage on U.S. capital markets while remaining outside the jurisdiction of the U.S. government haunted the SEC. It became the key to the SEC's running battle with Cornfeld, Cowett, and their successors, Vesco, Meissner, and Norman LeBlanc. In its lengthy investment company report to Congress,[3] published in December 1966, the SEC devoted an entire chapter to fund holding companies like Fund of Funds and asked that they be banned. FOF-type inventions, the report stated, held little utility for investors who were subject to double charges in sales, administration, and management.

The danger of misused control obviously increased if the fund holding company was resident in an unregulated foreign jurisdiction with conveniently strict secrecy laws. A most unique characteristic of IOS and its successor companies was that they were subject to very little external restraint. It must be assumed, consequently, that a large number of IOS's clients approved the notion whereby neither the SEC in Washington, the Department of Trade in London, the German and Swiss banking commissions, nor the various Canadian securities commissions had much influence over IOS's worldwide operations. Of course, none of these institutions was set up to provide this kind of international public service. There was, in fact, no organization that Cornfeld, Cowett, or later Vesco and his lieutenants had ever heard of that possessed that kind of authority.

By a totally different route of deduction that took them through law courts in Puerto Rico and Massachusetts at IOS's instigation, the SEC staff came to the same conclusion. Respecting IOS's claim to client secrecy, the U.S. regulatory authority finally admitted that the sprawling Geneva giant was, at least for the time being, outside its jurisdiction. In a decision made public in May 1967, the SEC opted for what it considered a second-best solution. It banned IOS from operating in the United States, prohibited the sale of IOS funds to Americans anywhere in the world, and set about insulating American stock markets as much as possible from the influence of the men who wielded power at IOS. This settlement was represented as a great victory at the time by Cornfeld and Cowett, and within days of the final order, Cornfeld sent this letter to his men in the field:

INVESTORS OVERSEAS SERVICES ● MUTUAL FUND
SPECIALISTS ● IOS

Bernard Cornfeld, President

May 27, 1967

Dear Associate,

After two long years of battle, we've finally made peace with the SEC. What's significant, however, is not simply that we have made peace but that we have done so honorably; that we didn't give the SEC any client information without the client's consent; that there were no

[3] Public Policy Implications of Investment Company Growth; House Report No. 2337.

findings of any wrongdoing in the settlement and finally that the settlement not only doesn't hurt our operation in any way but in many ways helps us and, as in the case of the FOF proprietary funds' move to Canada, makes more money for our clients.

We have enclosed the press release which we have distributed to many newspapers and magazines. Also enclosed for information is "Questions and Answers on the SEC Settlement."

We're glad the battle is over. I think, as a company, we've come out of the fight stronger and more convinced than ever of the basic soundness of our direction. You can take pride in the settlement and look forward to still broader horizons in the future now that one of our major problems has been satisfactorily resolved.

> Best regards,
> [s] Bernie
> Bernard Cornfeld

119 rue de Lausanne Geneva Cable: Oseasinvest Telex 22550

It was peace, but peace at a price. Still, Cornfeld was pleased. He thought his problems with the SEC were over. Actually they were just beginning. The SEC's "harassment" of IOS continued unabated and ultimately was blamed for wrecking a half-dozen attempts to rescue the group when it fell into beleaguered straits.

Cornfeld's remedy for the bad publicity generated by his fight with the SEC was to sponsor an international peace conference in Geneva. When asked why IOS was getting involved on a diplomatic level with a business that clearly it knew very little about, Cornfeld replied with irrefutable logic, "Peace is bullish."

Pacem in Terris II, with James Roosevelt as master of ceremonies, more than anything else launched the ill-fated era of the New Deal at IOS. Firmly scheduled for the last week of May 1967, it required courage, a touch of showmanship, a measure of genius, and $500,000 in brokerage give-ups to pull off.

By taking John XXIII's Papal Bull by the horns, Cornfeld was inevitably accused of attempting to make a circus out of diplomacy. This was a charge he vigorously denied. "Nothing could be more fitting than IOS, an international organization dedicated to the creation of financial security for people all over the world, lending its support to such a project. For without true, lasting peace, security of any sort is impossible in this nuclear age," he wrote in the *IOS Bulletin,* a glossy in-house publication that was distributed each month to the ever expanding sales force.

In spite of attracting some three hundred distinguished peace-lovers, including delegates from several Communist countries, a dozen foreign ministers, six Nobel laureates, six U.S. senators, two U.S. congressmen, an American Supreme Court justice, and others no less notable, *Pacem*

in Terris II became an early casualty of the June 1967 Six Day War
in the Middle East.

Nonetheless, IOS came out of it a winner, able to capitalize on an
association with the Vatican, the Secretary General of the United
Nations, and Pablo Casals, whose world-famed Peace Oratorio was
performed for the assembled notables, and gain the admiration of the
entire Communist bloc for providing a first-class forum in which to
denounce U.S. foreign policy.

IOS went on to develop the *Pacem in Terris* doctrine, carrying it as
a company symbol for quite some months. It even built an advertising
campaign around the theme "Peace Equals Prosperity," which stirred
comment in many places around the world where Cornfeld's band of
mercenaries did business. The main thrust of the campaign was carried
in a dark double-truck headline: "People Say There Can Never Be
Financial Security Without World Peace. Well, the Fact Is, There Will
Never Be World Peace Without Financial Security," which appeared
over some of the ads.

Although the Pope never did attend *Pacem in Terris,* Cornfeld eventually met His Holiness Paul VI in Rome about two years later. He flew
down to the Eternal City with a specially bound picture book on war
and peace, which the IOS Foundation had printed up, and presented
it to His Holiness as a token of esteem for being able to ride on the
coattails of a great Papal encyclical.

In the leadoff to the book, entitled simply *Pacem in Terris*, there
were full-page photographs—in this order—of Bernie Cornfeld, James
Roosevelt, Robert Hutchins of the Center for the Study of Democratic
Institutions, which organized the conference, and U Thant, the then
U.N. Secretary General.

Cornfeld brought his eighty-five-year-old mother, Sophie, along with
him to see the Pope, and a personal photographer. The Vatican protocol
officer firmly told Cornfeld that the photographer wasn't necessary.
The Holy See had its own.

The private audience was described in the *IOS Bulletin* as follows:
"Bernie told the Pope of the IOS Foundation's activities. . . . The
Pope agreed to Bernie's suggestion that the Foundation publish a
photographic essay on the papal encyclical, 'On the Development of
Peoples.'

"Mrs. Cornfeld recommended Israel's cause to Pope Paul. At the
conclusion of the audience, the Pope wished them well, saying 'Shalom,
Shalom.' "

Unfortunately, Cornfeld never did get any pictures of this historic
meeting, which IOS sales promoters were looking forward to in order

to give their marketing efforts in Latin America a boost. The Pope's photographer never showed.

However Cornfeld did receive a letter from Cardinal Villot, the Vatican's Secretary of State, thanking him for the munificent $15,000 offering plus the specially bound edition of *Pacem in Terris*, an unauthorized IOS Foundation recording of *El Pessebre*, Casals's peace oratorio, and a brochure on the activities of the IOS Foundation.

"For all these gifts, His Holiness is warmly grateful, and bids me assure you of His appreciation of the sentiments of concern for the needy and suffering which prompted you to make this outstanding contribution to His works of mercy and relief throughout the world.

"In return, He willingly invokes upon you, your Mother, your family and associates, an abundance of divine graces and heavenly favors."

7

Rape of the Moneycatcher

How Cornfeld at his zenith meets the Denver Natural Resources King, and the two of them restructure the Moneycatcher, acquiring it for 22 million acres of ice and snow in the Canadian arctic ~ The golden era of offshore finance closes with a $110 million underwriting of IOS stock, and a greedy time is had by all

Professional management, by definition, implies the prudent management of other people's money.

> The Fund of Funds Prospectus, May 2, 1968

All that can be required of a Trustee to invest is that he conduct himself faithfully and exercise a sound discretion. He is to observe how men of prudence, discretion and intelligence manage their own affairs, not in regard to speculation, but in regard to the permanent disposition of their funds, considering the probable income, as well as the probable safety of the capital invested.

> The Prudent Man Rule—JUSTICE SAMUEL PUTNAM, Supreme Judicial Court of Massachusetts, 1830

It was a typically gray and drizzly Geneva afternoon in early 1968, and I was sitting in Bernie Cornfeld's new, large-size seventh-floor office at 119 rue de Lausanne when the switchboard operator rang through with a call from Denver, Colorado.

Cornfeld got up from one of the velvet-covered lounge chairs placed around a mirrored coffee table and floated across a thick, pale blue Chinese carpet to switch on the conference telephone, one of three lined up on his imitation Empire-style desk.

"Helloooo," he called out once back in the lounge chair, one leg casually draped over the arm rest.

The voice coming out of the speaker-phone on the desk sounded slightly hesitant but eager. It was John McCandish King, chairman of the board of King Resources Company, calling with news of another daring venture in which he wanted IOS to participate.

Bernie, the mutual fund mogul, joked for a while with John M. King, the natural resources magnate. They made a good match, I remember thinking.

Cornfeld's office in those days represented the real command cockpit of the make-believe IOS world. People with all sorts of things to sell, some personal, some public, some small and some worth millions, were lined up in the corridor waiting for a few minutes of prime time with Bernie to get their thing across.

Bernie's pretty red-haired secretary, Didi Fischer, from Stuttgart, would rush in and out with telephone messages and reminders, while in the corridor the silent traffic jam never diminished.

The office was the size of a double living room in any comfortable town house. The décor was a combination of walnut paneling and soft blue velvet, of kitsch and bric-à-brac, with mementos of voyages around the world, including a miniature statue of a Siamese priestess, a Balinese mask, a Chinese horse, and a modern sculpture of a bull and bear.

It was comfortable, even if hectic, and with all the velvet and plush one had an eminent feeling of security. One floor after another, for six floors underneath, normal middle-class apartments had been converted into executive suites by a string of Cornfeld decorators so that IOSers could work more comfortably and more securely at making money for Bernie, for Bernie's clients, and of course for themselves.

With all that activity going on right underneath you, with all that money being made with every telephone call from London, Frankfurt, Hong Kong, Nassau, New York, or Panama, it had an immensely satisfying effect on Bernie and the people around him, especially those waiting in the corridor with something to sell him.

John King, I soon realized, was also working hard at selling Bernie a part of a rather high-risk enterprise. He was, one could tell by the buildup, someone very much like Cornfeld. They were both born in 1927 and, like Vesco, had started from nothing to become multimillionaires. Neither man drank or smoked, and they were both master salesmen with high-pitched egos to soothe. But the similarities went far beyond all that.

Once firmly astride the golden bull of their respective successes, both men maintained much the same flourishing life-styles. Bernie, at the time, owned five homes; King six. Bernie had a chateau in Switzerland and another in France with fifteen bedrooms and a stable of race horses; King owned a 400-acre ranch with a private airstrip, executive auditorium, beauty parlor, and bunks for 120 guests. King had monogrammed clothes specially made for him; Bernie owned 50 per cent interest in one of Guy Laroche's *haute couture* enterprises and designed most of his own sartorial finery.

Computerized petroleum exploration was John King's specialty, and he was one of the men helping the Israeli government extract oil from occupied Sinai at a rate that Cornfeld said would soon rival Kuwait's production.

"Have you heard of John King?" Bernie asked me. "He's an incredible guy—the largest wildcat oil driller in the world."

Quite understandably, glad-handing John King was irritated about being put on the "squawk box," a diabolical device whereby the person on the other end of the phone can speak to a whole room of people and the whole room can speak to him. This insidious gadget places the caller at a distinct disadvantage. He no longer has personal contact with the one with whom he is trying to communicate—in this case Bernie—and right away senses he is addressing an unseen audience.

Poorly performing sales managers and portfolio advisers were often dragged over the coals in this manner, being put through sessions of ridicule by Cornfeld and gallery of inquisitors who were not fully made known to them.

The purpose of King's present call was to interest Cornfeld and the IOS group in financing a large-bore oil pipeline, which the Israelis wanted to construct from Eilat to the Mediterranean, by-passing the blocked Suez Canal.

King was not able to close this particular deal with Cornfeld, but in March 1968, a few weeks after trying to interest Cornfeld in financing the pipeline, he joined with IOS to supervise a Natural Resources Fund account for The Fund of Funds, selling the Dollar-Crested Money-catcher myriad other, no less speculative ventures. King appeared on the scene at the acme of IOS's success and was to play a key role in raping its most successful venture, The Fund of Funds.

Few funds in the history of the investment industry had experienced the tremendous six-year growth record achieved by Cornfeld's brain-child. By 1968 FOF's $800 million success was so spectacular that it had outstripped the fund's original concept, transforming it into a monster unlike the creature first conceived.

When originally offered to the public The Fund of Funds was restricted from purchasing securities on margin, loaning securities, borrowing money, selling short, and purchasing, leasing, or otherwise acquiring real estate. The Fund of Funds, early investors were told, would invest in the U.S. economy through publicly offered mutual funds or fund management companies registered with the SEC.

By early 1970, or seven itchy years after its launching, FOF was already in steep decline. Just as the SEC had feared, the fund's original investment policies had been diametrically modified without share-holders receiving prior notification from management. Less than 5 per cent of its portfolio was invested in publicly offered mutual funds.

The history of what happened to The Fund of Funds was long and sad. Greeted with such tremendous enthusiasm by investors and sales-men alike when it first appeared, it soon became a Cornfeld-Cowett plaything that was tampered with, kicked about, and in the end used as an instrument for IOS's self-serving market maintenance practices before finally being run into the ground by the Vesco group.

Funny things started happening to The Fund of Funds in 1965. Three years after its launching it had $316 million in the kitty, and top-performing U.S. funds were becoming edgy about accepting further investments from the great Moneycatcher. In May 1965 managers of U.S. funds in which FOF had invested started receiving frequent queries from the SEC, and in some cases the SEC staff held up publication of a fund's prospectus—thereby preventing the fund from offering new shares to the public—until the fund's relationship with the IOS syndicate in Geneva was clearly spelled out.

To get around this roadblock, Cornfeld and Cowett created a series of "captive funds," which worked just like any other mutual fund ex-cept that they had only one client. That client, of course, was The Fund of Funds. To manage the captive funds Cornfeld and Cowett went out and hired some of the best go-go talent on Wall Street, agree-ing to pay them a special fee for the segment of FOF's portfolio which they managed. The fee system was novel—no money was paid to the portfolio managers if their part of the fund failed to perform, but a 10 per cent "bonus" was paid on all capital appreciation when business was good. A profit-sharing arrangement was typically tied into these agreements whereby the proprietary fund managers—generally referred to as "advisers" so as not to offend the SEC—were required to split their earnings fifty-fifty with IOS Ltd., in return for which IOS guaranteed a small fixed fee to the "advisers" sufficient to cover their actual expenses.

This bonus system became known in the industry as a "performance fee" and was heartily frowned upon by the SEC. But SEC reservations aside, some of FOF's faster-moving "advisers" earned more than $1 million a year under the new system. Cornfeld, of course, defended the bonus gimmick, stating that if his top investment managers performed like "artists" they deserved to be rewarded like artists for their talent.

For a long time the existence of these captive or proprietary funds was kept under wraps and out of sight of the investors. Casual reference was made to them in the IOS media, but very few details were given about them until the full glare of the 1967 SEC settlement order brought them to light, and only then was their method of operation explained to shareholders. Management's reluctance to detail how these "prop. funds" functioned was really due to the fact that they were a device for squeezing more client money out of The Fund of Funds. The income they produced kept IOS afloat and prospering for the next three years.

One of the key provisions of the SEC settlement required the removal from the United States of all FOF proprietary funds then in existence: York Fund, Alger Fund (named for Fred Alger, Jr., an investment expert then in his early thirties, who was the top-performing U.S. fund manager in 1965), Computer Directions Fund, and Financial Institutions Growth Stock Fund.

Fortunately, Cowett happened to have available an empty corporate shell in Canada—a company that existed on paper only, inasmuch as it had no assets—which was pressed into service to handle the SEC's dismantling order. The four captive funds were liquidated in the United States one day and reconstituted in Canada the next, becoming fund accounts in FOF Proprietary Funds Limited, a marvelous Cowett creation.

"You never know," said Cowett, "when you may need a spare corporation."

In the Moneycatcher's heyday, with assets booming to the $800 million mark, new proprietary fund accounts were opened and closed by Cornfeld and Cowett with the rapidity of dealers shuffling cards. The proprietary funds multiplied like money-making rabbits until there were more than twenty of them in the FOF portfolio at any given time.

Indeed, so many things happened to the once-gilded Moneycatcher that were never explained. In addition to a constant sapping of its assets by deducting double acquisition charges and sometimes triple management fees, the Moneycatcher purchased shortfalls or unsold portions of IOS-managed Eurobond issues. FOF also held accounts for which little or no information existed, and was used, one IOS money-manager insisted, to reduce the floating stock of friendly conglomerates.

Summit Growth was one short-lived account for which there was never any disclosure. It had assets of $12 million and lasted in the FOF lineup only one calendar quarter. No statement of investments was ever issued concerning the dispostion of Summit's $12 million. There one day, it was gone another, without any hint of who managed it or in what it supposedly invested.

Another quick shifter was listed ominously as the Kensington Organization, actually a Netherlands Antilles company. Kensington received a $50 million unsecured loan from FOF in May 1969, although the fund's investment restrictions prohibited the lending of assets except for the purchase of government bonds. Hardly coincidentally, prior to FOF's granting of the loan IOS Ltd. acquired 42 per cent of Kensington's outstanding common stock. Cowett said Kensington was to engage in special situations investing. An IOS subsidiary was also to have underwritten an additional $50 million offering of Kensington's securities —for which IOS would have received an underwriting fee. The underwriting never took place, however, and Cowett later said the $50 million was repaid to FOF, apparently with interest.

There was one little-mentioned speculation known as the Commodities Fund account, which invested in gold and silver bullion. No details of its operations were ever furnished either.

Another phantom in the closet was the Communications Media account, which invested in two London theatrical productions that had caught Cornfeld's fancy. This last account, it transpired, was never audited because its assets, listed at a cost of $174,000, constituted less than 1 per cent of FOF's total investment portfolio.

By the same measure, in June 1969 FOF invested $150,000 in a full length feature film called *Bloomfield*, to which Cornfeld's personal movie company, World Film Services, held the rights. Four years later these World Film "participation units," after being carried at cost, were assigned an honest market value of zero.

Performance fees, acquisition charges, and administrative costs combined, IOS Ltd. milked its great Moneymaker for more than $23 million during the four-year period 1967–70. The cost of investing with IOS had become exorbitantly high. And there was very good reason for this. IOS had to squeeze its richest profit center for a maximum to cover soaring costs.

By the end of 1969 the IOS sales force had grown to 15,191 associates.[1] But despite being the largest and supposedly the most efficient in the industry, it had been a money-losing proposition since 1966! Ten per cent of the salesmen accounted for 90 per cent of the sales. Every deadwood salesman cost the company $500 a year to service and maintain on the computerized associate records. Thus every 2,000 nonproductive sales creatures added $1 million per year to the operating expenses.

Looking at this problem from another angle, a million dollars saved in administrative expenditures was equal to increasing sales by $100 million a year. But these figures were known only to a handful of corporate planners who were powerless to do anything about it. No

[1] IOS Corporate Report 1969, prepared by Sales Management Information Services.

paring of deadwood salesmen was permitted. For Cornfeld, Cantor, and others, the sales force was sacred. Cantor even foresaw a time ten years hence when there would be, heaven forbid, 100,000 sales associates.[2]

To get an idea of how insanely the whole operation was run, it would suffice to look at the inefficient dream world in which IOS's "ambassador at large" operated. Roosevelt's aggregate salary over the next four years exceeded $450,000, which was not too bad on the world diplomatic scale. Then there were the expenses charged to IOS Development Company, which he headed, and these were astronomical. Yet Roosevelt was able to inform thirty-five IOS million-dollar associates who attended the first Advanced Training Seminar in early 1968 that "our first year has proven even more rewarding than we had hoped. . . . The team that we built of financial, diplomatic and legal experts covered close to half a million miles, touching every continent. I have been continually on the go—carrying on top-level discussions with the heads of state, government and banking officials, and ambassadors to international organizations. . . .

"In Spain, South Africa, Iran, Japan, Australia, Belgium, Pakistan, and Taiwan we have concentrated investigations. We are moving ahead in some thirty countries, and no two situations are quite the same," Roosevelt stated. And on the basis of this hot-winded marathon, he announced he was "confident that we have laid the groundwork for really explosive IOS growth over the next few years." And explosive it was.

When visiting the IOS ambassador's sixth-floor offices in Geneva, such an air of security had been achieved by Cornfeld's head decorator that one felt convinced Roosevelt had been purposely isolated from the mainstream of world developments by a trick of environmental control. For walking into his three-room executive suite was like entering a judge's office in a New England country courthouse. Only the fittings were perhaps finer, and certainly more flamboyant. Flanking either side of a large Regency conference table where Ambassador Roosevelt and his staff pieced together new strategy for IOS funds there was a silk Stars and Stripes and the bright crimson standard of a U.S. Marine Corps Brigadier General,[3] and on the walls were pictures and citations that spanned almost half a century of United States politics.

IOS still faced problems in Brazil, a hangover from the Armistice Day raids, so Cornfeld dispatched his roving ambassador to try and

[2] Allen Cantor, addressing the Thirteenth Annual IOS Managers Conference, Geneva, August 1969.

[3] James Roosevelt had seen active service in World War II as a Marine Corps colonel with Carlson's Raiders in the South Pacific. He retired from active service with the rank of brigadier general.

sort them out with some of IOS's "New Deal" hocus-pocus. The offer Roosevelt brought with him to Brazil was a strange one—not to say hypocritical—considering the company's past record in exporting flight capital from developing countries. Brazil possessed all the basic resources to build a diversified economy, but a chronic scarcity of domestic capital had hindered economic development. Now IOS, according to the Roosevelt proposal, wanted to form the required domestic capital by creating a Brazilian "People's Fund."

The old adage "once bitten, twice shy" might have come straight from the Mato Grosso, judging by the interest which Roosevelt was able to cull. He was graciously received by members of the government and given special treatment befitting a former ambassador of that great democracy to the north. Yet after several months of on-and-off discussions with the local authorities the idea of a People's Fund was finally shelved, and the charges against IOS for its earlier activities were never dropped.

As the shades fell on IOS operations in Brazil, Germany was developing into the new Dorado, replacing Brazil as the company's number one market. Cornfeld was obviously concerned that the Germans should firmly understand his "New Deal" concept. And so, one year after signing up Roosevelt, IOS gained another leading campaigner in the person of the prominent West German politician Dr. Erich Mende.

A Vice-Chancellor of the West German Federal Republic under Ludwig Erhard, "Erich the Fair" was brought into the Cornfeld stable for less than half the price paid to Roosevelt. He was soon joined by a host of New Dealers hired by Cornfeld to spread the word that IOS was no longer a runner of hot money but essentially a stable financial institution that was interested in offering the little investors of this world a better deal. According to this doctrine, the honest hard-working folk who placed their savings in a bank account at a fixed rate of interest were being exploited by the banks. While their savings were ravaged by inflation—which Cornfeld termed the Money Problem of the Twentieth Century—it was the bankers who made all the gains, investing their deposits at much higher rates of return. Cornfeld preached that this system was unfair to the forgotten man at the bottom of the economic pyramid. He said IOS wanted to democratize the investment of capital so that the little investor could share in the benefits of the capitalist system with the same rights and privileges as a Rockefeller or a Rothschild. This, Cornfeld said, was People's Capitalism, and this was the message his New Dealers were instructed to bring to the public's attention.

Most notable among IOS's New Deal recruits was Sir Eric Wyndham White, KCMG, former director general of the General Agreement on

Tariffs and Trade (GATT) in Geneva. Shortly after his retirement from the world trade body in May 1968, Sir Eric was asked by Roosevelt to become a consultant to IOS's regional development squad, an offer he gladly accepted. The appointment surprised a great many people in Geneva who were well acquainted with Sir Eric's track record at GATT. His autocratic running of the delicate international trade machinery had earned him the sobriquet the Mandarin of GATT. One therefore wondered how so strong a personality would mesh with the IOS jigsaw puzzle.

As the United Nations Development Decade ran out of steam at the close of the 1960s, the IOS New Dealers pressed on with their crusade, attempting to convince Third World and Socialist goverments that the free enterprise system was still the best. Roosevelt and Sir Eric flew off to Belgrade with a planeload of advisers to explain to President Tito how IOS could "contribute to solving some of Yugoslavia's problems."

"We had to listen to an hour-long speech about the advantages of Socialism, after which the people we met, including some members of the government, listened very intently to our Capitalistic proposals," Roosevelt told one group of IOS salesmen.

Quite obviously, different political systems were of little concern to men in Roosevelt's position as long as the money motive was firmly established. "Perhaps one day we shall see a national Hellenic Fund run by IOS," he said at another IOS meeting. "We don't mind about the ideological complications as long as there is a profit in it somewhere for us."

Apparently the Greek colonels felt there was a little too much profit-taking by IOS's self-serving management, and a few months later they ran the firm's representatives in Athens out of the country.

As Cornfeld's top political lobbyist, Roosevelt informed his fellow frontiersmen in his whistle-stop tours into the field how he kept IOS abreast of the latest international trends. "I recently spoke with our Secretary of State in Washington and we discussed the whole world situation. That's how we always stay on the ball," he told a meeting of IOS managers in Bremen.[4]

Roosevelt probably would have succeeded Cornfeld as chairman of IOS Ltd. in May 1970 instead of Sir Eric Wyndham White had it not been for an unfortunate incident in the summer of 1969 that compromised his credibility as IOS's ambassador at large. Late one evening at his residence in the quiet Geneva suburb of Cologny, Roosevelt was stabbed in the back by his wife, Irene, during a violent row over their son's former teacher at the International School in Geneva. Roosevelt,

[4] *Die Zeit* (Hamburg), May 2, 1969.

a large man well over six feet tall with a shiny bald dome, fled into the garden screaming for help.

Cornfeld, when he heard the ambassador had been stabbed in the back with his own Marine Corps bayonet, stormed about the seventh floor at 119 rue de Lausanne in a rage. "Why, that stupid so-and-so should be fired!" Bernie was heard to mutter.

After a period of convalescence in Geneva's Cantonal Hospital, Roosevelt pressed ahead with divorce proceedings against his wife and later that same year married Mary L. Winskill, an English school-mistress.

With Roosevelt no longer effective as a roving ambassador, many of his official duties were reassigned to Sir Eric. IOS's New Deal was over. Before it petered out, however, the Roosevelt era had established two distinct trends that greatly impacted upon the future viability of the company. The first was the appearance of IOS's second generation of funds to replace the aging all-purpose Fund of Funds and IIT. These new funds taxed IOS's investment management facilities beyond capacity and, after months of mediocre performance under admittedly unfavorable market conditions, their inability to live up to expectations contributed to a weakening of investor confidence in the group.

This was not to say that the new funds were unsound in concept, for that was not true. But in the arcana of IOS management their development costs spiraled beyond budget and that, combined with the lack of investment talent, placed a heavy burden on the corporate structure. In the vanguard of the second generation funds were:

Fonditalia International
Investors Fonds (Germany)
IOS Venture Fund of Canada
IVM Invest (Netherlands)
IOS Venture Fund (International) N.V.
Interfond (Svenska Internationella Investment Fonden)
Rothschild Expansion (France)
The Fund of Funds Sterling Limited

The second innovation of the Roosevelt era was an attempt to weight the company's sales activities in legal areas. This caused an ideological rift among the IOS directors. Cornfeld opposed the closing down of sales in black areas, but eventually it was decided with typical salesman's flair for compromise that most sensitive sales operations would be continued, but on a "restricted basis," while waiting for more national funds to come into service. It was sadly typical of IOS, however, that no one had charted what a shift to entirely legal business would cost the company in terms of fixed overhead expenditures since nobody seemed to realize that maintaining showcase front offices and large backroom staffs in major market areas such as Germany, Italy, Canada, the United Kingdom, and the Netherlands was a vastly more costly proposition than running briefcase operations on the fly in Africa, Latin America, and Southeast Asia.

People's Capitalism was in urgent need of refurbishment, and Cornfeld, consequently, was hard at work developing new doctrines to match the new operating methods. With the changing emphasis, Cornfeld's Villa Elma, a neoclassical mansion on Geneva's lakefront that Napoleon had built for Josephine, became the center of his new revolution.

Cornfeld had acquired the villa as his residence for $1 million in 1968, and like the company structure it was undergoing certain renovations that rendered life there somewhat hectic. An elevator was installed to the left of the main entrance hall for Bernie's mother, who had moved into a private apartment on the third floor. Crates of marble statuary arrived on Cornfeld's Convair aircraft from London, accompanied by cases of art copies representing some of the best works of the Great Masters to adorn the villa's walls. And Bernie, directing the traffic, had one of his lawyers lugging that statuary around.

"What do you think?" Cornfeld cheerily asked the lawyer about the bust of a nameless Roman senator installed on a pedestal in the pillared living room.

"More to the left," the lawyer replied, realizing that any critical appraisal would be considered an affront to Cornfeld's taste.

"I happen to like velvet," he once screamed at one of his assistants who remarked upon the acres of it lining most of his walls as well as hanging from the ceilings, with matching velvet window drapes, of course.

"Bernie likes velvet," one of the Villa Elma groupies echoed seriously.

"Really, I think you have less taste than Winthrop," the dressing down continued. Winthrop was Bernie's basset hound. So in the end it was easier to say, simply, "More to the left," and leave it at that.

Likewise, any criticism of his favorite decorator, Serge Mourreau, known as the Velvet Boy for his ability to hang more velvet per square foot on a wall or ceiling, than possibly any man alive, was considered a personal slur.

Visitors to Villa Elma were greeted as they entered the long front hall by an enormous six-foot by ten-foot copy on real canvas of Jesus having His feet washed before the wedding supper—one of Bernie's favorites. Two Roman generals in marble flanked the painting. A harpsichord stood off to the right toward Bernie's red plush office. To the left was a green bar designed by the Velvet Boy. Golden fittings glittered in the bathrooms, and the toilets were disguised as Louis XVI wicker armchairs.

When Bernie walked into the living room an air of nostalgia crept in with him. In everything he said and did there was a memory of the old days when things were not quite as complicated. His attention span had shortened over the years, and so had his temper. The rages were more frequent. Otherwise he stuck to old habits, told old jokes, relived past adventures, drank Coca-Cola with dinner, and was always late.

He turned up for an international business management conference in Cyprus, at which he was the main speaker, one day late, and for a reception in his honor in Athens, attended by several government officials, two days after the event. Wherever and whenever he did arrive, however, it was always with a coterie of Beautiful People attired in mod clothes and see-through dresses, the women with sun glasses as large as saucers to hide a permanently dissatisfied look in their eyes.

He had sold all but 15 per cent of his company to the people who worked for him; it had made him a vastly wealthy man. His fortune was estimated by various accounts to exceed $150 million, most of it in paper. All that money had made Bernie look a little sleeker, more elegant perhaps, even more soft-spoken between his famous bursts of ill temper, and certainly more restless. His tastes for fast cars driven at slow speeds, Guy Laroche clothes and sloe-eyed women at high speeds had all increased. It was Bernie's little universe. The big one outside hardly seemed to matter any more.

From the moment Cowett had launched the IOS Stock Option Plan back in 1960, IOS's entire corporate existence was focused on one day achieving a public market for the company stock so that insiders could cash in their paper at a tremendous premium. The stock market crested out in December 1968, with the Dow Jones touching the 1,000 mark for the first time in history, and it was then that the IOS directors decided to push for the long-awaited public offering.

In preparation for the underwriting, Cowett transferred IOS's place of incorporation from Panama, making it a non-resident Canadian corporation, with complete tax-shelter status offered to federally chartered companies that conduct their business outside Canada. He also rejiggered the capital structure of the company, creating a new class of IOS common stock and keeping back the nonmarketable preferred shares for Stock Option Plan issue only. Then, in spite of generally poor market conditions, the autumn of 1969 was chosen to float off 11 million of the newly created common shares—20 per cent of the quadrupled share capital—at the magic issuing price of $10 a share.

The timing could hardly have been less propitious. As the markets worsened instead of improving, an atmosphere of tension hung over the leading financial centers in late 1969—with the exception of Geneva, where a small patch of sunshine was carved out of the overcast above the IOS headquarters. There, under Cowett's command, a task force of sixty lawyers, accountants, and clerks was preparing feverishly for the September 24 issue date.

Cowett confidently told everyone who would listen that the underwriting would be, in typical IOS fashion, the largest, the best, the most glamorous. It was the largest—$110 million—in European financial history and third largest in the world as a stock issue after Comsat and General Motors. The most glamorous is debatable, although public bidding went up to $33 per share in the "when-issued" market weeks before the final offering terms were even set.

Like most Cowett creations, the underwriting structure was exceedingly complicated. It was a triple-tiered affair, with distributions held simultaneously in Europe, Canada, and the Bahamas. Representatives of the main European underwriting syndicate, made up of six of the finest names in the business, spent months in Geneva going through the IOS files with a fine-tooth comb. Still it seems doubtful, even after they had completed their inspection, whether the underwriters really understood what IOS was all about or how its internal mechanisms functioned. "It's remarkable," said Ken Klein, a junior IOS lawyer at the time, "that Ed Cowett could create a corporate animal capable of baffling six of the smartest houses in banking."

From the outset, the utility of so large an underwriting was open to question. Cowett had maintained on numerous occasions that IOS did not need the money. What other motivation was there, in that case, than personal enrichment?

Personal enrichment was indeed the answer. IOS had been taken over by the Ethic of Greed, and corporate venality was the company's undoing. Nowhere was this more apparent than in the underwriting exercise and its curious aftermath. Of the proceeds from the underwriting, a total of $53.9 million went directly into the pockets of 490 insiders who had converted a portion of their preferred stock into common shares for sale at the underwriting. Approximately $52.4 million was paid into the IOS treasury and supposedly became available for corporate development. But IOS, a company with virtually no financial controls, was not geared to digest such a huge influx of new capital.

The stock hit the market at $19 on a wave of heavy buying from Geneva. From this high point it gradually drifted lower during the months ahead. Nevertheless, an atmosphere of unrestrained euphoria persisted at IOS. In spite of a quickening downward trend in most markets around the world, everyone at IOS was sitting back expecting to get rich quick by buying large quantities of the company paper, on margin if need be.

Three months after the much-heralded September 1969 public offering—marking the first time the public at large was permitted to buy a piece of Cornfeld's golden-imaged holding company—the market price for IOS shares had fallen back a disappointing 30 per cent to around $13 rather than taking off to fantastic heights as the IOS command had expected. But Cornfeld and Cowett were convinced the IOS Ltd. stock would regain all of its promised zest and climb a lot higher if only they could post a year-end performance boost for IOS's flagship, Fund of Funds. Good performance meant increased advisory fees, which translated into a more attractive price-earnings ratio for the IOS stock. Therefore, something dramatic had to take place.

John King was consulted.

Cowett had been introduced to King in late 1967 by IOS's Washington lawyer, Myer Feldman, formerly counsel to John F. Kennedy both in the Senate and in the White House. Cowett and King immediately hit it off. Each had something the other wanted, and both knew it. "It was like watching two pickpockets having a go at each other. Both realized that one was lifting something out of the other's pocket but both were certain that they were getting away with the better bargain," one observer of Cowett and King in action reported.

King was looking for new money to sink into his oil drilling funds. Cowett wanted some unusually high returns for the Moneycatcher that were not conditioned by the ups and downs of Wall Street. One of King's senior executives remarked that the two men would play poker with the devil just for the pleasure of it.

According to Cowett, King was invited to fly down to Acapulco for the next Fund of Funds board meeting in April 1968 and make a presentation to the directors. One of the most convincing salesmen of the twentieth century, King without too much trouble persuaded Cornfeld, Roosevelt, Henry Buhl, and the other FOF directors that the rewards of searching for the earth's mineral treasures were immeasurable.

FOF's other directors were not dummies, but King, with a little help from Cowett, hooked them easily. Wilson W. Wyatt, former Lieutenant Governor of Kentucky; Eric D. Scott, senior partner of the Toronto stockbroking firm of J. H. Crang & Company (later Crang & Ostiguy); Pierre Rinfret, noted economic adviser to three U.S. Presidents; Edmund G. ("Pat") Brown, two-term Democratic Governor of California; and Allan Conwill, partner of Wendell Willkie's old law firm in New York—Willkie, Farr & Gallagher—and former head of the SEC's Division of Corporate Regulation—all were in favor.

According to Cowett, the directors said fine, but they would permit FOF to invest only in projects in which King Resources Company took a position as managing partner. Apparently none of them realized that oil and gas exploration permits, unlike stocks and bonds, carry work obligations that require the holder actually to do some exploring or the permits become void, and depending on where the concessions are located this may cost millions, in fact tens of millions, of dollars. In FOF's case—and it is doubtful whether the directors ever grasped this important factor—the fund became committed to work obligation payments in excess of $20 million as well as a 12.5 per cent profits royalty off the top in favor of King Resources in event of a discovery or sale of a property at higher than cost.

The main inconsistency in Cowett's account is that, by the time the directors assembled in Acapulco, FOF had already committed $10 million to the King-managed Natural Resources Fund account. Investors were duly apprised of this in Cornfeld's president's letter accompanying the March 31, 1968, quarterly report. However, no accounting of how the money was allocated reached the fund-holders for the next three years.

This was typical of the procedures that had crept into Fund of Funds bookkeeping. The FOF treasurer was required to effect payments to King Resources based upon memos from Cowett referring to one-page King Resources Company invoices. No one at IOS even looked at the exploration permits, titles to mines, or related documents. In fact, investment records of the Natural Resources Fund account were so loosely kept that, in an unheard-of stance adopted in 1969, Cowett and King forbade their independent auditors Arthur Andersen & Company to verify the existence of the Arctic permits, which by then had become FOF's single largest investment, or review the geological surveys upon which their value supposedly in part was based.

Of course there were investors and others who wondered what a supposedly solid fund like The Fund of Funds was doing with such highly speculative property, but that was another question. And it was not the type of question that bothered John King. He proceeded to sell FOF a total of more than $100 million worth of dubious mineral and mining ventures, including some 240 oil wells, of which two dozen were already drilled and found to be dry before being sold to the fund; an abandoned mining venture on Vancouver Island that had failed sixty years before but was termed a "$900 million profit prospect" by King; a questionable diamond mine; and portions of oil and gas exploration permits for acreage to which King Resources Company had little claim —all liberally seasoned with phony expense reports.

King's answer to FOF's lagging performance in late 1969 was to propose a part sale of the fund's interest in the Canadian Arctic oil and gas exploration permits. As a matter of policy King Resources Company had retained an undivided 50 per cent interest in everything it sold the fund. This meant in the case of the Arctic permits that FOF ended up owning an undivided 50 per cent interest in King's holdings covering 22.3 million net acres, much of it at excessive underwater depths.

Furthermore, King Resources Company retained a burdensome royalty right in the form of a 12.5 per cent interest in any operating profits on the natural resources investments it sold The Fund of Funds. This was on top of the 10 per cent "performance fee" due to IOS Ltd. as the investment adviser, so that FOF fundholders were piggy-backing two heavy corporate freeloaders along with them on their already rickety enough investments in natural resources properties.

The performance booster that King now suggested was a crafty revaluation of the Arctic permits. The revaluation was based upon a price FOF would receive for selling a fraction of its interest in the permits to outside purchasers. That portion of the permits retained by FOF would then be marked up in the fund's books to reflect the new "market" price.

Again the pliant auditors when consulted said all right, they would approve a revaluation provided it reflected an arm's-length sale (i.e., to outside purchasers) of at least 50 per cent interest in that portion of the permits held by FOF; eventually they said only 25 per cent would be acceptable if the sale were made to a major oil company such as Texaco.

Finally, despite the auditors' reservations, a 10 per cent sale of FOF's holdings was agreed to after the fact by the fund's directors as an acceptable minimum.

For Cowett and Cornfeld this method of goosing the Moneycatcher became their hope for counter-balancing IOS's sliding profit projections in late 1969. So they proceeded to give the tired-out Moneycatcher one last kick. And what a kick! The news release that accompanied their field goal attempt was another minor Cornfeld-Cowett masterpiece of misrepresentation.

IOS FUNDS SELL INTERESTS IN CANADIAN OIL AND GAS VENTURE

Geneva, December 29, 1969—The Fund of Funds, Limited, and IOS Growth Fund, Limited, today announced the sale of 10 per cent of the interest each fund holds in Canadian Arctic gas and oil exploration permits.

Based on the sale, after appropriate discounts and reserves, the value of the remaining acreage is being carried at US $8.01 net per acre. The acreage was originally purchased for prices ranging from US $0.75 to US $2.00 per acre. The gross sales price was US $14.12 per acre.

As a result of this transaction the assets of The Fund of Funds have increased by US $70.8 million.

The assets of IOS Growth Fund have increased by US $2.9 million.

The net value per share of the two funds was increased by 12.6 percent, as of December 26, 1969.

The funds have interests in oil and gas exploration permits which cover 22.3 million acres of the Canadian Arctic.

Oil and gas leases have been recently sold in the Canadian Arctic at prices ranging upwards from US $10 an acre.

The Fund of Funds and IOS Growth Fund also hold investments in diamond and titanium mines in South Africa, uranium properties in the United States and sulphur prospects in the Canadian Arctic.

To newsmen who received this communiqué two days before the end of the year, at least those who understood the language employed in the cryptic IOS release, the fact that FOF and its baby brother, IOS Growth Fund, owned oil and gas exploration permits covering thousands of square miles of ice and snow somewhere north of Baffin Island seemed like one of the best-kept secrets in the world.

For information and disclosure purposes the release did not, as Cowett might have said, come close to passing muster. It did not disclose the location of the permits, the purchasers, how payment was effected, or any other pertinent details that IOS, for reasons that were then not entirely evident, was eager to hide. But the release left little doubt that FOF's net asset value per share had been increased by 12.6 per cent on December 26, 1969, as a result of a sale that had already taken place when in fact there had only been a transfer of assets onto the books of King Resources Company, the managing partner, *in anticipation of a sale* that was not entirely to outsiders.

Although it was a most misleading document, the press release did tip off a few of the more alert professionals that a major liquidity crisis was looming at IOS. Only the full extent of the crisis was not yet known. By revaluing FOF's natural resources holdings five days before the end of the year, IOS had dealt itself a neat $9,737,000 performance fee on the net *unrealized* profit, which would only appear on the accounting ledgers of The Fund of Funds on the first business day after the New Year. As it happened, this performance fee represented 95 per cent of IOS's total profits for 1969.

Based on the terms of the 10 per cent sale, the FOF board approved the revaluation of properties acquired at a cost of $11,850,000 [5] to a new carrying value of $119 million—an increase of $107 million, which after taxes produced IOS's $9.7 million performance fee.

The actual cash proceeds to FOF on the sale, when it finally did occur, amounted to less than $600,000. A total $7.6 million more was to

[5] Report of Charles Baer, KRC Trustee in Bankruptcy, October 10, 1973, p. 5.

be paid in six semiannual installments beginning in 1973 and running through 1976. Thus the "performance fee" retained by IOS was greater than the entire proceeds of the alleged arm's-length transaction.

This land-office tour de force was not particularly appreciated by the auditors, who nevertheless managed to sign off the 1969 accounts with an ambiguous qualification.

Quite naturally, both IOS and King were reluctant to disclose who the supposedly arm's-length purchasers of FOF's 10 per cent interest really were. The only real hint came when Cornfeld claimed in a rhapsodic year-end letter to his salesmen that the purchasers were three independent oil companies. In fact they were nothing of the sort. Five months later IOS was pressured into disclosing their identity. The largest stake, amounting to 3.125 per cent of the entire FOF-KRC holdings, went to another Denver firm, Consolidated Oil & Gas, whose chairman, Harry Trueblood, was John King's neighbor in Englewood, outside Denver.[6]

Comparable sale agreements were entered into by King Resources Company with John M. Mecom, a Houston oil millionaire, and with John King personally, each covering 1.5625 per cent of the whole. A fourth sale involving .78125 per cent of the whole was made to Lakeshore Associates, a limited partnership formed by Bennett King (no relation to John King, but a director and senior vice-president of KRC) and Edgar Greenbaum, a Chicago investor. The four sales of working interests represented 7.03 per cent of the whole and not almost 10 per cent as FOF's audited annual report alleged. Clearly, once the details that IOS and King had attempted to hide became known the conclusion was hardly avoidable that the FOF sale contained all the characteristics of a sham transaction.

This conclusion was reinforced when it transpired that Consolidated made but one payment on the permits to King Resources and then annulled the agreement, bringing an action against KRC for breach of contract. Mecom, John King, and Lakeshore Associates also made small down payments in 1969 but no other payments thereafter. Mecom and King entered into bankruptcy arrangements in 1970 and 1971, respectively, and Lakeshore defaulted. All three contracts were rescinded.

The full details of the part sale of the Arctic permits, which marked the beginning of a long downhill slide in the fortunes of both IOS and King Resources Company, have never been clearly or concisely reported to the shareholders of FOF, its Global Natural Resources offspring, or King Resources Company. However, when investors got an

[6] Consolidated purchased its 3.125 per cent interest with only $443,550 cash and the balance of $4,774,692 in notes plus the assumption of 25 per cent of the work obligations.

early indication of what had occurred there was a rush of requests to redeem fund shares for cash. By then the crippled Moneycatcher had no less than $166.6 million of its total $623 million in assets—representing close to 30 per cent—tied up in illiquid "underground" holdings.

By early 1970 fund-holders were redeeming their FOF shares for cash at a rate of $2 million per business day. Obviously this hemorrhage couldn't go on indefinitely, as the Moneycatcher was bound to run out of cash, particularly in a heavy down-market. This critical situation had already cast a sickly pallor over IOS when a devastating crisis of confidence erupted in April 1970. The combination of heavy client redemptions and a runaway confidence crisis presented a situation that the spendthrift management in Geneva was unable to cope with. Then, when no reputable financial institutions would move to save the offshore giant from collapse, the door was left open for Robert Vesco and his band of corporate looters to step in and administer the *coup de grâce*.

8

Crisis Uncovered

Cornfeld learns of a crisis at IOS while playing backgammon at Eilat and returns to lead his troops in the defense of People's Capitalism ⁓ A few horrifying discoveries provoke panic in the ranks, and the search begins for a savior with clean hands

The complex scheme of events that brought Bob Vesco into a control position at IOS began in early April 1970 with a telephone call from Geneva to a quiet hotel overlooking the beach at Eilat in the south of Israel.

As the bearded, balding Cornfeld, rakishly trim for his forty-two years, was playing backgammon at a seaside cabana opposite the untidy Jordanian port of Aqaba, he received his first warning of a crisis at IOS headquarters in Geneva.

Cornfeld's deputy chairman, the soft-spoken, reflective Allen Cantor, head of the 15,000-man IOS sales organization, reached him with word of an apparent bear raid against the company's publicly traded common stock.

Unless support was found in the market place, Cantor feared the stock would fall through the $10 issuing price within a matter of days. He therefore urged Cornfeld to return immediately to Switzerland and resume control of his $2.3 billion financial planning empire.

Cornfeld, in a show of pique the month before, had stalked out of the IOS boardroom because his directors had rejected two of his pet projects—the acquisition of a pair of gambling casinos (one in Divonne-les-Bains, France, and the other in San Juan, Puerto Rico); and participation with his friend Hugh Hefner in a Playboy real estate venture in Florida.

For quite some months resistance had been growing in company councils to Cornfeld's free-wheeling ways, and Bernie, full of anger, had handed in his resignation from all posts save the topmost position of chairman, leaving control of the day-to-day operations in the hands of his two most trusted lieutenants, general counsel Cowett and sales chief Cantor—which is where it had been for the better part of two years anyway.

Cantor now reasoned that Cornfeld's presence back at the IOS control center was the only way to end the rumors circulating through the financial community that the flamboyant financier was dead, ousted from power, or committed to an insane asylum, or that he simply had absconded with the cash. Such scurrilous publicity, which Cantor imagined was part of a plot by West German bankers to bring the arrogant IOS to its knees, diminished public confidence in the company and its investment products.

IOS, unfortunately, was hoist upon its own petard—the hot air of untold mutual fund sales presentations and a windy stock promotion that had stirred the breezes of speculation. It was these same breezes that had caused IOSers to mortgage everything they owned to purchase company shares, as many as they could lay their hands on, when the IOS common stock first hit the market in the well-publicized public offering six months before. An astute salesman like Cantor knew very well that once the IOS stock started to deflate there was no telling where the giddy little trip might end. Cantor, it should also be noted, held an undisclosed block of 32,442 common shares himself and was as much concerned for his own financial well-being as he was for the welfare of the company.

In this uncertain atmosphere, then, Cantor's long-distance call held the same significance for Cornfeld as a call from Paris to Colombey-les-Deux-Eglises for General de Gaulle. IOS needed him; his month-long exile was over. He folded away his backgammon board, collected his entourage of long-legged minions, and left Israel that same night for Switzerland aboard his orange and white Jet Commander.

Bernie the Beneficent, his image as an international financier somewhat tarnished by IOS's record of having underwritten some of the worst dogs of the Eurobond market, was coming home. Next day, when he appeared in the corridors of the seven-story IOS headquarters in Geneva dressed in another of his extravagant costumes, word spread from floor to floor that "Bernie's back. Everything's okay."

This confidence, alas, was sadly misplaced, for Cornfeld was no financial genius—in fact, he was unable to read a balance sheet. His strength was as a master motivator who understood the combination of fear and greed that made top sales people.

Many insiders recklessly plowed their savings into the stock simply because Cornfeld had said the shares were likely to double in value before the following summer. That prediction, four years later, landed the bountiful Cornfeld in Geneva's 150-year-old Saint-Antoine Prison. But at the time the founder of IOS was riding high on the crest of success. He believed himself when he assured his faithful that profits were soaring, business had never been better, and hundreds of IOSers would become millionaires as a result. To show he meant every word, he ordered that each clerk and typist be allocated stock at the "bargain underwriting price." Furthermore, he insisted that these deserving people be loaned corporate money to assist them in paying for their allotment. Under Swiss law this could be defined as abetting speculation beyond an individual's means, which is a criminal offense.

Cornfeld's response to the situation, upon returning from Eilat, was a gut appraisal. He sensed the euphoria slipping in a direct ratio to the fall in IOS stock prices; his troops were apprehensive. After listening to the other members of the triumvirate he realized that the company was caught in a cash bind because of some "unauthorized loans." For several weeks he was unable to ascertain the exact figures, but he knew that the sums involved in these "unauthorized loans" were substantial. Nevertheless, he remained confident. "IOS had overcome worse problems before," he confided afterward. For Cornfeld, misquoting Victor Hugo, there was no stopping the momentum of "a great idea that had met its time." [1] What he didn't understand was that IOS's time had passed.

By April 1970 the company's twenty mutual funds and investment trusts had $2.3 billion of other people's money under management. Investment program sales in these funds were running at a record rate of $4.5 billion in face amount per year. The client roster had swollen to nearly 1 million from more countries than there were members of the United Nations. IOS's sales force was the largest of its kind in the world and had the potential of writing the same amount of cash business in a month as the entire U.S. mutual fund industry.

Still, IOS was more than just a marketing machine. Its network of banks held $101 million in customer deposits.[2] Its six major insurance companies had $1.13 billion of insurance in force.[3] Its real estate operations had a retail sales value of $80 million. Although its corporate structure—consisting of some 200 separate entities domiciled in jurisdictions scattered around the globe—was described by one high-ranking Swiss official as possessing the "clarity of a bottle of ink," its exterior image was brassy. Like it or not, this freewheeling, unregulated offshore monster, a financial maverick of the first order, had become the best known ambassador of American capitalism abroad,

[1] "No army can withstand the strength of an idea whose time has come."
[2] IOS Ltd. Underwriting Prospectus, primary issue, p. 22.
[3] *Ibid.*, p. 26.

pumping more dollars back into the U.S. stock markets in any ninety-day period than all other foreign investors combined. Thus IOS's sudden collapse would have not only a very large emotional impact on the investing public, but a very material one as well.

Cornfeld was therefore persuaded that IOS and governments one day would end up as partners in the financial planning concept he had sired under the slick sounding name "People's Capitalism."

"Governments, by and large, are now on our side. They recognize that they need us," he told his executives at a meeting in Geneva a few weeks later.

Typical of the frame of mind then rampant at corporate headquarters was that of Christian Henry Buhl III, by then an eight-year veteran of People's Capitalism under Cornfeld. Fluffy and affable, the thirty-nine-year-old Buhl was one of the very few IOS directors to have risen through the ranks of management without any sales experience. As the company's senior investment officer, his compliant manner in management matters was one that well suited the triumvirate. And Buhl, a highly paid executive by any standards, wanted it kept that way. He had less than two years remaining under the stock option plan agreement before becoming vested.[4] Based on Cornfeld's estimate of what the stock might be selling at—and $20 a share seemed reasonable to some—Buhl was well on his way to becoming a multimillionaire. His mountain of IOS Ltd. shares would have been worth in excess of $8.3 million.

Of course, socially eminent C. Henry Buhl III never really had to worry about working for a living. His mother was one of the largest individual shareholders of General Motors, and so there would always be plenty of food in the cupboard for Henry, even if mother was a little tight with his annual stipend. Independent of the Buhl family fortune, however, Henry's secret desire, once vested, was to retire from the heights of offshore finance and enter American politics.

Unfortunately, time was running out for Henry, too. As long as he held onto his IOS stock he lived under a golden hammer. In IOS's terms this meant he had a large loan outstanding at one of the company banks. This $128,000 note[5] placed his ability to act independently—as a president and director of several of the IOS mutual funds—in con-

[4] Under terms of the IOS Stock Option Plan, holders of preferred shares were granted the right after completing ten years with IOS to convert 10 per cent annually of their preferred shares into common shares that then could be sold on the open market. However, if they left the company's service before the qualifying ten-year period, they were obliged to sell their shares back to the company at the going formula value.

[5] IOS Annual Report, 1970; IOS Financial Holdings Limited and Subsidiaries, note 2, p. 23.

siderable doubt. In fact, Henry was content to maintain little more than a general overview of IOS's worldwide fund management activities, having abdicated much of his responsibility to others.

Therefore Buhl's first reaction when tipped off by one of the accountants late in the afternoon of Thursday, April 9, 1970, that nearly $50 million in corporate cash had disappeared was also—like Cornfeld —to deny the existence of anything that could be labeled a major crisis. Having classified this turning point in IOS's history as a nonevent, his next move was to pass the information along to the company's new "all-weather" consultant, Professor George von Peterffy.

A big teddy bear of a man, von Peterffy was one of the few executives at IOS who could analyze a balance sheet. He had been an associate professor at Harvard University Business School, where he gave courses on long-range corporate planning and business-government relations, before joining the IOS board of directors a few months before. Since then he had worked in the Geneva offices making suggestions for cutting costs, which were ignored, and recommending the introduction of financial controls, which nobody wanted imposed. But Bernie figured the company needed a long-range planner, and earnest George was his selection.

Von Peterffy had spent most of that Thursday afternoon at Villa Elma, Cornfeld's neoclassical residence on the Geneva lakefront a half-mile east of the IOS headquarters, listening to Bernie explain how he was going to finance a Guy Laroche fashion boutique and nightclub along the rue de Lausanne through a tax-free "philanthropic" device known as the IOS Foundation. He had just returned to his offices and was talking with fellow director Sir Eric Wyndham White when the call came through from Buhl.

"Henry asked if I knew that IOS's cash position was as low as it was. I said no, that I had no idea what our cash position was. I was quite surprised at the figure, which Henry gave as $4.5 million," down sharply from $53 million in November of the previous year, von Peterffy noted that evening in a diary he kept of the crisis.

> Henry also reported he had heard that in the last week between $12 million and $14 million had been paid to a Beta Corporation, though no one seemed to know what this expenditure was for. It seemed to me that the board of directors or the executive management committee has to give approval for payments in the magnitude of $12 million or $14 million. I had never heard of this corporation. Henry did not know anything about it either.

Shocked, von Peterffy returned to Sir Eric and discussed the situation with him. The two of them decided to go and see Henry immediately.

They arrived in his first-floor offices just as Buhl was leaving to join Cornfeld and Cantor in Cowett's office on the sixth floor. "We spoke only for a few minutes. Each of us had arrived at the conclusion that we had no faith in what we were told by the three men at the top," von Peterffy noted.

Thus, the great IOS crisis was uncovered. Cowett's reaction when confronted with the facts about the missing money was perfect serenity. Trouble was suspected, however, by traders across Europe. The day before, the stock had fallen for the first time below the $10 issuing price after IOS refused to pick up 30,000 shares from a Zurich bank. A short rally on the morning of April 9 brought it back above the $10 mark, but by late afternoon, as Buhl spoke with von Peterffy, the steady decline had resumed. Within a week it was at five dollars and change, but heading lower, much lower. The big squeeze was on.

The next day was Cowett's fortieth birthday, a somber occasion under the circumstances. But IOS's bearded chief operating officer and acting financial vice-president steadfastly refused to acknowledge the existence of an irrevocable crisis. The problem, he said, was inadequate reporting, which prevented him from properly forecasting the company's cash requirements. But to von Peterffy Cowett's explanation made no sense. "If his finance department lacked figures it was because the internal procedures involving disbursements were such that Ed Cowett carried much of the needed information in his head. Something is badly amiss here," he remarked in his crisis diary.

To employees, shareholders, and members of the financial community, Cowett told another story. He spoke of bigger profits, better sales, and expanded operations when exactly the reverse was taking place. He told reporters in a series of press briefings that IOS had never been more liquid. In a front-page article in the April 20 edition of *The IOSer,* the staff newspaper, he wrote: "We have, within the past month, embarked upon a planned expansion program to put approximately $40 million to work in a series of new mutual fund, insurance, banking and real estate projects." But it wasn't true.

The same day Cowett's reassuring report came out in *The IOSer,* banks across Europe started calling margin loans on IOS stock. The atmosphere of euphoria slipped to one of deep gloom as top executives and stockroom clerks saw their dreams of the Good Life fade.

Von Peterffy, Sir Eric, and Buhl, now convinced of the seriousness of the situation, pressured Cowett into calling an emergency meeting of the thirteen-member executive management committee for the following week to review the company's financial position. The executive management committee when it met appointed a seven-member crisis committee, or Krisenstab, as it soon became known, to take control of the management of the company and conduct a full-scale investigation. The Krisenstab consisted of Buhl, von Peterffy, and Sir Eric on the side of the angels; the by then chastened but still obstinate triumvirate of Cornfeld, Cowett, and Cantor; and a chairman-moderator in the person of plodding, indecisive Richard M. Hammerman, head of IOS's insurance operations.

The forty-four-year-old Hammerman had flown in from London the moment he suspected the company was floundering. He seemed the right person for the job of Krisenstab chairman since in his plodding fashion he had successfully managed IOS's British subsidiary, International Life Insurance Company (U.K.) Limited, and had built it into one of the more solid components of the IOS group—a feat that had always baffled Cornfeld since he claimed Hammerman was both pompous and incompetent. Hammerman was just as critical of Cornfeld's operating methods and often said so. There were in fact few subjects on which the two men could see eye to eye. And, to add further to the friction, Hammerman held the same mistrust for Cowett's sharp practices.

The first action the Krisenstab undertook was the issuing of a supposedly definitive press statement to set matters straight in the public eye and calm the troubled waters. Laying out what the Krisenstab considered the proper facts, the communiqué said in part that "the IOS group of companies (as distinct from the cash in the funds we manage), presently has a cash position in excess of $30 million being held at interest, in addition to other corporate assets. We are proceeding with a selective program of corporate investments and projects this year."

The two-page document was a crude piece of work. It sought to replace rumors with outright lies. IOS was facing unprecedented redemption requests from clients who wished to exchange their mutual fund shares for cash that within days would push the company into a net negative cash flow from which it never recovered. But more immediately serious, the $30 million in corporate funds alluded to as "a cash position being held at interest" simply did not exist. The total "free deposits," or cash that could be readily drawn upon for that date —April 22, 1970—were no more than $6,053,000,[6] not sufficient to cover the following month's payroll and trade creditors' notes. The program of corporate investments had come to a grinding halt.

The Krisenstab dispatched Cowett to the United States for talks with Charles Bluhdorn of Gulf & Western and Cowett's friend and fellow conspirator John King, the Denver oil tycoon. The same windy wheeler-

[6] IOS Ltd. Liquidity Summary as of April 22, 1970, prepared by the Cash Management Department.

dealer who served as FOF's natural resources portfolio adviser was a former vice-chairman of the Republican Finance Committee and a close personal friend of Richard Milhous Nixon. Just a few weeks previously, the President had named King the United States Ambassador Extraordinary to the 1970 World's Fair in Osaka, Japan. It was thought that King's high-level political contacts might help in mounting a support operation and also in softening the SEC's hostile attitude toward IOS. The SEC, which had banned offshore IOS from operating onshore in the United States under the terms of its 1967 Settlement Order, was to play a key role in the months ahead in discouraging reputable American-based saviors from wading into the cesspool over in Geneva, effectively signing IOS's death warrant.

Cowett, the bespectacled *éminence grise* behind IOS's unfolding crisis, had actually developed a secret scheme that would have left King in control of a major portion of the Cornfeld empire. Although it was as yet unknown to the other directors, King was already the second largest shareholder in IOS Ltd. after Cornfeld himself.

With tricky Ed out of town, Hammerman began to ferret into company accounts, concentrating on the Cowett sector. The investigation confirmed his worst fears. The $30 million to $40 million that Cowett had announced was available for corporate development simply could not be found. One of the things Hammerman did uncover, however, was a classic stock support operation that had cost the company more than $20 million. As it was illegal for a Canadian corporation to purchase its own stock, Cowett had run most of the orders for the IOS shares through a Cornfeld account at Overseas Development Bank, the IOS bank in Geneva. Cornfeld had been away at the time, but when he learned upon his return that 680,000 shares had been purchased at prices ranging between $13 and $15—thereby running up a sizable deficit in the account—he almost had apoplexy. Cowett promptly reversed 650,000 shares out of Cornfeld's account and divided them between a King family trust and a Cowett "charitable trust" in the Bahamas. Corporate funds were loaned out to pay for the stock—$2.8 million to the Cowett trust and $6.7 million to the King trust.

The Krisenstab sat in almost continuous meetings over the next ten days while preparations were made to call an emergency meeting of the full twenty-three-member board of directors for the first week in May. During the Sunday session on April 26, Art Feder, an IOS lawyer who had been sent to Washington to take the temperature there, telephoned with a report that the White House was extremely concerned about what was happening in Geneva. Feder had learned from a member of the Board of Governors of the New York Stock Exchange that

"President Nixon himself" had called the SEC that very day to discuss the implications of an IOS failure.

Von Peterffy, Buhl, and James Roosevelt, president of IOS Development Company, were sent to the States to reassure the NYSE Board of Governors, the SEC, and the White House. The next day, Monday, April 27, the Dow Jones dropped twelve points, closing at 744. Wall Street was uneasy with rumors rolling out of Europe that IOS was selling large blocks of American securities to meet client redemptions. Those three letters carved in gold in Geneva had become stretched in many people's minds to read K-r-e-d-i-t-a-n-s-t-a-l-t, and the mood was 1929 all over again.

Buhl and von Peterffy, when they arrived in New York, immediately put through calls to Peter M. Flanigan, a White House aide who later became embroiled in the ITT scandal, and Maurice Stans, the Secretary of Commerce. Stans, an IOS friend of long standing, was away in South America and unreachable, but Flanigan, when he returned the call, nervously requested clarification on whether IOS had been flooding the market with orders to sell. Von Peterffy assured him the wave was coming out of Germany, not Geneva; Flanigan, he said, sounded relieved.

At its Sunday meeting, the Krisenstab gave its first serious consideration to obtaining outside support. Nearly four dozen potential candidates were suggested to participate in a rescue operation. Robert Vesco's name was not among them, although Henry Buhl, who had kept in touch with the New Jersey entrepreneur on a continuing basis since their first meeting in early 1968, contacted Vesco personally for some advice on how to handle the fast deteriorating situation. That was the only opening the Dark Horse needed.

The Krisenstab finally settled on two official candidates: John King and Banque Rothschild in Paris, a member of the lead underwriting syndicate that had brought IOS public seven months before. Cowett was the architect of the package proposal under which IOS would offer the rescuers 10 million shares of its principal subsidiary, Investors Overseas Services Management Limited, a nonresident Ontario corporation listed on the Toronto Stock Exchange, as collateral for $40 million in emergency financing.

Cowett was instructed to contact King with details of the package, while a separate approach was made to the Rothschilds by Allen Cantor. The junior member of the triumvirate drove to a secret meeting at a three-star restaurant near Lyon, France, for talks with the general manager of the Paris bank. Before Cowett left for New York and Denver, the Krisenstab stipulated at Cornfeld's insistance that no deal with King would be considered unless it was preceded by repayment of the nearly $10 million in loans to the King and Cowett trusts.

Upon his return to Geneva a few days later, Cowett insisted that, as frayed as it was, the King thread would hold up. As far as he was concerned, IOS's main need was cash, not credibility, and the money, according to Cowett, King could readily supply.

During the tense Krisenstab meetings Cornfeld, who wanted no part of a deal with King, remained apart from the discussions except to shout, occasionally, "For God's sake, we've got to kill the shorts!"— his remedy for IOS's problems. He was referring to the suspected short selling of the IOS stock by hostile West German bankers to drive the market price lower.

Cornfeld saw no reason why IOS could not look after itself, as it had done in the past when confronted with serious adversity. However, if his board of directors resolutely decided that outside help was needed, then, he said, it must come from members of the financial Establishment and not a promoter like John King.

The Krisenstab's arrangements to call an emergency session of the salesman-dominated IOS Ltd. board of directors were urgently completed. Telegrams went out to board members around the world summoning them to Geneva for the first Sunday in May. It was the key meeting, the one that sealed the fate of IOS and with it the viability of investments belonging to 1 million people.

The tragic bickering and appalling indecision of the IOS directors resulted in a loss for investors on the topside of $1 billion. Although no sum can be accurately attached to the public's aggregate losses, many investors—including hundreds of genuine hardship cases, unsophisticates who had been oversold into placing everything they owned in IOS— were wiped out, while a good proportion of the directors were able to retire as rich men on that portion of their wealth they were able to salvage from the wreckage.

The sad truth is that strong, experienced, and ethical management could have saved IOS from total collapse, whereas the incompetent, greedy, scared, and self-interested group of individuals who actually controlled the company only assisted its ultimate demise. It took three years, finally, to put IOS in its grave, and who knows how long thereafter to properly bury the stripped-down cadaver. That so large an institution with a fiduciary responsibility to safeguard the savings of so many people was permitted to remain under the domination of such inept and unclean hands for so long represents in itself one of the great crimes of financial history.

9

The Bella Vista Coup d'Etat

Crisis-bound IOS is overcome by a corporate death wish, which first becomes apparent at a seven-day board meeting, a masterpiece of indecision, that ends in the purging of Bernie and his Blue Sky expert

The company minutes officially recorded that "a meeting of the Board of Directors of IOS, Ltd., was convened on Sunday, May 3, 1970, at Bella Vista, 308 route de Lausanne, Geneva, Switzerland, at 10 A.M."

For the introduction to an epic confrontation without precedent in IOS's fourteen-year history, the wording was routinely anodyne. Thus, on a warm and sunny May morning, while the rest of Geneva braced itself for the debut of the tourist season, one of the most rocambolesque board meetings ever held commenced at a pleasant lakeside property three miles outside the city, on the main road to Lausanne.

The meeting had been called against the wishes of the IOS triumvirate, without any fixed agenda, in an atmosphere of growing crisis.

It lasted seven days.

Seven days of indecision.

During that time internal dissension shattered the company's technical structure, deprived the employees and sales force of leadership, and paralyzed all but the most mechanical of operating procedures.

The seven-day Bella Vista marathon left the affairs of IOS in turmoil, setting the stage for Vesco's slippery but easy entry as the group's purported savior. Only Vesco was not the portrait of the savior he painted of himself. He was seeking urgently needed financial muscle to keep his own International Controls empire from collapse. Confronted with a decreasing cash flow, International Controls was having difficulty meeting the charges on its large debt structure. Vesco quickly capitalized on the mood of deep depression inside the Bella Vista board-room to place himself in a controlling position within the corporate structure so that he could manipulate to his advantage the vast store-house of IOS assets without resistance or restraint.

However, the carefully worded minutes carried no hint of the panic and paralysis that gripped the IOS board but blandly continued: "The Chairman of the Board, Mr. Bernard Cornfeld, took the Chair . . . and began the meeting with a description of the IOS stock slide, rumors, sales volume and cash flow."

Times were tense the world over. Just four days previously, for the first time in the drawn-out Indochina conflict, President Nixon had ordered American troops into Cambodia. On the economic front, credit was tight and Wall Street was reeling under one of the biggest sell-offs in its history.

To add to the general malaise, word had circulated for several weeks among bankers and brokers that IOS fund managers were dumping large blocks of securities to meet a steadily increasing wave of client redemptions. These same reports spoke of negative cash flows as large as rivers and huge operating deficits that high-flying IOS could not long sustain. As a result, the company stock continued to tumble—from 30 per cent to 50 per cent below its $10 issuing price, to 70 per cent below, where support was fleetingly found.

London's *Sunday Telegraph,* in a curtain raiser to the Bella Vista marathon, commented: "There is one key factor overshadowing the stock markets of the world at the present time. It is not the rate of inflation, nor even the threatening Cambodian situation—even though a full-scale war there would have grave effects on the American economy.

"The plain fact is that a more settled mood in world markets is unlikely to emerge until the whole IOS situation has been resolved." [1]

The very next day the *Telegraph* article found a resounding echo on Wall Street. As newspapers carried the first on-the-spot reports of the Bella Vista round, the New York Stock Exchange experienced its sharpest decline since the November 1963 assassination of President Kennedy. The Dow Jones, during a hectic session, fell 19.07 points to a new interim low of 714.56, compared to the last bull market crest at 985 some eighteen months earlier.

But the Dow Jones was still heading lower. Before the end of May, in a mood of selling hysteria, it would bottom out at 631, the lowest level in eight years. Similar reports of market jitters came from London, Toronto, Tokyo, Amsterdam, Paris, Frankfurt, and Johannesburg, as

[1] Patrick Hutber (business editor), "IOS, the Question over the Markets," *Sunday Telegraph* (London), May 3, 1970.

IOS fund managers received directives to liquidate up to 50 per cent of their existing portfolios.

The minutes made no mention of this wholesale dumping. They continued almost cryptically: "Mr. Cornfeld indicated that as a result of these factors [the supposed bear raid and rumor campaign "inspired by the German banks"], redemptions were up sharply in the last weeks. He also indicated that there was major illiquidity in the corporate area."

For many of the out-of-town directors who had responded to the emergency call, mention of "major illiquidity in the corporate area" was the first confirmation they had received that the company had serious problems. But what astounded them most was that such problems should occur in the area of corporate finance. After all, only the previous autumn IOS had completed a $110 million flotation of its common stock.

"Hell, we have money coming out of our ears," said an IOS spokesman only weeks before. And the president himself, the ever smiling, serenely confident Ed Cowett, had maintained repeatedly as the tide of public confidence receded that profits for 1969, when audited, would be in the $24 million range, when in fact without the contrived revaluation of FOF's Arctic permits they would have been closer to zero.

There was no sign of crisis, either, on the faces of the board members as they arrived at Bella Vista for Sunday's opening session. They drove up to the three-story gingerbread mansion in custom-built limousines and racy, grand touring cars—the Ferraris, Maserattis, and Lamborghinis outshining by far the Cadillacs and Lincoln Continentals—that measured accurately the mood of opulence and splendor still reigning in company circles.

"What crisis?" one of the directors pompously responded when asked to comment on the deteriorating situation by a group of journalists standing on the sidewalk in front of Bella Vista's tall green gates.

Other directors joked casually among themselves and smiled at the reporters before slipping past the security guards at the gates, clutching as they went their slim leather briefcases, part of the corporate uniform. The very presence of the journalists in front of Bella Vista on that bright Sunday morning indicated to what extent the financial community was gripped by the IOS crisis and wanted news of decisions that it hoped would soothe the markets and restore public confidence.

In addition to "major illiquidity," Cornfeld quickly identified slipping credibility as another corporate problem. "The Chairman pointed out that the [executive committee] was seeking groups outside the Company which could induce confidence in the field, and would provide interim capital while the Company made liquid some of its assets," the minutes continued.

Cowett next took the floor and explained that the executive committee had worked out what was thought to be "an acceptable proposal to offer outsiders." He said it was open to more than one institution and provided for funds to be immediately available, adding that Chemical Bank had "expressed an interest in participating; and possibly Continental Illinois."

While this basic package circulated through Western financial capitals in search of possible takers, the IOS boardmen sat in their Bella Vista vastness arguing about who should resign and at what price their stock would be repurchased by the company for resale to the outside consortium of rescuers. While this farcical debate continued, the stock option plan, once hailed as an outstanding asset, suddenly became a $175 million liability as discouraged associates and executives, or the banks to whom they had pledged their stock, rushed to sell their preferred shares back to the company at the prevailing formula value. The pressure became so great that the stock option plan was quickly suspended, thereby destroying one of the holiest myths in the IOS pantheon.

Certainly it was difficult to imagine a more unlikely setting for a boardroom drama that contributed so significantly to the mood of tension in the major international market places. A large Victorian villa with many gables and high chimney pots, Bella Vista was purchased by the company in 1964 for $250,000 from a branch of the Colgate family. It was renovated thereafter by Cornfeld's decorator, the Velvet Boy, who turned it into a plushy upholstered haven for tired financiers and master mutual fund salesmen.

Throughout the week-long round of meetings, hot coffee and finely catered buffets were served around the clock by a staff of white-coated waiters in the villa's main dining room. This impressive salon, with polished beams and an eight-foot-tall blue porcelain Bavarian heater, could have been taken from a Charles Addams cartoon, complete with an elegant bay window with a view of Mont Blanc.

A private park ran along the water's edge to a boathouse and port, where IOSers were allowed to keep their sailboats and sunbathe during the summer weekends. Across the garden stood the former stables and carriage house, which, at a cost of another $250,000, had been turned into the velvet and oak-paneled IOS boardroom and caucus chambers.

The IOS board was divided into two classes of directors. The voting majority was reserved for the "inside" directors, who made up two-thirds of the board and were elected by the preferred (insider) shareholders. The "outside" directors formed the other class, consisting of no more than one-third of the board, and they were elected by the common (public) shareholders.

Among the prestigious outside directors were Count Carl Johan Bernadotte, youngest son of the late King Gustav VI Adolph of Sweden;
Wilson Wyatt, the Kentucky politician who served three U.S. Presidents;
Pasquale Chiomenti, a well-placed Italian lawyer; George von Peterffy,
soon to leave IOS for an appointment with the U.S. State Department;
and the austere British merchant banker Martin Montague Brooke,
representing Guinness Mahon & Company Limited, a member of the
primary underwriting group.

On the insiders' portion of the board, in addition to the triumvirate,
were Henry Buhl, Dick Hammerman, and George Landau, as well as
Malcolm Fox, an ex-tennis pro who was general manager in the Far
East; Roy Kirkdorffer, a former air force lieutenant who was the sales
chief in the United Kingdom; and Ira Weinstein, the man in charge of
Canadian operations. Among the nonsales types were three members
of the diplomatic brigade—James Roosevelt, Erich Mende, and
Sir Eric Wyndham White—and two divisional technicians, Barry Har-
mon Sterling, a sad-eyed, ineffectual-mannered attorney from Los
Angeles who was the group's leading banker, and Martin ("Montana
Marty") Seligson, the real estate boss.

Sterling, a past treasurer of the California division of the Democratic
National Committee, was brought to Geneva by Jimmy Roosevelt to
become general counsel of IOS Development Company. Later promoted
to president of IOS Financial Holdings Limited, he was in charge of
Investors Bank, Luxembourg, the manager of a number of disastrous
Eurobond offerings that cost IOS fund-holders an estimated $50 million
in losses and write-offs.

Sterling was the architect of IOS's biggest investment banking fiasco:
$40 million in debt financing for a pallid Beverly Hills conglomerate,
Commonwealth United. Incestuous business relations had a way of
creeping into IOS's affairs, and Sterling was responsible for one of the
classic examples. The year before, Commonwealth United began a
merger-mad expedition by taking over Sunset International Petroleum
Corporation, a debt-ridden oil and real estate company closely con-
nected with the Sterling family. The deal was arranged by the Hollywood investment banking firm of Kleiner, Bell & Company, which acted
as investment adviser to the Beverly Hills show-biz conglomerate. Sterling's wife, Audrey, a former head of the California Fair Employment
Practices Commission, was a limited partner in Kleiner, Bell. Her husband's Los Angeles law firm, Hindin, Sterling, McKittrick & Powsner,
had Kleiner, Bell as a client.

Before its expulsion from the New York and American stock exchanges
and the withdrawal of its broker-dealer license by the SEC, Kleiner, Bell
had a number of intricate financial dealings with Commonwealth United

that only came to the surface sometime afterward and were professionally unethical if not downright dishonest in light of Commonwealth's subsequent financial difficulties. Kleiner, Bell had prepared a confidential research report on Commonwealth, which became the basis of IOS's decision to bring out a $30 million Eurobond flotation followed by a $10 million private placement in early 1969, when the junior conglomerate was already in deep financial trouble. One year later Commonwealth filed under Chapter X of the Bankruptcy Act, and in 1971 the company was officially declared insolvent.

In announcing disciplinary action against Kleiner, Bell, by then heading into ignominious liquidation, an Amex official charged that the firm had "publicly recommended that Commonwealth United stock be bought while at the same time selling it on the basis of bearish inside information."

The ethics of profiting from insider knowledge never bothered IOS's top banker. When news of the pending sale by Fund of Funds of a 10 per cent interest in its Arctic holdings was disseminated internally in early December 1969, Sterling and his wife were among the numerous insiders who made investments in FOF just prior to the sudden 12.6 per cent jump in share value. Their profit on the quick in-and-out investment was a modest $3,642.99. Some months later, when Sterling was asked to forfeit this insider gain, he protested bitterly.

This was perfectly representative of the high moral fiber of the men at the helm of IOS. Certainly no exception was the character of windy, high-pressured Montana Marty Seligson. When the IOS board of directors decided in the summer of 1965 to enter the land development field, Seligson was the man Cornfeld selected to lead the assault.

A former dude rancher and folk singer from New York City, Seligson's main experience in real estate prior to joining IOS had been as the head of a syndicate that planned to develop New York's Breezy Point, an 800-acre tract of ocean front across the bay from downtown Manhattan. Seligson and his Atlantic Investment Company intended to put up 15,000 apartment units, five shopping centers, four schools, six churches, and a couple of beach clubs on the site, but, after they had spent $20 million on land acquisition, surveys, and preliminary construction, Breezy Point was expropriated by the City of New York, and the project became embroiled in lawsuits.

As president of IOS Real Estate Holdings Limited, he was responsible for the conception of IOS's two major real estate projects: Playamar, a self-contained resort community of twenty-one fifteen-story apartment buildings next door to Torremolinos on Spain's Costa del Sol, and the

Hemispheres, four luxury apartment buildings at Hallendale, on Florida's Gold Coast, just north of Miami Beach.

Both projects were primed with Fund of Funds money and then transferred to Investment Properties International Limited. (IPI), a $100-million closed-end investment company that the IOS sales force sold to the public at $10 a share in July 1969. Seligson was also president of IPI, another unmitigated IOS fiasco.

Serious questions had been raised about the Playamar project. It was suggested that the contractual concept used in selling Playamar to the public was fraudulent. The prospectus was replete, one legal expert retained by IOS noted, with contradictory affirmations that had the smell of sharp U.S. real estate practices about them. The clients were not given clear title to their apartments but ended up owning a Bahamian bank account instead. "All the characteristics of swindling are present," said the expert in his detailed legal opinion.

In the days following the Bella Vista directors' meeting, the attention of the recast Krisenstab was drawn to a glaring conflict of interest between Seligson and IPI. Under questioning by the committee, Seligson admitted that he had been a "junior partner" in several of the real estate projects acquired by IPI. For example, it was disclosed he owned 15 per cent of the Waterways, a land development project adjoining the Hemispheres, when IPI acquired the Waterways for its portfolio. Seligson then sold his interest in the Waterways to IPI for a tidy $80,000 profit. A similar arrangement existed at the Meadows, a 573-unit rental apartment complex in Los Angeles. Both Seligson and IPI were limited partners in the property. IPI invested $250,000, Seligson $25,000.

Another all-star was a former New York schoolteacher, Bob Sutner, one of Cornfeld's earliest sales captains. In the middle of one board session, when it was suggested that fellow director Eli Wallit had sold his IOS stock short, Sutner leaped from his chair, lunged at Wallit, threatening to strangle him, and had to be immediately restrained.

Wallit, who held the rank of Super GM in charge of German sales coordination, had been Cornfeld's first supervisor when the IOS founder started his career as a mutual fund salesman in New York City. He admitted that with Cowett's approval he had sold a batch of his stock for delivery at a forward date in order to raise cash for a new $500,000 villa he wished to purchase on the opposite shore of Lake Geneva.

There was nothing illegal about this transaction provided it was declared to the appropriate Canadian authorities as an insider trade, but it showed certain lack of judgment on Wallit's behalf since it was assumed he was either abandoning ship or speculating on a further decline in IOS shares by selling short.

Cornfeld, Cowett, Kirkdorffer, and Sutner were among those who, in addition to Wallit, sold large blocks of IOS stock during the crisis period in transactions that were kept carefully hidden from the public. Cornfeld was the heaviest seller. With Cowett in mid-April 1970 he jointly sold 390,000 preferred shares at $4 to his close friend and supporter Meshulam Ricklis, chairman of Rapid American Corporation. Cornfeld had done the Israeli financier one or two good turns in the past, and Ricklis found a way to sluff the shares off on Canadian Schenley, a foreign subsidiary of Rapid American. Cornfeld separately sold 30,000 common shares at $2.25 in July 1970, and 348,400 preferred in August 1970. Kirkdorffer unloaded 17,000 undeclared common shares in the first five days of May 1970 as the directors meeting was in progress, and Sutner cast off ballast totaling 199,600 preferred shares during the summer at prices ranging from $1.50 to $2.75.

The twenty-third member of the board, Harvey Felberbaum, a one-time New York taxi driver and time-study engineer who became the chief of IOS's Italian operations, had suffered a relapse of hepatitis caught while selling illegally for IOS in India; he had to follow the board's deliberations by telephone from the Geneva Cantonal Hospital.

Felberbaum had become a legend around IOS for his unorthodox management methods. On occasion he chaired top-level meetings at his expensively decorated offices atop Rome's Monte Savello literally from the floor—that is, seated cross-legged on the carpet with his Italian lieutenants clustered around him. It was not unknown for Felberbaum, who had a remarkably short attention span for so successful a sales executive, to take out a shoeshine kit during these discussions and begin polishing the shoes of his managers. Unorthodox perhaps, but Felberbaum's operation accounted for 24 per cent of all IOS's business in 1969, with sales pouring into Geneva from Italy at a rate of $40 million a month in face value.

When the board session opened Sunday there was an unmistakable scent of revolt in the air. Cowett, more confident since his return from Denver, was able to forestall an early attempt at impeachment by laying on the table a $40 million "Letter of Offer" from John King. That very day a King courier had arrived from the United States with a little black satchel. He met with Cowett upstairs at Bella Vista for a brief time, then spent the next four hours at Belle Haven, Cowett's home across the lake, waiting for a return flight to New York. All he would say in a rather tired voice was, "I'm the mailman. I'm leaving tonight, back to New York."

Cowett returned to the boardroom with a $10 million check to cover the "unauthorized" loans to his and King's offshore trusts. The money, which the King-Cowett trusts had borrowed from Delafield Capital

Corporation of New York at 11 per cent interest, provided IOS with desperately needed short-term liquidity, permitting the company to meet the May 1970 payroll. On Wednesday the mailman was followed to Geneva by the grand master himself, carrying further details of his $40 million offer of support. But meanwhile Cowett launched into a report of the Krisenstab's meeting the previous week with representatives of the underwriters. His report was not rosy.

Because of IOS's past problems with the SEC, the six underwriters who made up the lead syndicate that managed the IOS public offering— Drexel Harriman Ripley and Smith Barney & Company in New York; Guinness Mahon and Hill Samuel, two of the most respected merchant banking houses in London; Banque Rothschild of Paris; and Pierson Heldring & Pierson of Amsterdam—had been extremely cautious in handling the offering, keeping the SEC abreast of every development.

The noted Wall Street law firm of Shearman & Sterling had acted as counsel for the underwriters and gone over every word of the offering prospectus and underwriting agreement. In a highly unusual move, the underwriters had even hired the chartered accountancy firm of Price Waterhouse to check the work of their competitors, Arthur Andersen, to make doubly sure the accounts were accurate. Price Waterhouse's opinion, marked private and confidential, had stated that nothing "came to our attention during the course of our work for you that caused us to believe that the examination of the financial statements of IOS Ltd. at December 31, 1968, by Arthur Andersen & Co. was not made in accordance with generally acceptable auditing standards or would give you any reason not to rely on such examination." It added most cautiously, "As part of our original undertaking with you, it was agreed that no reference, public or otherwise, would be made to our firm or our participation as a member of your investigating team."

Not very nervous! And with reason. A reconciliation of IOS's consolidated cash flow for the final quarter of 1969, had it been available, would have shown that without the proceeds of the underwriting the company was approximately $23 million in the red (see Appendix 1 on page 367).

Even a bare-bones estimate of the last-quarter 1969 cash situation was sufficiently depressing to present the underwriters—now referred to by IOSers as "the undertakers"—with a very sticky reconciliation of their own. Indeed, it was with some embarrassment, even anger, that the underwriters announced in their meeting with the Krisenstab that, after all, they were concerned with the accuracy of the offering prospectus and felt there had been little justification for bringing out the IOS common stock at $10 a share. Sir Kenneth Keith, chairman of Hill Samuel, had been most appalled by the financial condition of the company and took the lead in demanding the immediate ouster of Cornfeld and Cowett. Moreover, the underwriters wanted 51 per cent of the preferred stock placed in a three-year voting trust, which they would control, and the existing board replaced by a caretaker board of directors. This, Cowett now said, amounted to placing the company in receivership. The underwriters were concerned that IOS was already bankrupt.

It was Chiomenti and Count Bernadotte who opened the real debate. They repeatedly pressed Cowett for an answer to the key question: Where had all the money gone? They pursued him with it until Cowett gave them the sketchiest of answers. He presented IOS's over-all financial position at April 30, 1970, as follows:

The Sept. 1969 public offering, net of expenses, had brought in:	$47.2 million
Already on deposit from ILI:	$ 1.0 million
Total cash position at Oct. 1, 1969	48.2 million
IOS deployed these assets as follows:	
ILI repayment	$ 1.0 million
Purchase of Canadian Channing mutual fund group	$ 6.5 million
Increase in capital at ODB	$ 2.3 million
Increase in capital at Orbis Bank, Munich	$ 1.5 million
Cologne Training Center	$ 0.4 million
Building improvements at Ferney	$ 0.5 million
Real estate acquisitions	$ 1.1 million
Loans to Commonwealth United	$ 6.5 million
Repurchase of IOS Management stock	$ 3.9 million
Acquisition of a Canadian insurance company for ILI	$ 1.9 million
State of Israel war bond	$ 1.0 million
Support of IOS common stock by the IOS Stock Option Plan Ltd.	$ 3.2 million
Paid to Bear Sterns arbitrage account	$ 1.0 million
Cash on hand (including repayment of the King-Cowett loans)	$12.0 million
	$48.2 million

But Cowett's cash schedule was as deceitful as it was incomplete. It didn't take into account, for example, the situation at the IOS banks. The banks were nearly as illiquid as IOS itself, and it was feared that a run on their resources might develop. Cowett had omitted all mention of tax shelter schemes, the shortfall in the IOS underwriting, and the myriad loans extended to insiders and friends. In all, there were fourteen more items:

Tax shelter schemes for senior IOS officers, directors and friends:

Beta Foundation Equipment Associates, a tax shelter formed to acquire and lease oil-drilling equipment	$ 4.6	million
Foundation Equipment Associates (same as Beta)	$ 0.5	million
Advance to a King company (Regency Income) for the purchase of three Handley Page Jetstream aircraft as tax write-offs for Felberbaum, Kirkdorffer, and Wallit	$ 1.6	million
Advance by IOB to Colorado Corp. (a privately held King company) for purchase of net operating profits interests (NOPIs) for the accounts of various IOS directors and officers	$ 1.6	million
Additional loans to Colorado Corp.	$ 3.5	million
IOS Financial Holdings guarantee of back-to-back loans shared by Wells Fargo and Western American Bank in connection with Beta	$ 5.0	million
	$16.8	million

Other corporate undertakings:

Shortfall in IOS underwriting purchased by the IOS Foundation	$ 8.6	million
Additional exposure on Commonwealth United	$ 2.4	million

Plus loans extended by IOS banking subsidiaries to insiders and friends:

Officers, directors, associates, and employees, mainly for the purchase of IOS common stock	$ 6.7	million
John King personally, secured by unregistered KRC voting stock (when ODB called this loan, King defaulted)	$ 1.8	million
David Meid, manager of San Francisco–based Winfield Growth Fund, also ran FOF's Meid Fund account (it was suggested that this loan be written off)	$ 0.25	million
Denver junior conglomerateer William M. White, chairman of Great Western United	$ 1.5	million
Dean Melosis and Carlisle Jones, former FOF sub-advisers	$ 0.85	million
Contingent liabilities in connection with ODB guarantees for Cornfeld's purchase of a BAC 1-11 jet, a Jet Commander, and a Convair 240	$ 4.9	million

Grand total of loans, guarantees, and contingent liabilities	$43.8	million

This supplemental list confirmed the real reason for IOS's liquidity crisis; it laid bare an extraordinary record of corporate generosity to insiders and friends. Moreover, it raised a number of delicate questions that had to be carefully broached by the board members for fear of coming face to face with the elements of a major fraud. For a starter, Cowett mentioned that it was a corporate policy to assist senior executives with their tax problems. About all that could be said for that as a defense was $16.8 million represented impressive assistance. More impressive still, it was accomplished without the board's approval and in most instances without even the knowledge of the principal recipients.

Then, too, under what conditions were proceeds from the underwriting used to purchase Israeli war bonds? The offering prospectus, after all, had stated that the increased working capital would be used "to develop and expand the company's activities, primarily in the banking and insurance areas."

How also were $11.8 million used to support the stock of IOS (a total of $21 million, if the stock purchases by the Cowett and King trusts were included), when normally a Canadian-registered company was prohibited from trading in its own stock?

Cornfeld said afterward that some directors reacted out of pure self-interest to protect their own skins and reputations, that one or two were motivated by genuine concern for the shareholders and fundholders, while the majority panicked and were stampeded into a deep crisis psychosis from which they and the company never recovered. Chiomenti, the Italian lawyer who looked like somebody's kindly aunt, was so horrified by what he heard that he threw his arms in the air and asked to be relieved of his functions. He requested that his director's honorarium and stock option be disposed of at the board's discretion, then left Bella Vista in a dither.

In the course of the long and suspenseful days that followed, when white knights were said to be riding to the rescue with saddlebags full of gold, a prim-looking receptionist in a tight blue suit sat at the switchboard in the front hall of Bella Vista calmly reading her way through *L'Histoire d'O* while the world of IOS collapsed around her.

Out on the front lawn during the board's recess periods, the directors and other insiders gathered in groups according to their financial situations and the factions they supported. On the periphery were those who had already lost their shirts by having bought IOS stock on credit and were not able to cover the margin calls from their bankers and brokers and those who were still hanging on, but only just.

Ironically, the group promoting the hottest deal—King's $40 million offer of emergency financing—found itself in the weakest position, and by Wednesday night Cowett, its leader, with only two dissenting votes in his favor, was asked to resign. He withdrew from all further meetings.

On the other side of the lawn was Dick Hammerman's group, which included, more or less, George von Peterffy and Sir Eric Wyndham White. They opposed a deal with King and wished to postpone any decision pending further consultations with the underwriters.

Standing alone in the outfield, where he was viewed by some observers as a possible dark horse candidate to succeed both Cornfeld and Cowett, Henry Buhl was biding his time.

Cornfeld, increasingly isolated, was for once on the extreme right wing, favoring the piecing together of a broadly based consortium headed by the Rothschilds, to join in a partnership with IOS. Scurrying back and forth was Allen Cantor, acting as liaison between the Paris Rothschilds and the board, which placed him halfway between the Hammerman and Cornfeld camps.

The knights with the bulging saddlebags, of course, were the two Rothschilds—Baron Guy in Paris and Jacob in London—heading an unformed consortium of mainly European banks, and Big John King, who claimed he had support from the Bank of New York, Fidelity Insurance Corporation of Richmond, Virginia, and a major German savings bank. However, Samuel Woolley, chairman of the Bank of New York, denied a few days later that his bank had any intention of joining the King rescue group, and Fidelity confirmed that it was interested in placing $5 million with a consortium, but independently of King.

The week-long meeting had progressed into its third day when the Denver Croesus, with an impressive delegation of troubleshooters, flew to Geneva at the board's request to elaborate on the terms of this $40 million Letter of Offer. When King and his team arrived at Bella Vista they found the lakeside villa invaded by the Afrika Korps, a ragged group of general and regional managers from south of the Sahara. The sales operation in Africa, once an IOS gold mine, had been wiped out, they reported, because of bad press and the spreading credibility gap between IOS management and the public.

Combining forces with a deputation of moaning German sales managers, who were already negotiating their desertion to the competition, the Afrika Korps gathered around the old carriage house and stables demanding to know what was going on inside the boardroom. They cornered Cornfeld during a coffee break and started shouting at him. Cornfeld lost his cool.

"You guys are eating my guts out," he yelled back at them. "Why the hell don't you go back to work and start selling again?"

The atmosphere was tense and crackling. Cornfeld, wearing more of a conventional suit and less of a costume for the first time in almost two years, told those who wished to listen how he had built the company virtually on his own, how it had prospered under his management until he had turned over control of day-to-day operations to his two chief lieutenants, and how when things got a little tight a bunch of scared children wanted to take it all away from him.

When his speech was over there was silence. The Cornfeld charisma had lost its grip. His shoulders hunched, he ambled on, alone, except for the two security guards who now accompanied him wherever he went. A number of threats against his life had been received. The most serious came the week before, when the Israeli *Shin Bet* and Swiss counter-intelligence received independent reports that Cornfeld was on the *El Fatah* blacklist and an attempt would be made by the Palestinian guerrillas to kidnap and hold him for ransom.

King's first appearance before the board was dazzling, but the Rothschilds, meanwhile, had come up with their first counter-proposal:

(1) immediate resignation of Cornfeld and Cowett
(2) consideration of $15 million in debt financing
(3) the $15 million debt convertible into preferred stock at $1 per share
(4) issuing 10 million warrants to purchase additional preferred stock at $1 per share
(5) setting up a three-year voting trust which would give the Rothschild group outright voting control of IOS affairs
(6) no deal with King

The warrants were to be used by the Rothschilds to attract "name" banks or institutions to join the consortium. The Dresdner Bank in Germany, the Banca Commerciale Italiana, and the Rockefeller-backed International Basic Economy Corporation (IBEC) were said to be interested.

Seligson and Roosevelt, who had taken over leadership of the Cowett camp, were particularly outspoken against the Rothschild offer. Seligson termed it "unthinkable." Roosevelt said he hated to see IOS "subjected to daily management by a banking group, bringing in unknown managerial talent." This, of course, was their way of clouding the issues of corporate survival with the interests of each director's pocketbook. The Rothschild offer was vague on the amount of financing the consortium of European banks might provide, whereas IOS directors were impressed by King's apparent hard offer of $40 million in emergency funding. But even more impressive, the King proposal recognized a $4 per share valuation of the IOS preferred stock (held only by insiders and not publicly traded), while the Rothschild offer implied a valuation of $1 per share for this same stock.

Almost everyone agreed—Martin Brooke, Sir Eric, and Dick Hammerman included—that acceptance of the $1 per share for the IOS preferred stock would cause havoc in the field. The then current stock option plan value for the insider shares was just above $4, and salesmen had worked hard to earn the right to purchase them at that price, think-

ing their holdings would double in value—based upon past performance
—at least once every year.

The board members, the overwhelming majority of them large preferred shareholders, reasoned that if they accepted the Rothschild contention that the preferred shares were worth only one-quarter of their
last computed formula value this would further demoralize the sales
force and increase the wave of defections. But they blindly refused to
consider that one-quarter of the existing formula price was better by
far than 100 per cent of nothing, which is what the shares were worth
three years later.

John King had correctly sensed the mood in the boardroom and
realized the importance of not tampering with the $4 formula price
when he talked about converting KRC's proposed $40 million financing
into IOS stock. By maintaining this exorbitantly generous share price
he played heavily upon the sentiment of greed that motivated a large
majority of the board. In a very narrow sense he was right, of course.
IOS had been built on greed, and upon greed it would fall.

The sixth day of debate was decisive. It had been confirmed to the
directors that the company, after running up a first-quarter 1970 deficit
of $2.5 million, was operating at a daily loss of $250,000. Thousands
had abandoned the sales force. Redemptions were mounting; the net
negative cash flow from the funds had attained a rate of $7 million to
$10 million a day. Consequently a decision had to be made, and made
quickly, before "the whole damn works disappears down the tubes,"
the board was warned.

With Cowett out of the picture, Roosevelt became the key man in
swinging the board away from the Rothschild offer and behind the King
proposal. Roosevelt stated that his Washington contacts indicated a
reconciliation with the SEC was feasible with King at the helm as long
as Big John had with him Establishment partners.

Furthermore, it was suggested that King was operating with tacit
White House backing. This supposition was given substance by the
knowledge that King was in contact with the White House and had been
a close personal adviser to Nixon before the California Republican became President.

Cornfeld, by threatening to publicly expose Cowett and King for
having sought to purchase control of IOS with the company's own cash
unless they immediately repaid their "unauthorized" loans, already had
saved IOS from instant insolvency. Now, in spite of strong opposition,
he made one last attempt to rally his board around him.

He had spoken by telephone with Baron Guy de Rothschild, seeking
advice. Baron Guy had studied the IOS problem in depth and come to
the conclusion that the company had been hit, above all, by a crisis of

confidence, Cornfeld reported. Furthermore, Baron Guy had convinced Cornfeld that he must resign as chairman. Later Cornfeld said this phone conversation had left him with the impression that once he did resign the Rothschilds were prepared to come in and assume control.

The directors were by then exhausted. Their meetings had gone on past midnight several days running. It was near the end of another heated sixteen-hour session; tempers were short. There was no way, Cornfeld told his fellow board members, that King could meet with the kind of acceptance IOS needed. Money, he said, was of secondary importance; it was credibility that counted. In a dramatic move, having torn up an earlier letter of resignation dictated to him by the board, Cornfeld voluntarily stepped down as chairman. However, he strongly urged the directors to close with the Rothschilds on the following terms:

(1) appointment of a new board with a majority of independent directors
(2) three-year voting trust
(3) the company would make available 20 per cent of its voting stock, including 30 per cent of Cornfeld's total holdings, for sale to the new control group at $2 a share (double the original Rothschild offer)
(4) the Rothschilds would consider some form of limited interim financing.

Although it was the one solution that would have assured IOS's survival, the board refused to take any action on it. Instead, in a touch of negotiating mastery, King re-entered the boardroom and maneuvered around Cornfeld's final stand. He emphasized the importance of maintaining the $4 formula price for the preferred stock. He also pledged that IOS funds would not be permitted to make investments in King-related companies and that there would be no new natural resources investments unless approved by a majority of the non-King directors.

For those board members who were concerned about the value of their preferred share holdings, King's reaffirmation of the $4 formula rating crushed any remaining doubts they still harbored, and in the vote that followed only Hammerman, von Peterffy, and George Landau, although not aligned with Cornfeld, prevented a landslide vote from going King's way. Then, in a final window-dressing effort, Cornfeld remained obstinately opposed in his defeat to accepting a deal with King. The Denver oil "millionaire," he said, would be bankrupt within a year. But no one listened. The coup d'état was now complete.

Casting around for the most prominent name they could find, the directors elected Sir Eric Wyndham White as "interim" chairman to replace Cornfeld, and a separate negotiating committee was set up to deal with King.

It was a Pyrrhic victory for the new politburo at IOS. The trouble was that their battle for control had gone on too long. Four million dollars of boardroom talent had bumbled and bickered its way through a seven-day masterpiece of corporate indecision that was to characterize the rest of IOS's operations.

Why had that point been reached? Why had IOS's arrogant and aggressive management suddenly lost its nerve? No one had the answers. The company had been overtaken by a corporate death wish.

In an effort to get the head office staff back to work, Cornfeld, Sir Eric and John King, along with Dick Hammerman, the leader of the palace revolt, addressed a meeting of executives at Bella Vista after the debris of the board meeting had been cleared away. Cornfeld introduced John King not as the savior of IOS but as a partner in the ongoing struggle to bring People's Capitalism to the masses.

"Remember something," Cornfeld told the executives. "This company was not built by large amounts of money or by large institutional partners. It was built by the people who worked for it." Which was true, for, remarkable as it was in the age of the conglomerate, IOS had, until the King deal was signed, no corporate debt.

Meanwhile, John King was handing out chuckles and charm to everyone in sight. "I have a deep emotional attachment to IOS," he told the executives at Bella Vista.

That was just the point. People were beginning to realize the full extent of his attachment. It involved a $31 million investment which the IOS funds held in King Resources Company and its affiliates. In addition to being a major KRC shareholder, IOS was KRC's largest client and also King's largest provider of low-interest money. Apart from the direct loans at below prime rates of interest, two years earlier the IOS banking group had underwritten a $15 million Eurobond issue for King Resources Capital Corporation, N.V., with two-thirds of the issue ending up in the IOS funds. Hence, by almost any standard, it could be considered a deeply emotional attachment indeed. In fact King definitely needed IOS kept afloat to keep KRC's high-leverage operations turning over at an acceptably healthy rate.

Implementation of the complex fifty-four-page agreement by which KRC agreed to lend IOS $40 million was staggered in several phases.

The "front money" was already in place. This $8 million King's lawyers had immediately paid over to IOS. According to a 1973 report by the KRC trustee in bankruptcy, though, the $8 million was withdrawn from the KRC treasury without the authority of King's board of directors.[2]

The next phase expired at the end of May 1970 when King was required to name at least two institutional partners and pay over $12 million more. But by then KRC had run out of cash, and the deal collapsed.

King blamed SEC interference. However, his company was then operating at a $15.7 million loss, which by the end of the year would be stretched into a net deficit of $53 million. With the flow of IOS moneys turned off forever, the only action remaining to King Resources was the filing of a petition in bankruptcy under Chapter X of the U.S. Bankruptcy Act. King himself, who was required to step down as KRC chairman three months after his abortive IOS takeover attempt, requested court protection under a Chapter XI bankruptcy proceeding in meeting his personal liabilities.

King's problems aside, IOS was again up for grabs. The search for now corporate partners began, but with every day that passed IOS's situation visibly deteriorated. During May 1970, the IOS funds experienced their worst month ever, losing close to $100 million in client redemptions.

Throughout the seven-day Bella Vista marathon and the ensuing King imbroglio, Bob Vesco had been carefully studying developments in Geneva while structuring in his own mind a play for IOS.

Two days after the news was released that King had withdrawn, Vesco flew off to Geneva with Dr. Milton Meissner, a high-powered financial consultant whom Vesco had known at Olin Corporation in New York, where Meissner once served as a divisional vice-president. The purpose of the Geneva visit was to conduct a quick on-site survey of the situation so that Vesco could submit, uninvited, his own Letter of Offer to the IOS board of directors.

[2] Report of Charles E. Baer, KRC Trustee in Bankruptcy, October 10, 1973, p. 12.

10

Our "Front Man" in Geneva

In which Vesco flies to Geneva with the brilliant Dr. Meissner and proposes a dramatic plan to rescue IOS with the supposed backing of the Bank of America and the Prudential Insurance Company ~ How IOS accepts his offer and how he uses IOS's own cash to collateralize the $5 million in "emergency financing," which he provides through the good offices of his debt-ridden Fairfield operation

Henry Buhl was emphatic. Bob Vesco had contacted him several times during the early days of the crisis to ask if the could be of any help in Geneva.

"But I kept on telling him no," Henry insisted.

Vesco, however, said it had worked the other way around. It was Henry who did the calling, wanting to know "could I come over and see if I could be of assistance," he told the SEC.[1]

Buhl, in fact, knew—because Vesco had told him—that the astute Fairfield financier sometimes engaged in "investment banking" activities in an independent capacity. Notably, the Prudential Insurance Company of America had experienced anxiety pangs over one or two of its junior investments and invited Bob Vesco to come in and analyze the troubled corporations with a view to sorting out their problems.

One of Sir Eric's supporters had a slightly different version, though. "Henry repeatedly mentioned Vesco's name to Sir Eric, saying we needed him to come over and see us," reported Hal Vaughan, a fair-haired former U.S. Information Service career officer who had served as Cowett's Boy Friday and now was executive assistant to the new IOS chairman.

For balance—and perhaps this is the most faithful reflection of what

[1] Vesco's SEC testimony, April 1971, p. 75.

happened—a Fairfield executive remarked, "Henry asked Vesco for help and Vesco said he would undertake a study of what the situation was at IOS, and what could be done with it. By the end of this study, Vesco had become quite interested in IOS. He knew in his own mind exactly what IOS was worth to him as an investment."

One thing was clear from all this: Vesco was already standing on IOS's doorstep when John King "came in like gangbusters." However, he decided not to get into a bidding contest with the Denver promoter and quietly withdrew while continuing to observe the latest developments from a distance.

Thus, at an International Controls board meeting on June 9, 1970, Vesco announced that he had been having "discussions concerning the possible investment with a European financial institution, but that those discussions had been terminated because of arrangements that institution had made with another party.[2]

Vesco, when he addressed his board in early June 1970, already knew the King deal had aborted as Buhl had telephoned him with the news and had asked that Vesco make a move. Vesco had in fact gone over to Geneva for a second look but decided not to press matters just yet, as during the second week of June 1970, Banque Rothschild had called an emergency meeting of bankers at its Paris offices to discuss IOS's plight. The Rothschild meeting was attended by representatives of some of the most prestigious names in finance, and IOSers were hopeful that something positive would result.

Conducted behind closed doors, the two-day reunion was reported to have been called at the behest of the United States Treasury. The Treasury was so concerned about the effects a sudden IOS collapse might have on the U.S. balance of payments situation that two of its top men were standing by ready to intervene. After all, the Geneva syndicate was credited the year before with pumping nearly $800 million belonging to foreign investors back into the American market.

Among the potential members of an eventual international rescue consortium attending the Paris meeting were senior officers from Bank of America, Barclays Bank of London, Chemical Bank New York Trust Company, Banca Commerciale Italiana of Rome, Marine Midland Bank, and German's Dresdner Bank. But nothing came out of the gathering.

Vesco followed the Paris talks intently. He knew, for example, that the bankers had received a report from Sir Kenneth Keith of Hill Samuel & Company, the London merchant bankers, on the state of IOS's finances. However, this particularly gloomy report, as far as Vesco had determined, was "totally inaccurate," and he and his tag-

[2] International Controls Corp. Board of Directors minutes, June 9, 1970.

along consultant, Dr. Meissner, both felt "there's more vitality here than might appear." Vesco, of course, had done his homework. At any rate, the Paris group never reconvened. Thus a second rescue attempt came to naught, though one member of the group—Marine Midland—continued negotiations with the IOS board for a short while thereafter.

Vesco's keen interest in the troubled affairs of IOS was motivated by his need to come up with another major acquisition to keep International Controls one step ahead of its huge debt structure. In spite of his remarkably calm front, there was little doubt that the situation in Fairfield—where sales had fallen by 30 per cent but earnings appeared to be holding up as a result of Vesco's rich imagination for devising a steady stream of noncash "extraordinary" income items—was more critical than in Geneva.

International Controls had already acquired a new company in June 1970 when it took over All American Engineering, the Wilmington concern that seven years previously had attempted to hire Vesco away from Captive Seal. The young Vesco had disappointed the All American directors on that occasion by staying with Captive Seal, which not long afterward he had merged into his infant International Controls conglomerate. But still through Malcolm McAlpin, a director of both All American and International Controls, Vesco had kept in touch with the situation in Wilmington. Over the next few years the observation was not lost on McAlpin that Vesco's operation had grown from virtually nothing until reaching the $100 million level in sales, while All American had stagnated with sales of $7 million annually. Hoping to cash in on some of that elusive growth potion which Vesco apparently had discovered, All American finally agreed to become an 81 per cent–owned subsidiary of International Controls in exchange for $31 million in ICC assets. But the only potion Vesco otherwise had to offer was a change of name for the Wilmington concern to the slightly glossier sounding All American Industries Incorporated.

Ironically at this point International Controls itself had no administrative talent to speak of and a cash flow too meager to support Vesco's grandiose designs. The costly takeover of Electronic Specialty in 1968 had overtaxed Vesco's managerial talents and his tiny executive team of Dick Clay, the marketing vice-president; Ralph Dodd, the general manager in charge of production; Frank Beatty, the financial vice-president; and Shirley Bailey, the corporate secretary, had hardly any concept of how to run a big corporation. Therefore, upon the advice of his board, Vesco asked Laurence B. Richardson, Jr., the chief executive officer at All American, to come up to Fairfield and initiate a professionally developed administrative program.

"With his creative accounting, Bob had programmed away enough deferred income to stave off immediate disaster. But he had to take over a company bigger than International Controls to keep the operation from ultimately collapsing, and he had to do it quickly," Richardson said. Vesco was after companies for the cash they could generate.

Early in the spring of 1970 Vesco had brought New York management "specialist" Milton Meissner, whom he had known vaguely at Olin Mathieson, to Fairfield to study various possibilities. Prior to any indication of a crisis at IOS they both decided that Commonwealth United, then on the brink of bankruptcy, was worthy of a rip-off attempt. Vesco was a firm believer that situations of obvious corporate distress provided many exciting opportunities for those who were fast enough to grab them and run.

With "Bud" Meissner's assistance, Vesco concocted a plan which demonstrated his genius for financial legerdemain. He suggested that All American buy from Commonwealth United's creditors a portion of the troubled conglomerate's staggering corporate debt and turn it back to Commonwealth in exchange for its only valuable asset, the Seeburg Corporation. Seeburg was America's leading manufacturer and distributor of juke boxes, pinball machines, and coin-operated vending machines and, unlike the rest of Commonwealth, was making a good profit. However, to swing the deal All American needed $5 million in cash.

To raise the necessary financing, then, Vesco proposed that All American create a new class of stock which he termed "funny preferred" and sell it to an IOS mutual fund for $5 million. Among the "funny" qualities of this new-styled preferred issue were various "if-earned" and "if-declared" conditions which virtually insured that the company would never have to pay any dividends.

"He had written into the draft issuing prospectus a bunch of cute definitions as to what constituted earnings and under what conditions dividends could be declared. It was really quite an evasive document," Richardson noted with a touch of wonderment.

The Seeburg deal bogged down in the mire of the IOS crisis. Just before it fell through, however, Buhl came over to New York and stayed at the Regency Hotel for secret talks with Vesco. The president of International Controls had reserved a double suite at the expensive midtown Manhattan hotel and came into New York to join Buhl, announcing to his staff that he mustn't be disturbed and above all that no one from the office should be seen hanging around the hotel.

Out of their cosy Regency get-together came a proposal letter to Louis Nicastro, president of Commonwealth United, in which Vesco explained that All American would issue $5 million worth of its preferred stock to an unnamed IOS fund. The proceeds were to be used to purchase from another IOS entity a substantial amount of Commonwealth United's indebtedness, which would then be offered back to Commonwealth in exchange for Seeburg.

Real progress was being made on the Commonwealth proposal when Buhl called Vesco from Geneva with news that the King deal had collapsed and IOS was up for grabs again. Seeburg was shifted onto a back burner; Meissner was reassigned to gather intelligence material on IOS's crisis-bound state.

When Vesco next returned to Geneva with Meissner in early June 1970, he had the impression that the disintegration Buhl described had penetrated deeply. "It was pure chaos," he said. "Cornfeld was trying to start a proxy fight. Wyndham White was fighting with someone else. All the kids were in the sandbox."

Hammerman, the leader of the previous month's palace revolt, had just resigned as president after a heated quarrel with the reconstituted executive committee over his insistence that a $50,000 ceiling be imposed on all executive salaries. Hammerman returned to London, bitterly disappointed, convinced that IOS was doomed. Although it was of no consequence, Erich Mende had stepped down that same week as head of the shipwrecked German operation, and George von Peterffy also had resigned.

Sir Eric now turned to Buhl, and for the next few weeks Henry became acting chief executive officer. Buhl informed Sir Eric that Vesco held the confidence of the Prudential as well as major U.S. banks and therefore might be of assistance.

At Sir Eric's request, Marvin Hoffman, a $14,000-a-year accountant who was IOS's newly appointed financial vice-president, and Jay Leary, a member of Cowett's decimated legal brigade, were delegated by the executive committee to meet with the gentleman from Fairfield.

From discussions with Hoffman and Leary, Vesco quickly reappraised the situation and prepared a Letter of Offer from International Controls which he submitted to the IOS directors. It indicated a willingness by International Controls to provide up to $10 million in emergency financing plus a standby line of credit of an additional $10 million.

"It is not our intent," Vesco's letter stated, "to assume control of IOS, but simply to benefit by what may be an attractive investment opportunity. . . . To this end we do not insist upon control of the board of directors, or selection of the principal officers of IOS. We do, however, expect to have representation and to be in a position to understand proposed office alignments, as would any major institutional lender under the prevailing circumstances."

After giving consideration to the International Controls offer, the committee decided to reject it. The effect of the warrants to purchase IOS Ltd. stock which International Controls would have received under the proposed agreement, if exercised, meant giving up one-third of the company for a mere $20 million. This was still far below what the IOS directors were prepared to accept. At the IOS public underwriting the year before, one-third of IOS's equity had been given a value of $150 million. Though their dream world had already become a nightmare, the IOS mini-men still clung to yesterday's values. Ironically, in two months' time they would turn over control of their company to the same Robert Vesco for the price of a $5 million loan.

In the meantime the committee had two other offers before it that were deemed more serious. So Vesco was informed that the proposal "in its present form did not meet the IOS problem." But Henry Buhl was requested to follow up the Vesco offer just in case there was a change. Furthermore, Buhl suggested that Vesco was "an appropriate and competent person to examine the Commonwealth United situation" [3] since IOS was still uncertain what its exact exposure was on the loans the IOS group had made to the feverish Beverly Hills conglomerate. This was a somewhat underhanded proposal by Buhl under the circumstances. But the committee, knowing nothing of Vesco's plans for the All American "funny preferred" stock issue, agreed and charged Buhl with the task of following that one up as well.

Although his second attempt to capture IOS hadn't worked, once back in Fairfield Vesco wrote Sir Eric another letter "to keep the ball rolling," in which he confirmed that International Controls was ready to extend $5 million in immediate financing to IOS if it would help the troubled offshore giant meet some of its more pressing commitments while more permanent financing was arranged in the weeks ahead. This was the height of impudence but illustrative of the sharp tactics Vesco employed. While cashless International Controls was proposing to lend IOS $5 million, Vesco was secretly cooking up a deal with Buhl to raise $5 million from one of the IOS funds.

Events now moved swiftly. In quick succession, IOS published its long-delayed 1969 annual report; Cornfeld was voted off the board of directors at the annual general meeting of shareholders; and the two hottest rescue deals fell through allegedly because of obstructive SEC pressures.

IOS's heavily qualified annual report showed a technical profit of $10.3 million for 1969—half the $20 million that Cornfeld and Cowett previously had predicted, and the last profit, technical or otherwise, in IOS's now measured lifespan. Of that total, $9.7 million came from

---

[3] IOS Executive Committee meeting minutes for June 17, 1970, 9:30 A.M.

the special performance fee that IOS had dealt itself as a result of the Arctic revaluation.

Two weeks later IOS held its first annual general meeting as a public company. The meeting took place in Toronto on June 30, 1970. Strangely—almost eerily, since neither was present or even concerned any more—it marked the culmination of the Cowett-King conspiracy.

When the IOS proxy material had been in preparation two months before, Cowett shifted Cornfeld's name onto the "outsider" slate of directors, the one-third portion of the board elected by common shareholders. Cornfeld was unaware that this shift represented a prize bit of scheming by Cowett. But it did, since the Cowett and King offshore trusts effectively controlled the common class of stock—at least for voting purposes.

Cowett's plan had been to vote Cornfeld off the board at the Toronto meeting and with King assume control of IOS. The plan would have worked beautifully but for the crisis, which came to a head in May 1970 with the result that Cowett was resigned from the board and King ran out of money in his attempt at rescuing IOS that followed.

When Sir Eric, as interim chairman of IOS, saw the significance of Cowett's maneuvering, he voted the common stock proxies held by management—including those that had been owned by the King-Cowett trusts—against Cornfeld. Much to Cornfeld's surprise, he found himself removed from the board. Elected in his stead was Marvin Hoffman, the barrel-chested thirty-six-year-old accountant with a sergeant major's bark who had been appointed a member of the Vesco reception committee. Known as "Yogi Bear" by his peers in the accounting department because of his generally shaggy appearance and erratic bear-like gusto, Hoffman would now play a decisive role in bringing Vesco into the company.

The month of July 1970 was critical for the survival of IOS. Two reputable groups were seriously interested in coming to its rescue. Then, in the space of a tension-packed ten-day period, both Marine Midland and Loeb Rhoades & Company, the New York investment bankers referred to as the "Rosy Loebs" by the boardroom wits at IOS, dropped out.

"Marine Midland was going to bring in their own management; it was all set and ready to go, but they backed away at the last moment because of an unexplained decision by their board of directors. The decision was influenced to no minor extent by the SEC's obstinate position," said Vaughan, himself newly elected to the IOS board.

Under the terms of the SEC's 1967 Settlement Order with IOS, any company that owned 1 per cent or more of the outstanding shares of

IOS could be classified as an "affiliate" and therefore could be precluded from engaging in the securities business in the United States or from selling its securities either in the United States or to U.S. citizens. That was a powerful deterrent for U.S. companies, even though there was some doubt whether such an order could technically be enforced.

The "Rosy Loebs" had thought they could convince the SEC of their sincerity in wanting to bring IOS back onshore in the best interests of the shareholders, fund-holders, and U.S. securities markets. It was difficult to grasp the SEC's reasons for rejecting this proposal. Whatever they were, if IOS could have been saved as a legal operation—and that was doubtful—the obdurate stance adopted by the SEC played a predominant role in preventing its survival. The unbending SEC staff assured the "Rosy Loebs" that if they became directly involved in the affairs of IOS then their books would be examined with the same "care and diligence" as the SEC had paid to IOS's. Following this bit of news the "Rosy Loebs" backed away, having clearly gotten the message.

"This was the critical breaking point for the board," said Vaughan. On the following Monday the deal was to have been signed and a press release, already prepared, was scheduled for issue. "The collapse almost broke Sir Eric," commented Buhl. "And from then on the Vesco offer was treated seriously."

Vesco and Meissner returned to Geneva at the end of July to continue work on the "Green Book"—their study of the company and its predicaments. Vesco later told the SEC he had been "minding his own business and visiting friends" when he got a new panic call, this one from "Yogi Bear" Hoffman.

"We really don't know what's happening. Cornfeld's making a bid for control," Hoffman told him, according to Vesco. He therefore agreed to visit Hoffman at the accounting offices in Ferney-Voltaire for urgent discussions.

The meeting took place during the first days of August, and Hoffman, Vesco later said, asked if International Controls would make a firm proposal to the board at its forthcoming meeting, because he felt that a deal with Vesco was the only way IOS could survive.

"So I told Hoffman that we would take it under advisement," Vesco said.[4]

Cornfeld's reappearance on the scene in midsummer of 1970 with his own set of proposals to get IOS back onto its feet had caused considerable confusion in the IOS boardroom. He still possessed the strongest will among the Old Guard, and the mouse-like rebels who had ganged up to remove him from power were in no way inclined to accept him back. They were scared to death of him.

[4] Vesco's SEC testimony, April 1971, p. 118.

Such pandemonium suited Vesco perfectly. "Cornfeld was jumping out of boats and trying to crash gates and a few other odds and ends, so it was not the usual environment that you would expect for a corporate enterprise," he remarked snidely.[5]

The Cornfeld comeback camp was a motley cast of characters. It included Jeff Hollander and Mike Freedman, two washed-out IOS salesmen from Canada; several secretaries; two Playboy Bunny sisters from Chicago; Leslie, a former Elvis Presley groupie; a new legal adviser to replace Ed Cowett; and Seymour ("the Head") Lazare, a short, pussycat type with a matador's pigtail who described himself as the world's only hippie arbitrage expert.

Cornfeld had spent the time between his disappearance from Geneva in mid-May until IOS's August board meeting putting together new financing, a new product for the shattered sales force to market, and even a new company as the levers intended to assist him back to power.

The new product was called Cinema City. It was said to cover 10,000 acres of Southern California desert near Palm Springs, which would be developed as the movie-making capital of the world. Initial investment in Cinema City, for which Cornfeld held the land options, was estimated at $50 million. Cornfeld planned to raise the money by selling 10,000 participations of $5,000 each through the crumbling IOS sales force. But Cinema City was merely a diversionary ploy in his comeback campaign.

Like many other Cornfeld dreams, it never saw the light of day, but it did at least serve a transitory purpose. While IOS sank deeper and deeper into its morass of problems, there was hectic activity at Villa Elma. A steady stream of disenchanted or out-of-work IOSers kept turning up at the front door looking for a job with the Cornfeld comeback camp.

On Friday, August 7, 1970, Cornfeld made his comeback presentation to the board. His proposals were turned down, described as pie in the sky, badly thought out, with poor-quality visual renderings of his Cinema City jewel. At one time the directors burst out laughing. Cornfeld lost his calm. He came back to Villa Elma thoroughly depressed.

Cornfeld returned to the boardroom at least twice the next day, Saturday, and asked to address the directors. Both times he floated into Bella Vista's harbor aboard his houseboat, the upper deck crowded with a crew of Cornfeld girls in bikinis.

"All right, Bernie, if you really feel you must," Sir Eric said the first time around. "But please be quick about it. We have work to finish."

Bernie started telling the directors they had to give him back his

[5] *Ibid.,* p .301.

company. This was received with stone-cold silence, and so Cornfeld started to warm up. "If you don't give me my company back I'll have you all thrown in prison," he screamed. "As a matter of fact, I'll have Guy Laroche come over and design you special prison suits, and I'll fly you to jail in my BAC 1-11."

"Bernie and his status symbols," someone sighed. John Templeton, who had been offered Sir Eric's job as chairman but refused, got hold of Bernie outside the door. "Be reasonable," he told Cornfeld.

"Be reasonable!" Cornfeld screamed back. "How can I be reasonable when these maniacs are trying to destroy my company?"

Earlier in the day Bob Vesco had gone over to Villa Elma to have a chat with Cornfeld at the board's request. Vesco had made his own presentation to the directors and was about to conclude an agreement in principle to lend IOS $5 million, with provision for an additional $10 million to follow. Things seemed to go well at their first meeting, and Cornfeld invited Vesco back for dinner that evening.

"The evening meeting was much less constructive," Vesco said later. When asked to be more specific, he replied, "We didn't feel at all that the conversation in the evening was on the kind of business level we were accustomed to dealing with and that it was not as conclusive."

No wonder. The way Cornfeld told the story it sounded as if Vesco had been lucky to escape with his life.

"Bob Vesco came to see me on Saturday and we had two meetings, and at these meetings I was trying to understand exactly what his interest in our situation was," Cornfeld said. "When I discovered exactly what his interest was, namely to control our company based on a $5 million uncollateralized loan, I decided I wouldn't support him. In fact, when I learned just what he had in mind, I told him to pick up his marbles and get the fuck out of my house, and that I didn't want to see him around here again."

Somebody suggested that their difference had begun when Vesco informed Cornfeld he didn't want petulant Bernie back on the board because that would constitute a default under the proposed loan agreement.

"Well, he indicated last night that if he had complete control of the company he really wouldn't care all that much if Adolf Eichmann was in as chairman," Cornfeld replied.

With that said, Bernie Cornfeld renewed his declaration of war on interim management. He already had solicited more than 23 million "irrevocable" proxies, which he kept locked up in his basement safe. Now he dictated a letter to Sir Eric demanding that a special meeting of the preferred shareholders be called within the statutory forty-five-day limit. He also brought a barrage of lawsuits against IOS, its directors, and International Controls to declare the Toronto shareholders meeting invalid and prevent Vesco from concluding the loan agreement.

Vesco in the interim had encouraged Buhl to think there was a pressing cash crisis at IOS when there really wasn't one at all. This feeling of financial catastrophe stalking the company seemed confirmed by "Yogi Bear" Hoffman, who was pessimistic about the company's ability to meet the September payroll unless outside financial help immediately was found.

The shell-shocked directors, impressed by Vesco's direct approach during the preliminary discussions, also appreciated Meissner's fine background. The lanky, gray-haired, fifty-six-year-old Vesco sidekick came across as a thoughtful, well-versed corporation fix-it man. A Rhodes scholar and doctor of philosophy from Oxford, Meissner had helped run Mexico's electric industry when both Cornfeld and Vesco were still in knee socks. "He had a lot of quiet savvy about him," one board member recalled.

"Vesco was cool, tough, straight. Not a guy who would walk in and bullshit you to death," said Vaughan. "He told us the loan agreement was going to be very tough, but he said the circumstances warranted it. It was indeed extremely onerous, but it was negotiated under terrible pressure, and as the previous six deals had all misfired the manic board of directors was ready to sign anything on any terms."

The critical moment in the debate came when Hoffman assured the board that by September 15 the company would be out of cash. "That was the real breaking point," Vaughan continued. "Yet by October we knew that we could have made it on our own."

Vaughan blamed this tardy realization of the true cash situation on an "archaic" accounting system. But not everyone concurred— particularly not some of those in the accounting department. "Hoffman was a committed Vesco man on the inside. There is no doubt he was suppressing at Vesco's request cash reports that should have been destined for the board of directors," one accounting executive said. And for this Hoffman would receive his due reward.

Meanwhile Vesco had enlisted the aid of Hogan & Hartson, his attorneys from Washington. They worked themselves red-eyed for the next two weeks forging one of the toughest commercial documents in the history of free enterprise. But, as Vaughan so aptly pointed out, the directors were ready to sign anything, for they were all in a state near cataleptic shock.

When Cornfeld learned what was afoot he almost went berserk. "Aside from a rare imbecile like Buhl, I can't understand who would want to have dealings with a hoodlum like Vesco," he roared.

Then, at one of the many press conferences called in his dining room at Villa Elma, Cornfeld released more bombast against Sir Eric "Windmill" and his "marionette" board of directors, many of whom had been required to sign undated letters of resignation.

"A deal with International Controls makes a deal with King Resources look like a deal with the Bank of America," he said. The IOS founder was standing at the head of his imitation Baroque dining table with a marbleized plastic top and strutting like a peacock. He was in full demagogic swing in the style that once held his board in thrall.

"I opposed the King deal vehemently, and as such my attitude about the International Controls deal is very resolute indeed. I think the aftermath of the King deal has been catastrophic for the firm and it is obvious that the board hasn't learned anything from that experience and are proceeding at this moment into a kind of situation that is even grimmer.

"I have always taken the position that the company doesn't need money. But if this management remains in much longer, no amount of money will be of any help because of the nature of the destruction that is being wrought."

There was no humor intended by Cornfeld. But while he was sounding off, Vesco was informing everyone he met that both the world's largest bank—Bank of America—and the world's largest insurance company—Prudential—were International Controls's prime lenders. Which in fact they were. Then, confidentially, he told Buhl and Sir Eric that he was acting as the Bank of America's "front man" in Geneva. That capped everything.

Buhl in the meantime had informed Sir Eric that, because of his long-standing friendship with Vesco, he did not want to be part of the *ad hoc* negotiating committee and withdrew from further discussions with the team from Fairfield. But Buhl had already served the Vesco cause well, and for this there was a measure of recompense.

On a previous trip to the Far East, Buhl had fallen in love with the island of Bali and, along with Malcolm Fox and a few others, had bought a tract of land there, intending to develop it as a holiday resort with a luxury hotel and beach cottages. King, one of the charter venturers in the project, had dropped out for lack of cash, and so on August 11, 1970, one day after the IOS board had agreed in principle to accept the International Controls offer of financing, Vesco personally invested $39,000 in Buhl's Bali adventure.

On the same day, IOS's ever-helpful IIT fund agreed to exchange $7.3 million principal amount of International Controls's lackluster Eurobonds, sold to the fund in 1968, for a new higher-interest series with a sizable reduction in face value. Thus, IIT received $4.4 million of the new International Controls Eurobonds bearing 9.5 per cent interest, four points higher than the interest rate of the old bonds. The $2.9 million difference in principal amout represented a reduction in International Controls's long-term debt that was quickly entered as a noncash profit item on the firm's balance sheet—one of several small dividends Vesco extracted from the Geneva fund group while promising to provide it with emergency financing.

In his dealings with the IOS board, as part of his negotiating tactics Vesco had been purposely deceptive on a number of key points. But the IOS directors increasingly had become spellbound by his cool, self-assured approach to seemingly insurmountable problems. And, too, they were impressed when Mel Rosen, deputy head of IOS's investment department and one of the leaders of the *ad hoc* negotiating committee, assured everyone, "Mr. Vesco is one of the keenest and cleverest financial men of our times. This man has done some very clever, some extremely imaginative things."

Such rabid praise for the greatest corporate looter of modern finance was surely an inspired piece of work—inspired, that is, by the prospect of a nice fat payoff. Even Vaughan, who voted for the acceptance of Vesco's proposal, admitted, "With Bob there was always a great deal of innuendo." Actually, it went much farther than that:

- Vesco had suggested that the Prudential Life Insurance Company of America was interested in taking over IOS's insurance operations in some form of partnership arrangement. The Pru, though, never did become involved.
- Vesco made idle promises of being able to bring in senior management and outside financial institutions to participate in the reconstruction of IOS.
- He also maintained that he could use his considerable influence in Washington to improve relations with the SEC.
- He told the directors that his intentions were to put IOS back on its feet financially and continue to see it run as an operating company.
- And, of course, he insinuated that he represented the Bank of America.

Offstage, Vesco cautioned Buhl and Sir Eric that the whole Bank of America connection was so hush-hush it would probably be denied by the bank if anyone attempted to check it out. It might even cause B of A to withdraw, he explained, since the bank did not want to be embarrassed by adverse publicity surrounding IOS until the transaction could be presented as a *fait accompli.* And they believed him.

Nevertheless, to demonstrate Vesco's good faith to the board Sir Eric, as a matter of formality, requested confirmation that International

Controls had $5 million to lend. Vesco coolly instructed his people in Fairfield to transfer all available corporate cash to the firm's account at the Bank of America. He then had the bank cable him in Geneva confirming the balance.

The telegram that the Bank of America returned made Vesco hopping mad. It said that International Controls had a cash balance in excess of $5 million but that the money was not available for withdrawal. Furthermore, it warned that the intended loan transaction with IOS appeared to violate the loan agreement International Controls had outstanding with Bank of America.

Rejected by the Bank of America, Vesco turned instead to Butlers Bank in Nassau, which had a net worth of $5.2 million, pleading technical problems with the complex loan agreement to Sir Eric for the delay.

Money was pouring out of the Bahamas at the time, and Butlers was having difficulty attracting new deposits to replace the trust accounts it was losing. The bank, with total deposits down to around $35 mililon, seemed in a perpetual liquidity squeeze at a time when Allan Butler was gearing up his staff for new accounts that were essential to the bank's long-term survival. Therefore in terms of available capital Butlers was not in an ideal situation to help. Vesco, however, intimated that by helping him gain control of IOS the bank could expect substantial amounts of new business to flow its way.

Butlers returned a cable to Geneva on August 25 affirming that International Controls held $5 million on account in Nassau but neglected to mention that it was a back-to-back deposit against a loan that had been extended as a tax gimmick to capitalize another International Controls subsidiary, and as such the money was not available for deployment to IOS.

In spite of this tenuous situation, Sir Eric advised the board on August 28 to accept Vesco's offer of "interim financing." He told the uneasy directors that reports from "one of the leading banks in the world" indicated that, although Vesco was a hard businessman to deal with, he was a person of impeccable integrity who had "gone against the financial establishment in the United States and won."

The following day Vesco informed Buhl and Sir Eric that the B of A had backed out. Deeply depressed, Sir Eric might have been influenced by this development when he concluded within forty-eight hours a cease-fire with Cornfeld that led to Bernie's temporary return to the board of directors. In exchange, Cornfeld agreed to cease all legal harassment and consented to abide by the board's decision on the necessity of obtaining financing from Vesco. Cornfeld had by then come up with an alternate source of financing, since he now realized that the board would not feel secure unless it thought it was receiving an emergency cash infusion. Cornfeld's new backer was identified as the conservative British merchant bank of S. G. Warburg & Company.

The Cornfeld peace talks were moderated by Harold Lever, the man who had negotiated Britain's swap arrangements with the International Monetary Fund, and Wilson Wyatt, a supposedly neutral member of the board. Lever, a Labour millionaire, Cabinet minister in Harold Wilson's government and Chancellor of the Duchy of Lancaster, was as impressive and impartial a figure as could be found—in fact, remarkably so under the circumstances—and he was asked to address the waiting directors at their crucial board meeting on August 31, 1970.

Lever strongly advised the board against accepting the International Controls financing. He told the directors that he knew the Bank of England was favorably disposed to Warburg's making an offer and would be willing to provide whatever support was needed to bring it off.

The meeting was carried over the following day when Gil Bennett, IOS's Canadian counsel, recommended rejecting the International Controls deal. Hammerman, the fallen Krisenstab leader, also belatedly rallied to Cornfeld in opposing Vesco. In the tense balloting that followed, the board voted twelve to ten in favor of Vesco. "From that moment on," Cornfeld later confided, "I knew that IOS was lost."

The loan agreement was signed on September 3, 1970, between IOS and ICC Investments Limited, a newly formed Bahamian subsidiary of International Controls. Under the 110-page agreement ICC Investments undertook the following:

(1) make available on September 17, 1970, $5 million in the form of an unsecured loan repayable on May 24, 1971, one week before the $8 million King loan fell due
(2) provide an additional $10 million in financing at a later date if needed

The agreement also stipulated that:

(3) IOS would issue 4 million five-year warrants to purchase IOS common stock at discount prices
(4) IOS agreed to pay $350,000 as a "front-end" deduction on the first $5 million for legal, auditing, and other out-of-pocket expenses, "irrespective of the actual amount of such expenses"
(5) IOS was liable to a penalty of 15 per cent ($750,000) if the loan were repaid before May 24, 1971
(6) the company would hire Ulrich Strickler as a management consultant at a monthly salary of $2,000 (plus expenses and housing),

and place two International Controls nominees (Vesco and Meissner) on the board of directors and the executive committee

(7) a five-member finance committee would be created to control all the company's major financial activities; the committee would have two members from International Controls, two from IOS, and one "neutral" acceptable to both parties; the acceptable neutral was designated as Marvin Hoffman

(8) in the event of a default under one of the thirty to forty negative covenants, IOS was obliged to pay "liquidated damages" of $3 million should the company be prevented by "applicable law" from repurchasing the warrants at 74 cents apiece [6]

Hence in a series of transactions that catapulted Vesco to international prominence, he caused International Controls to lend IOS $5 million that International Controls itself had to borrow.[7] Then, in a masterly touch of financial hocus-pocus, he arranged for IOS to collateralize that loan by maintaining an equivalent $5 million at Butlers Bank.

The operation's extreme craftiness indicated that Vesco knew something that no one else—except Cornfeld—had been able to figure out: IOS may have needed a lot of things, but money was not first among them. His preliminary investigation of the company's finances had determined that sufficient corporate funds existed if one knew where in the in-house tangle to look for them. But Vesco didn't tell that to Sir Eric or his "puppet" directors. The panicky boardmen in Geneva, few of them with any financial background, actually believed that IOS was about to go bust.

International Controls's net worth was then stated at $42 million, which was less than half IOS's pre-crisis net worth. In fact, IOS probably had more cash on hand than International Controls, and that was the ludicrous side of the deal. But management in Geneva was in a state of irreversible shock; the corporate beast had given up and surely would have lain down and died of sheer nervous exhaustion had not Vesco come along.

When questioned by the SEC about his use of deception in bamboozling the IOS board, Vesco denied any impropriety. He said, "The intention [was] that we would go in, unravel the mess, get rid of the

[6] As Canadian companies are prohibited by law from repurchasing their own securities, there was some polemic over whether this provision was entirely legal; if illegal it could have rendered the loan agreement null and void.

[7] Hale Bros. Associates Inc. provided the interim financing to ICC Investments Ltd. for a six-week period. Subsequently, on November 6, 1970, ICC Investments borrowed $5 million from Butlers Bank on a nonrecourse basis while IOS had agreed to deposit a like amount in Butlers Bank.

skeletons, put a bow tie around the package, and deliver it to the B of A, who would subsequently make an offer for the entire company."

There was nothing in writing between him and the bank's San Francisco head office, Vesco testified, and when the Bank of America finally backed away from the deal he said he found himself left with a multimillion dollar obligation and no financial backing.

"You've got to give me that again," insisted Stanley Sporkin, the then assistant director of the SEC's enforcement division, who later would head the SEC investigation of Vesco.

"The B of A did not want to show publicly as getting involved with IOS. So our approach to the B of A, the general deal was that we would form an offshore subsidiary, B of A would lend it all the money that was necessary for it to, in turn, lend to IOS and we would split the equity, with the understanding that once a comprehensive review and clean-out job at IOS had been accomplished, that the B of A would presumably come in and buy the darn thing."

"That B of A would actually go in and buy the whole operation? Is that what you're saying?" Sporkin asked again, just to be certain.

"Or whatever. Take control of it somehow. We did not get involved in those specifics," Vesco replied somewhat vaguely.

"Did you ever put anything of this in writing?" Sporkin wanted to know.

"No."

"No correspondence between you and the B of A concerning IOS Ltd?"

"I don't think so, no."

The tone of their dialogue was somehow unreal. It seemed inconceivable that Big Business in the United States could adopt such a cavalier approach when discussing major transactions of this nature.

Sporkin inquired again, a few questions later: "And what is it that ICC would get out of the transaction?"

"We in effect would have gotten half the deal for nothing. They were going to put up all the money and we were going to split the warrants," Vesco replied coolly.

With this commitment firmly in place, then, at least in his own mind, Vesco explained how he went ahead and made a presentation to the IOS board of directors in August 1970. "We proceeded diligently to actively negotiate the final details of the loan agreement, and simultaneously Dr. Meissner kept doing his homework, and everything was going along fine and great" until the B of A called him in Geneva and, in Vesco's own words, said, " 'Hey, we changed our mind.' "

"What was the next thing that happened after you learned from the B of A that they weren't going through with it?" he was asked.

"I had a serious case of indigestion.

"I think the thing I did was, you know, spend a long weekend on the telephone with various people at B of A using a few foul words."

When excerpts of Vesco's testimony were made public in federal proceedings the following year, the Bank of America promptly denied that it had planned to take over the ailing IOS.

A spokesman for the bank labeled Vesco's sworn statements before the Commission staff as total nonsense.

"Mr. Vesco's claim to be a so-called 'front man' for Bank of America is absolutely untrue. We did not make any kind of a verbal agreement with him and we had no plans for a 'takeover' of IOS."

11

Chinese Laundry

Vesco uses a "Chinese laundry" to buy Cornfeld's shares ~ Our daring financier attempts his first raid on the funds but is forced to fall back on a couple of third-line banks in Zurich and Nassau instead

Vesco moved quickly to consolidate his control over the Cornfeld empire. Although the September 1970 loan agreement did not give International Controls a stock holding in floundering IOS until the Fairfield concern chose to exercise its warrants, it contained no less than fourteen pages of negative covenants that bound the company over to the lender in virtually every important matter of corporate life.

The covenants covered a multitude of situations, such as minimum working capital provisions, limitations on distribution of dividends from IOS or its subsidiaries, and a prohibition against the issue or sale of stock in any subsidiary. They also prevented IOS from entering into certain types of contracts or purchases and forbade any merger or sale of assets without the consent of the lender. The famous finance committee dominated by Vesco was the watchdog body to ensure that these covenants were respected.

The negative covenants, or insecurity clauses as Cornfeld persisted in calling them, were far from the "boiler plate" that Buhl's assistant, Mel Rosen, had suggested to the board of directors. They were exactly what Cornfeld had described them as weeks before the arrangement was signed: "At any time they feel insecure about their loan—if Vesco decides, well it's Thursday, it's gray, and I'm really not feeling very secure—as such the loan is immediately recallable," Cornfeld had warned. Everyone snickered. No one believed him. "That is an untruth," Rosen responded. "Simply an erroneous statement."

Cornfeld continued to stir up problems with repeated semihysterical warnings that Vesco was a financial hoodlum out to bleed the company dry. It was imperative to Vesco's grand looting scheme that all resistance be stamped out. This he proceeded to do with customary directness, instituting a reign of terror that left employees who opposed him fearing for their jobs if not for their physical well-being.

At the October 1970 board meeting in Geneva it was announced that a new chief executive officer had been hired. Robert E. Slater, a fifty-four-year-old former president of John Hancock Life Insurance Company, the nation's fourth largest insurance company, had been found by a New York headhunter and agreed to come aboard the sinking ship for a modest salary of $150,000 a year.

Vesco was furious when he heard the news. He feared a real powerhouse was moving in to cramp his style.

"The man looked good on paper; we knew he had resigned from John Hancock the year before in a policy dispute. We didn't know why. Then when he arrived in Geneva he turned out to be a blithering idiot," said Vaughan, whose head was soon to be on the Vesco chopping block. "Vesco met the man and immediately found him acceptable. From then on, Slater took orders straight from Fairfield.

"By then Eric had come apart. He was out of his element—not at all business oriented. He was used to being surrounded by a clockwork bureaucracy. He couldn't stand the long hours day in and day out. He was dealing with tired, discouraged, nervous, and in some cases evil and vicious people. Eric took to Bob Slater like a life preserver."

Said Sir Eric, "We've hit paydirt with our new president." [1] Slater lasted eleven months before resigning. Under him, Vesco pushed for the appointment of forty-two-year-old Malcolm Fox as head of the stagnating sales company. Vesco had taken Fox under his wing and counted him among his staunchest supporters from the splintered Old Guard ranks.

The first spark of revolt came at an executive committee meeting later in October when Vesco asserted that he would exercise full authority in running the company until proper management was found.

Allen Cantor, the only member of the triumvirate remaining in an operating position, objected to Vesco and his group of "consultants" acting as shadow management. There was no clause in the loan agreement, Cantor argued, that gave Vesco, Meissner, Clay, Straub, Strickler, and other members of the Fairfield task force the authority to meddle in the day-to-day affairs of the company.

Vesco merely brushed aside such criticism and continued delving into the mysteries of the IOS structure. Sir Eric, meanwhile, had shifted his

[1] *The IOSer,* October 23, 1970, p. 1.

efforts to achieving a 51 per cent sale of the Italian operations to Istituto Mobiliare Italiano (IMI), a state-controlled credit institution. The transaction was concluded in early December 1970 after four months of difficult negotiations. It paid the IOS group $10 million in cash and placed the $250 million Fonditalia under the shelter of the largest medium and long term credit bank in Italy, thereby preserving it from the rapacious intentions of Vesco. This achievement, according to Vaughan, was a negotiating masterpiece and became Sir Eric's only notable success during his eight-month tenure as IOS chairman.

Vesco watched these negotiations intently. The partial sale of Fonditalia Management Company S.A. and the Italian sales operation was obviously contrary to the negative covenants of the loan agreement. Therefore he used it to tighten the noose around IOS's neck by requiring a substantial renegotiation of the loan contract. Thus, in November 1970, he announced to the executive committee that he would permit the Italian sale to go forward provided that the proceeds were blocked in banks of his choice to guarantee repayment of the $5 million loan.

The banks of his choice turned out to be (1) that paragon of banking practices in the Bahamas, Butlers Bank, which received no less than $4 million, and (2) Bank Cantrade, Zurich, for redeposit with Union Bank of California, Nassau. And so began the first of several costly bootstrapping operations to save Butlers Bank from collapse—at the expense of IOS.

Allan Butler, the jet-set chairman of Butlers Bank, had launched his operetta-style banking operation on an ill-conceived expansion program that left it overextended and tottering on the brink of financial disaster. Butler's visions of banking grandeur were pursued without regard to balance sheet considerations. One of the empty corporate shells in the Butler Bank pyramid he used to purchase a Sabreliner for personal use. The tanned, dashing-looking Harvard graduate and international-class skier used the private jet to bolster his image as a high-flying international financier of a type after Vesco's own heart.

During 1970 Butlers Bank had also purchased for $4.5 million a downtown office complex known as Charlotte House for its future headquarters. Still under construction, the opulently modern four-story structure cost another $2.5 million to complete. It was described as "the largest and most prestigious office building in the Caribbean." Until then, the bank's headquarters were located at the top of Charlotte Street in a small, almost storybook colonial cottage appropriately named Gresham House. Gresham's Law holds that bad money drives out good. This adage, attributed to Sir Thomas Gresham, the sixteenth-century financier who founded London's Royal Exchange, may well have had nothing to do with Butler's fortunes, but after two years of dealings with Vesco, Butlers Bank had no money at all—good or bad!

While Butler, the playboy banker and Consul General of the Netherlands in Nassau, was wheeling and dealing with his wife's money—part of the fabled Sir Harry Oakes gold mining fortune—the sinking condition of the bank went largely unnoticed and unattended for the better part of a year. But Vesco had plans for Butlers Bank since it was an established and operating institution. The loose Bahamian Banking Act permitted many more sleight-of-hand operations than the tighter Swiss Banking Code, and both were equally secretive. He discussed with Allan Butler and his managing director, Frederic J. Weymar, the possibility of the tiny Nassau bank's becoming the custodian for the various IOS funds. He also suggested that Butlers Bank come under the umbrella of IOS Financial Holdings Limited, which would give it more working capital.

In the short term Vesco promised to push IOS deposits of up to $20 million through Butlers. Meanwhile, pending receipt of the proceeds from the Italian sale, International Controls put up $4 million in a thirty-day certificate of deposit in Butlers to alleviate the pressing liquidity problems. This $4 million was withdrawn over the next six weeks as IOS fed in $4 million raised through the Italian sale.

Cornfeld fought Vesco bitterly on these cash transfers once he learned that they were taking place. He accused Vesco of extreme imprudence at best in tying up such sizable amounts in a bank of no consequence. But the money IOS transferred to Butlers continued to grow until by early January 1971 it was more than double the $5.2 million net worth of the bank.

As Cornfeld was the source of most of the friction inside the company, it became obvious to Vesco that his removal had to be engineered at any cost and as quickly as possible. The outspoken IOS founder was still the largest shareholder, owning approximately 15 per cent of the preferred stock, or some 6.6 million shares. Taking Cornfeld out of IOS, Vesco imagined, would be the straw to break the back of the group that later called themselves the dissidents. He foresaw the Old Guard plunging into a state of disarray with Cornfeld out of the picture.

So Vesco constructed a trap into which Cornfeld walked, difficult as that is to imagine, as innocently as a freshly shorn lamb. Vesco used Cornfeld's new appointment as chairman of the almost inanimate sales subsidiary, which Vesco had verbally sanctioned, as the needed pretext to spring the trap shut by calling the International Controls loan to IOS in default. Any operational role given to Cornfeld without written consent from International Controls technically constituted a breach of the loan agreement. After provoking Cornfeld into a shouting match at a meeting of the executive committee in mid-December 1970, Vesco angrily announced that the company was too small for both of them to remain in it together. Either Cornfeld had to sell out his stock or find the necessary cash to meet IOS's obligations to International Controls.

"Fine," said Cornfeld. "What's your price?"

Vesco responded that it was not an appropriate matter for discussion in front of the committee. When the meeting ended he drew Cornfeld into one of the Louis XVI salons adjoining the IOS boardroom and asked how much he wanted for his stock.

"Around a dollar a share," Cornfeld said he replied. "How much do *you* want?" he asked of Vesco, meaning the price International Controls would exact for withdrawing from IOS affairs. Vesco's answer was that IOS would have to retire the loan forthwith, thereby incurring the penalty foreseen under the loan agreement, and buy back the 4 million warrants issued to International Controls as a premium for arranging the loan.

"How much does that come to?" Cornfeld inquired.

A total of about $9.5 million, came the reply. The matter was left there for the moment.

The next day Vesco handed Slater a formal letter notifying IOS of its alleged default.

One week later Vesco telephoned Cornfeld in Palm Springs, California, with news that he had a hidden purchaser for the stock at 65 cents a share. Cornfeld rejected the offer. A few days later Vesco came back and said the purchaser was prepared to go as high as 92 cents a share.

The mystery buyer was portrayed to Cornfeld as an "institutional purchaser of whom you'd be proud," but still was not identified. Later Vesco said that he would let him know who the buyer was when Cornfeld was ready to sign.

In negotiations that followed in New York and Geneva, Cornfeld got the strong impression from Vesco's hints that the purchaser was the Union Bank of Switzerland, the biggest Swiss bank. UBS was purported to be acting through a subsidiary, Bank Cantrade of Zurich.

Cornfeld by this point had expended a veritable fortune attempting to regain his dominance in IOS's affairs but was still without an audience in the boardroom. In fact, the alienation between him and the other directors had only increased. He therefore reasoned that the most responsible action was to sell his shares and withdraw from corporate life, hoping his action might reunite the company and give it new impetus to meet the crises that he knew lay ahead.

Cornfeld had no idea, however, that Union Bank of Switzerland refused to touch IOS with an eleven-foot barge pole and would have been quite happy to see the scandal-ridden Cornfeld empire slide into the River Rhône and disappear forever. According to UBS's general manager, Dr. Nikolaus Senn, IOS was already dead and had no chance of recovery. "Their reputation in the investment trust business is completely shattered, and it is well known in financial circles that a good reputation can be lost only once. In its last phase IOS constituted a handicap for the entire investment trust industry and would again in the case of renewed operations," said Senn in a letter written weeks before Vesco began plotting Cornfeld's final overthrow.[2]

But the use of deception, by then a practiced Vesco standard, was essential in structuring the $5.5 million purchase of the Cornfeld stock for four very good reasons. First, it was necessary for International Controls's image to maintain that the sale was to an outside financial institution; second, Vesco hoped by maintaining that the purchaser was a foreign bank and not International Controls he would avoid an SEC probe; third, the purchaser grossly overpaid for the stock by some $3.5 million at the then unofficial market rate, and this had to be hidden from International Controls shareholders.

But more importantly, Vesco still hadn't given up the hope of being able to drag in other institutional partners by selling them a part of the Cornfeld block, and so he needed to convey the impression that another major bank was involved.

Vesco had acquired from a Bank Cantrade subsidiary, Consulentia Verwaltungs A.G., an off-the-shelf dummy corporation—one of the specialty services offered by Consulentia, a financial consulting firm, to its wealthy international clientele. The shell that Consulentia sold Vesco had the unlikely name of Linkink Progressive Corporation S.A. Linkink was conveniently incorporated in Panama. Vesco eventually identified Linkink as the prospective purchaser, suggesting to Cornfeld that the Panamanian company was controlled by a number of banks. However Linkink was later discovered to be owned by another Panamanian shell company with the even more unlikely handle of Red Pearl Bay S.A.

The Cornfeld camp moved back to Geneva in early January 1971 and was entrenched at Villa Elma when it was learned from Henry von Maur, IOS's top portfolio manager, that an attempt had been made by Meissner to divert $6.2 million from one of the IOS funds to a numbered account in Germany. Immediately it was suspected that Vesco was attempting to use IOS fund money to buy Bernie's stock.

The thirty-five-year-old von Maur, from Davenport, Iowa, was some-

[2] Letter from Dr. Nikolaus Senn.

thing of a hero around IOS. Beginning in June 1969 he had placed the IOS funds (except FOF, over which he had no control) in a highly liquid cash position well before the Great Bear Market took hold. In the nine months leading up to April 1970 the IOS funds had raised on his instructions $500 million in cash. It was a daring course of action that no other fund group in the world could match, and it was the salvation, for the time being, of the IOS funds. Without it they would not have survived the summer, when corporate problems and falling securities markets brought over $250 million in net client re- demptions flowing into Geneva.

Von Maur's call to Villa Elma four days before the scheduled closing with Linkink sent the Cornfeld camp into a tailspin, and after a tumultuous all-night meeting Cornfeld and his lawyers announced they would break off negotiations and bring legal action against Vesco unless he came up with a logical explanation. Von Maur made one other call that day—which threw Vesco into a violent rage when he learned about it—to Sy Lewis, president of Bear, Sterns in New York.

What had occurred, in fact, was not enveloped with the usual subtle Vesco veneer but was rather brutal in execution. Early Monday morning, January 11, 1971, IOS financial vice-president Marvin Hoffman called one of his subalterns and asked if $6 million of IOS or IOS Insurance Holdings cash could be available within hours for a deposit. The answer was negative. Then before noon the same day Meissner called up Henry Buhl's department and gave one of the new portfolio man- agers, Marty Solomon, instructions to transfer immediately $6.2 million from an unspecified fund to a numbered account at Manufacturers Hanover in Frankfurt. Meissner said the money was needed as a "break" deposit. As Solomon had only been at IOS for a month he asked Buhl what procedures should be followed to effect the transfer. Buhl told him to speak with someone in accounting at Ferney-Voltaire. Eventually the request was cycled back to Hoffman, who gave instruc- tions to put it through fund accounting, and late that afternoon a telex went out to Credit Suisse in Zurich, the custodian of cash, to make the transfer from IIT's account.

The next morning Credit Suisse responded that it had refused to execute the transfer on the grounds that ownership of the Frankfurt account could not be ascertained.

Vesco was indignant when confronted by a ranting Cornfeld and denied any impropriety had been intended. He promised before the intended closing to provide Cornfeld with letters from Bank Cantrade, acting for the purchasers, and Manufacturers Hanover that no corporate or fund moneys were involved in the purchase of his stock. Vesco's innuendo machine then went into high gear, letting it be known discreetly inside the company that the Frankfurt numbered account belonged to Union Bank of Switzerland and that the transfer had been intended as a normal fund transaction, first to establish a relationship with UBS, and second to avoid a Swiss withholding tax on interest payments on cash deposits.

The letter from the Manufacturers Hanover branch office in Frankfurt, which Vesco later presented to Cornfeld, was worded in such a manner as to suggest that the mysterious account really might have belonged to UBS.

> January 13, 1971
>
> To whom it may concern:
>   This is to confirm that a major international financial institution carries an account with this bank under the number 172-5285.
>   At the request of this institution and due to the banking secrecy laws in its jurisdiction we are not in the position to reveal the name of the said institution.
>
>> [s] Thomas H. Potschek
>> Manager and Vice President

The account in fact belonged to Butlers Bank—hardly a major international financial institution. Vesco had originally intended for Butlers to lend the money to purchase the Cornfeld stock, which would then be warehoused with Bank Cantrade until a suitable buyer was found for it. But the $5.5 million needed for the Cornfeld buyout represented more than 15 per cent of Butlers's total deposits, and the Nassau bank didn't have the necessary liquidity on hand. The result: Vesco had to find the cash for Butlers before going forward with the closing.

Vesco told Frederic Weymar, a managing director of Butlers Bank who had come to Europe to handle the banking end of the closing, that Linkink was a "grandson" of UBS, but that the big Swiss bank was nervous about the unholy publicity surrounding IOS and wanted to wait thirty days before putting up the cash. Vesco therefore wanted Butlers to bridge that gap. Butlers was agreeable but needed help. New York stockbroker Arthur Lipper III provided that help.

Vesco raised the $5.5 million "swing money" from Lipper. Although an SEC hearing examiner later recommended that Arthur Lipper Corporation have its broker-dealer registration suspended for one year for kicking back over-the-counter brokerage commissions to an IOS subsidiary, Lipper was still at that time dependent on IOS for the lion's share of his business. Lipper had $5.5 million in offshore cash available, and he transferred it to Butlers Bank in Nassau in a demand deposit.

Before the money was received, Weymar wrote Georges Philippe, the Bank Cantrade manager, that everything was set.

January 13, 1971

Gentlemen:

    This letter will confirm that the undersigned is advancing US $5,500,000 to Linkink Progressive Corp. S.A. in connection with the purchase of six million preferred shares of IOS Ltd. The undersigned further represents that the funds being used for such transaction are in no way being supplied by IOS Ltd., its subsidiaries or its mutual funds.

BUTLERS BANK LIMITED
[s] Frederic J. Weymar
Managing Director

Vesco now insisted that the closing take place in strictest secrecy in London in order to separate Cornfeld from his clique of meddlesome supporters in Geneva. The weekend before he left Geneva, Bernie was asked by a worried Allen Cantor who really was buying his stock. A perplexed Cornfeld confided that he really didn't know. "It's a Panamanian company with a Chinese-sounding name," he said. "Its shares are supposedly held by six banks, one of them Swiss, and the darn thing will probably turn out to be owned by Bob Vesco's grandmother."

Vesco later told the SEC in sworn testimony that "I, Robert Vesco, and ICC or its subsidiaries [are] not a party of any agreement in relation to, or tied into the Cornfeld transaction." [3]

Although Cornfeld truly wanted to believe in his heart of hearts that the purchaser was Union Bank of Switzerland—for that would have meant in all likelihood the survival of his creation—even he was not convinced. He privately reasoned that if in fact the purchaser turned out to be Vesco this would not necessarily be bad for the company. The chairman of International Controls then would be more inclined, as a major shareholder, to see IOS prosper. And since Vesco's equity position would be less than 15 per cent, Cornfeld estimated that half a dozen of the Old Guard directors—if they united in a common front—could at any time outvote him. Theoretically, therefore, control of the company would remain in the hands of the Old Guard.

Before Cornfeld left Geneva for London, it was then thought perhaps never to return, I called at Villa Elma to say goodby. The house was quiet and nearly empty. Bernie looked absolutely worn and beaten. The little hair he had hung down over his collar in unwashed strands, which he twisted nervously between his fingers.

Anyone who knew Cornfeld well could sense the real torment

[3] Vesco's SEC testimony, April 1971, p. 204.

hidden behind his deep-rimmed eyes. Nights without sleep, the see-saw battle with his board, the screaming rages and frantic negotiations, and the fear of losing everything—his women, wealth, and power—had left him muttering into his untrimmed beard, trusting no one, contemptuous of the world.

We were seated in the front hall of Villa Elma, and Bernie was idly talking about the future. The phone rang every two minutes, but the IOS founder, exceptionally, wasn't taking any calls. Occasionally, however, he interrupted himself to give instructions to one of the secretaries who were busily collecting files and legal documents in preparation for his final retreat, first to London and later to California, where he would purchase a baronial mansion in elegant Beverly Hills.

It soon became apparent from our conversation that about the only Cornfeld trait that had not suffered during the bitter siege was his overweening pride. Although he had been deserted by his closest associates, and removed from all positions of power in the empire he created, Bernie was still intent on maintaining the living Cornfeld legend 100 per cent intact.

One part of our conversation went something like this:

"What will you do once the deal is signed?"

He tugged at a bit of bread before answering; then, with the trace of a stutter that always returned when he was tired or under stress, he said quite softly, "I'll be watching how things develop. I can't engage in any solicitation of proxies, but if I don't like what's happening there are other ways I can react."

He paused, perhaps still trying to rationalize his sellout to himself and not quite succeeding. "Anyway, I've got enough money to live comfortably for the rest of my life. Nobody need worry about me. But I'm tired of fighting everyone else's battle without any help from those schmucks. Let them fight on their own now, and find out what it's like."

The next day in London forces from both camps assembled for an exchange of documents and the final signing of the contracts, of which there was not one, but three. Under the first contract Cornfeld sold his 6 million IOS preferred shares to Linkink at 92 cents a share.

The second contract concerned the settling of Cornfeld's indebtedness to the IOS banks for an amount of $2 million and the transferring of his $4.9 million bank guarantee for his BAC 1-11 jet and two other planes elsewhere.

The third was a twenty-one page agreement between Cornfeld and IOS whereby the corporation undertook to indemnify him against losses, claims, damages, fines, costs, expenses, or liabilities (including amounts paid in settlement, attorneys fees, and other costs incurred in connection therewith) resulting from his past activities with the IOS group.

There was a last-minute delay at the London closing when Vesco forgot the documents in a taxi and a new set had to be flown in from Zurich. The originals were returned a day later by the cabbie and was rewarded with a £5 tip, which probably was the lowest "finder's fee" Vesco ever paid.

The closing finally took place in the early hours of Saturday morning, January 16, 1971, in the offices of Freshfields, the London solicitors. Cornfeld was given two checks: one for $2 million, which was paid over to Overseas Development Bank of Geneva, and the other $3.5 million, which he kept.

Prior to signing the three contracts, Cornfeld was shown two letters from Bank Cantrade. The first, which he was allowed to keep, stated:

> In connection with moneys which we will receive on behalf of Linkink Progressive Corp. S.A., and in respect of the latter's order to pay the amount of up to $5.5 million which we are to receive, we confirm that we have in our possession a written representation from the bank that is advancing the moneys to Linkink that the moneys being advanced by the bank are in no way supplied by IOS Ltd., its subsidiaries or any IOS mutual fund.

Vesco, according to Cornfeld, produced a second letter written on Bank Cantrade stationery, stating that a subsidiary of the bank was purchasing the stock for its own account. Cornfeld's lawyers and others have testified to the existence of this letter. However, Vesco refused to leave a copy of it with Cornfeld because, according to Cornfeld, Vesco said that Union Bank of Switzerland did not want its interest disclosed. He did, however, leave Cornfeld with a copy of UBS's latest annual report.

The question was later raised whether the second Bank Cantrade letter was a forgery. UBS, in response to an inquiry almost three years later, said that "no such letter was written by or on behalf of Bank Cantrade (or any of its subsidiaries or affiliates, including UBS) and the statement said to have been made in the letter to the effect that a subsidiary of the bank was purchasing the Cornfeld stock for its own account was not a correct statement." [4]

Within hours of signing the Linkink deal Cornfeld, with his usual coterie of long-legged minions, boarded a jet for Cuernavaca, Mexico, where his friend Seymour "the Head" Lazare had a sumptuous hide-away villa, for the first rest after ten months of uninterrupted crisis. Vesco's public relations vice-president, Dick Clay, thoughtfully prepared a statement in Cornfeld's name, which was released later in the day.

"I have today after much deliberation sold my preferred shares of IOS and resigned from my positions in the company. I cannot disclose

[4] Letter from the UBS legal department to the author, December 6, 1973.

the terms of the transaction nor the purchaser. However, I can say that the purchaser is affiliated with a major international financial institution. I sincerely hope that this will prove a valuable new association for the company," the statement said in part.

Meanwhile, Allen Cantor belatedly voiced concern that everything might not be legitimate with the mystery buyer of the Cornfeld stock and asked Sir Eric to call a special meeting of the executive committee "to clear the air." It was a typically damp and foggy winter's day in Geneva that Saturday, and Vesco had considerable trouble flying back from London. When he finally arrived he was in a state of ill-concealed fury. The meeting began late in the afternoon and went until 2 A.M. Sunday morning.

"The unnecessary publicity [surrounding the suggestion that an attempt was made to use fund moneys for the purchase of Cornfeld's stock] has resulted in almost incalculable damage to IOS," Vesco told the committee. He said he could not "conceive how such a conversation [by IOS fund manager von Maur] with Mr. Lewis [of Bear, Sterns] could benefit the fund-holders, especially as all Wall Street and the European banks were now on their guard and distrustful.

"Had von Maur acted within the normal chain of command in IOS, the problem and loss of possible involvement by a major financial institution could have been avoided. If employees did not trust management, they could leave."

Demonstrating yet another instance of Vesco's skillful use of deceit, IOS's interim president Robert Slater reported to the committee that as a result of his inquiries he was satisfied the controversial $6.2 million deposit was intended for a UBS account at Manufacturers Hanover.

"Unfortunately, last week during the negotiations there were many malicious rumors circulated in and outside the company. They were investigated and have been found to have no basis in fact," he said. How far Slater carried his investigations was not clear. At any rate he apparently accepted Vesco's word that the attempted transfer of the $6.2 million was part of Meissner's efforts to establish a working relationship with UBS. Both Vesco and Meissner said they had been actively courting large and conservative UBS to take over as custodian of the funds. Vesco told the committee what he had told Cornfeld: that the purchaser of Bernie's stock was "a major international financial institution" but that he was not at liberty to disclose the name.

Sir Eric, looking for an easy way out, stressed the need for complete frankness among members of the committee. Vesco expressed his total agreement. He pointed out that von Maur evidently did not trust management and that this type of atmosphere had to be "eliminated" if the company was to prosper in the future.

Von Maur, who only months before was praised as a manager of great courage and foresight, was fired *sur-le-champ* as an example to others not to cross Bob Vesco. Following the von Maur incident four other members of the accounting department where "eliminated."

The Cornfeld "default" was the excuse for a further modification of the loan agreement. On January 25, 1971, it entered into its third phase, with even more sinister implications. Vesco accepted to withdraw his previous allegation of default on condition that:

(1) the company deposit an additional $1.5 million in Butlers Bank to cover the full amount of the loan plus interest
(2) management agreed to submit to shareholders for approval by July 31, 1971, a proposal to sell substantially all of IOS's assets and virtually none of its liabilities to a new corporation in which ICC Investments Limited or its shareholders would have at least 25 per cent interest
(3) if this "reorganization" was not approved by the shareholders on or before July 31, 1971, ICC Investments had the right to sell back to IOS 3 million (of the 4 million) warrants acquired under the first phase of the loan agreement at almost double the price
(4) IOS agreed to deposit a further $3.6 million in Butlers Bank to secure its obligation to purchase the 3 million warrants
(5) the company's promissory note to repay the original $5 million loan was made payable on demand
(6) the prepayment penalty was reduced to $500,000
(7) IOS agreed to reimburse International Controls and its employees for all travel expenses or other out-of-pocket expenses incurred in connection with activities pertaining to IOS and conducted at the direction of Vesco

This last amendment permitted Meissner to submit bills totaling thousands of dollars for dog food for his prize German shepherd, shipped to Geneva at the company's care and expense. However, Meissner's dog food was insignificant when compared to the $840,000 in travel expenses, $615,931 in legal expenses, and $156,434 in general administrative expenses—totaling $1,612,365—which International Controls billed IOS in 1971. Another $3.2 million was expensed to IOS in 1972 but remained largely unpaid. IOS was then without resources.[5]

The rape of IOS had begun. Meissner was placed on the IOS payroll with a yearly "consultant's fee" of $90,000 plus expenses and housing. Colonel Walter A. Howkins, a retired British army officer and a

[5] Securities and Exchange Commission *v.* Robert L. Vesco *et al.* (72 Civ. 5001), Frank G. Beatty affidavit, February 11, 1973, pp. 19–20.

chartered surveyor, was engaged as Meissner's batman at $2,000 a month, plus expenses and housing. And Clay and Straub were to be paid an allowance of $25,000 per annum and expenses while in Geneva or "working on projects approved by the chief executive officer of IOS Ltd."

Whatever else it accomplished, the Cornfeld buy-out definitely left Vesco in the driver's seat. Soon afterward Dick Hammerman sold his 968,000 preferred shares to ICC Investments. Hammerman, however, was paid nowhere near the same 92 cents per share that Cornfeld received. Vesco would only agree to 22 cents a share, setting a new market low for IOS preferred stock.

Within a month Sir Eric resigned, Hal Vaughan was out, and Cantor was removed. Bob Vesco seized the title of chairman of the board in addition to his other positions as chairman of the executive and finance committees.

"Affiliate of a major international financial institution," the term used for the purchaser of the Cornfeld stock, was perhaps a kind way to describe Linkink, a company that Cornfeld privately referred to as a "Chinese laundry." Disclosure of whom Linkink, through Red Pearl Bay, actually represented was never made to the Canadian authorities and was withheld from shareholders of IOS, which is an offense under Canadian law.

Lipper withdrew his swing money in April 1971, and a new search began to replace it. J. H. Crang and Company, the Toronto stock-brokers, put up $100,000; Global Natural Resources, by then firmly under Vesco's thumb, put in $1,250,000; and IOS Reinsurance Limited, $750,000. Where the remaining $3.1 million came from, as far as is known, was never disclosed.

The stock meanwhile was warehoused in a safety deposit box at Lombard Odier, the Geneva private bankers—with Straub and Strickler holding the keys—until Linkink finally resurfaced four months later. In May 1971, as Vesco prepared for a hot proxy battle with the Old Guard dissidents, Linkink was sold, along with the 6 million Cornfeld shares—its only assets—by Red Pearl Bay to American Interland Limited, a newly purchased Canadian subsidiary of International Controls. The price American Interland paid for Linkink was 50,000 shares (one-quarter of 1 per cent) of American Interland's 20,500,000 authorized shares.[6] The disposition of those 50,000 shares was for a long time unknown. Finally, in December 1971, they were bought back by International Controls for $50,000. The $50,000 was paid to an account of unknown ownership at Finabank S.A., a small Geneva bank controlled by Michele Sindona, the enigmatic, super-powerful Italian

[6] International Controls Corp. Form S-1 amendment of October 8, 1971, p. A4.

financier. In effect, International Controls ended up with Cornfeld's $5.5 million worth of IOS stock for an outlay of $50,000.

Had the Canadian Department of Consumer and Corporate Affairs intervened at some point along the way to force proper disclosure, as required under the Canada Corporations Act, then IOS Ltd. shareholders and clients might have been saved from much of the later shenanigans that reduced their investments to instruments of paper without financial value but with a certain collectors' fascination.

Instead, the task of policing IOS was passed from jurisdiction to jurisdiction with mixed results until the final SEC intervention of November 1972, when civil fraud proceedings were filed in New York. But it was only one year later, in November 1973, that a Canadian court finally reacted to a shareholder's petition and ordered the forced winding up of a raped and ruined IOS.

12

Revolt of the Old Guard

*Rebellion stirs the old-time magicians at IOS, which prompts
Vesco to call in default the $5 million loan ⁓ The Fairfield Fin-
agler employs mendacity and muscle to win a tumultuous proxy
battle over the Old Guard at the 1971 annual general meeting in
Toronto ⁓ Rewards for the faithful*

With Cornfeld no longer around to stir up trouble, Vesco
thought his problems with the increasingly suspicious Old Guard at IOS
had ended. In fact they were just beginning.

Within weeks of the Linkink transaction a full-scale dissident revolt
broke out. It started when Larry Rosen, a junior Cornfeld assistant
from Louisville, Kentucky, dared to question the accounting principles
used in IOS's 1970 corporate audit, which had been completed under
Vesco's careful supervision. When Rosen persisted in his criticism he
was physically removed from his office on the seventh floor of 119 rue
de Lausanne by a pair of burly IOS security guards and barred from
the building.

What Rosen was attempting to alert other insiders to was the fact
that in one swift slash Vesco had reduced IOS's net worth from the
$98.5 million stated in the 1969 annual report to the $35 million that
appeared in the financial statements for 1970. Accordingly, under
Vesco's severe auditing treatments, IOS's net loss for the year was stated
at a staggering $60.35 million, whereas Rosen calculated that a loss of
$13.7 million would have been more realistic.

This meant, according to Rosen, that the 1970 net worth of IOS
should have been much higher—around $82 million. He deduced, there-
fore, that Vesco and his associates were writing down the assets so that
when IOS was "restructured" the shareholders would not seem to be
getting such a bad deal. Conversely, Vesco, at no cost, would be getting

the difference between the higher net worth and the written-down value when he exchanged these assets for the shares of a successor corporation that he planned to create. This new version of IOS appeared on paper as the "ABC Corporation." And ABC, company wags suggested, stood for "After Bernie Cornfeld."

According to the broad outline of the restructuring plan, at least one quarter of ABC Corporation was to be owned by International Controls, "and recognized financial organizations shall also [be offered] in the aggregate substantial interests." But descriptions of how Vesco intended to reorganize the company, in printed form at least, were rarely much more explicit or meaningful than that.

Vesco's immediate concern, once Cornfeld was out of the way, was to assure his absolute control as quickly as possible over every avenue of IOS life. The independent auditors were a matter of particular concern to him. The Arthur Andersen team had listed so many instances in the 1970 audit where they couldn't make a valuation that they had declined to express an opinion on the financial statements as a whole. Vesco replaced them in 1971 with Coopers & Lybrand, whose U.S. affiliate, Lybrand, Ross Brothers & Montgomery, handled the International Controls account. Coopers & Lybrand was one of the international Big Eight, handling such prestigious clients as AT&T Ford Motor Company, Atlantic Richfield, Firestone, Sun Oil, and Alcoa. Vesco felt infinitely more comfortable with them since he knew exactly how they worked, how far they would bend, and over precisely what kind of issues they could be expected not to give an inch.

Before proceeding with the dismantling of IOS, Vesco made but one effort to appease the senior preferred shareholders by inviting them to a conference in New York early in March 1971. The meeting was held chiefly at Allen Cantor's insistence, and Vesco had promised he would there unveil his formalized plans for a Restructured IOS. But Vesco had little intention of taking the IOSers—most of whom he regarded with extreme contempt—into his confidence. The plans he unveiled were as foggy as ever, and the arrangements to which the senior shareholders were subjected firmly alienated most of them, giving birth to the first organized dissident resistance.

The meeting was set for the Regency Hotel in New York on the day of the Muhammad Ali–Jerry Quarry fight. But when newspaper reporters arrived at the hotel before the meeting, the twenty-five shareholders who together owned about 15 per cent of the preferred stock suddenly were ushered out the back door by a man in a foreign service raincoat and hustled into a waiting fleet of rented Cadillacs that were lined up at the curb. They were driven across the George Washington Bridge and taken to a motel somewhere in eastern New Jersey. Dick

Clay contended that "legal considerations" rather than a desire for secrecy had prompted the change of venue.

The meeting lasted about one hour in a small, overheated conference room, in the company of a handful of henchmen Vesco had brought with him from Fairfield. There were no introductions, and Vesco's crowd, said one of the IOS participants, "did not look like a New Englander's idea of Capitalism."

Vesco put on a mediocre performance, full of little jokes that didn't work, which tended to depress the situation even more. Addressing people who had come, in most cases, 5,000 miles to see how they could protect their nonexistent fortunes, Vesco began brutally: "There is a rumor about that I have stolen your company from you. Well, rest assured, it hasn't happened—yet."

He went on to say he wasn't quite sure why the meeting was being held. He had nothing much to tell them, he said, because he honestly didn't know what the final form of a Restructured IOS would be, at least not as of that moment. There was some fuzzy description of how IOS might be reorganized under ABC Corporation, but very few people understood the mechanics involved.

Then "these institutions that we get, if any, to come in and lend us money, we're going to give them a big con job and get them in permanently [which is] the object of our maneuvers," Vesco told his by then hostile audience.

"Once it was over, you left the motel checking to see if you still had your underwear," said one former IOS director who later sold his stock to Vesco just the same.

A few weeks later Vesco started making the rounds of institutions he hoped might participate in the new IOS. He met in Toronto with Earl McLaughlin, chairman of the Royal Bank of Canada, and indicated to him that Linkink was owned by Union Bank of Switzerland but that Vesco had a gentleman's agreement to take UBS out of the deal. McLaughlin wasn't interested. Vesco also contacted United California Bank, Salomon Brothers, Investors Diversified Services, Eastman Dillon, Canadian Imperial Bank of Commerce, Jefferies & Company, Wells Fargo Bank, Lehman Brothers, and Union Bank of California, but they all turned him down.

Larry Rosen was not invited to the New Jersey meeting. Soon afterward, however, he joined forces with Allen Cantor and six other Old Guard captains to form a dissident directorate that sought to block Vesco's bid to steal the company and presented their own plans for refinancing the crisis-torn financial services empire. Dedicated to the resurrection of the golden-image IOS of old, the dissident directorate was headed by Morton Schiowitz, who until 1968 had been Cornfeld's chief financial officer.

Less than a month before the second annual general meeting on June 30, 1971, in Toronto, the dissidents engaged in a desperate proxy contest to oust Vesco from IOS. This attempt from the ranks of former management to regain control brought a bitter response from Vesco in the form of a black publicity campaign with no holds barred.

"Seemingly, it is the desire of those responsible for the splendor, and wreckage, of IOS to once again work their magic," said IOS president Bob Slater in a letter to shareholders warning them not to be taken in by the dissidents' proxy solicitation.

Among the "old-time magicians" leading the attack against new management Slater noted Allen Cantor, a participant in two private tax-avoidance foundations that owed the company $5.5 million. Also on the dissident slate was George Landau, who belonged to the same two private foundations as Cantor.

Slater stated caustically in his letter attacking the dissidents, and justly causing them some embarrassment, that no doubt "the opposition group can supply urgently needed financing for the company. All they need to do is cause the ventures in which they participate to repay the money presently owed to IOS and to assume the liabilities which IOS has been forced to undertake on their behalf."

Other tactics employed by Vesco in his fight with the dissidents included, predictably, once again calling IOS in default on its $5 million loan agreement with International Controls.

Pursuing this tactic, Vesco notified the IOS board of directors in mid-June 1971 that because of the statutory forty-five-day notice period for calling a special meeting of shareholders it was physically impossible to approve a restructuring program—if indeed one existed at all—before the July 31, 1971, deadline.

This contention by Vesco certainly was outrageous since it had been up to him to present a reorganization plan, and also call the meeting to vote upon its acceptance. But Vesco conveniently failed to do so. The absence of a plan gave him the opening he needed to demand that IOS repurchase, for $3.6 million, 3 million of the warrants the company had issued as a premium to International Controls.

Then, as failure to approve a restructuring plan constituted another default, Vesco also demanded in his June 1971 letter that IOS pay back the loan and repurchase the remaining warrants it had outstanding at 74 cents apiece. Thus the minimum amount repayable by IOS for the "emergency" $5 million financing it had received through International Controls would have been as follows:

Outstanding principal amount of loan	$5,000,000
Interest	400,000
Repurchase of 3,000,000 warrants at $1.20	3,600,000
Repurchase of 1,250,000 warrants at $.74	925,000
Total	$9,925,000

As a result of one of the most onerous loan agreements ever negotiated, IOS owed International Controls almost twice the sum originally borrowed just nine months before.

"Conflict of interest!" cried the dissidents. Vesco, as chairman of International Controls, claimed to be acting in the best interests of his American shareholders in calling the loan. In the same breath he also maintained that as chairman of IOS Ltd. he was defending the best interests of the Geneva-based company against a group of irresponsible insurgents. The inconsistency was obvious.

Schiowitz ineffectively attempted to exploit the situation by bringing a damages suit against Vesco and International Controls in the Superior Court of New Jersey alleging that the Fairfield group was taking advantage of "beleaguered IOS in order to loot and plunder its assets." Vesco retaliated by filing a $20 million defamation suit against Schiowitz and the other dissident leaders. It stayed before the federal courts in New Jersey for two years before finally being thrown out. The dissidents, meanwhile, had not pressed their action.

Three days after dispatching the third default letter, Vesco, the chairman of International Controls, and Vesco, chairman of IOS, agreed to delay enforcement of the June 1971 default claims until after the annual general meeting of IOS shareholders. The chairman of International Controls then said the default claims against IOS would be dropped at that time if two-thirds of new management's nominees were elected to the IOS board of directors at the annual meeting, which by then was only one week away.

The stick-and-carrot routine was flaunted even more flagrantly at a ten-hour session of the IOS board that same day, when Vesco promised to provide $10 million in new financing if re-elected by a comfortable two-to-one majority. Where Vesco was to obtain the $10 million remained bound in very iffy speculation and in fact was never elucidated, as the proposal quickly evaporated in the summer mist over Lake Geneva.

However, what caused real panic among the ranks of the dissidents was Vesco's use of any pretext to call the personal loans of former management that were still outstanding at IOS's banking subsidiaries and seize their IOS stock that collateralized the loans. Only those who sided with Vesco, turning a voting proxy for their shares over to him, were spared.

One ex-director, Richard Gangel, who withheld his proxy too long for Vesco's liking, was thrown into immediate bankruptcy. The high-living Gangel, once the overlord of IOS's sales operations in Britain, had bought a $250,000 home in London's fashionable Rutland Gate district of South Kensington and spent almost $750,000 remodeling it.

Gangel, a onetime New York union organizer, estimated his fast fortune, mostly in IOS paper, at $7 million. He thought he was a wealthy man and built up a wealthy man's overdraft at IOS's Overseas Development Bank in Geneva, exceeding $1 million when the 1970 crisis erupted. Unsuccessful in creating a carbon copy of IOS with some of the early sales force defectors, he was soon in financial ruin with debts of $2 million when Vesco called his loan. Others who feared a similar fate backed away from the dissidents and attempted to conclude a deal with "Uncle Bob."

Where had some of the other old flowers gone? Sir Eric Wyndham White, who had never been a large shareholder, unloaded his modest holdings at a substantial loss when he resigned from the company. Sir Eric took no interest in the proxy battle. His first attempt at rehabilitation in the real world outside IOS, the formation of a company called Wyndham White & Associates, was a financial washout. It was intended as a consulting service to teach developing countries how to extract the most benefits from the U.N. system for the least input, but not one of the governments canvassed expressed anything more than cursory interest.

Next Sir Eric opened a small art gallery in Geneva's Old Town just down the hill from the Saint Antoine prison. Galerie Cinq was another disaster. "I haven't sold a painting in months," he confided to a former GATT associate who came to visit him. The gallery finally closed at the end of 1973, and Sir Eric left Geneva for Marrakech. IOS had been a personal tragedy for the ex-mandarin of GATT.

Cowett, meanwhile, had set up his own financial and legal consulting bureau in Geneva, Emco Financial Services S.A., with IOS and Vesco as two of his earliest clients. But Cowett fled town in late 1971 when it looked as though the Swiss would issue a warrant for his arrest. Early in 1972 he found employment with Cavanagh Communities Corporation, a Miami Beach property development concern listed on the New York Stock Exchange. To help tide Cowett over some financial difficulties, Vesco interceded with Butlers Bank, enabling the Blue Sky expert to obtain a $300,000 loan that was in part guaranteed by Henry Alba Teran, Duc d'Antin, a convicted international swindler.

Eli "the Bear" Wallit, the architect of IOS's sales breakthrough in
Germany, had also formed a Geneva-based company, F & M Consultants, and was looking for free-lance work. At the time of the Toronto
meeting Wallit had joined forces with ex-IOS banker Barry Sterling in
a scheme to sell cancer insurance to British housewives. This slick venture was called the Blue Seal Cancer Plan, and the product was to be
sold door to door by out-of-work IOS salesmen.

"Tell as many lies as you like on the doorstep, but get in and make the
sale," Blue Seal recruits were instructed.

All went well until this "callous" and "appalling" business was exposed by Britain's *Daily Mail* in July 1971.

In the weeks leading up to the all-important Toronto meeting Vesco
was able to dispose of a good number of the dissidents. Nevertheless, a
hard core of discontented shareholders remained impervious to his
strong-arm measures and continued to support the dissident directorate
with abject resignation. To many it was unclear which of the two camps,
once elected, would destroy IOS the faster, in which case why not place
your chips with an old acquaintance rather than a newcomer to the game?

Because they maintained this support right up to the opening ballot,
the dissident directorate was supremely confident in spite of constant
internal wrangling that Vesco faced certain defeat and that the company
was all but back in their hands. They had obtained an injunction from
the Supreme Court of Ontario, which they served on Vesco the day of
the meeting. It prohibited the voting by IOS management of a key block
of stock held by the IOS Stock Option Plan that Vesco needed to maintain his control.

The court injunction, covering 3.6 million preferred shares, spelled
doom for Vesco unless he found a way to circumvent it. The situation
was that desperate. Failure to maintain control of IOS probably would
have pushed Vesco into instant bankruptcy. His desperation was underlined by his decision to run a major risk in ignoring the court order and
by the series of blatant lies he dished up to the more than 300 shareholders packed into the blue-draped Ontario Room at the Royal York
Hotel in downtown Toronto.

The acrimonious meeting spanned two days and was several times ad-
journed. Vesco, in the chair, had trouble controlling the proceedings
and on one occasion requested uniformed Pinkerton guards to evict a
troublesome shareholder who protested too loudly.

In his up-beat opening report to the angry shareholders, Vesco portrayed IOS as having reached the break-even point on its road to recovery and announced that with stable management it would be once

again turning a profit by the end of the year. Concerning relations with the SEC, he remarked:

> We believe that the SEC's primary concern with IOS back in 1967 was the fact that they lacked jurisdiction over the funds. And our solution to that was the essence of simplicity and that was to simply offer to register the funds with the Securities and Exchange Commission which we have offered to them in writing.[1]

However, a spokesman for the SEC later denied that any specific proposal for registration of the funds was ever received from IOS, Vesco, or International Controls. Even if one had, it is doubtful that it would have been accepted.

Concerning his relations with the Swiss and French governments, he went even farther:

> We have had a series of contacts with them and indeed have worked out a *modus operandi* that will allow the company to proceed uninterrupted. . . . I understand that it appeared in the Swiss press just today, and I do not know the accuracy of this statement, but presumably what was stated there was an unofficial comment by the government of Switzerland that if the management slate is not elected, that they would take a much different view. And indeed, it appeared also in the French papers yesterday, the same thing. In summary we have been successful in developing a working relationship with both governments and I believe that the difficulties that were expressed in the press are now resolved.[2]

The articles Vesco referred to were something of a mystery, since as far as could be ascertained no such representations had appeared in print in Switzerland or France. In fact, the Swiss had made it perfectly clear that IOS's continued presence in Switzerland was incompatible with the new Swiss law on foreign mutual funds.

And about the "beneficial" loan agreement:

> It operates for the benefit of the shareholders for one simple reason, that we are the major shareholders. We find that it has been quite effective in protecting the company from certain spurious actions that might have otherwise been contemplated had not the umbrella of protection of the loan agreement surrounded the assets of the company.[3]

But Vesco through this all-protective loan agreement held such tight control over the management of the company that the only "spurious"

[1] Transcript of IOS Ltd. Annual Meeting, June 30, 1971, p. 31.
[2] *Ibid.,* p. 49.
[3] *Ibid.,* p. 65.

actions it could ever get involved in would have to be of his own making.

The first item of business on the agenda required a vote approving amendments to two bylaws proposed by Vesco, the most important of which was the reduction of the board of directors from twenty-seven to seventeen members. Changes to the bylaws needed a two-thirds majority to be accepted. The vote was also an interesting test, for it showed how many proxies each side held before going on to the crucial issue of electing directors. There was a three-hour adjournment while the votes were counted. The results rocked Vesco:

For	17,282,015
Against	17,998,140

Had that been the vote for the election of directors, Vesco would have lost control. He immediately sent his agents out onto the floor to buy more shares while craftily withholding the exact figures of the balloting but simply announcing that the motion was defeated since it had failed to obtain the required two-thirds majority.

Once armed with more shares, Vesco permitted the election of directors to go forward. It was just before midnight. This time, based on a simple majority vote, his team managed to squeak through. Only three dissidents—George Landau, Don Q. Shaprow, and Samuel C. Welker— were elected; the rest were members of the Vesco camp.

When the complete results were announced on the following day, H. Bernard Mayer, the dissidents' Toronto lawyer, asked Vesco if the Stock Option Plan shares, which the dissidents had legally enjoined management from voting, had in fact been voted by management or anyone else for that matter.

Vesco answered, "I understand . . . that the shares owned beneficially or of record by the Stock Option Plan were not voted."

This was a half-truth at best, because those shares had been voted, but by a new owner. Twice more he stated, "To the best of my knowledge . . . shares registered in the name or beneficially owned by IOS Stock Option Plan Ltd. . . . were not voted."

This was again reiterated by an employee of the Montreal Trust Company, official scrutinizers and transfer agents for IOS. "The shares of the IOS Stock Option Plan were not voted at this meeting," said Rudi Hegele, a regular counter of votes at IOS meetings.

"Are those 3.6 million preferred shares still registered on the record under the name of the IOS Stock Option Plan Ltd.?" Meyer asked.

"The preferred shares were transferred yesterday," Hegele responded.

"To whom were they transferred?"

"I would have to check the records. I don't know."

At which point pandemonium broke out on the floor, prompting Vesco to remark wryly, "It's like the Vietnam War in here."

"To whom were those shares transferred, Mr. Chairman?" Meyer shouted.

"Well, I am not in a position to answer," Vesco replied evasively. "I don't have full knowledge of the questions you've asked." Considering that he had made the sale himself—transferring the shares from his left hand to his right back pocket, so to speak—his reply was less than candid.

The dissidents pressed for an immediate examination of the ballots and proxies. Vesco ruled them out of order. Meissner stood up and moved that the meeting adjourn. Slater seconded the motion. It was defeated by 17,170,296 votes to 16,906,100. Once the results were announced Marvin Hoffman jumped up and without a pause proposed that "due to the closeness of the vote, I move that we terminate the meeting and have another polling."

One of Vesco's legmen, Dibo Attar, had fallen asleep in his chair the first time around and failed to vote the Italian proxies he was holding. But they were not sufficient to close the meeting. Vesco's management team had found 66,000 additional votes in the interval between polling for an adjournment and Meissner's motion that the meeting be terminated.

A New York attorney representing the dissidents, Martin A. Coleman, leaped to his feet and objected to the termination motion.

"If you continue to talk you'll be ejected from the meeting," Vesco responded snappishly.

"We protest—" Coleman, still arguing, shouted back.

"You may protest—" Vesco started to answer but was drowned out by continued shouting. Finally he called for the Pinkerton guards and ordered, "Will you please have this person ejected for being unruly."

The astonished New York lawyer was bundled from the room, and a new poll was held. This time the votes were 17,202,483 in favor of Vesco management, 17,104,316 against. The meeting was declared over. Vesco had scraped through in the end by a mere 98,000 votes.

A post-meeting statement in a printed press release distributed by Vesco's associates disclosed that Hemispheres Financial Services, an International Controls subsidiary, had bought "various blocks" of IOS preferred shares just before and during the meeting, including the 3.6 million shares from the IOS Stock Option Plan. Vesco added orally that the shares, as suspected, had been voted for management. He of course knew this all along. His trusted lieutenant, Dick Clay, held the proxy.

Content that victory was his, Vesco wrote to IOS shareholders informing them of the highlights of the Toronto meeting. "Present management very definitely retains control," he said. He did not mention that to do so management had circumvented an Ontario court order restraining it from voting the IOS Stock Option Plan shares—which had been the margin between victory and defeat. He then added with an ominous hint of things to come that "with [the proxy fight] behind us, we are now addressing ourselves to the income side of the ledger."

Almost unnoticed in the general rumpus, the Ontario Securities Commission placed a ban on trading of the IOS common stock—the second in just over a year—that was never lifted. A contempt of court action charging that Vesco had violated the Ontario Supreme Court order was filed by the dissidents in Toronto. But Vesco denied that he had violated any such court order pertaining to the voting of those shares. As for circumventing the injunction—well, that was another story.

He had obtained in the interim a written opinion from a partner of a prominent Toronto law firm stating that he had acted within the letter of the injunction if not actually within its intent. "The injunction was directed towards the voting of those shares by the IOS Stock Option Plan Ltd. and it was accordingly my opinion that, on a careful and literal reading of the injunction, a sale of those shares would not constitute a violation thereof," the exculpatory opinion stated.

Although outflanked and dispirited by their setback, the Old Guard continued to fight. Mort Schiowitz flew down to Saint John, New Brunswick, where IOS Ltd. maintained its registered offices on a bookshelf in a local law office, and requested a new and more sweeping injunction from the Supreme Court there. Schiowitz charged that he and his teammates had been the victims of "constructive fraud."

An *ex-parte* injunction was granted, this one restraining Vesco and his fellow IOS directors and officers from transacting any but routine business pending trial. The day before the New Brunswick order was granted, Schiowitz unveiled his heavy artillery with the announcement that Meshulam A. Ricklis, chairman of Rapid American Corporation, one of the largest U.S. conglomerates, whose interests ranged from apparel to liquor, had joined forces with the dissidents. Ricklis, who the year before had been "sandbagged" by Cornfeld into buying 450,000 preferred shares at $4 apiece, said he would provide $10 million in financial aid for IOS "on terms judged fair and equitable in the business community." All Ricklis wanted, Cowett suggested from the sidelines, was to be taken out of his stock position at cost, in which case he would drop the dissidents flat and step aside.

But Vesco sat firm. He was furious, of course, because the dissident injunction in New Brunswick was more encompassing and effectively interfered with his restructuring plans. In a new default letter dated July

15, 1971—this one signed by International Controls vice-president Frank Beatty—IOS was reminded that it remained in default of the loan agreement. Repayment of the $5 million loan plus almost $5 million more in penalties and charges was now demanded by July 26—in ten days—unless the New Brunswick injunction was vacated before then.

In addition, the Beatty letter required that a long list of items, including all outstanding stock in the key IOS subsidiaries, constituting virtually all the worldwide listed assets of IOS Ltd., be delivered to Butlers Bank in Nassau as security for the loan, its premiums, penalties, and other obligations.

Slater, in a rare show of independence, replied firmly that Vesco's attempts at intimidation were unjustified and without foundation. "It is our present position that such defaults and events thereof do not exist," Slater responded in a return letter to International Controls.

There followed three months of legal infighting as Vesco's lawyers argued on the one hand to have the New Brunswick injunction lifted and attempted on the other to enter into an out-of-court settlement with the dissidents in which Vesco proposed to purchase their stock at a generous above-market price. Meanwhile, as added insurance in case the results of the Toronto meeting were declared invalid, he instructed Hemispheres Financial Services to continue purchasing whatever other IOS preferred shares were available. Thus over the next four months Hemispheres bought an additional 5.2 million shares at an average price of 22 cents each. When added to the shares bought in June 1971, International Controls had spent a total of $2.8 million on IOS stock, giving the Fairfield concern about 32 per cent of the outstanding equity, which at last placed Vesco in an unassailable control position.

Meanwhile Vesco's lawyers had successfully appealed the New Brunswick injunction, which was lifted on October 1, 1971. This obviated the necessity of reaching a handsome settlement with the dissident captains, since they no longer constituted a threat to Vesco's plans. And so, after lengthy negotiations to purchase their stock for $2.3 million—Vesco's best offer—a settlement was never concluded.

However, the three former Old Guard directors who had supported Vesco throughout the dissident attack—Bob Sutner, Malcolm Fox, and Henry Buhl—were duly rewarded.

The following year a newly incorporated Sutner venture capital company, Dominion Guarantee, was loaned $1 million from The Fund of Funds. Only a portion of this loan was actually disbursed prior to the SEC's filing its massive fraud complaint in November 1972, spelling Dominion's early retirement from the venture capital field, but Sutner remained a defender of Vesco right up until the bitter end.

Malcolm Fox, who replaced Cantor as IOS's new sales chief, resigned in mid-1971 to set up an independent sales operation in London—Growth Financial Services—which received a sweetheart contract from IOS worth close to $1 million for its marketing and client services capabilities.

Henry Buhl also resigned from IOS and then formed his own company to construct and sell to foreigners some 800 Swiss chalets on a tract of Alpine pastureland that his in-laws owned. Vesco promised to invest $200,000 in Buhl's chalet development, the Domaine de Belvedere S.A.,[4] and actually arranged for International Controls to transfer $50,000 to Buhl's numbered account at a Geneva bank in early January 1972.

However, when the Swiss government's surprise anti-inflationary measures banning the purchase by nonresident foreigners of real estate in Switzerland were imposed in mid-1972, the Belvedere project was wound up at a loss. Buhl said that after the dissidents' defeat Vesco had agreed to purchase his 376,000 preferred shares, which by then had been transferred to his wife's name. The apparently agreed-upon price for the shares was $140,000—slightly above the going rate for other "friendlies." The $50,000 already received by Buhl became a part payment for his (wife's) stock. He later testified that the remaining $90,000 was paid in May 1972 via bank transfer from the Bahamas.

Reverting to the dissidents, it was quite understandable under the circumstances that an International Controls spokesman should announce that Bob Vesco felt "gratified" by the October 1971 decision of the three-judge appeals panel to lift the New Brunswick injunction. It was a triumph of justice over the forces of corporate disorder, the excellent Fairfield innuendo machine suggested. And so, out of a pigeonhole in Geneva, came a more daring "Plan B" for a Restructured IOS.

By the same date just one year later IOS was "restructured" to a point where, virtually insolvent, it hardly existed any more. As one disgruntled employee described it, all that remained of the once-mighty offshore giant was a "ragbag full of headaches and some 250 lawsuits around the world."

[4] C. Henry Buhl III, SEC testimony, October 30, 1972.

13

International Vendetta

Enter the U.S. Securities and Exchange Commission with an investigation that Vesco considers unjustified harassment — While battling with the U.S. regulatory authorities he attempts to restructure rickety International Controls, then decides to mount his own investigation of the SEC and bribe or otherwise compromise its agents

With Vesco devoting nearly all of his time to the affairs of IOS, International Controls was suffering from neglect in early 1971 and required a general rethinking of its corporate objectives. Sales were falling, and Vesco, occupied on the transnational front, had little time for refurbishing old profit centers, then carrying through with the kind of tough administrative program that would ensure a continued smooth functioning. The man selected for this task was Larry Richardson, a tall fifty-year-old aerodynamics engineer whose executive background mingled well with International Controls's varied activities and made him ideally suited to be Vesco's number two man on the domestic front.

Richardson was the son of a U.S. admiral with a distinguished record as a pioneer naval aviator. Laurence, Jr., had followed his father into the navy as a career officer. After graduating from the U.S. Naval Academy in 1943 in the top 7 per cent of his class, he was assigned to heavy cruiser duty and saw action in the Pacific, later becoming a naval fighter pilot. In 1951 Richardson received a masters degree in aeronautical engineering from Princeton, and in 1955 he became chief test pilot at Chance Vought, then joined LTV Aerospace Corporation as vice-president for marketing.

After consenting to become chief executive officer at All American in 1969, Richardson attempted to pull the Wilmington firm out of the doldrums. Then, with the 1970 takeover of All American by International Controls, he moved up to Fairfield to help Vesco put the lagging Fairfield conglomerate back on its feet as a viable, forward-moving enterprise.

Vesco's plan at this time called for the transformation of International Controls into essentially a holding company conducting its operations through three publicly traded subsidiaries, of which All American Industries became the first.

Radiation International Incorporated was selected as the second operating arm of the new-look International Controls. In September 1970 Vesco completed plans to transfer to this newly incorporated shell two "advanced technology" divisions formerly belonging to Electronic Specialty. The assets of Radiation Machinery Corporation, an existing but insolvent concern, were then acquired in exchange for Radiation International stock. Radiation became an 80 per cent controlled subsidiary of International Controls.

One month after the Radiation deal was consummated the Fairfield group entered into a letter of intent with Datron Systems Incorporated, a financially troubled manufacturer of computer accessories in Mountain Lakes, New Jersey. The plan was to merge the data-processing and automation controls division of International Controls into Datron for stock and convertible debentures. This resulted in Datron's becoming an 81 per cent controlled subsidiary of International Controls.

Vesco, in his year-end letter to stockholders, launched into one of his hyperbolic descriptions of the reorganization plan without really telling shareholders anything. "Despite the predicted drop in 1970 sales volume, the company's level of earnings before extraordinary gains was maintained. This creditable performance was accomplished in part by excellent profit-center performance, a successful company-wide cost control program, and increased interest income," the Vesco letter stated.

In this obscurely worded passage *"increased interest income"* held the key. Although no indication of its source was given, without this mysterious animal International Controls would have operated at a loss in the final quarter of 1970 and was clearly in failing financial health.[1] In fact, and again it went unstated in the annual report, the "increased interest income," a purely noncash item that had little to do with real money in a more conservative accounting sense, accounted for $1.5 million, or 35 per cent of the company's net income *for the year* before taxes.

But even more baffling to International Controls shareholders was the question, Where did this cashless income item come from? Here again Vesco succeeded in shrouding the facts, for it was born from

---

[1] By virtue of the increased interest income, fourth-quarter 1970 profits sustained only a 42 per cent decrease from $534,000 the year before to $250,000.

the $3.6 million in warrant income International Controls stood to collect if the reorganization of offshore IOS was not approved and completed according to a stipulated schedule. However, in Vesco's notice to shareholders no direct reference was made to the company's relationship with IOS either, because that might have tipped his hand to the other players and bystanders in this treacherous game of corporate poker.

Under the $5 million loan agreement signed in Geneva in September 1970, IOS gave ICC Investments Limited 4 million warrants as a premium for arranging the loan. In the first amendment to the agreement, however, IOS's directors agreed to buy back 3 million of the warrants at $1.20 each, for a total of $3.6 million, if an unspecified reorganization plan was not ratified by IOS shareholders on or before July 31, 1971, and completed by the end of the year. Conversely, if the reorganization was achieved on schedule, IOS was given the right to buy back all the warrants for $750,000.

As it turned out, neither of these alternatives happened, although Vesco took the full $3.6 million as noncash income into the International Controls accounts. His method lay hidden in the almost incomprehensibly worded explanations that accompanied the audited financial statements.

Buried in the footnote material to the 1970 annual report, International Controls explained that it hadn't consolidated the accounts of ICC Investments Limited, and by becoming a financial sleuth the interested investor through one or two cross-references was able to uncover a balance sheet for ICC Investments Limited in footnote 2, which appeared as follows:

Notes receivable from IOS Ltd.	$5,000,000
Other current assets	411,964
Investment in IOS Ltd. warrants	3,600,000
Deferred charges	110,131
	$9,122,095
Current liabilities	255,289
Bank loan due January 15, 1972	5,000,000
Unamortized loan premium	2,088,000
	$7,343,289
Net equity	$1,778,806

The net equity was listed under assets on International Controls's own balance sheet. The ICC Investments Limited balance sheet carried the IOS warrants as an asset at a value of $3.6 million. As this was the amount that IOS was obliged to pay if the reorganization was not approved and implemented by the end of 1971, it seemed to indicate that from the outset Vesco had no intention of submitting a reorganization plan to the IOS shareholders. Indeed, he needed to make use of that warrant income. But this is how the situation was explained in footnote 2 of the International Controls accounts:

> The investment in warrants to purchase IOS Ltd. common stock received in connection with the loan is carried at the estimated fair value of the warrants given consideration to all related factors, including contractual terms for their repurchase. The loan premium based on such valuation of the warrants is taken into income over the original term of the notes, from September 17, 1970, to May 24, 1971.

By deduction, then, the amount taken into income from the funny warrants for 1970 was $1,512,000 (the full carrying value of the warrants less the "unamortized loan premium"). The balance of $2,088,000 shown as "unamortized loan premium" was therefore to be taken into income during the first two quarters of 1971.

Footnote 2 went on to explain that International Controls had applied the $1,512,000 as a reduction of interest expense in the consolidated statement of operations for International Controls. That statement showed International Controls's interest expenses had dropped from $3,485,018 in 1969 to $1,927,645 in 1970.

This was, of course, an awful lot of Chinese accounting. Finally, Frank Beatty, International Controls's financial vice-president, in response to an astute question from the *Wall Street Journal*'s Scott Schmedel, admitted that about $775,000 represented the net effect after taxes of the IOS warrants for the final quarter of 1970.

The remaining chunk of now you see it, now you don't income was brought on stream during the first half of 1971.

The treatment of the funny warrants was too much for the SEC investigators, who were by then hot on the trail of the magic instant-cash assignats of the Vesco regime.

An April 1971 SEC memorandum declared:

> International Controls in one breath states its present intention is to pursue the reorganization of IOS and in the next breath reports warrant income of $1.5 million which it will receive only if the reorganization does not proceed as scheduled. If the reorganization does succeed IOS will have the right to repurchase the IOS warrants for only $775,000. . . . If International Controls didn't expect the reorganization plans to materialize, it shouldn't have reported the warrant income.[2]

Yet Vesco's curious treatment of the warrant income didn't seem to bother International Control's independent auditors, Coopers &

---

[2] Robert L. Vesco and International Controls Corp. *v.* Securities and Exchange Commission *et al.* Defendants' trial memorandum, p. 11.

Lybrand. In the company's annual report, the auditors made ritual reference to "generally accepted accounting principles" without qualifications when signing off their audit.

A few weeks later International Controls disclosed that its first-quarter 1971 net income was 90 per cent attributable to the amortized value of the warrants. The amount brought in from the funny warrants was $555,000 in the first quarter, which meant that International Controls's actual earnings from continuing operations were a miserable $68,327 and shrinking. Things were not good.

An additional sum of $489,000 in warrant income was brought in during the following quarter, which meant that *all* of the first-half 1971 profit came from funny noncash items.

Vesco defended his fantastic financial plumbing. The warrant treatment, he said, should be placed "in context" with other "noncash book-keeping items" such as tax provisions that exist one year, when deemed appropriate, then are said not to exist the next, and "deferred gains" and other such gimmicks. That was really creative accounting.

It bewildered even the most knowledgeable investors; International Controls stock no longer found favor in the market place. When the complicated treatment of the noncash items was made public by Scott Schmedel in the *Wall Street Journal* in one of the best pieces of analytical financial reporting of the season,[3] International Controls stock fell to a new low of $7.125 a share. Vesco was furious and assailed the *Wall Street Journal* article as "a gross misrepresentation."

However, "gross misrepresentation" was a more accurate description of the line Vesco was feeding the IOS shareholders. Capturing the full amount of the dubious warrant income, thereby saving his Fairfield flier from dipping into the red, was perhaps the main reason why he had no intention of presenting a formal reorganization plan to the IOS shareholders for approval before the July 31, 1971, deadline. Even more significant, he had wanted the purely hypothetical revenue derived from the warrants so badly that he started taking it into income eight months before the July deadline expired.

But scoring his duplicity more deeply, though he lusted for the warrant income Vesco did not want the warrants themselves to expire. They were very unusual pieces of paper and a key backup in his scheme to maintain control of IOS by stealth, an image of wealth, boardroom muscle, and financial chicanery.

"The slickest thing about the warrants was that they were powerful and remarkable instruments—with the same covenants written on the back of them as the loan agreement. Had IOS managed to prepay the loan, the warrants would have continued with the same negative control

[3] *Wall Street Journal,* June 2, 1971.

clauses written into them," International Controls president Richardson explained. He was frankly puzzled that the IOS board and IOS's various counsel had ever allowed them to come into existence.

Richardson, when he first moved up to Fairfield in the December 1970 management reshuffle—with Vesco assuming the title of chairman of the board with a salary of $120,000 a year—was astonished by the mess he found. He discovered that International Controls had twenty-three manufacturing units, which were uniformly poorly managed from an over-all corporate standpoint.

Virtually every one of Vesco's original operations had to be sold, discontinued, or consolidated in the clean-up process. The box score at the end of 1971, Richardson's first full year with the company, was three unprofitable units sold, five liquidated, and the transfer or consolidation of four others. Among the victims were Captive Seal, Special Corporation, and Drewes Manufacturing.

"Vesco made more bad mistakes—Datron, Radiation, Drewes, Special—one after another. He became enchanted with the products they had and thought he could use them as the basis for a stock promotion deal," Richardson said.

"In technical areas he was easy to con into an oversold position. The advanced technology deals became promotional devices in his mind. But they never got airborne. I've also seen his kids con him on occasion. Otherwise he was a tough guy to fool and he could charm the socks off you if he tried."

Both Radiation and Datron, two of the three new operating subsidiaries under which he intended to restructure the group's affairs, were insolvent tax-loss deals. They had aggregate losses of $8.2 million between them when Vesco acquired them.[4] Radiation was a bail-out situation, which he undertook as a "favor" for Will Snipes at American National Bank & Trust (the former Trust Company National Bank) in Morristown. Radiation owed American National $1.2 million, which Vesco agreed to make good provided the bank would lend Datron $600,000.

Datron, according to Richardson, was over $1 million in debt. It had a system for coding plastic credit cards and identification cards that was a failure. Eventually the original shell—Datron Equipment—was shut down and replaced with other International Controls assets. Still, Richardson said, Datron never worked.

Radiation Equipment had a process for turning solid waste into bricks through radiation treatment. The process worked all right, but it was the most expensive way in the world to make bricks, Richardson re-

[4] International Controls Corp. 10-K report, December 31, 1971, pp. 13 and 15.

marked. But Vesco liked it. The idea was catchy, was in vogue, and sounded good.

Another discovery Richardson made when he came to Fairfield was that Vesco had International Controls so highly leveraged it needed a cash flow of between $8 million and $9 million a year just to service its debt structure. In 1971 the company's main operating subsidiaries had a bad year. The cash flow was off sharply. But Vesco was spending more, using the company as a private bank to cover the expenses of his intercontinental ambitions.

Advances for travel were costing International Controls at least $200,000 a month, although most of it was billed back to IOS at some juncture. Vesco personally drew $200,000 a year in expense money, never going anywhere without a roll of corporate $100 bills in his pocket and rarely accounting for it to the company.

From a corporate standpoint the situation was intolerable. Frank Beatty, the chief financial officer at Fairfield, was not known to refuse a Vesco request. As a former Lybrand senior partner, he was no accounting dummy and knew how to bury more items in an accounting ledger than most experienced certified public accountants could shake a pencil at. There was never any question of personal gain: Beatty did it out of loyalty to Vesco; he felt that somehow Vesco would pull it all together. And Vesco did, raking in the required funds from IOS.

Vesco's relationship with IOS and International Controls was so rife with conflicts of interest that the SEC would have been accused of gross negligence had it not intervened to demand greater disclosure for the sake of the U.S. investor. Fast-moving Vesco did not have to wait beyond the first quarter of 1971 for the SEC to challenge his actions, and then, supremely confident of his consummate sophistry, he decided to take on the U.S. government.

Three weeks after his investiture as chairman of IOS Ltd. in the first quarter of 1971 Vesco was no doubt still congratulating himself on having made it onto an equal footing—or so he might have imagined— with the chairmen of the world's major financial institutions. After all, his horizons were no longer limited to Wall Street; his dark, piercing eyes now scanned the world at large for the best invesment opportunities.

By his own admission this had been his goal since leaving the Holly Body Shop in Detroit's Saint Claire Shores, and now he had arrived on schedule some eighteen years later. His all-consuming ambitions were challenged and then checked by a U.S. regulatory agency whose staff, in his own mind at least, comprised third-rate lawyers disgruntled with their jobs who earned salaries that were one-tenth of his own. And this, in Vesco's view, was definitely not the way the capitalist system should work.

He was fairly out of his mind with indignation when in March 1971 the SEC issued an order instituting investigative proceedings to determine, among other things, whether Vesco, International Controls, Butlers Bank, and others had violated the antifraud provisions of the federal securities laws in connection with the takeover of IOS, the sale of the Cornfeld stock, and the subsequent plans for a reorganization of the sinking offshore combine.

When asked by a federal judge to support its reasons for ordering a full-scale inquiry, the SEC responded that for a starter IOS had received "a $5 million loan solely by use of its own credit and without recourse to International Controls, while International Controls, without expending any money, gained control of IOS and stands to reap substantial profits whether or not IOS is reorganized. Surely these are facts that warrant investigation." [5]

Vesco was first subpoenaed to appear before the Commission enforcement staff on March 22, 1971. He was given a list of documents to bring with him. He did not make an appearance until April 12, 1971, when he submitted some of the documents requested but said the rest were withheld on the advice of Swiss and American counsel. He appeared before the Commission staff three more times in the two weeks that followed.

In these hearings Vesco borrowed a page from Cowett's handbook on how to stymie the SEC and, in addition to withholding certain documents, refused to answer more than sixty of the questions put to him by the enforcement staff by invoking Swiss banking secrecy. If he satisfied all the SEC's demands for information, he alleged, this would expose him to heavy fines and possible imprisonment under Swiss law.

"I can't believe that Swiss secrecy is meant to control the world. I just can't believe that," retorted Stanley Sporkin, associate director of the SEC's enforcement division at the time, after running into the same roadblock every time he confronted Vesco with a halfway delicate question.

"It just doesn't make any sense that you can use London banks, and you can use Bahamian banks, you can use U.S. citizens, and we are told that all this is bound by Swiss law. I don't think we can accept that kind of thing," Sporkin said.[6]

On April 26, 1971, Vesco countered the SEC's demands by bringing suit in the U.S. District Court for New Jersey. He sought an injunction

[5] Robert L. Vesco and International Controls Corp. *v.* Securities and Exchange Commission *et al.* Defendants' Trial Memorandum, p. 13.

[6] Vesco's SEC testimony, April 1971.

Robert Vesco speaks to Walter Cronkite and the rest of the
nation from his Costa Rican hideaway, April 1, 1974.

Courtesy CBS News

Bella Vista—scene of the seven day coup d'état, a marathon
of corporate bloodletting   *Courtesy Freddy Bertrand*

Natural resources magnate John M. King

Courtesy George Crouter/Empire/Denver Post

**James Roosevelt and his third
wife, Gladys**   *Courtesy UPI*

Vesco with
Wilbert Snipes and
Shirley Bailey on
the first day of
International Controls's
listing on the
American Stock
Exchange

Courtesy Howard A. Singer

The Al Smith Memorial Dinner, 1968

Vesco demonstrates his form for Pat and the kids
in Geneva, August, 1970.

Courtesy Kelvin Brodie
/Sunday Times of London

Norman LeBlanc aboard
Big Bobby's "Big Bird"

Courtesy UPI

Safe on the ground in San José,
Costa Rica, Vesco relaxes in his
plane, a corporate 707 with
the world's only flying sauna.

Courtesy Wide World Photos

"Yogi Bear" Hoffman, IOS Ltd. financial vice-president

Maurice Stans
Courtesy Wide World Photos

Harry L. Sears
Courtesy Wide World Photos

John N. Mitchell
Courtesy Wide World Photos

F. Donald Nixon
Courtesy UPI

Bernie Cornfeld in the
defendant's chair
in Geneva

Courtesy Freddy Bertrand

From his home in
London's Belgravia,
Cornfeld plots
his revenge
on Vesco.

*Courtesy
London Daily Express*

Don-Don Nixon, Richard's nephew

Courtesy
The Reasoner Report,
ABC News

Vesco's N11RV at San José Airport, Costa Rica

Courtesy Anne Groer,
Tico Times

"Groundskeepers" guard Vesco's compound in the Bahamas.

Courtesy
Wide World Photos

prohibiting the SEC, its five Commissioners, seven of its staff members, and the Attorney General of the United States from pressing the investigation. The SEC, in turn, cross-claimed for subpoena enforcement to compel Vesco to complete his testimony.

At the court hearings before Judge Reynier J. Wortendyke, Jr., the following month, Vesco's lawyers maintained that International Controls and its officers were not bound by the 1967 Settlement Order between the SEC and IOS, since they had not been a party to it. Therefore, Vesco's high-powered Washington attorneys requested that the court order the SEC to stop harassing their client.

The SEC's associate general counsel, Robert E. Kushner, explained the Commission's perplexity that, every time an attempt was made to obtain full disclosure from Vesco or International Controls, as required under U.S. securities laws, they "deliberately sought to cloud the complex underlying facts of their involvement with IOS in an atmosphere of secrecy." [7]

Sherwin Markman, one of the more colorful litigators in the Washington law firm of Hogan & Hartson and Vesco's lead attorney, protested vehemently. "There is nothing to hide insofar as we are concerned. . . . There is not one whit of this information which is embarrassing to us. We were brought in as a new broom to sweep this thing clean. That is what we are trying to do. But our concern—we are faced with the immutable law of Switzerland that as a director of a bank or director of this corporation if we testify to these facts we are criminally liable." [8]

Already he had painted a gushing picture for the judge that made it sound as though Vesco had acted out of a highly developed sense of public spirit in coming to the rescue of IOS, indeed having almost to be dragged to the scene of the impending disaster to accomplish the Herculean task of sweeping the stables clean over in Geneva.

> IOS was in deep financial trouble because of the machinations of its former managment. . . . The corporation was floundering. It needed help. It had investors and has investors all over the world and they came to Mr. Vesco and asked him for his help, as the records will show, and Mr. Vesco came in and negotiated an arm's-length transaction where he provided $5 million in funds and agreed to serve on the board and on the finance committee and on the executive committee, because Mr. Vesco is an extraordinary human being. At the age of thirty-five he has done wonders with himself and his company, and this kind of talent is what this company needed, because both the SEC staff and its board recognized that the company was in trouble and was in need of help. [9]

[7] Robert L. Vesco *et al. v.* Securities and Exchange Commission *et al.,* transcript of proceedings, May 24, 1971, p. 13.

[8] *Ibid.,* p. 50.

[9] *Ibid.,* pp. 36–37.

Judge Wortendyke ruled almost at the start of the proceedings that he could not be concerned with foreign secrecy laws in rendering a decision on whether the SEC should be permitted to complete its probe into the dealings of an American company and its American chairman. The plaintiffs met this loss of protective "secrecy" cover with a quick tack to starboard, suddenly challenging the objectivity and indeed the propriety of the SEC staff in its handling of the Vesco investigation.

Pursuing this line, Vesco's lead counsel Markman asked for Stanley Sporkin, the SEC's chief enforcer, to take the witness stand. As the "third-rate lawyer" heading the investigation, Sporkin had become the target of special Vesco enmity.

Emotions were running high around Fairfield. Because of the scope and breadth of the SEC's subpoenas and the effect the investigation was having on third parties, particularly creditors and customers of the company, Vesco was quite vocal on the fact that he was being victimized by a strait-laced bunch of "overzealous civil servants."

This feeling of unwarranted SEC harassment had caused him to bristle in a manner that inevitably led to a deterioration of relations between Fairfield and 500 North Capitol Street, the SEC headquarters in Washington. Vesco's reaction to the problem was not the most diplomatic, although consistent with his growing sense of power and fortune. If those small-minded bureaucrats wanted to be shitty with him, it could become a two-way street, he informed his Boonton lawyer, New Jersey state senator Harry Sears. And so it did. Vesco told Sears he wanted to get a "message" to Judge Wortendyke and let him know "that I am not a bad guy just because I am suing the Government." [10] Sears said he couldn't help. There was no way he wanted to be placed in the position of having "bought" a federal judge for Vesco.

Now Vesco's blue-ribbon trial lawyer Sherwin Markman proposed to demonstrate to the court what he said was Sporkin's "nonobjective interest" in the case, which, for reasons that were implied but remained unexpressed, had degraded the investigation into a personal vendetta.

"Are you impugning this gentleman's fidelity to his office as an employee?" the judge asked.

"I am impugning his objectivity. . . ."

"Do you charge that he should be ousted from his office?" the judge asked.

"No, sir, I do not. I merely state that insofar as the consideration of the issues before this court that there has been an abuse of discretion

[10] United States of America *v.* John N. Mitchell *et al.* Sears testimony, March 6, 1974.

by the defendants . . . and they have gone beyond their authority in such a way that the subpoenas in these instances . . . should not be enforced." [11]

It was a weak wicket to go to bat on, but it was obviously the best that Vesco and his lawyers could manage. Anyway, Markman alleged that Sporkin, in taking testimony from Dick Pershing of Hale Brothers, had said in substance that "so long as Vesco was involved with IOS there was no chance of IOS doing business in the United States." [12]

Sporkin denied any recollection of such a statement, but that was beside the point. It was consistent with Markman's endeavors to show by inference or otherwise that Sporkin had a marked hostile animus toward his client.

This attempt to discredit Sporkin and other members of the SEC staff backfired, as one might have expected, and only served to put up the backs of the SEC to an even greater degree.

Probably it was Vesco's old friend and early supporter, Malcolm McAlpin, who best understood what had gone wrong.

"When the SEC came in and started poking around he should have cooperated with them instead of fighting them. Hell, they make the rules in the securities business, and if you don't abide by the rules then you can't play the game.

"But he's a fighter, and this was the action he took. Unfortunately, he lacks humility. He wants to be bigger than the government.

"Vesco went too far too fast; I think that really sums up the whole thing."

The combination of highhanded tactics and under-the-table maneuvers Vesco employed to get the SEC off his back so that he could proceed unmolested with the plundering of IOS only worsened his position and increased the SEC's resolve to press on with a meticulous and resolute investigation.

His fatal error was the hiring in the summer of 1971 of a private detective to check on Sporkin's private and governmental actvities. He could not have chosen a worse target, for the then thirty-nine-year-old Sporkin was a tough and tenacious investigator. The son of a Philadelphia judge, with a strong background in accounting as well as law, Sporkin was rated by some members of the securities industry as "probably the best enforcement officer the SEC has ever had."

According to one member of the Vesco task force in Geneva, it was New York attorney Howard Cerny who arranged Sporkin's undercover

[11] Robert L. Vesco *et al. v.* Securities and Exchange Commission *et al.*, transcript of proceedings, May 24, 1971, pp. 159–60.
[12] *Ibid.*, p. 169.

surveillance and hired the private detective to handle the job. Cerny, however, when questioned under oath about this pleaded client-attorney privilege and refused to answer.

The private detective incident, so arrogantly stupid, backfired. Nothing was produced to cast the slightest shadow of doubt on Sporkin's activities or motives. A man who took great pride in the achievements of the enforcement division, Sporkin did not take kindly to this attempt at intimidation. Convinced that Vesco had something to hide, he threw himself into the case with more determination than ever and was credited inside the Commission with having played a principal role in developing the theories that ultimately led to the SEC's filing its well-documented civil fraud suit in November 1972.

Vesco's strategic error was not immediately recognized. In fact, in Geneva senior IOSers close to the Vesco camp boasted that "Uncle Bob" had a pipeline into the SEC's highest councils. In some instances it was said that Vesco knew within hours what decisions had been taken at private staff meetings concerning his case. When it was learned from Vesco's source inside the SEC that two SEC attorneys would come over to Geneva in early 1972 to make some inquiries, the IOS security men were placed on full alert.

The Vesco "plumbers" in Geneva wanted to put a tail on the two attorneys and find out whom they talked to and what questions they asked in order to determine the thrust of their investigation. Cerny was excited and followed the events closely. The dates of their visit to the Geneva area had been ascertained well in advance. One of the SEC travelers was known to be Thomson von Stein, a young lawyer in the enforcement division, but the identity of the second attorney traveling with him was unknown, which made the task of the Geneva "plumbers" that much more difficult.

At a strategy session conducted by Gil Straub and Dick Clay at Geneva's Intercontinental Hotel, one of the participants remarked, "Dammit, there must be some way we can compromise those guys."

"How about bribing them?" another member of the group suggested.

But that idea was quickly discarded. Finally it was decided to fix up the two attorneys, both married men, with "a couple of broads."

The first problem was to locate the unsuspecting SEC investigators. Going on the only name they had Bob King, one of the IOS security officers, phoned a buddy of his on the Geneva police force and asked if he could check through the nightly hotel registration slips to find out where this Mr. von Stein was staying. Sure enough, a von Stein was found registered at a second-class downtown hotel.

King rounded up two cooperative call girls he occasionally did business with, furnished them with hidden miniature tape recorders from the IOS security stores, and dispatched them to the hotel to make contact with the SEC agents.

After a brief conversation with the hotel concierge, *les girls* discovered that the Herr von Stein in question was a sixty-five-year-old Liechtenstein businessman and he was traveling alone. Back to the Intercontinental they went for further instructions from King.

What the IOS "plumbers" didn't know was that the two SEC sleuths, so as not to upset the Swiss, had taken the precaution of staying at a hotel in Annemasse, just across the border in France. When by chance the IOS security squad did locate them at a meeting away from their hotel it was reported back to headquarters that the unidentified person with von Stein was some "bald-headed old man." The supposedly decrepit-looking mystery man was none other than a spry thirty-five-year-old G. Bradford Cook, the future SEC chairman for a brief ten-week spell, balding indeed, and bespectacled, but hardly suffering from a *coup de vieux*, as the French would say.

But the missed von Stein connection showed to what lengths Vesco was willing to go to frustrate the official investigation of his arrogation of power and usurpation of control over the still important, though fast dwindling, IOS empire.

At the June 1971 International Controls annual general meeting in New York's Commodore Hotel Vesco again demonstrated his arrogance, which tended to confirm an early impression that he believed himself beyond the reach of the law.

Replying to a shareholder's question, he stated that an unfavorable court decision in New Jersey or further SEC sanctions would have "no impact whatsoever on our plans" to control IOS.

"Will we divest ourselves or otherwise disengage from IOS?" he asked rhetorically. "No, we will not. I can't think of any circumstances anywhere, by anyone, that would cause us to." [13]

When, early in July 1971, Judge Wortendyke, acting on the SEC counter-claim, ordered Vesco to comply with the subpoenas, Vesco's lawyers went to the U.S. Court of Appeals in Philadelphia. A bitter blow to Vesco's plans to thwart the SEC investigation came that August when the Court of Appeals denied his application to stay further testimony before the SEC staff. Vesco's lawyers took their case to the Supreme Court of the United States, where Supreme Court Justice Thurgood Marshall also threw it out. The Fifth Amendment was now the only escape route left.

The pressure, meanwhile, had become too much for Robert Slater, IOS's supposed new-broom chief executive. At a board meeting in Nassau in September 1971 Slater resigned as president and a director

[13] *Wall Street Journal,* June 3, 1971.

of IOS Ltd. Officially Slater blamed continued dissident interference in plans to restructure IOS for his decision, but his sincerity had to be doubted. The Swiss had refused him a work permit, and for months he had been working, principally on insurance-related matters, from his room at the Hotel du Golf in Divonne-les-Bains, France, making trips across the border to Geneva as infrequently as possible.

Milton Meissner, Vesco's artful and charming master of chaos, replaced Slater as president.

14

Restyling IOS

Introducing Nasty Norman the Burble, a Montreal accountant who becomes Vesco's trusted lieutenant ~ In which Vesco and the Burble tow the IOS wreckage from offshore into deep-sea waters ~ Their plans for a restructured IOS lead to the creation of two "dividend" companies, and the early travels of "the Flying Bishop"

Norman P. LeBlanc was indignant. "Canada should do away with this type of nonresident operation," he said, and his pudgy face fairly bulged with rage above the nattily cut, lightweight suit. He hunched over his desk in a securely guarded office at Charlotte House in downtown Nassau, his right hand occasionally creeping under his suit jacket to scratch his chest. This distinctive habit, limited to a single patch just below his left nipple, was so frequent that frayed threads marked the spot on his finely knit shirts.

"The Canadian Government has no business registering companies it cannot regulate," he went on, "no business at all." The upper lip trembled with moral fervor, the ever glowing cigarette described punctuating circles in the air, and Montreal's own Nasty Norman the Burble, sometime accountant, newly-minted millionaire, and self-acknowledged financial wizard, screwed his indignation to the sticking point.

"It's completely ludicrous," he said, "that IOS was allowed to sit offshore, footloose and fancy-free, and operate around the world under the shield of a Canadian company. I believe that companies should be regulated in the territories where they are incorporated and that control over those companies should be in those territories."

He fixed me with a challenging glare. I was enchanted. This, after all, was the principal partner, financial aide, and disciple of Mr. Rip-Off himself, Robert Lee Vesco, then emerging as the self-appointed investment banker to the Third World. And the piquant point of LeBlanc's argument was not only that he was dead right but that the company he was citing, IOS Ltd., was one that he and Vesco were in the process of dismantling with the precise intention of frustrating whatever future designs the Canadian authorities might have entertained regarding their regulatory responsibilities.

LeBlanc in fact was advocating the end of offshoreness and its replacement with a concept that was positively deep-sea by comparison. The great proliferation of companies that rose from the ransacked ruins of Cornfeld's empire was the most noticeable, and confusing, result of this new concept. He and Vesco had created a Sargasso Sea of corporate shells for the purpose of moving assets out of IOS and its funds and into extraterritorial waters beyond the limits of national jurisdiction. Administration of this loosely structured corporate condominium was conducted from tiny meridional republics and newly independent dominions where regulation was not the same sharply defined proposition that existed in the Northern democracies.

Almost exactly the same age—LeBlanc was one month older than Vesco—the two men also shared broadly similar social backgrounds. LeBlanc's father was a Canadian Pacific Steamships clerk who worked his way up to executive level, becoming head of the catering department before retirement. Norman had been raised in the Park Extension working-class district of Montreal and, after graduating from the Town of Mount Royal High School at seventeen, joined a nationally prominent accounting firm and spent the next five years attending night school at McGill University. He wrote his final exams in 1956, winning the Governor General's gold medal for the highest accounting marks in Canada. At twenty-six, a Sunday school teacher on the side, he became a junior partner in his accounting firm, specializing in mergers and acquisitions but also undertaking some auditing work in underdeveloped countries for the World Bank.

Then in 1969 he ran into his first trouble. He was the partner in charge of a major account that went bust amid a cloud of criminal charges. Almost until the very end, when a junior partner auditing a relatively minor Toronto subsidiary of the Montreal parent uncovered something he didn't understand and refused to certify the accounts, LeBlanc had insisted on giving the ill-fated group a clean bill of health.

The collapse of corporation Foncière de Montréal (Cofomo), which controlled the $50 million Bank of Western Canada (which never opened), caused a national scandal. The Royal Canadian Mounted Police were called in to investigate. Cofomo's two top officers endured legal wrangles. LeBlanc was called upon to do some explaining. Soon after, he decided to leave Montreal for a year or so "to broaden his horizons" in Europe. He arranged for his firm, McDonald, Currie & Company, to transfer him to the Paris office of its overseas affiliate, Coopers & Lybrand.

He was working in Paris in September 1970 when he received a call from Coopers & Lybrand's Newark office asking him to fly to Geneva for an urgent meeting with an important client, the president of International Controls Corporation. LeBlanc recalled, "I had had many of these calls before—somebody from America wanted to buy a business in Europe, particularly with the European Common Market opening up—and so I went down to Geneva expecting, you know, a sixty-year-old executive who wanted to buy some company and I find a thirty-four-year-old fellow who controls quite a big company and he said, 'I'm getting involved with IOS and need some auditing help.' At that point . . . I almost fell off my chair.

"I said, 'Well, what do you want me to do?' And like he wanted Coopers & Lybrand to make a complete investigation. I said by when, you know, and he said, 'Well, like yesterday.' And so I spent from September through till April or May commuting back and forth from Paris to Geneva, working virtually inside the IOS empire with a staff that ranged up to forty-five professional accountants."

The audit, LeBlanc said, disclosed that "at that point in time IOS had no financial controls at all. Management had no idea what was going on. . . . I found three warehouses—they didn't even know they owned them. And in one there was a pink Rolls Royce, and in the other there were two Fords . . . with a whole lot of stuff, material they didn't know was there."

"That's nonsense," huffed Cornfeld when questioned about it in Beverly Hills. "We had a corporate Rolls Royce limousine. It was black. LeBlanc might have painted it pink, but we knew every one of the cars the company had. I'm sure there were huge amounts of relatively small items that were used as contest prizes that were kept in storage. One of the things that happened when new management came in, a lot of the items that were in storage were taken out of storage and distributed to friends and family of the new management."

In the general 1971 house-cleaning, company accountants uncovered no less than twenty-one IOS warehouses spread over the countryside in the Geneva-Nyon-Ferney triangle. They contained everything from rolls of unused velvet to an old-fashioned circular bank vault door weighing several tons and included 200 tons of bonded IOS notepaper.

One astonished IOS quartermaster witnessed a $350,000 raid on the contest prize depot on Geneva's Avenue Blanc, behind the old IOS headquarters, by Vesco's men, including LeBlanc, who helped themselves to the stores. The prizes included more than 200 IOS gold watches worth over $1,000 each, large sterling silver candle lighters, hand-tooled leather backgammon sets, Polaroid Swinger cameras, gold Dunhill cigarette lighters, electric toothbrushes, Sony cassette recorders, James Bond briefcases, video tape machines, and special travel bags in which to carry away the loot.

Vesco's jet, parked at Geneva airport, was loaded with the booty and flown back to the United States. Also shipped to decorate the Vesco home in Boonton were cases of paintings and statuary from the offices, including a bronze Balinese dancing girl that once stood in Cornfeld's office. Eventually dozens of the gold watches were shuttled on to a new bonded depot in Nassau rather than remain in New Jersey, where Vesco would have been required to pay duty on them. Before the booty left, however, Vesco handed out the IOS "millionaire" watches to friends around Fairfield. One of the recipients was young Donald Nixon, Jr., the President's nephew, and another was Ted Simmons, then a senior vice-president at Prudential in Newark and the contact man on the International Controls account.

Toward the end of his investigative audit, and after putting in motion the programs that slashed IOS's operating expenses from an annualized rate of $90 million at the time of the crisis to $22 million twelve months later,[1] LeBlanc was offered the job of IOS's financial vice-president at an annual salary of $85,000. This entailed replacing "Yogi Bear" Hoffman, who had outserved his usefulness. Hoffman was directed into semiretirement with a $100,000 termination package and a $100,000-a-year sinecure as head of an "independent" service operation in Amsterdam.

LeBlanc accepted Vesco's offer and was appointed to his new functions on July 1, 1971, the day that Vesco won the bitterly fought proxy contest against the dissidents in Toronto.

At the time of the LeBlanc audit, IOS Ltd. represented the summit of a pyramid that managed more than $1.2 billion in other people's money. The parent company presided over five top-line subsidiaries, one for each of the main operating fields: sales, fund management, banking, insurance, and real estate. Under these five key subsidiaries came the more than 250 other companies around the world that made up the incredibly complex corporate maze known as the Investors Overseas Services group.

LeBlanc's tendency to "burble" when he talked earned him the unloving sobriquet "the Burble" among the drones who worked under him at IOS. The profession of accounting, to which he was introduced by his captain in the Montreal Boys' Brigade, he regarded as a vehicle that would lead him to the Good Life, with all the accoutrements of

[1] IOS Ltd. Annual Report for 1971, President's Letter.

power and influence that money could buy. Which was the antithesis of his upbringing. His forefathers were hardy Norman sailors from the French fishing village of Honfleur. His mother was of staunch Scottish Presbyterian stock. She brought up Norman, his younger brother (also an accountant), and a sister with a healthy respect for the Protestant work ethic. Where Norman's respect for generally accepted accounting principles went is hard to say.

"Norman was a very effective administrator. But there was one major problem; he had no conception of the difference between right and wrong," said a young lawyer in the IOS legal department who turned down a stock bribe to continue the cruise into deeper offshore waters with the Burble and his crew.

LeBlanc's almost boyish exterior manner hid the cool inner instincts of a gambler. An exceptionally gifted accountant, he was a specialist at "untracking" difficult loans, passing control through a "daisy chain of companies," "rolling back" maneuvers, the "exing out" of unwanted entries, "mushrooming" the independent auditors, and "dividending out" the hard assets of a corporation on a Chinese paper route into a regulatory vacuum—delectable methods he had been able to observe firsthand while working on the Cofomo books.

"Everything has a price, and if the price is right, I'll sell it," was his self-professed philosophy.

Whether justly or not, LeBlanc took credit for the restructuring plans that slowly emerged from the shambles in Geneva. The theory behind these efforts was to divorce IOS's hard assets from its considerable liabilities by placing as much "Chinese paper" between the two as possible (a technique to be described in detail later).

The plans started taking shape in June 1971 with the transfer of a major portion of IOS Ltd.'s assets and corporate functions to its principal subsidiary, Investors Overseas Services Management Limited (IOSML). This was important, for it put the various pieces of the IOS group in place for the coming spin-outs, which would leave IOS Ltd. an empty shell.

LeBlanc's rationalization for transforming IOS Ltd. into a passive holding company was the hostile legislation recently elaborated against the Geneva-based combine in several European countries, particularly its home base of Switzerland, as well as a number of technical considerations such as the $8 million King Resources Company loan which Vesco had no intention of repaying.

Under the new Swiss law on foreign mutual funds, which became binding in August 1971, the federal authorities no longer tolerated the marketing, management, or administration of mutual funds from a Swiss base unless the funds in question were registered with the Federal

Banking Commission. There was no chance for the IOS funds to obtain registration—structurally they were unable to comply with the new regulations.

A search for a new operations base initially centered on Britain, but as early as April 1971 it was concluded that the sweeping provisions of the British Prevention of Fraud (Investments) Act of 1958 precluded a move to London for all but a fund management service unit.

"The wording of this legislation is drawn so widely that in many instances it is innocently breached by highly reputable U.K. operations," an internal fifteen-page memo on the subject stated.[2] Obviously this would not do for Vesco, as his intentions were anything but innocent. Nassau was the chosen alternative with the result that the Bahamas became the front line of defense in the ensuing battle with the SEC and other regulatory bodies.

Meanwhile, the transfer of assets and operating functions to IOSML went ahead as planned. This cunning shift of some of the corporate goodies, but also most of the corporate expenses from the parent to the income-rich subsidiary was presented in such a complex manner that few people understood its double intent.

IOSML's initial public offering in 1968 of 600,000 shares—representing 20 per cent of its issued share capital—had been devised by Ed Cowett as the appetite-warmer for the IOS Ltd. underwriting one year later. The IOSML stock was relatively low-priced at less than nine times earnings to find favor with investors, and Cowett had structured the company in such a way that no operating expenses were levied against its income. The income resulted entirely from the management fees of the major IOS mutual funds; the management contracts of the funds were IOSML's only assets.

The IOSML stock came out on the Toronto Stock Exchange at $12.50 and within months had soared to $125 a share, split three-for-one, and kept on climbing till it hit $210 a share in pre-split terms. Thereafter the stock slipped gradually backward as IOS fund redemptions increased in early 1970 to catastrophic proportions, and it eventually ended up trading around $2 a share.

The cash flow that IOSML received from the funds ran straight through the company and was dividended out the other end—80 per cent to the parent company, IOS Ltd., and 20 per cent to the public shareholders.

Over the next two years, IOSML paid a total of approximately $6.6 million in dividends to its public shareholders, and in Vesco's esprit this represented an awful lot of money needlessly lavished upon the

---

[2] Report on Possible Move of Functions to London, April 15, 1971. Memorandum prepared by Michael Rogers.

gullible public investors that could be diverted usefully to other ends. But in 1970 an even more compelling reason emerged for altering IOSML's dividend policy. As security for the $8 million loan from King Resources Company, IOS had pledged four million IOSML shares which were deposited with the First Jersey National Bank of Jersey City as the pledge-holder. The dividends on this stock should have flowed to the pledge-holder, which meant parting with an additional 33 per cent of IOSML's net income.

Vesco's strategy was to curb this outpouring of cash. On the pretext of turning IOSML, which he renamed Transglobal Financial Services, into an independent operating unit so that "in the future it did not have to fear any repercussions from the difficulties facing IOS," certain assets said to be "essential to the continued functioning of the corporation" were transferred from the parent to Transglobal.

Included in these "assets" were virtually all the operating expenses which up to that point had been paid by IOS Ltd., such as fund accounting, custodial bookkeeping, portfolio management, computer costs, and assorted legal fees. The allocation of these expenses against Transglobal's gross cash flow effectively meant that there would be no more income available for dividends, thereby depriving the public shareholders of any hope of further return.

Expenses should be shifted to where the income lay, and in the long run this would represent a better deal for the shareholders—such was the announced reasoning for the redeployment of these "assets." "Which was so much bullshit," said a LeBlanc accounting mechanic. In reality the minority (public) shareholders, plus the pledge-holder of the King Resources Company loan, had been short-changed by a basic altering of the charge structure.

"Suddenly the public shareholders, after having had an interest in pure jam, found they had an interest in pure shit," the accountant stated, unable to conceal his lightly muffled amusement.

The July 1971 New Brunswick injunction brought by the dissidents following their defeat by Vesco in Toronto came in the middle of LeBlanc's restructuring plans, forcing a pause in the replumbing work. This interruption allowed Vesco and LeBlanc time to sit back and study once again how they were going to rip off the banks, insurance companies, and real estate components.

Vesco was outraged. The injunction caused them to shift into the drafting of "Plan B for a Restructured IOS" which reflected in part International Controls's increased equity participation in IOS itself brought on by the dissident revolt.

"Plan B" foresaw the creation of two "dividend" companies into which the remaining assets of IOS would be transferred. The shares of these two companies were to be distributed as a dividend to the stock-holders of IOS, with Vesco's company receiving the control block. One dividend company was to be in banking with the name International Bancorp Limited, and the other was to operate in insurance and real estate under the name Value Capital Limited.

Vesco was fascinated by IOS's commercial and investment banking operations and the possibilities that an international banking network would offer a man of his talents. The reasons for his fascination were threefold. The banks had apparent and solid value. Also, he needed a banking pillar to use as a future depository for the funds. And there was this scheme—almost a mania with him—to merge IOS's banking assets with Butlers Bank and make Allan Butler a major world banker. World banker, perhaps, but one well tied to the skirts of Uncle Bob Vesco.

Allan Butler and his wife Shirley had come to Geneva in early 1971 for talks with Vesco and LeBlanc concerning the proposed marriage, and plans were drawn up to sell them a controlling interest in IOS Financial Holdings for $4 million in cash "and some short-fused notes."

Shirley Oakes Butler was the handsome daughter of Sir Harry Oakes, the legendary American-born prospector who staked his claim in 1912 to a Kirkland Lake property in northern Ontario that became Lake Shore Mines, often described as the world's richest gold strike. Irascible old Sir Harry was murdered in Nassau in July 1943. Staunchly opposed to the introduction of gambling to the Bahamas, his unsolved murder, according to one theory, was ordered by the Mob.

Of the four surviving children, his second daughter Shirley inherited most of the old man's single-minded determination. She also inherited one-fifth of the Oakes fortune, which made her one of the richest young women in North America. After graduating at the top of her class from Yale Law School, she worked for a while as a lawyer in New York. However, her pursuit of a legal career ended when she married Allan Butler, the son of a Boston doctor, later setting him up in the banking business with the purchase by Lewis-Oakes Limited, a family holding company, of a banking shell, which became Butlers Bank Limited.

Preliminary contracts were drawn up for the sale of the IOS banking operations to the Butlers, with Vesco retaining virtual veto power over board decisions in this new association of interests. But the contracts were never executed. Last-minute political considerations and a general disenchantment with Allan Butler as a world banker caused Vesco to back away.

In the late summer of 1971 a British lawyer on the IOS payroll in Ferney-Voltaire by the name of Michael Rogers went down to Nassau to begin the legal spadework. Rogers, a hefty former RAF water polo champion with a deep-dimpled chin and the pious manner of a country clergyman, traveled back and forth between Nassau and Ferney so often that summer that his colleagues at IOS dubbed him "The Flying Bishop." With the Bishop on the spot gathering material for recasting the IOS banking network, it emerged that Butlers Bank was in worse condition than originally thought. This cemented the need for a change in concept, which brought another Harvard alumnus, Frederic Weymar, to the fore.

The existence of "Plan B"—the spinning out from IOS of the dividend companies—was kept a carefully guarded secret inside the company and certainly was never disclosed to shareholders, who were given no opportunity to approve or modify its contents. Of course, in most jurisdictions such a massive restructuring of the corporate undertaking would require shareholder approval.

But IOS shareholders were so geographically dispersed that Vesco and LeBlanc obviously felt this was not necessary. And then, who among the shareholders would know that bylaw four of the company's revised statutes stated under clause (3) (a) (iv) that "none of the shares in the capital of the company may be subdivided, consolidated, reclassified, or changed into a different number and/or class of shares," and (v) "the company shall not voluntarily wind-up its affairs, surrender its charter, sell, lease or otherwise dispose of its assets and undertaking as an entirety or substantially as an entirety or take other steps with a view to the discontinuance of its business" without a two-thirds approval of the holders of each class of shares.

Nevertheless, just twenty-two days after the New Brunswick restraining order was lifted in October 1971, the inception of International Bancorp Limited was announced, along with the transfer to it of all IOS's European and Caribbean banking interests. In exchange for contributing its banking assets, IOS received 5,643,000 common shares of Bancorp, representing 70 per cent of the 8.1 million outstanding shares and $8,655,000 of Bancorp debentures.

The first IOS shareholders learned of this development was through newspaper reports informing them that a stock and debenture dividend had been issued. The mechanics of the dividend were such that shareholders would receive one share of International Bancorp and $1 face amount of Bancorp debentures for every ten shares of IOS common and preferred stock.

A letter from IOS president Meissner to shareholders followed a few weeks later setting out some of the more intimate details, including news that International Bancorp had been formed in the Bahamas the week before the dividend was declared. It emerged from the letter that 30 per cent of the Bancorp stock had been shunted out under unclear circumstances in return for some hard-to-evaluate assets.

In effect the IOS board of directors, having approved the spin-out at a meeting in Nassau in early October 1971, had dealt 22 per cent of the banking cake directly to International Controls, 48 per cent to the other IOS shareholders, and the remaining 30 per cent to banker Frederic Weymar in exchange for 100 per cent of a spanking new Nassau bank, Bahamas Commonwealth Bank, whose only assets appeared to consist of its rather grandiose name and the Bahamian loan and investment portfolio of troubled Butlers Bank.

Weymar, who was then appointed International Bancorp's president, was well versed in the complexities of international banking. The founder and former chairman of Bache & Company's German subsidiary, Bankhaus Bache GmbH, in March 1968 Weymar had the shock of discovering that a sizable fraud had taken place in the German offices of Bache. Two of Bache's German salesmen were found to have opened dummy trading accounts and were using them in the hope of hidden profit. Weymar had no involvement in these shady dealings, but the fraud had occurred in a rapidly expanding operation where he was the allied partner in charge.

The incident contributed heavily to the deficit shown in Bache's 1968 accounts, and the firm feared it might become the target of disciplinary action by the New York Stock Exchange under rule 405, "Diligence as to Accounts." Protectively, therefore, the local allied partner's head was placed on the block, and at the end of December 1968 Weymar resigned.

Weymar, who was in his late thirties at the time, left Bache a wiser man. Very persuasive, immensely popular among his peers in the Bache organization, and "a hell of a good salesman," on January 1, 1969 he joined Butlers Bank as one of its three managing directors.

Bache and Butlers had enjoyed a lengthy and profitable relationship. The Nassau bank was Bache's single largest international client, and Shirley Butler for a time had been a registered representative in Bache's branch office in Nassau, "handling" the Butlers account.

Three years after joining Butlers, Weymar hitched his banking career to the Vesco bandwagon, hoping to turn a quick profit on the International Bancorp stock he had picked up in the process and which Vesco had assured him would benefit from the floating of a planned Bancorp public issue in Amsterdam the following year. Events conspired against Weymar, however, and the offering never took place.

How Weymar acquired the Bahamas Commonwealth Bank shell was not disclosed to IOS shareholders, but had the information been made available it would hardly have reassured them. In fact, Weymar purchased the empty BCB carcass from Butlers Bank only days before

International Bancorp's creation. He paid a total of $1.8 million for the shell—Bahamas Commonwealth Bank's initial capitalization—but only $300,000 was in cash. The $300,000 was raised by selling his Butlers Bank stock back to the Lewis-Oakes holding company. The remainder was paid in two short-term promissory notes. He then traded the Bahamas Commonwealth Bank stock for 30 per cent of International Bancorp's stock having a book value of $2.5 million.

In this exchange Weymar was not required to accept any of Bancorp's debentures, which left IOS holding roughly $3 million in excess International Bancorp debt that had not been distributed to IOS shareholders. These debentures, Meissner said in his November 5, 1971, letter to shareholders, "will provide an additional element of liquidity to IOS and thereby add stability to the continued holdings and operations of IOS." This statement showed monumental hypocrisy on Meissner's part, since the placing of IOS's banking assets in International Bancorp was the second of three operations (the first being the Transglobal contrivance) which doomed IOS to destruction, a fate the sophisticated Meissner could hardly have ignored when he wrote his November 1971 letter.

What eventually became of that $3 million in International Bancorp debt was in itself an interesting episode. Six months later the debentures were taken over from IOS by Bahamas Commonwealth Bank in exchange for $3.2 million in subordinated capital notes. As it turned out these notes were subordinated to every existing debt at Bahamas Commonwealth Bank, causing them to be jocularly referred to by staff at the bank as the "insubordinate dentures." In July 1973 the notes were removed from the IOS offices in Geneva and taken to Bahamas Commonwealth Bank on the pretext that they "needed the bank's corporate seal put on them." Needless to say that was the last anyone in Geneva saw of the insubordinate dentures. They were never returned.

The slippery Meissner letter to shareholders indicated that the new bank holding company had assets of $100.8 million, but upon analysis of the details given under the heading "liabilities and stockholders' investment" it was discovered—although not readily apparent from the information provided—that all but $7.4 million of these assets were counter-balanced by liabilities.

In addition, IOS shareholders were charged a well-padded $406,000 starting-up fee relative to International Bancorp's formation expenses, a bit steep when one considered that the charge for registering a company in the Bahamas was less than $500, but which in part reflected the cost of doing business in the tax-free but payola-prone island commonwealth. As a rule of thumb, one Bancorp director explained, it cost $20,000 under the table for every three-year work permit acquired, and Bancorp required at least seven for its foreign personnel. This conceivably accounted for $140,000 of the starting-up costs, but most of the remainder allegedly was accounted for in a "rollback" exercise that later became associated with the New York phase of Watergate.

Weymar, meanwhile, had brought with him from Butlers Bank a loan portfolio of an unstated amount along with liabilities of $3.4 million. The loan portfolio included a $200,000 mortgage to Lynden O. Pindling, Prime Minister of the Bahamas, and another to Paradise Bakeries, a Bahamian bakery owned by Pindling's relatives. Both Pindling concerns were in arrears on interest payments, insiders said, but were allowed to lie dormant for political reasons.

Other loans soon extended by Bahamas Commonwealth Bank included $100,000 to Dick Clay, a director of the new bank, for the purchase of a home in Bernardsville, New Jersey. Weymar, who had gone to Europe to manage International Bancorp's operations there, stated, "The first I knew of the Clay loan was when I read about it in the newspapers."

IOS director James Roosevelt also borrowed $150,000 from Vesco's new Nassau bank, collateralized in part by a collection of his father's memorabilia.[3]

Although one might have wondered how, Bahamas Commonwealth Bank did manage to attract some reputable names onto its board of directors. In addition to Vesco, Weymar, Straub, and Clay, there was Arthur McZier, a thirty-seven-year-old black American who was assistant administrator of the U.S. Small Business Administration in Washington. McZier, a graduate of Loyola University, Chicago, was in charge of a $250 million program to build a stronger minority business community in America. Vesco groomed McZier as the acting chairman of the bank, a post he filled for only a few months until the heat of the SEC civil fraud proceedings forced him to resign. McZier returned to the fold one year later, however, when he left his Small Business Administration post to become chief executive officer of General Bahamian Companies Limited, a pint-sized conglomerate acquired by the Vesco group in later dealings with Allan and Shirley Butler.

[3] In testimony before the SEC in early November 1972, Vesco's New York attorney Howard Cerny said of this loan and its unusual collateral: "[Roosevelt] had an action pending in England. The proceeds from that, if any, were put up as collateral. . . . It was an action against a newspaper, in relation to a libel action, as I recall it. And that action was pending, and it was felt that the action had merit, and the proceeds, if any, [were] put up as collateral. And I think that all of the personal stuff he had in his house involving his dad was put up for collateral because I know there was an itemization, an appraisal with an itemization. . . . He was tied up in knots, I know, on that one, because I thought it was a very strenuous agreement as far as he was concerned. In other words virtually everything that he had was tied up to collateralize the loan." Howard F. Cerny testimony, November 2, 1972, SEC file No. HO-520, pages 153–54.

Also on the Bahamas Commonwealth Bank board were Harry L. Sears, the Boonton lawyer who had been Republican majority leader in the New Jersey Senate and chairman of New Jersey's Committee to Re-elect the President, and Will Snipes, senior vice-president of American National Bank & Trust of Morristown. For several months Snipes performed as BCB's acting managing director.

The completed International Bancorp operation left IOS shareholders puzzled but silent. This complacency on the part of the shell-shocked majority seemed to augur well for the New Jersey financier and possibly encouraged him to incorporate more brazen designs into his plans for a stripped-out IOS.

After letting the dust of the International Bancorp spinoff settle, Vesco flew back to Geneva at the end of November 1971 to continue with Plan B's stage-two launching. He agreed to be interrogated by the dean of Geneva's examining magistrates, Judge Robert Pagan, concerning a stockholder complaint.

This small but dangerous time bomb was a criminal action brought against Vesco, Meissner, and Ulrich Strickler. The complaint by former sales manager David Tucker alleged that Vesco and the other two IOS directors had illegally removed 56,000 IOS Ltd. preferred shares from Tucker's account at Overseas Development Bank in Geneva and sold them to American Interland, that ubiquitous Canadian subsidiary of International Controls. The unlawful transaction took place exactly four days before the 1971 annual general meeting in Toronto.

Vesco considered the Tucker case a patently minor affair, designed and brought against him purely for nuisance purposes. Tucker, originally from Memphis, Tennessee, had been listed as a member of the dissident slate of directors. It was his misfortune, however, to have a loan of about $35,000 outstanding at Overseas Development Bank, collateralized in part with his IOS stock. Tucker's shares were "inadvertently" included among the 135,000 shares Vesco and Strickler, on a visit to the bank the Saturday before the Toronto meeting, had physically removed from the vaults.

Tucker was tipped off to what had happened and flew to Geneva from his home in Paris. His shares, he was told at the bank, had been sold that same afternoon to American Interland at 22 cents a share so that Vesco could vote them in Toronto. Tucker threatened to go to the police and report this "theft" forthwith. Realizing that he had overstepped his authority as a director of the bank, Vesco ordered the shares returned to ODB in time for Tucker to vote them himself.

Two weeks later Tucker brought suit in Geneva, alleging improper conduct, fraud, and attempted embezzlement by the IOS command.

In his session with Vesco on the last day of November 1971, Judge Pagan concentrated on establishing beyond a flicker of doubt that the Fairfield financier and his henchmen had physically removed the 135,000 shares, Tucker's included, from the ODB offices when the bank was closed for business instead of disposing of them through normal banking procedures.

It mattered very little to Judge Pagan that Vesco and his cohorts controlled the company that owned the holding company that controlled the bank, nor that all three were directors of the bank. It further did not impress him that Vesco had obtained legal opinions from two of the most respected members of the Geneva bar which approved the share sales provided certain criteria were met. "Anyone," the judge remarked curtly, "can buy a legal opinion."

What was later characterized as a "dialogue of the deaf" continued for about two hours in Pagan's office at the Palais de Justice, with Vesco endeavoring to impress upon the crusty old judge his importance as a businessman, the extent of his international connections, and the value of his time. Pagan, short of patience, finally responded by signaling his clerk to call for a gendarme.

Pagan turned back to Vesco and, choosing his words deliberately, announced in French, "You have endangered the reputation of Swiss banking by your actions. I intend to set an example in your case to demonstrate that Swiss justice knows no double standard. . . . *Il est dans votre propre interêt, donc, que je décerne contre vous un mandat d'arrêt.*"

Vesco, who spoke no French, was perplexed and asked the interpreter, "What did he say?"

"He said you're under arrest," the interpreter replied flatly.

"What, what?" Vesco reportedly stammered, unable to believe his ears.

"He said you and your colleagues are going to jail," the interpreter repeated.

As Vesco was led from the judge's office by a uniformed police officer he turned to Tucker, who stood across the room, and was heard to remark, "Well, you got me that time, you bugger."

A bail hearing was set for the following afternoon. Before then nothing could be done; an examining magistrate's decision in Switzerland is beyond appeal until it comes before the Chambre d'Accusation. This meant that the three executives were doomed to spend the night in Geneva's 150-year-old Saint Antoine Prison.

When news of the arrest was carried back to IOS, shock and consternation spread among the remaining troops—there were then about

700 of them still in the Geneva area, down from a pre-crisis high of 2,500, but there would be fewer than 150 by the following year. The Swiss authorities, it appeared, wanted Vesco and company out of the country, and this was their blunt way of putting the message across.

Meanwhile, behind the scenes the machinery of influence began to rumble. As soon as word was relayed back to Harry Sears in Boonton, he put a call through to the U.S. Attorney General, John N. Mitchell, to see if he could do anything to help. Vesco boasted a warm relationship with Mitchell, and his numerous contributions to the Republican cause were not to be forgotten. Thus Mitchell, after hearing from Sears, immediately put through a call from his office at the Justice Department to the American Embassy in Berne and spoke with the counselor, Richard Vine.

"All possible pressure must be applied in the appropriate Swiss quarters to secure Vesco's earliest release," an astonished Vine was reported to have been told. A second call was put through to the Vesco home in Boonton to assure Pat Vesco that everything possible was being done to win her husband's freedom. Mitchell later called back Harry Sears in Boonton to say that he believed Vesco would be released on bail the following day.[4]

In the crowded Geneva courtroom next day, Vesco's Swiss lawyer, Maître Alain Farina, characterized Judge Pagan's arrest order as "unprecedented, inadmissable, and of exceptional gravity." Nevertheless, the assistant public prosecutor for the Canton of Geneva requested that the arrest warrants be maintained. The assistant prosecutor did agree, however, to bail upon the posting by Vesco of a $125,000 bond and bonds of $25,000 each for Meissner and Strickler.

A black limousine from the bank was parked outside the courthouse containing two IOS security officers and over one million dollars in cash. When the bail was finally fixed the money quickly was posted and the three directors were released that same night. They were driven across town to the IOS duplex apartment at 147 rue de Lausanne, a block away from the old corporate headquarters. A coming-out dinner of sorts was ordered in from the IOS Bull and Bear Pub a few doors down the road. Vesco, a member of his entourage said, savored more than usual his favorite drink of Crown Royal whisky that night as he began planning his revenge.

"If they are going to treat me like a criminal, then I'm going to act like one," he told a number of his closest collaborators.

Said another associate, "After his night in prison, the IOS reorganization plan changed drastically. It became 'Full Speed Ahead Irregular.'"

[4] Harry L. Sears, SEC testimony, New York, February 20, 1973, p. 70.

Next day Vesco left Geneva with the intention of never returning. Meissner moved across the frontier to France and for many months ran the company from a hotel room in the gambling resort of Divonne-les-Bains. Strickler was transferred to Munich, also out of Judge Pagan's immediate reach.

Vesco's arrest and subsequent departure from Geneva led to significant modifications of the plans for a Restructured IOS, even though the restructuring continued without an apparent change of pace.

As a preliminary maneuver, within days of Vesco's release from Saint Antoine IOS was caused to repay the $5 million lent to it by ICC Investments Limited just over a year before. The repayment schedule, including of all outstanding default claims against IOS by the lender and the repurchase by IOS of the remaining warrants, amounted to $6,367,420. A small portion of this amount—$517,420—went to Hale Brothers for their early help in putting the initial loan package together. In addition, IOS was required to issue not 4 million but 6 million common shares as a premium to ICC Investments Limited against retirement of the bulk of the warrants. This boosted International Controls's equity participation in the offshore complex an extra 6 per cent, from 32 per cent to 38 per cent, just in time for the second spinoff, which took place the very next day.

In this second hiving off of IOS's assets, most of the group's insurance operations along with substantially all of the real estate holdings were transferred to another newly formed Bahamian shell company, Value Capital Limited. Sixty-two per cent of Value Capital's stock went to individual IOS shareholders as a pro-rata dividend. The remaining 38 per cent was paid to International Controls.

The IOS accountants gave the assets received by Value Capital a scant $1.3 million book value. Yet within four days of this transfer the former IOS assets were written up in Value Capital's books to around $20 million on a basis which Coopers & Lybrand refused to accept. "The valuation of such assets is not susceptible to substantiation by auditing procedures," the auditors' report to Value Capital shareholders stated.[5]

The $5 million loan principal repayment, incidentally, went traveling on a circular route through Butlers Bank and back to IOS. In effect, IOS had "rescued" itself with its own money. It was an achievement virtually unique in the annals of international finance, and one which the interim IOS directors under Sir Eric Windmill, who after all had made it all possible by accepting the onerous loan agreement, could feel somewhat less than proud. They had handed over the assets of a giant public

[5] Value Capital Limited 1971 Report, Coopers & Lybrand report to the shareholders, dated August 31, 1972.

corporation that controlled the investments of close to a million people to a band of financial marauders. At least Cornfeld, with all the egg on his face, had been correct in that respect.

"The impression I had of Vesco at the time we first met was that I would hesitate to leave any loose change around, let alone put him in a position where he had an active voice in a major corporation like IOS that was in the fiduciary business and that was responsible for the management and safekeeping of other people's money," said a vacant-looking Cornfeld in early 1973, a few weeks before his own arrest by the authorities in Geneva.

The two spinoffs—International Bancorp and Value Capital—left IOS with only three assets: International Life Insurance Company (UK) Limited, which was transferred to Value Capital the following year and then sold to a British banking group, some real estate in Geneva and Ferney-Voltaire, and its stock in Transglobal Financial Services.

There was considerable debate at the Nassau board meetings that approved the International Bancorp and Value Capital dividends over whether IOS was solvent at the time. So concerned were the dummy directors about attaching their names to the transactions that they abstained from the voting, leaving it to the committed Vesco men to push the motions through with only mute misgivings.

Article 85 (5) of the Canada Corporations Act was in the forefront of their thoughts. It states:

> Where the directors of the company declare and pay any dividend when the company is insolvent, or any dividend the payment of which renders the company insolvent, or that impairs the capital of the company, they are, until repayment of the dividends so declared and paid, jointly and severally liable to the company and to its creditors for the debts of the company then existing or thereafter contracted, but such liability is limited to the amount of such dividends and interest that have not been repaid to the company.

With International Bancorp and Value Capital safely in place, Plan B for a Restructured IOS was completed, permitting a deeper phase of corporate rape to begin in the new year.

Not long afterward it was disclosed that IOS's losses for 1971 were reduced to $10.57 million from the previous year's record deficit of $60.35 million. At first this 84 per cent "improvement" in operations was portrayed as one of new management's more positive achievements. But the company already had divested itself of most of its underlying assets "so as to protect the shareholders' interests." Therefore, Meissner thoughtfully cautioned in his president's letter accompanying the 1971 annual report that "no meaningful comparison can be made with the previous year's financial results." In fact, so well were the underlying assets "protected" that by the time the IOS winding-up proceedings began in 1973 official Canadian liquidators envisaged up to ten years of legal battling in numerous jurisdictions to win them back again.

15

Flying High in a Mortgaged 707

*"Big Bobby" buys himself a $2 million plaything and, with a
nephew of the U.S. President as factotum/flunky, sets out to impress rulers and other important people in faraway places ⁓
Vesco meets with a New Jersey mobster to ask a favor, cavorts
with London strumpets, gets arrested in Geneva, and then insti-
gates a conspiracy of intelligence-gathering and blackmail to have
the charges against him dropped*

"Hey, Alwyn, I've been looking all over for you," the man in
the mauve shirt, well-cut slacks, and Gucci shoes said excitedly as he
bounded through the doorway into the air-conditioned lobby of the
Halcyon Balmoral Beach Hotel on Nassau's West Road, a few miles
from the airport.

Captain Alwyn Eisenhauer was standing at the front desk glancing
over his bill before checking out. He was neatly dressed in tropical
uniform, coatless with a short-sleeved shirt, epaulettes, and navy blue
trousers. Beside him on the counter lay a black briefcase marked
N11RV.

"I've gotta great guy outside I wantcha to meet. His name's Dick
Nixon," exclaimed the near-breathless young executive. He was holding
a small walkie-talkie with a whip antenna that danced up and down
in front of him as he approached the desk where Captain Eisenhauer
was standing. He stopped, peering intently at Eisenhauer from behind
mirrored aviators' glasses, hoping to detect a reaction.

There was none. Obviously Eisenhauer had been through similar
routines from the same source before and had grown used to them.

"Not the *real* Dick Nixon," the exuberant, collegiate-looking executive quickly added. "My kid cousin. He's outside in the car, just about
to leave. Come on out, it'll only take a minute."

"Look, Don, I have to hurry. Bob wants the aircraft ready for takeoff right after the meeting. I've got to get out to the airport."

Just then the walkie-talkie crackled into life. "Don-ya-there-Don?" the little box asked.

Donald A. Nixon, the twenty-six-year-old nephew of the President of the United States, responded affirmatively.

"For Chrissakes, willya get your ass out to the Island on the double? Bob wants to see you," the box commanded.

"Okay, okay," Don Nixon replied, his feeling of self-importance in no way diminished by being treated with the same amount of respect one might show a prairie dog.

Vesco acquired Don-Don Nixon and a personal Boeing 707 at about the same time—in mid-1971—and used them both unfailingly to win influence and attract attention in his quick rise to international notoriety. Don-Don had come into the Vesco camp through the good offices of Gilbert R. J. Straub, the director of European services for International Controls, as a personal favor to his father, F. Donald Nixon, the President's then fifty-five-year-old brother.

"Junior," as Straub called Don-Don, recently had completed his military service as a drill instructor at the Great Lakes Naval Training Center in Illinois and was not at all interested in earning a living.

According to Straub, the Nixons were worried about young Donald's future. He had been "off in the hills" of California living with a hippie commune and was generally giving the family some concern, particularly since his uncle at the time was blaming the hippies for stirring up resistance to his Vietnam policy.

Anthony Ulasewicz, the former New York City detective who was a member of the White House Special Investigations Unit, was sent into the hills to retrieve Junior and bring him back to the San Clemente White House, where top Presidential aide John Ehrlichman informed him of the Vesco job offer.

Straub, Vesco's short and paunchy good-humor man, had offered to take Junior over to Europe as his personal assistant. In a memorandum to International Controls headquarters in Fairfield explaining the details, Straub wrote, "With the agreement of Robert L. Vesco I have secured the services of Don Nixon Jr. . . . Per our recent conversation we have agreed to compensate him monthly as a 'consultant.' "

Before leaving for Europe, Don-Don was given a lengthy lecture by Ehrlichman, who told him to behave himself overseas. Ehrlichman warned young Nixon not to tell the world he was working for Bernie Cornfeld's ex-outfit. International Controls was not yet the "International Disaster" of one year later, although it was under SEC investigation at the time, and Ehrlichman instructed Don-Don to reply to anybody who asked that he worked for the Fairfield complex in Europe. Don-Don was given a contact number to call at the White House any hour of the night or day should he need help or advice, and was sent on his way, entrusted to the good care of Gil Straub.

Don Nixon, Jr., turned up in Ferney-Voltaire in July 1971, announced he was a "real estate executive" working for Straub, and apparently was placed on Indevco's payroll for a while, although Indevco, IOS's chief operating subsidiary in the real estate field, was overstaffed and laying off bodies wholesale.

The IOS security staff was given instructions to treat Don-Don with special care, make sure that he kept out of trouble, and report any hint of same to "Gauleiter" Straub, as Vesco's close confidant became known as a result of his stern babysitting demeanor. And trouble soon developed.

At a house party in France given by one of the Ferney employees, Don-Don turned up uninvited and announced to David Tucker, who was in the process of bringing criminal charges against young Nixon's employer, "I'm traveling incognito, but you know who I am, don't you?"

Tucker, who had never seen Nixon before, replied no, he had no idea. Don-Don didn't keep Tucker in suspense but immediately told him, as was his custom upon meeting someone for the first time, that he was the President's nephew. Tucker found that very interesting and asked what Don-Don was doing in the Geneva area. The next day Don Nixon, Jr., was reported to the police as working illegally in France. He was quickly shifted to Munich while red-faced IOS officials requested a temporary work permit for him in Ferney.

When Don-Don returned to Ferney a few weeks later, Gauleiter Straub ordered him to stop his after-work drinking with the crew of young IOSers that hung out at The Club, the gatehouse of Voltaire's chateau transformed by Cornfeld into a discotheque for the IOS staff; Don-Don talked too much. When his relationship with one of the Ferney secretaries became too intense, the attractive young Frenchwoman was told to break it off.

Although described as "a fast-car fiend" (he claimed to have a Porsche and Sting Ray back home), Don-Don was only given a powder blue Volkswagen to drive in Europe. While "Dangerous Don" stormed on to new and more reckless conquests in the rented VW, his White House contact number was used by Straub for a variety of untoward purposes such as setting up meetings with Ehrlichman on Vesco's behalf.

Vesco prided himself on being "the tutelary mentor" of Don Nixon, Jr. Aside from young Nixon, the IOS payroll included other examples of Vesco's political largesse. He had inherited the services of Jimmy

Roosevelt, who became a leading Democrat for Nixon during Vesco's tenure of the IOS purse strings. Vesco also wanted Seymour Halpern, the Republican Congressman from New York, to go on the board of his Nassau bank, but Halpern, doubtless alarmed by the charges of fraud hanging over Vesco's head in early 1973, politely declined after receiving a congratulatory cable from Bahamas Commonwealth Bank notifying him of his appointment. Still, there were others who didn't mind the soiling effects of a Vesco association, and a case in point had occurred two years before through Vesco's seeking favor with prominent New Jersey Republicans.

In the summer of 1971, when Regina Cahill, daughter of William T. Cahill, then Republican governor of New Jersey, wanted to spend a year in Europe, Vesco arranged that she be given a job with IOS. The security department was instructed to accord her special VIP treatment, and she was provided with the IOS transit apartment in Ferney as lodgings.

Known around IOS as the "gubernatorial body" for her striking looks, Regina was put to work in the legal department under Kenneth "King" Klein, a wispy New York show-biz attorney who a few years before had fled to Europe to escape the wrath of George Huntington Hartford II. Klein had been seeing altogether too much of Hartford's estranged third wife, fashion model Diane Brown, for Hartford's liking, and the heir to the great A&P food-store fortune wanted the young lawyer out of town. Klein found refuge with the Cornfeld circus. Having survived the downfall of the Old Guard, Klein rose to head the busy IOS legal department under Vesco until Robert Foglia, a desk-thumping associate of Howard Cerny, was sent over from New York to take charge.

In June 1971 Vesco decided to add to his image of success, as well as his personal comfort, with the purchase of an eleven-year-old Boeing 707 from Pan American World Airways for $1,375,000. International Controls advanced $343,750 for the 150-seat aircraft and issued a five-year first mortgage to Pan Am for the balance. It was the only corporate 707 in America.

Vesco never obtained approval from his board for the purchase of this grand version of the executive jet. However, he attempted to charm the directors into accepting it on a *post-facto* basis by inviting them and their wives aboard for its maiden North Atlantic crossing under International Controls's colors.

The occasion was the July 1971 International Controls board meeting, which Vesco elected to hold at Bella Vista in Geneva so that his directors could become personally acquainted with the IOS setup. After all, the Geneva financial services group had become the company's largest investment, and the trip gave his directors a chance to meet some of the

IOS bright lights. They were impressed by Norman LeBlanc, the new financial vice-president, and also heard reports from Colonel Howkins, IOS general counsel Ken Beaugrand, and IOS director Murray Howe, a senior partner of the Toronto brokerage firm of Crang & Ostiguy.

The Geneva junket, McAlpin recalled, "was a fantastic affair." A senior Pan Am pilot was at the controls on the flight over, checking the plane out before turning it over to Alwyn Eisenhauer, International Controls's director of flight operations.

McAlpin "steered" the plane for part of the way across the Atlantic and was "absolutely delighted," never having taken the controls of a jet before. In Geneva the directors were taken on a tour of the administrative complex in Ferney-Voltaire, which impressed McAlpin because he thought it resembled "a junior Pentagon." A rebellion by Ralph Dodd and Will Snipes over Fairfield's deepening involvement with IOS was successfully matted. By the time Vesco had completed his charm campaign everyone was convinced. "We got the impression that in fact there was a recovery under way within IOS as a whole," Stanley Hiller, the chairman of Vesco's executive committee, later told the SEC.[1]

Cocktails were served on the terrace at Bella Vista. Clay acted as cruise director. Straub, the "legwork man," was present. And "charming" sales master Malcolm Fox addressed the group, undoubtedly explaining IOS's Year of New Directions, though he found time to regale the Fairfield chieftains with stories of the fantastic parties that Cornfeld had hosted at the old Colgate mansion. "He even showed us where the wild animals were kept in cages for one of the orgies," McAlpin remembered, his eyes alight.

At the next International Controls board meeting in December 1971 the directors were asked to approve a backdated resolution authorizing the purchase of the white and blue Boeing 707 and the concluding of a five year leasing contract committing the company to rental payments aggregating $3.8 million. Vesco assured the board that the plane would not cost International Controls one penny. Everything, he said, would be charged back to IOS.

Ownership of N11RV, the new registration of the aircraft, was in the name of Skyways Leasing Corporation, a subsidiary of Fairfield Aviation, which in turn was a subsidiary of Fairfield General, a company created in 1972 and spun off to International Controls shareholders as a stock dividend. As Vesco was the largest shareholder of International Controls, he naturally became the major shareholder in Fairfield General.

Under the rental contract, International Controls was responsible for all operating costs of the aircraft, including servicing, maintenance, scheduling, and personnel. Its tail emblazoned with an American flag,

[1] Hiller Testimony, October 19, 1972, p. 100.

the International Controls corporate logogram, and the identification letters N11RV, the big plane was sent down to Fort Worth, Texas, soon after its first Geneva trip for extensive modifications.

The remodeling included a forward cabin and dining area with accommodations for fourteen. Furnishings consisted of a four-place divan, a circular conference table, two console tables, fitted cabinets, and a bookcase with instrument panel for an air-speed indicator, interior and exterior temperature gauge, altimeter, and compass heading indicator. There was a master console with a high-frequency intercontinental telephone system so that Vesco, if he wished, could telephone his wife when leaving Europe to warn her he'd be home in Boonton Township for dinner, or hold midair telephone conferences with aides dispersed around the globe from Beirut to Nassau, London, or Amsterdam.

Immediately aft of the forward cabin was a discotheque with bar, hardwood dance floor, two easy chairs, two leather lounge chairs, sofa, two coffee tables, wine rack, movie projector and screen, rhythmic lighting "providing a dynamic sweep of endlessly shifting patterns in vari-colored lights," stereo hi-fi equipment, and cassette deck player.

Farther aft was Vesco's office, with six chairs, a large divan, master desk, one console table, a coffeemaker, and two secretarial desks with typewriters. Behind that were a master bedroom, a guest bedroom, and an "exercise area" complete with sauna bath for two and shower.

The refurbishing cost, Vesco said, would be limited to $350,000. But when the final bill came in from Qualitron Aero Incorporated, the custom designer-decorator, the sum was grossly in excess of $600,000.

The renovations transformed the airplane into a "pleasure palace" designed to satisfy Vesco's personal tastes and rendered it "commercially useless by decreasing its capacity to thirty-three seats," complained new management at International Controls two years later in a suit charging Vesco with wasting the corporate assets. Belated ratification of the lease was obtained by concealing from the board certain details, the suit further alleged. Both Richardson and McAlpin affirmed in separate affidavits that they would not have voted to accept the lease had they known all the facts concerning the termination and modification provisions "which were key elements in Vesco's plan to convert the Boeing 707 to his own use."

The "termination" article provided that the agreement could be canceled at the option of Skyways on five days' prior written notice, while the "modifications" article stated that any "alterations, modifications, additions, or improvements to the aircraft" requested by the lessee would become the property of Skyways.

According to Don Nixon, Jr., the refurbishing was well worth it.

Vesco's Boeing 707, he said, made his uncle's Air Force One "look like a Piper Cub."

Although the sober Swiss were not impressed by Vesco's "Big Bird" —they threatened to impound it in a tax dispute—Vesco used N11RV and Don Nixon, Jr., to bedazzle heads of state, prime ministers, Middle Eastern potentates, London prostitutes, and European royalty. Even Vesco's personal pilot carried a famous name, and, although he spelled it differently, claimed to be related to the late United States President.

Vesco, now accustomed to the high life, was seen on his travels in the company of some of the most expensive international call girls. One of his accountants remarked that it was not unusual for the Fairfield financier and a few associates to spend $3,000 for a night on the town in sleepy Geneva. In London he, Straub, LeBlanc, and Clay were known to wine and dine buxomy bedroom blondes in a most lavish manner and afterward hold all-night parties in Vesco's six-room suite at the Inn on the Park.

Norma Levy, the English strumpet whose goings-on caused two Conservative Cabinet Ministers to resign in 1973, had nothing but praise for Vesco's gallantry. The biggest spender of all among her select clientele, she said, "and from my point of view one of the nicest, was, to use the politest applicable term, international financier Robert Vesco."

In her book, *I, Norma Levy . . .* , she recounted with obvious delight how

> . . . sometimes thirteen or fourteen of us would go round [to his hotel suite]. We would arrive there about eight o'clock and . . . stay until the late small hours of the morning.
>
> He used to live it up like no one else I have ever met. As you walked into the sitting room, there would be about a dozen bottles of Dom Perignon champagne on side tables round the room and to one side an enormous silver bowl of the finest Iranian caviar. In the middle of it all, rather like the ringmaster at a circus, was the ebullient figure of Vesco himself.
>
> With him would be a collection of international bankers, mostly South American, but some Swiss and a few Americans. . . . I can't remember seeing one without dark glasses.

It was Vesco's desire that this woman's auxiliary be "instantly available to whoever wanted us at any time during the evening," she continued. "You would see one of the men going off with one of the girls. They would lock themselves in one of the bedrooms in the flat and then come back to join the party twenty minutes or so later."

Norma Levy was also impressed by Vesco's generosity. "He always acted with us as if money did not mean anything at all. I have sometimes seen twenty girls at a party. He would give us $1,000 each if we stayed until midnight and another $300 if we had to stay later."

But the parties aboard the Boeing 707 impressed her as being "the most spectacular." She said a convoy of cars would be laid on to take about twenty people, including eight call girls, from the hotel to the London airport, where the airliner would be lined up on the tarmac ready for instant takeoff. "The party would go on for two or three hours while we flew round Western Europe at 600 mph at 30,000 feet and then we would come back to London airport where we had started from without even landing anywhere else." [2]

International Controls president Larry Richardson was not nearly so impressed with N11RV as some of Vesco's fellow members in the 30,000-foot club. He termed the Big Bird a "financial albatross." It chalked up tens of thousands of miles in 1972, generating some $2 million in billings, with the cash advanced by International Controls, though the aircraft carried on an average six passengers per trip.[3]

From its home base of Newark the Big Bird visited such faraway destinations as Bangkok, Beirut, Bombay, Cairo, Damascus, Hong Kong, Kuwait, Nairobi, Osaka, Rabat, and Singapore. Less far-out ports of call included Acapulco, Amsterdam, Las Vegas, Lisbon, London, Luxembourg, Madrid, Nassau, Nice, Porte au Prince, Reno, Rome, San José de Costa Rica, Stuttgart, Toronto, and Washington's Dulles Airport.

Don-Don was a frequent passenger aboard the Big Bird. On one memorable trip he flew down to the Dominican Republic for discussions with President Joaquin Balaguer concerning the setting up of an industrial free zone in the area. He tagged along on visits to other heads of state as "Big Bobby," Don-Don's affectionate handle for the boss, rushed against the SEC clock to establish himself as his own head of state with his own government and a tract of extra-territorial land to govern either very far offshore or in some inaccessible banana republic.

Vesco's access to high political circles began on November 1, 1968, when he had International Controls issue a bearer check for $25,000. He converted this check into five cashier's checks for $5,000 each, drawn on the Trust Company National Bank (predecessor to American National Bank & Trust) of Morristown. He dispatched the five checks to the Nixon-Agnew finance Committee with a covering letter to Jack

<hr />

[2] *I, Norma Levy* . . . (London: Blond & Briggs, 1973), pp. 105–8.

[3] When IOS treasurer Edward Whitcraft prepared a memorandum for Norman LeBlanc analyzing the cost differential between first class commercial fares and the Skyways billings—$167,000 for August 1971, excluding an additional $17,248 in crew layover charges, compared to $22,000 for scheduled first class air fares— LeBlanc returned the memo to him with the scribbled annotation, "I really don't think this is a relevant comparison."

Gleason, the Republicans' chief fund-raiser in the 1968 campaign, instructing that they be allocated to five different subcommittees.

A few ardent Republicans among International Controls's 9,000 shareholders might have been delighted had they been informed of their firm's $25,000 contribution, but it was hardly a proper use of corporate funds. Corporations are prohibited by law from contributing money or services to political campaigns for federal office. Of course, that did not prevent Maurice Stans as Nixon's 1972 finance chairman from soliciting $100,000 campaign contributions from a long list of major American firms. And Vesco quite definitely wanted his Fairfield creation to be considered in that "élite" category.

Vesco once claimed he was totally apolitical until caught up in the excitement and intrigue of the 1968 Presidential campaign.[4] It was as a result of attending that autumn's Alfred E. Smith Memorial Dinner with Buhl, Roosevelt, Humphrey, Johnson, and Nixon that his interest in the political affairs of the nation was suddenly stimulated.

"Now this was during the last weeks of the race. I decided that Nixon was a good guy—or of the two he was the better. That doesn't mean that I think Nixon is the greatest President in the world, and I don't think he'll ever be," Vesco told a New York acquaintance in 1969. "I got involved in the race in the last weeks. I wandered around to Nixon's campaign headquarters at the Waldorf. I was interested and intrigued. I sat around and watched the returns come in."

"He was right there with Nixon," the obsequious Clay interrupted.

"I don't know whether you know it or not," Vesco continued, "but I am an adviser to the Youth Commission and my feelings about President Nixon are a little bit stronger now than when I voted for him."[5] But his appointment to the White House Commission on Youth was yet another fabrication. The White House staff indicated that Vesco "was never appointed to any commission by President Nixon." In fact there was no such thing as a White House Commission on Youth.

Interesting insight into how Vesco operated was given by one of his former employees. The incident occurred before Vesco became involved with IOS. One of Gil Straub's early associates, a vice-president of the Executive Growth Fund operation, asked if Vesco could pull some strings for a friend who desperately wanted a beer route license in eastern New Jersey. Vesco said he would see what could be done and a few weeks later arranged a Saturday morning meeting at his office in Fairfield between the interested party and "Bayonne Joe" Zicarelli, the

[4] Schwebel tapes, no. 2, p. 38.
[5] *Ibid.*, p. 40.

Mafia boss of northern Hudson County. The party never got his beer license, though.

"Bayonne Joe" was a real powerhouse in New Jersey. He had his finger in many pies and was an astute investor besides. In 1971 Zicarelli was found guilty, along with the Republican chairman of Hudson County, John B. Theurer, of conspiring to gain appointment of a county prosecutor who would protect the Mob's gambling interests in that area of the state. Zicarelli was also indicted on charges of evading federal taxes on more than $1 million in income during a two-year period. He was sentenced to a twelve-year term at Trenton State Prison for conspiring, through use of political influence, to protect Mafia interests in Hudson County.

"Everything has a price on it in Hudson County," said U.S. Attorney Frederick Lacey, the federal prosecutor on the Zicarelli case, who later moved to the federal bench. Vesco would have disagreed with the geographical limitation. As far as he was concerned, everything anywhere had a price on it.

Perhaps because of his association with such eminent investors as Bayonne Joe, Vesco was able to learn the art of proffering a payoff at an early stage in his career. There was, for example, a cash gift of $15,000 to Harry Sears for the call Sears made to Mitchell on Vesco's behalf in November 1971, when the financier was incarcerated overnight in Geneva. Sears was still serving as majority leader of the New Jersey Senate, although his retirement was only a few weeks off. Vesco's expression of gratitude, Sears no doubt was interested to learn, had been paid for with corporate funds.

Certain stylistic similarities surrounded the delivery of a small brown package by an IOS courier to Richard D. Vine, the political counselor at the U.S. Embassy in Berne, after Vesco's release from jail in Geneva.

According to Robert King, an IOS security officer, Vine had been helpful with "one or two problems" IOS had with the Swiss federal authorities. Vine also had fielded the call from John Mitchell requesting that "all possible pressure be applied" to spring Vesco from the pokey.

King later claimed that one of the packages delivered to Berne—it seemed there were several—contained legal documents relating to the Tucker affair.

But Vesco became furious when he thought the SEC had intervened with the State Department to have the Embassy in Berne turn its back on further requests for assistance. In an August 1972 letter to Brad Cook, SEC general counsel at the time, Vesco accused the staff of unwarranted interference in matters that were in no way related to the enforcement of securities laws.

Another example of Vesco's influence-building efforts was the placing of a pair of leased brown and yellow helicopters at the disposal of New Jersey CREEP during the 1972 campaign. The helicopters were used to ferry Harry Sears and other GOP officials back and forth between electioneering meetings. Although by no stretch of the imagination could this be considered a corporate expense, Fairfield Aviation billed International Controls for the flight time.

In another vein, Vesco's contempt for due legal process was clearly demonstrated by the manner in which the Tucker affair was handled. Once released from Geneva's Saint Antoine Prison after his overnight detention, he set a task force of a dozen Swiss and American lawyers to work to have the charges against him dropped—by any means, fair or foul.

It was Cowett who made the classic remark concerning Judge Pagan's November 1971 decision to arrest Vesco. "These people are crazy," he said of the Geneva justice. "They just don't understand the morals of this business."

"Pagan would not have acted so harshly had it not been for certain events," IOS secretary Ken Beaugrand was informed by one of his Swiss contacts. This implied that more forceful evidence had compelled Judge Pagan to issue warrants against Vesco, Meissner, and Strickler. But these compelling reasons were never disclosed.

It was thought, however, that maybe Pagan had been influenced by the reign of terror Vesco had instituted at Overseas Development Bank in Geneva during June and July 1971. The bank was subsequently placed under the surveillance of two Federal Banking Commission observers, and Vesco and Meissner were required to resign from the board.

But at the time Vesco wanted the bank to lend $5 million to an International Controls affiliate, which the three Swiss directors would not authorize. There were repeated threats to fire the managing director for refusing to act in the generally acceptable manner of a hired hand, and other efforts were made to intimidate the unruly ODB board members into obeying his command. Vesco's tactics included bringing criminal slander charges against the three obstinate Swiss when they continued to oppose him, and he even went before a local magistrate to demand their immediate arrest in order to protect his reputation from being maliciously damaged. This was accompanied by an absurd attempt—almost comical—to collect $25 million in damages from each of them by sending formal *Commandments de Payer* through the post office. Under this peculiarly Swiss system a person served with such papers can immediately contest the validity of the cash claim, although sometimes the procedures involved can be extremely annoying.

"But we were just applying a little pressure," Beaugrand protested. "Hell, in the States it's normal practice in suits like this."

Seen from that angle, Cowett was probably right. The Swiss just did not understand the business morals of men like Vesco and Cowett. Whatever unsavory talents the Swiss might possess, shooting from the hip in boardroom brawls is not among them.

The repercussions of Judge Pagan's action were not long in manifesting themselves. The widespread publicity the case received fanned the latent fears of IOS's remaining fund-holders into a new blaze of redemption requests.

Vesco, in spite of his Swiss setback, never ceased to maintain a confident front. Nevertheless, overnight he had become the laughingstock of the European banking establishment. As a result, many of the larger financial houses with which he had hoped to develop close working relationships closed their doors to him forever.

His reaction was typical. The moment he was released from custody he vowed in private to repay Judge Pagan for the humiliation he had suffered. Vesco owed this revenge to his family, a member of his entourage suggested.

"Don't ever cross Bob Vesco," one of his security staff advised. These were not idle words.

The U.S. Attorney's Office in New York lost no time in capitalizing on the situation either. An important gold-trading case had been pending against IOS and Cornfeld for more than two years. Lawyers were close to working out a settlement involving acceptance by the defendants of a $10,000 fine when news of Vesco's arrest was released.

Instead of settling, the U.S. Attorney's Office decided to throw the book at IOS. Thus, in another flurry of international publicity on the day after Vesco's release from jail in Switzerland, the United States accused IOS and Bernie Cornfeld of violating the rarely invoked 1934 Gold Reserve Act and demanded payment of $76 million in civil penalties.

The initial reaction of the defendants was pained horror. IOS lamely tried to shrug the matter off by claiming it was a situation inherited from original management and therefore had nothing to do with the new control group.

According to the complaint filed with the U.S. District Court for the Southern District of New York, IOS had unlawfully purchased and sold $31.9 million in gold for the IIT fund during the March 1968 gold rush in Europe. Later, the complaint added, Cornfeld personally caused The Fund of Funds to acquire some $6.2 million in bullion. Neither party, it said, had acted with a U.S. Treasury license. Under the 1934 act it was illegal for Americans or companies controlled by Americans to trade in gold without such a license.

The news that IIT and FOF had bought and sold some twenty-five tons of gold came as a surprise to most IOS fund-holders. Nowhere at any time in the official fund reports had the bullion transactions been disclosed.

In fact, not only were IOS investors unaware of the 1968 gold dealings, but some of the company's senior officers appeared to have been kept in the dark as well. Jimmy Roosevelt, on an IOS image-building tour in England at the time of the 1968 gold fever, had some harsh words to say about gold speculators. "It is rather unfortunate that, at a time when the world should be seeking stability, there are elements in our economic community which would seem to be bent upon creating confusion and lack of security in people's minds," Roosevelt told newspaper reporters in Birmingham. He was convinced, he said, that the United States would take the necessary steps to "end this more or less wild spree of speculation." [6] And so it did—more than three years later.

Judge Pagan, in the meantime, had not been sitting on his hands. Two other major IOS-related criminal suits were before him—the so-called suit of sixty-eight, brought by sixty-eight Swiss ex-employees of IOS who alleged that they had been hustled by management into buying IOS stock at the underwriting, and a Fund of Funds suit by a group of Swiss fund-holders, which singled out Cornfeld, Buhl, Cowett, and Roosevelt for high-level fraud proceedings.

In mid-December 1971, Judge Pagan issued a magistrate's order subpoenaing Cowett. The Blue Sky expert, however, had arranged to be out of the country on business and informed the judge that he could not be present.

Judge Pagan's reaction was again unexpected. He drew up a series of international arrest warrants for some of the more prominent names on the list of defendants in the two suits. International warrants must be issued through the Federal Department of Justice in Berne. The federal authorities, however, were conscious of the stir the new warrants would cause and placed a "hold" order on them while they huddled for consultations.

As it happened, one of Cornfeld's defense lawyers, Raymond Nicolet, was in Berne that day on unrelated business. When word of the warrants reached him, Nicolet—perhaps the shrewdest criminal lawyer in Switzerland—wasted no time in suggesting to the Justice Department officials that Judge Pagan's "pieces of paper" were ineffectual unless they contained more detailed information concerning the charges being brought against Cornfeld and the other defendants.

Nicolet succeeded in having the warrants returned to Judge Pagan for clarification and immediately raised the alarm by contacting at-

[6] *Evening Mail*, Birmingham, England, March 15, 1968.

torneys of the defense cabal in Geneva. He had several months before advised Cornfeld not to return to Switzerland until all litigation of a criminal nature had been settled. The mood of the Swiss judiciáry was such, he said, that there was no telling what might happen next.

Now the same advice was passed on to other Old Guard defendants in the two criminal actions. With Pagan's treatment of Vesco fresh in everyone's minds, a general panic developed and led to a hurried exodus from Switzerland.

Although Cowett's office said he intended to spend the Christmas holidays with his family at Belle Haven, the mansion he rented in the Geneva suburb of Cologny, his return was repeatedly postponed with every new reading he received of the local situation. Christmas drifted into New Year's, and the two-secretary staff of Emco Financial Services in downtown Geneva presently announced that the Blue Sky expert was closing down his Geneva office and would remain permanently in the United States to help his newest client, Cavanagh Communities Corporation, plan a European sales drive.

Cowett telephoned his wife, Betty, and told her to pack everything she could, crate all the modern art, sell the bulky household fixtures to raise extra cash, move their two children out of school, and join him in Florida.

When Maître Claude Gautier, lawyer for the plaintiff fund-holders, heard of Cowett's move he sought and obtained a Geneva court order blocking tricky Ed's assets in Switzerland pending judgment of the lawsuits against him. A court clerk and bailiff rushed over to the Cowett home, but all that remained for them to attach was a handful of personal items valued at $5,000.

Marty Seligson, IOS's former real estate boss, was working at his Hampton Corporation office across the border in Divonne-les-Bains when his lawyer telephoned with the news. He immediately called his wife, Beverley, and told her not to ask questions, just pack a few things and get on a flight to London. He'd join her there.

Seligson's Divonne-based real estate company had not been successful in marketing limited partnerships in two Topeka, Kansas, garden apartment projects and was in the process of being wound up anyway, enabling Marty to slip out of town ever so quickly. He traveled first overland to Paris and then by air to London. Not long afterward he moved into a smart Eaton Square townhouse and started operating anew from business premises in London's Jermyn Street under the name Vancastle Limited, "specialists in financing, real estate, and acquisitions."

Roosevelt, too, fled Geneva, claiming that new business commitments demanded that he spend more of his time traveling between Los Angeles and New York. Hence when the panic button was pushed in Geneva, Roosevelt called from the States and instructed his wife to close up their residence at Jussy, outside Geneva, pay off the domestics, and join him at their new home in California.

Allen Cantor, who lived in a magnificent country manor at Versoix, on the road to Lausanne, also left town for a prolonged skiing holiday in Megève, the fashionable French Alpine resort, and from there went to Paris, where his real estate sales operation with David Tucker was booming. Sometimes he would return home for brief unannounced visits, but even these stopped after the unexpected arrest of Cornfeld in May 1973.

Howard Cerny, the sometime attorney to the Nixon brothers, was placed in charge of Vesco's task force of lawyers assembled in Geneva. He brought with him a member of his New York staff, Robert Foglia, who took over direction of the IOS legal department. Foglia, originally from the Fort Hamilton section of Brooklyn, the youngest of thirteen children whose father was a penniless immigrant from the south of Italy, became known around IOS as "the consigliere" because of his conspiratorial manner.

The plan Cerny and Foglia devised in concert with Vesco's Swiss counsel, Alain Farina, was a three-pronged effort (1) to reach an out-of-court settlement with Tucker; (2) to persuade the State of Geneva to drop the criminal charges against Vesco, Meissner, and Strickler; and (3) to engineer the censuring of Pagan by the Geneva College of Magistrates.

A private detective was hired in Paris to keep Tucker under surveillance. A file was compiled of Tucker's past commission statements with a view to turning it over, if necessary, to the IRS and the French fiscal authorities. The intent was clear. Should there be any discrepancy between Tucker's declared income and his commission earnings as a salesman for IOS, then he was likely to find himself in the soup.

A senior police official in Paris, Commissionaire Divisionaire Emile Benamou of the Sûrêté National, was primed on the situation by the IOS security staff. Tucker began to feel the pinch.

Direct negotiations started soon after. Tucker was offered a generous package settlement if he would withdraw his complaint. Clay and Straub, meanwhile, had taken charge of the anti-Pagan squad. "How are we going to get Bob off the hook?" they asked. The familiar suggestion was trotted out: luring Judge Pagan into bed with a woman of easy virtue. But this idea was quickly dismissed. Other plans were in store for Pagan.

Bribing Geneva's Attorney General was also discussed but discarded. One does not bribe senior justice officials in Switzerland. But, again according to Bob King, a scheme was dreamed up to make a discreet approach to the Swiss through a high-level West German political contact. Before this plan got into high gear, however, the Geneva charges against Vesco mysteriously were dropped.

Tucker had his arm twisted into accepting an $80,000 cash settlement in return for withdrawing his accusations against Vesco. Simultaneously, Vesco's lawyers negotiated with the Geneva Attorney General's Office to withdraw or, more precisely, "suspend" the charges handed down by Judge Pagan—without even informing Pagan. The agreement was reached on March 8, 1972, and announced from Fairfield before sufficient time had elapsed for the prosecuting attorney in Geneva to inform his superior, the Geneva Attorney General, that the final *classement* of affair No. 2074 had been signed. The official reason for dropping the case was that "the complaint having been withdrawn, the charges were not established." The bail money was refunded.

Judge Pagan was furious when he learned that his recommendation to indict Vesco had been rejected. "You don't think I laid charges without sufficient grounds, do you?" he said to inquiring newsmen. "If this sort of thing continues, pretty soon one won't be able to prosecute criminal fraud charges in Geneva," he told one reporter. Unfortunately, Pagan had fallen into the Vesco trap.

When contacted by a small Geneva press and public relations agency, Allpress, Judge Pagan declared that the charges against Vesco had been solidly proved but that the plaintiff had been bought off. He went on to mention a "white-collar Mafia" and then insisted "it is law and order which is being scoffed at" by these people.

Judge Pagan reconsidered what he had said and requested that Allpress treat his remarks as "off-the-record" and not for attribution. But Allpress had no such intention. Allpress was in the pay of Vesco interests and previously had been used to pump out thinly disguised Vesco propaganda.

The Geneva Attorney General was immediately informed of Judge Pagan's statements, which were published next morning in *La Suisse*, a local daily newspaper. Pagan was censured for poor professional conduct by the College of Magistrates, disqualified from handling IOS cases, and almost thrust into early retirement for breaking an examining magistrate's bond of absolute secrecy in conducting criminal investigations. Thus, from the dean of the examining magistrates the IOS affair was handed to the youngest of the magistrates, thirty-one-year-old Pierre-Christian Weber.

Vesco had gained his revenge.

Impressed by the benefits of operating one's own security force, Vesco directed Hal Simpson, one of his two Geneva-based "plumbers" —holdovers from Cornfeld's Keystone Kops—to give him a rundown on IOS's remaining security network worldwide. They were flying together in the refurbished Big Bird, destination unknown. Vesco's idea was to create a separate corporation out of the IOS security department, furnish it with service contracts from various group affiliates, and then spin it out to the IOS shareholders in the form of a stock dividend.

Simpson, a retired U.S. Army major, had been the head nark of the Sixth Criminal Investigation Division of the U.S. Army in Europe before joining IOS in 1969. An easygoing operator, Simpson had excellent contacts with European police forces. Through an assistant superintendent of police at Scotland Yard, for example, he was able to warn Vesco in 1971 that he was under investigation in Britain—which was another good reason for not shifting IOS's headquarters to London.

Simpson's sidekick in Geneva was Bob King, a mild-mannered U.S. Army warrant officer with the reserve rank of captain. King had worked under Simpson at USAREUR headquarters in Heidelberg and was an expert on counterfeiting. He had joined IOS two years before Simpson and was responsible for bringing his former superior into the company.

IOS's security force once numbered more than 100 persons, including guards, but by early 1972 the effective had dropped to twenty-five, of which very few were capable of performing special "investigative" work. Nevertheless, they could handle intelligence gathering chores and other useful "security" services, with personnel located in Geneva, Ferney, London, Amsterdam, Munich, and New York.

Fine, said Vesco after hearing Simpson detail his department's effective. He ordered Simpson to make it the subject of a written memorandum and, turning to an aide, added, make sure John Mitchell gets a copy.

Mitchell had not yet taken up his duties as chairman of CREEP and was still at the Justice Department. True, the process leading to Watergate had already begun in earnest. On January 27, 1972, the famous million-dollar meeting occurred in the office of the Attorney General with CREEP campaign director Jeb Magruder and Presidential counsel John Dean III present. The purpose of the meeting was to hear a proposal by G. Gordon Liddy for an "intelligence" assault on the Democratic National Party.

There is no indication that Mitchell solicited a report on the status of the IOS security network from Vesco, or in fact that he ever received one. But that Vesco, early in 1972, apparently already knew of Mitchell's special interest in the intelligence gathering field was surprising to say the least.

Or perhaps not. It was suggested that Vesco become overseas fund-raising chairman of CREEP—it was not clear who made the suggestion, or, again, whether it was only entertained by Vesco as a possibility. In any case, Judge Pagan's handiwork put a stop to all that.

16

The Washington Bag

*How to hire an honest politician from New Jersey and send him
down to Washington with a briefcase full of money to gain favor
with influential people*

Harry L. Sears stood tall among Republican supporters of
Richard Milhous Nixon. At the August 1968 GOP Convention in
Miami Beach, the soft-spoken forty-eight-year-old state senator from
New Jersey led the Nixon raid on the New Jersey delegation that was
successful in breaking the hold of favorite son Senator Clifford P. Case.
The Northern liberal Case lost control, and Sears brought in eighteen
of the forty New Jersey votes for Nixon. The Sears raid broke the
back of the Rockefeller camp and left California's Ronald Reagan as
Nixon's only serious competitor in the runoff for the Republican
Presidential nomination.

Sears had an easy smile and warm manner that made him a popular
figure in the community. Known as New Jersey's honest politician, he
was serving his first year in the state Senate after having spent six
years in the state Assembly. He had come into the Nixon fold
reluctantly after meeting John Mitchell, Nixon's law partner and campaign manager, in New York in early March of that year. New Jersey
was a heavy Rockefeller state, and Sears, an alternate delegate-at-large
at the convention, was strategically placed to swing votes in Nixon's
favor.

"In that campaign I developed a high regard and personal friendship
for John Mitchell," Sears said.

It was that relationship which Vesco so defty decided to exploit,
setting up Sears as his influence-wielding politician-on-a-string. And
so it seemed strangely natural somehow that this relationship, born of
political scheming, ultimately should lead to the 1973 indictment of

Mitchell and Sears, along with Nixon's campaign finance chairman, Maurice Stans, on charges of criminal conspiracy, obstruction of justice, and perjury.

Sears went upward quickly in the Republican machine after Nixon's election in 1968. He became the majority leader in the New Jersey Senate and chairman of its appropriations committee and, in 1969, was asked to run in the state primary for governor. Accordingly, in February 1969 he became the fifth entrant in a five-man field. It was a hopeless battle from the start. But, loyal to the party machine, he had agreed to run and did extremely well under the circumstances. It was his second year in the Senate; he had no statewide recognition; he had trouble raising campaign funds. Yet Sears finished third.

Sear's finance chairman during that primary campaign was an executive vice-president at American National Bank & Trust in Morristown, William Smith. Smith had solicited contributions from everyone at the bank and was running short of new sources to tap when another American National vice-president, Will Snipes, volunteered to introduce the gubernatorial hopeful to Bob Vesco.

Sears had known of Vesco for about eight years. His third daughter, Judy, and Vesco's oldest son, Danny, had been classmates at the Wilson School in Mountain Lakes, where the Sears family lived, but Sears had never actually met the founder and chief executive officer of International Controls.

"I knew Vesco was a very successful businessman who had put together International Controls—a lot of people around here invested in ICC back in those days because they believed in Bob Vesco," Sears said one morning over breakfast at the Parsippany Holiday Inn, a few miles down Route 46 from the International Controls headquarters.

Sears also knew that Vesco had contributed $25,000 to the 1968 Nixon campaign. He had, prior to the gubernatorial primary, last seen the Vescos at the Inaugural Ball in Washington in January 1969, where Vesco had purchased a $1,000 box. "Pat came running over to us in the crowd and said hello. She's a wonderful, down-to-earth, very ordinary sort of person."

In April 1969 Sears was taken out to the Vesco home on Old Denville Road and talked with him for about an hour concerning his campaign and the financial problems it was encountering. Without committing himself to any amount, Vesco agreed to contribute.

As it turned out, Vesco was an extremely generous contributor by the standards of that campaign, giving $20,000. On election night he drove over to the Sears campaign headquarters—just as he had gone the year before to the Nixon headquarters at the Waldorf in New York

—with his wife Pat and two oldest sons, Danny and Tony, to watch the results come in.

The predictable loss to William Cahill for the Republican nomination was confirmed, leaving Sears with a "very substantial campaign deficit."

"Traditionally and logically, the way you handled those things [was to] have some kind of a fund-raising effort, and the money is raised and the debts are paid off," Sears explained.

"But, because there was a gubernatorial general election in 1969, after conferring with my finance people I made the decision that no fund-raising affair should be held in 1969 because I felt that it would compete with and, indeed, conflict with the fund-raising efforts on behalf of the Republican candidate whom I was actively supporting.

"And so it became a question of finding some way to hold that debt until such time as an affair or some fund-raising effort could be made in order to pay it off.

"It was my preference that creditors not be kept waiting and that bills be paid, and the way the matter was handled was by my borrowing from American National Bank & Trust Co. $50,000." [1]

Because of his almost sheepdog eagerness to satisfy demands made on him by forces inside the party, Sears was left with a heavy financial burden on his back and no way of having it absorbed by the GOP's state treasury. This rendered him wide open to approaches by influence-seekers like Vesco willing to assume that burden in return for political favors, a fault in the American system of financing electoral campaigns that Vesco knew exactly how to exploit and turn to his own advantage.

As soon as Vesco heard of Sear's financial plight he called and offered his help. Sears was an important personality in Trenton, the state capital, and Vesco also knew that the "honest politician from New Jersey" had Cabinet-level contacts in Washington. Sears was obviously a worthwhile investment.

It was hardly surprising, then, that Vesco should have indicated he was willing to arrange the loan for Sears at American National Bank & Trust, which he agreed to carry until such time as the Sears finance committee was in a position to pay it off.

"I, of course, was delighted at the opportunity of putting this thing in a limbo posture for a period of time so that we could have a breather, as it were," Sears later testified. "And so a loan was arranged, and I signed, and I was the only signatory on the note of the American National Bank & Trust Co. for $50,000."

The understanding Sears had with Vesco was that the Fairfield financier would meet the interest payments on the loan until such time

[1] Sears's SEC testimony, February 20, 1973, pp. 61–62.

as the Sears finance committee could raise the funds to pay off the note. Meanwhile the proceeds of the loan were used to settle his existing obligations resulting from the primary campaign.

"Once the note was reposed at the bank, so far as I was concerned . . . I simply had no more to do with it," Sears later said.

Then in June 1970 a traditional event in the political life of Harry Sears was organized by the Citizens for Sears Committee, a group that was designed solely to support his political efforts.

"Citizens for Sears that year held, I guess, the fourth annual Harry Sears Golf Outing, the proceeds of which amounted to $2,500," he said. The chairman of that committee drew a check to Vesco for the full amount which was paid as an account on the interest due to the bank.

No further payments were made by Sears on the American National loan until the following year. But the interest installments continued to be carried, as far as Sears was concerned, by Vesco.

By early 1971 Sears had tired of public life. It was a demanding existence, and he figured that ten years in politics had been a big investment; he felt it was time to leave the political arena. He had five children and was already a grandfather.

"The years between forty and fifty are prime years in a man's lifetime and I was spending between sixty and seventy per cent of my time on legislative matters, earning a salary of only $10,000 and breaking my back in my law practice to keep everything together. I sat down with my wife and we talked it over and I reached the decision to retire. It was an easy decision for her, of course, but more difficult as far as I was concerned."

Thus in March 1971 Harry Sears publicly announced his retirement from the New Jersey Senate to take effect at the end of the current term. There followed a Sears testimonial dinner at the Chanteclair in Milbury, New Jersey, at which John and Martha Mitchell were the guests of honor. As a fund-raising effort it was "a resounding success," Sears said. His by then ardent supporters Bob and Pat Vesco attended, and it was the first time, according to Sears, that Vesco met John Mitchell.

Following the Chanteclair testimonial, the Sears finance committee drew a check for $50,000 and delivered it to American National Bank & Trust to retire the two-year-old note. Sears said he inquired at the bank what the total interest on the note had been and, after deducting the $2,500 already paid by the Citizens for Sears Committee, wrote another check for the full outstanding amount—$3,600—which he presented to Vesco.

In a two-day deposition made in New York in February 1973, which blew the lid off Vesco's secret 1972 campaign contribution to the

Republicans, Sears told SEC associate general counsel Robert Kushner how later he learned that the interest payments on the note had been met not by Vesco "as I thought," but by International Controls.[2]

Sears served out the remainder of 1971, getting ready to return to private law practice on a full-time basis. He received a number of interesting propositions to go on the boards of companies, which led to his acceptance of directorships with New Jersey Bell Telephone Company and Midlantic Bank Holding Company, a medium-sized New Jersey banking corporation with assets of $1.6 billion.

But the most interesting offer, he said, came from that respected international businessman Robert Vesco. Vesco wanted Sears to become associated with International Controls as general counsel and a member of the board of directors.

To executives at his Fairfield headquarters Vesco made no bones about why he wanted the Boonton lawyer on the payroll. It was, Vesco was reported as saying, because of the Mitchell connection. Mitchell was a figure of pre-eminent power in Washington, and for a direct pipeline into the U.S. Attorney General's office he was prepared to hire Sears at almost any cost.

Vesco in his talks with Sears outlined the widening scope of International Controls's activities, not only its standing as a diversified electronics and fluid controls manufacturer with annual sales of between $75 million and $100 million, but also its development in the offshore world. Vesco suggested, as an added enticement, that since the demand for in-house legal talent was constantly increasing the Boonton attorney would be able to hire his own staff to assist him, and, too, Vesco dangled a directorship with Bahamas Commonwealth Bank in Nassau.

"He felt that . . . my reputation and my stature in the community would be of some immediate benefit as far as International Controls was concerned . . . and that, from my standpoint, there was a business opportunity which would be worthy of my consideration," the honest politician from New Jersey noted with surprisingly few illusions.[3]

The SEC investigation was by then more than half a year old, but, after listening to Vesco's version of events, Sears said he decided the agency's interest in International Controls was "somewhat narrower in scope" than actually proved to be the case. Nevertheless, he had been concerned enough several months previously to contact John Mitchell in Washington on Vesco's behalf and ask for Mitchell's direct intervention in the case. Sears wrote Mitchell two letters in May and June 1971 asking him to feel out William Casey, the SEC chairman, about a

[2] *Ibid.*, p. 68.
[3] *Ibid.*, pp. 21 and 22.

possible "winding down" of the investigation. Significantly, because of the sensitive nature of the request, Sears sent these letters to Mitchell's residence at the Watergate East apartments and not directly to the Office of the Attorney General at the Justice Department (see Appendixes 2 and 3).

How the U.S. Attorney General reacted to Sears's first efforts to involve him in the Vesco affair was not disclosed, but at least Mitchell was well aware that Vesco was under federal investigation when four months later he was next contacted by the New Jersey Senator on Vesco's behalf. After Vesco's return to Geneva in November 1971, Sears received what he characterized as a "panic call" from International Controls vice-president Ralph Dodd advising him that Vesco had been jailed in Switzerland.

Sears immediately got on the line to Mitchell at the Justice Department and explained the situation. "It was represented to me," he said he told the U.S. Attorney General, "that Mr. Vesco had not been able to contact the people at the Embassy, and I asked him if there was anything that he could do . . . under these circumstances.

"[Mitchell] indicated to me that he would attempt to contact officials at the Embassy [in Berne] to find out what the situation was and would get back to me and let me know whether or not he could be of assistance."

Sears said Mitchell called back within a couple of hours to say that the Embassy people in Berne were looking into the matter and that he would be in touch as soon as he had something definite.

"He did get back to me finally, indicating that he believed Mr. Vesco would be released on bail by the Swiss officials." [4]

About a month after Vesco's release from custody, Sears received in the mail a check drawn on IOS for $5,000. Since he had no relationship with IOS, he asked Vesco about the check and was told that it was "his way of saying thank you for the favor that I had done, insisted indeed that I retain the check, and I didn't insist otherwise, and so I did, and that was it."

Only it wasn't. A second check followed from International Controls for $10,000. Vesco told Sears that it was a gift—"in other words, it was not for legal services, but out of gratitude for what I had done for him." [5]

Sears, contrary to the image of an unsophisticated country politician which he projected, was reputed to be an exceedingly cunning legal and political strategist. But he had committed a major error in letting Vesco know how badly he was hurting financially.

[4] *Ibid.,* pp. 69 and 70.
[5] *Ibid.,* p. 71.

On the Morristown–Mountain Lakes cocktail circuit, once all the dirt had surfaced, his friends used to ask him how he could have become involved with a financial thimblerigger like Vesco. "I developed a stock reply," he said. "It was, 'Look, the Prudential checked him out and they decided to lend [International Controls] $20 million. They must have thought he was pretty substantial. Well, so did I.' "

In December 1971 Sears finally accepted Vesco's offer to become associate counsel and a director of International Controls, as well as a director of Bahamas Commonwealth Bank, for an over-all monthly retainer of $5,000. No sooner was the arrangement agreed to than Sears requested from Vesco an advance of $35,000. Vesco made him sign two demand notes for the money, then set Sears to work on problems in Washington. Everyone was delighted, especially Vesco. He charged Sears's monthly fee to International Bancorp Limited in Nassau, and for many months nobody was any the wiser.

At the time Vesco was deeply involved in an attempt to acquire a troubled Middle Eastern banking complex—Intra Bank—and he sent Sears down to Washington to attend a meeting with Vesco's sideman Gil Straub in John Ehrlichman's office at the White House to solicit the backing of the Nixon Administration for the project.

Ehrlichman handled this request by drafting a memo to Mitchell asking that the U.S. Attorney General "make some calls to various embassies" on Vesco's behalf.[6] Mitchell apparently did not know what was required of him and asked Sears to a January 12, 1972, meeting at the Justice Department.

Sears arrived with a briefcase full of documents including a memorandum from Vesco in which the wish was expressed that various U.S. embassies in countries where Vesco had business interests be told that the financier was "a reputable American." Vesco particularly asked that the embassies in Beirut, The Hague, Hong Kong, and Luxembourg answer favorably when they received inquiries about him, Sears said. Of this list, Sears specifically requested that Mitchell call the U.S. Embassy in Beirut, where the Intra Bank headquarters were located, to vouch for Vesco's integrity, SEC probe and Swiss arrest order notwithstanding. This Mitchell did, angering the local U.S. Ambassador, who immediately protested to the State Department.

The other major problem on which Sears was put to work was the widening SEC investigation. The threat of SEC litigation represented the only remaining barrier between Vesco and free access to IOS's millions. A master of the Nobody Knows Theory, Vesco was quite aware that nobody else but the SEC really knew what he was up to

[6] *United States v.* John N. Mitchell *et al.* Sears's testimony, March 6, 1974.

at that point. But the SEC in early 1972 had only the vaguest notion of his ultimate intentions.

Sears had no qualms about trying to remove this barrier, which Vesco intended to circumvent anyway if everything else failed. And Sears continued to work away at it even after SEC general counsel Brad Cook informed him at one of their later meetings that "to be quite candid, Mr. Sears, I think your client has been less than candid with us. I'll give you some good advice. This [investigation] is not likely to stop at the Commission."

Sears maintained that the SEC's concern had given him "some reason to pause," but he also was aware that "emotions were running high on both sides of the investigation—that this was a two-way street." Vesco and others, he said, had expressed a "fear that there would be at some point a finalization, a report and recommendation [by the SEC staff], and before International Controls knew it, they would be in court without having an opportunity to present any material to the Commission in defense of some of the . . . allegations that might be made.

"And so . . . it was determined that I might be useful in opening a line of communications within the SEC to the Commission for the sole purpose of obviating that possibility, and at least having an opportunity to explore . . . the possibility of settlement," Sears said in his February 1973 SEC deposition.

This was an ingenious portrayal of his role, of course, as Hogan & Hartson, a Washington law firm with great experience in handling matters related to the SEC, had represented Vesco and International Controls before the SEC since the investigation began in March 1971. Hogan & Hartson knew, as do all law firms with any SEC practice, that they could present their client's position to the Commission at any time. Hogan & Hartson had in fact done so for Vesco. But Hogan & Hartson claimed they didn't know that Sears was attempting to set up a meeting with SEC chairman Casey, as Vesco hadn't bothered to tell them.[7]

It therefore seems likely that Vesco, in using Sears in an attempt to get directly to Casey, had a more devious plan in mind. Later it was disclosed that he was prepared to threaten the head of the SEC with legal action for alleged securities fraud violations in connection with Casey's past involvement with a company that subsequently went into bankruptcy.

Before joining the SEC, lawyer Casey had been the founding director of Ivanhoe Associates Incorporated, later renamed Multiponics Incorporated. The principal investor in Multiponics, acquiring over one-third of a $3.5 million public offering floated in 1968, was IOS's IIT

[7] United States *v.* John Mitchell *et al.,* Sherwin Markman testimony, April 8, 1974.

fund. According to Vesco, Multiponics had been organized "to take over personal interests of Mr. Casey and others in certain farming operations . . . at values subsequently determined to be inflated." Shortly thereafter Multiponics was declared insolvent. "The receiver subsequently has advised IIT fund that . . . there are apparent violations of the Securities Act of 1933 as a result of fraudulent representations by Mr. Casey," an unsigned Vesco *aide-memoire* stated. But Vesco never got his private audience with Casey, and IIT never brought its action. Vesco declared his reason for withholding it was to avoid "an unfavorable impact" on the Administration.

All things considered, that hardly turned out to be a favor. On the contrary, Vesco's continuing efforts to thwart the SEC investigation, making liberal use of Harry Sears as his paid agent in Washington, became one of the major scandals of the Nixon Administration, resulting in the 1973 indictments of John Mitchell and Maurice Stans, the former Commerce Secretary who became chairman of the Finance Committee to Re-elect the President, for allegedly conspiring to obstruct justice. And Vesco's efforts by no means stopped at the CREEP headquarters; they continued up Pennsylvania Avenue and into the White House, involving top Presidential aides John Ehrlichman and John Dean III. Even the President's two brothers, Donald and Edward, were called to testify at the New York conspiracy trial that followed.

Also mentioned in those proceedings was trusted Nixon legal adviser Murray Chotiner, who was the President's oldest political ally until Chotiner's death in January 1974. Only one name was missing, that of the President himself, until a former IOS secretary disclosed that Gil Straub once boasted of a Vesco meeting with Nixon in Salzburg, Austria, as the President was en route to Moscow for his May 1972 summit with the Soviet leaders. The White House denied that the Salzburg meeting took place, but as IOS founder Cornfeld gleefully remarked, "It wouldn't be the first time that a White House denial was later declared 'inoperative.' "

At his January 1972 meeting with Mitchell, Sears also gave the U.S. Attorney General a file detailing what Vesco claimed was evidence of the SEC's "harassment." With this in hand, Mitchell called SEC chairman Bill Casey and asked whether Casey was aware of what was going on. Casey, in later testimony, said Mitchell feared the SEC investigators were showing "excess zeal" in their handling of the case. Casey responded by sending Mitchell a copy of an internal SEC memorandum giving a rundown of the staff's findings as of January 24, 1972. The memo was fairly condemning. It stated that Vesco, in gaining control of IOS, "did not hesitate to engage in fraudulent and deceptive practices." Moreover, it concluded that, for all his self-righteous indignation, Vesco had lied to the SEC staff about his role in the purchase of Cornfeld's IOS stock by Linkink Progressive Corporation. Mitchell passed the memo on to Sears. Sears handed it directly to Vesco.

Again in mid-February 1972 Sears brought up the subject of SEC "harassment" with Mitchell. The meeting in Mitchell's Justice Department offices, he later testified, was primarily to discuss the handling of the Presidential election campaign in New Jersey. As Vesco was a member of the New Jersey Republican Finance Committee, Sears brought him along.

"John," he said to Mitchell, "this is Bob Vesco. You met him at my dinner." [8]

The two men greeted each other, Sears said; there was some small talk between them, then Vesco apparently sat through the remaining discussion of campaign matters by the two politicians as happy as a cat in a fish shop.

A few weeks previously Gil Straub was returning to New York on a commercial flight from London when he recognized and struck up a conversation with Daniel W. Hofgren, a onetime stockbroker and former White House aide who was vice-chairman of the Finance Committee to Re-elect the President. Hofgren in the course of their conversation casually asked when the committee could expect a contribution from Vesco. Straub said he would take it up with the boss.

Shortly afterward Vesco claimed to Sears that he had been approached by Nixon's finance committee directly and asked what he intended to do about another contribution. At least so Sears testified. Vesco then claimed he had "a personal desire" to continue supporting the President's political efforts and that he wanted to be known as "a substantial contributor." His reasons, it turned out, went beyond any direct interest in influencing the SEC investigation. He knew that John King had been appointed an Ambassador Extraordinary by Nixon after making a $250,000 contribution to the 1968 campaign. Vesco now thought he could seek a similar diplomatic status and maybe even immunity, if not at home then at least in his foreign travels.

"He was in a position where he was traveling on a worldwide basis almost on a daily and weekly basis, and he had a desire to be what he termed a roving ambassador—at least with that kind of status," Sears said.[9]

Former Commerce Secretary Stans was by then in the thick of raising an unprecedented $60 million for the Nixon re-election drive. Almost one-half of this total was solicited before the new law on federal

[8] United States *v.* John N. Mitchell *et al.,* Sears's testimony, March 7, 1974.

[9] Sears's SEC testimony, New York, February 20–21, 1973, p. 99.

elections went into force on April 7, 1972, with its more stringent reporting requirements. A good portion of it was solicited with an assurance to contributors that their identities would not be disclosed. In particular, about $1.7 million in cash was thought to have fallen through the month-long reporting gap between the expiration date of the old Corrupt Practices Act and the introduction of the new legislation, when absolutely no disclosure was required.

Vesco, accompanied by International Controls president Larry Richardson, flew down to Washington in early March 1972 to discuss the nuts and bolts of his attempt to buy political pull from Mitchell and Stans. As a senior partner in a Wall Street investment banking firm that had done a lot of business with IOS prior to the SEC's 1967 Settlement Order, Stans was familiar with IOS's long history of regulatory problems with the U.S. government. And he was undoubtedly aware that Vesco had yet to resign as chairman of IOS. But as head of the Nixon finance committee it would be difficult for Stans not to have been influenced by his responsibility to raise as much money as possible for the President's re-election campaign.

The problem of accepting a contribution from Vesco was obviously the delicate matter of where to draw the line between an honest political donation and an attempt to impede justice. As Stans was a true professional in his field, he knew exactly where to draw that line while giving Vesco the come-on. Vesco, according to Richardson, did in fact think he was buying influence. Although Stans did not offer any discouragement, he knew how not to transgress the boundaries of criminal liability.

Vesco explained to Stans that he wanted to be "a front-row contributor" and was prepared to give $250,000 immediately and another $250,000 toward the end of the campaign. But Vesco, according to Richardson, also mentioned that he wanted some help in getting the SEC off his back. Stans later denied that Vesco had said any such thing.

Stans, Richardson continued, brushed off the SEC aspect of the problem but proceeded to describe the confidentiality feature of the changing campaign financing laws, stressing the loophole provided by the month-long reporting gap. Stans—and Richardson was emphatic about this—then said he wanted the first half of the contribution "in currency" before the April 6, 1972, cut-off date. The term "currency" in reference to cash became a standing joke around the International Controls headquarters in the weeks that followed.

Once back in Fairfield, Vesco informed Sears that the contribution apparently was required "in currency."

"What did Stans mean?" Vesco asked.

Sears said he wasn't sure.

At a meeting in Vesco's office on March 29, 1972, with Richardson, Sears, and New York attorney Howard Cerny, Vesco said they had better check it out once again. "It was decided that Mr. Cerny would call Ed Nixon, the President's brother, and ask if he would verify this," Sears said, referring to whether Stans had specified cash as the form in which the contribution should be made.

Cerny called the CREEP headquarters in Washington and was informed that Ed Nixon had just left on the shuttle flight to New York. It was decided to intercept him when he landed at La Guardia and fly him over to the International Controls headquarters in one of the firm's leased helicopters.

Sears left the meeting just as Ed Nixon arrived but was later told that the President's brother had called Washington and confirmed that cash was the form in which the contribution was desired.

However, Ed Nixon testified for Stans at the New York trial that Stans had told him "to remain anonymous, the contribution would have to be made before April 7 . . . that if Mr. Vesco was really concerned so much about anonymity, it should be in cash, but as far as the committee was concerned, it made absolutely no difference at all." [10]

Sears, meanwhile, had suggested that Vesco give only $200,000 secretly prior to the April 6 deadline, and $50,000 overtly at a later date through the New Jersey finance committee. As chairman of the New Jersey CREEP, Sears reaffirmed this procedure when he flew to Washington on Monday, April 3, to make final arrangements with Stans. He told Stans that Vesco had indicated he was raising the funds from "personal sources" offshore and that the money would be available during the week. [11]

On April 5, the day before the deadline, Ralph Dodd called Sears at his Boonton law offices to tell him that the $250,000 was on its way. Dodd, recently resigned from International Controls, had bought into the small, financially strapped New York brokerage house of Ross, Low & Bull, Incorporated. The firm's president, Robert Bull, had been acquainted with Vesco for several years. Dodd was instructed in a call from the Bahamas to pick up the money at Barclays Bank International, which was in the same building as the Ross, Low offices, and deliver it to Fairfield.

Sears notified Stans that the cash was en route. But Stans had "bad scheduling problems" that took him out of Washington on April 6, and therefore physical delivery of the money was delayed until the

[10] United States *v.* John N. Mitchell *et al.* Edward C. Nixon testimony, April 7, 1974.

[11] Sears's SEC testimony, New York, February 20–21, 1972, p. 111.

following week. However, as the cash had been on hand by the cutoff date, CREEP later attempted to maintain that it had been "constructively" delivered within the secrecy period and failed to report it.

On the next day, April 6, Howard Cerny, who was involved in the transfer of the money, hired a 270-pound private detective, Philip Beck, to accompany Dodd to Fairfield with the cash. Armed for the assignment, Beck entered Barclays's Wall Street branch with Dodd just before the 3 P.M. closing and saw the cash stashed in a corner behind the tellers' cages. It was in $100 notes bound in brown paper wrappers.

The notes were loosely placed in an old brown leather briefcase that Dodd had brought with him. The two men then walked to Dodd's Cadillac, still registered in the name of International Controls, and the briefcase was tossed onto the back seat. They drove through the mounting rush-hour traffic across the Hudson River, west along Route 80 to Fairfield Airport, adjoining the International Controls headquarters, where a taxi was waiting to take Beck back to the city. As he left, Beck said he saw Dodd driving off with the money in the direction of the New Jersey hills.

The SEC investigators were not able to ascertain exactly where the $250,000 went from there, although they had strong suspicions, until Sears was subpoenaed to make his deposition in February 1973, three months after the SEC had sued on November 27, 1972.

Dodd drove the money to Vesco's office and left it there. Originally Dodd was supposed to have accompanied Sears to Washington to deliver the money. But the former International Controls vice-president was arguing with Vesco over his termination package and at the last moment refused to go. So late Friday Vesco called Richardson and asked him to act as the courier. He also instructed Richardson to give Stans a message—that he expected the SEC to be ordered to halt its investigation.

On Monday, April 10, Sears and Richardson flew down to Washington in a Cessna 310 belonging to Fairfield Aviation. They went directly to Stans's office at 1701 Pennsylvania Avenue. Richardson's instructions were to be as brisk as possible, so he placed the briefcase on Stans's desk and said, "Mr. Stans, here is your currency." He opened the top of the briefcase a couple of inches and, tilting it toward Stans, asked if he wanted to verify the $200,000.

Stans glanced at the largest cash contribution collected for Nixon and replied, "No, that won't be necessary."

No receipt was demanded; no receipt was given.

Sears said some light conversation followed, which he noted was the "propensity" in that kind of situation "because you kind of feel its like a cloak-and-dagger kind of atmosphere."

Richardson, according to Sears, made a remark to the effect that "we sure hope we might get some proper help somewhere along the line, if possible." According to Richardson, the remark was much more direct.

Sears claimed he immediately cut this avenue of conversation short by interposing, "Look, let us not kid about this. This is nothing but a political contribution. It has no relationship to any matter, and it has been worked out hopefully within proper bounds." [12]

In other words, there was to be no *quid pro quo*. Which really didn't matter, Stans later testified, because he hadn't interpreted the remark that way at all. Which was fine, except that Stans quickly added in reply to Richardson, according to court testimony, that the *quo* for the *quids* were not his baliwick anyway, but belonged in John Mitchell's department.

It was a very pregnant five minutes that ended just after 11 A.M., when Sears and Richardson left the CREEP headquarters. Richardson flew on to Wilmington, and Sears remained in Washington for a luncheon appointment, after which he paid a visit to Mitchell, the man supposedly in charge of the *quid pro quos*. During that meeting Sears admitted there was "some discussion" about Vesco's problem with the SEC.

"Some discussion" in fact resulted in the President's chief political strategist picking up the telephone and getting Sears an appointment with SEC chairman Bill Casey later that same afternoon.

Such quick action by Mitchell, however, was just as quickly out of mind. At his trial in New York two years later Mitchell said that, while he didn't dispute the government's evidence, he had no recollection of the telephone call to Casey or even the visit from Sears.

Sears nevertheless did meet with Casey that day. SEC general counsel Brad Cook also attended the meeting in Casey's office and noted that there might be a perjury case against Vesco in the offing. "If he lied to the staff, then we have to consider the possibility of a criminal referral," Cook stated.

Sears, shocked, asked Casey if there was any way to be assured that Vesco could present his side of the case before any charges were filed. He said Casey repeated, "We [the Commissioners] don't rubber-stamp staff recommendations around here." [13]

On May 11, 1972, Sears again met with Casey and Cook, then on May 31, 1972, another meeting took place with Cook alone. Finally, on June 27, 1972, ten days after the Watergate burglary that Vesco's cash

[12] Sears's SEC testimony, New York, February 20–21, 1973, pp. 120–21.
[13] United States *v.* John Mitchell *et al.,* Sears's testimony, March 7, 1974.

helped finance, Cook and Sporkin met again with Vesco and Merle Thorpe, International Controls's senior counsel from Hogan & Hartson. But Vesco never did get his private audience with Casey.

Sears met Casey once more in Miami Beach during the GOP Convention that August. He went around to the Hotel Doral, where the SEC chairman was staying, and talked with Casey for about thirty minutes in the SEC chairman's suite. Before leaving, Sears later told the SEC's Robert Kushner, he received what he thought was an undertaking from Casey that the entire Vesco/IOS/International Controls matter would be given a thorough review just as soon as the Commission chairman got back to his desk in Washington. However, after several weeks had elapsed and he hadn't heard back from Casey, he again contacted the chairman and was told that the case had become too big and was much more serious than Casey had imagined.

Vesco contributed, as planned, $50,000 through the New Jersey CREEP. This time it was delivered by check, and it figured in reports filed with the General Accounting Office's Bureau of Federal Elections. The only record of the $200,000, however, appeared in the Nixon finance committee's secret cash books under the coded entry "J.M."—meaning, Stans testified, that the donation was arranged anonymously by a friend of John Mitchell.

"What the hell did you do that for?" Mitchell was quoted as saying when he heard about it.

Stans, a member of the Accounting Hall of Fame, justified this cryptic bookkeeping technique by insisting that "Vesco made the contribution in private, and privacy was his constitutional right under the law."

The two thousand $100 bills were placed in a wall safe in Stans's office, and the money was used by campaign treasurer Hugh W. Sloan, Jr., the U.S. government's bill of particulars implied, to make at least three secret payments to campaign aide G. Gordon Liddy, CREEP's general counsel, who also served as operations head of the White House "plumbers."

A disbursement of $70,000 was given from Stans's secret cache to White House aide Frederick C. LaRue, one of Mitchell's closest political advisers, for purposes unknown. That transfer came two weeks after five men were arrested in the Watergate headquarters of the Democrats. This apparently illegal transfer was approved by Stans and was used for noncampaign purposes.

The contents of Stans's wall safe were one of three secret Nixon re-election funds that were uncovered during investigations into the Watergate cover-up. The others were the "Haldeman Account" containing $350,000 and kept in a safe at the White House, and the

"California Account," which contained up to $500,000 and was kept in a Newport Beach, California, branch of the Bank of America in the name of Herbert W. Kalmbach, the President's personal attorney.

A fourth account—the largest of all—was widely rumored to have existed in Switzerland, containing up to $1 million for "advertising" and other media expenses overseas. According to sometime Jimmy Hoffa "lawyer" William L. Taub, Vesco made additional substantial contributions to the Nixon campaign through the Swiss account.

The story of where Vesco's $250,000 came from is itself an intriguing sidebar to this Watergate curlicue. On April 5, 1972, Bahamas Commonwealth Bank transferred the money to Barclays Bank International in New York. At the time the transfer was debited to a suspense account tentatively labeled the Howard Cerny loan account at Bahamas Commonwealth Bank, since nobody was certain from which account the money should be withdrawn.

Finally, in mid-July 1972, LeBlanc instructed that the transfer be charged to International Bancorp Limited, along with the accrued interest from the date of remittal. Then by back-dating the transfer it was included as of December 31, 1971, in International Bancorp's organizational expenses account as an asset item; hence the inflated organizational expenses of International Bancorp helped finance the Watergate scandal. Not unexpectedly, this version of events contradicted Vesco's claim that the $250,000 was a personal loan extended to him by Trident Bank.

Trident was an alternative Vesco-LeBlanc banking arm in the Bahamas. It was itself the product of a rip-off, as once it had been part of IOS Financial Holdings Limited under a series of different names. Trident had no auditors, so who was to know any better?

The entire $250,000 was belatedly returned to Vesco in January 1973 by the Committee to Re-elect the President with a letter stating that, in view of the charges against him and his firms in connection with the looting of IOS, "we believe it is in your best interest, as well as ours, that the contributions be returned." The money was recouped not by International Bancorp but by a Vesco account at Trident.

The disclosures made by Harry Sears in his 371-page deposition taken by SEC counsel Robert Kushner were devoured with great interest by the U.S. Attorney in New York, who empaneled a federal grand jury to investigate. This resulted in the May 1973 indictments against Mitchell, Stans, Sears, and Vesco for conspiring to obstruct justice by attempting to fix the SEC investigation. Mitchell and Stans, who faced possible jail terms of fifty years and fines of as much as $75,000 if found guilty, were acquitted one year later after a dramatic ten-week trial. Sears, who refused to testify on the grounds it might incriminate him, was then granted immunity from the prosecution and became an embarrassed and reluctant government witness. Vesco, who had fled the country by then, faced a possible term of twenty years and a fine of $25,000 if ever he stood trial and were found guilty.

17

Looting the Funds

*The shell game begins in earnest — Vesco resigns from IOS —
International Controls sells its offshore holdings to a group headed
by Nasty Norman, and $280 million is siphoned from the four
IOS dollar funds into the Sham of Shams and similar investment
situations*

The collapse of IOS was one of the most significant factors in
undermining public confidence in the entire mutual fund concept. The
real *raison d'être* of mutual funds, later perverted by the go-go performance cult popularized by Cornfeld, was that they offered modest
and unsophisticated investors the possibility of pooling their savings for
the purpose of sharing in the same benefits of diversification and professional management normally available only to the very rich.

Part of the appeal of mutual funds was the notion that at any time
the investor could convert his or her shares back into cash. It was an
open-ended investment concept whereby the mutual fund stood ready to
buy back or "redeem" its shares for cash upon demand. To be able to
do this, fund managers were required to invest the assets of their fund
in readily marketable securities.

One of the unfortunate realities of the investment business, however,
is that anybody who handles large sums of other people's money is
open to the temptation of using some or all of that money for personal
gain. And since the range of potential abuses is wide, the U.S. Investment Company Act of 1940 was passed into legislation. To protect
investors from being bilked by dishonest or unscrupulous promoters it
requires that publicly offered mutual funds build a system of checks
and balances into their structures, administration, and operating procedures.

Under the act it is mandatory for a fund to have independent auditors and independent custodian banks as the depository of cash and securities. It prohibits fund management from dealing with affiliates or affiliates of affiliates without proper authorization and then making full disclosure. It establishes maximum investment limits that a fund can make in a single security. It also requires that statements be issued regularly to the fund-holders.

Summarized briefly, some of the more obvious abuses which the Investment Company Act was intended to protect the public investor against were:

(1) the improper placing of client money in companies in which fund management, affiliates, or associates held an interest
(2) certain back-to-back type contrivances, such as putting fund money on deposit with a "friendly" bank on condition that the bank make a compensating loan for the benefit of the fund managers, their associates, or affiliated companies
(3) using client money for classic bootstrapping operations or to support the stock of related or affiliated companies
(4) accepting kickbacks on brokerage, making reciprocal deals with brokers, or other types of financial backscratching to the ultimate benefit of the fund managers
(5) undisclosed or unnecessarily burdensome charges for management, advisory, and administrative charges
(6) locking up large portions of the fund's assets in "investments" that impair the fund's ability to redeem its shares
(7) interpositioning additional layers of brokerage in a fund portfolio transaction, permitting at least one extra broker to "scalp" the fund for extra commissions

Vesco and his associates abused their fiduciary responsibilities to the IOS mutual fund clients by systematically proceeding to do *all* of these things.

The first indication that he was moving in this direction came on November 15, 1971, when IOS sent out a "Dear Client" letter to its remaining 400,000 fund-holders informing them that "certain procedural changes" had been instituted that would affect future payments into their investment accounts. Little did anyone suspect that this letter introduced the final act in the sad IOS spectacle, with its long history of unsafe performances, fraudulent misrepresentations, and swindling sideshows.

The procedural changes referred to in the November 1971 letter were of the utmost significance, for they gave Vesco and his group the first of the levers needed to drain the funds by transferring huge sums of money to the Bahamas and from their investing the converted cash in a collection of self-dealing ventures and shady lockups.

The first "procedural change" was a shift in the receiving bank for the dollar funds—Funds of Funds, ITT, Venture International, and IOS Growth Fund—from Credit Suisse, Zurich, to Overseas Development Bank, Luxembourg.

The replacement of Credit Suisse as cash receiver was forced upon IOS by Switzerland's new legislation on foreign mutual fund operations. Federal Banking Commission officials in Berne frankly admitted that the new law had been designed to force IOS out of Switzerland. The IOS funds, it was known in advance, would be unable to comply with the strict registration requirements of the 1971 decree.

Thus the listing of a Swiss bank on sales literature by an unregistered fund became an unlawful act of solicitation. Similarly, processing on-going monthly program investments through a Swiss mailing address was also considered an offense. IOS, at the time, still received an estimated $1 million in monthly remittances from contractual plan-holders who apparently were immune to the continuing bad publicity about the company and its investment products.

Hence the "Dear Clients"—a gullible lot at that—were told to make their checks or bank drafts payable in the future to Overseas Development Bank in Luxembourg and send them not to the bank, as one might have expected, but to P.O. Box 10331 in Amsterdam.

Value Capital Limited, the IOS "dividend company" to which were assigned the rights to the IOS Investment Program, set up a service operation in Amsterdam under the direction of former IOS financial vice-president "Yogi Bear" Hoffman to pre-process the continuing client accounts. To help smooth the way for Value Capital in Amsterdam, Vesco contributed $28,000 of corporate cash to Prince Bernhardt of the Netherlands' favorite charity, the World Wildlife Fund.[1] Thereafter IOS client program payments were mailed to the post office box in

[1] In February 1972 Vesco heard that Prince Bernhardt, president of the World Wildlife Fund, was in West Palm Beach, Florida, on a fund raising campaign. Vesco flew there aboard his Boeing 707 and attended a World Wildlife auction, bidding $18,000 for a painting of a clouded leopard—the highest price of the day—and met Prince Bernhardt at a cocktail reception afterwards. He paid another $10,000 to become a member of the 1001 Nature Trust, an endowment fund formed by Prince Bernhardt to finance the World Wildlife Fund's activities. Other members of the "1001 Club" include the Aga Khan, Stavros Niarchos, the younger brother of the Shah of Iran, the Duke of Bedford, John Loudon, the head of Royal Dutch Shell, Sir Max Aitken, owner of Britain's Beaverbrook newspapers, Giovanni Agnelli of Italy's Fiat group, and Walter Annenberg, the millionaire U.S. ambassador to London. For Vesco, membership in such a prestigious association was exceptionally good value. However, in 1973, after being charged with fraud, embezzlement, and obstruction of justice, his membership fee was returned and his name struck from the "1001 Club" registry.

Amsterdam, then transferred to the appropriate fund account at Overseas Development Bank in Luxembourg, and the computer data updating individual client accounts were forwarded in bulk to Geneva.

The November 1971 letter informed the clients, with a total lack of candor, that "Overseas Development Bank Luxembourg S.A. is, like all other banks which perform services for the IOS Investment Program, unaffiliated with IOS Ltd. It is a subsidiary of International Bancorp Limited, a worldwide banking group with operations in Munich, London, Geneva, and the Bahamas, with total assets of approximately $100 million. Thank you for your cooperation."

The letter neglected to mention that just three weeks before International Bancorp had been created out of the shambles of the IOS banking network and could hardly be described as totally independent. But it was important to create the fiction that it was an independent entity, for ODB Lux was to become the first way station on the circuitous route that siphoned the IOS fund moneys into such sunny investment havens as the Bahamas, Costa Rica, the Dominican Republic, Lebanon, and Panama.

When Vesco joined the IOS board of directors in September 1970, the four dollar funds had combined assets of $667,786,564. By early 1972, as a result of client redemptions and poor market performance, these assets had dwindled to $440 million. Vesco meanwhile had swept out the old IOS investment department and installed a new fund manager brought in from New York, fifty-four-year-old Stanley Graze.

A former economics lecturer, Graze looked more like an unsuccessful bookmaker than a reasonably sharp investment manager. But he had been a vice-president of, successively, the Wall Street brokerage firm Love, Douglas & Company and BWA Incorporated, the West Coast broker-dealer in which Vesco once held an interest.

Graze first came to Vesco's attention in April 1968 when he wrote a dazzling brokerage house report on Vesco's young and little-known International Controls Corporation. Vesco spotted Graze as a man of talent when in that fourteen-page report he characterized International Controls as a rapidly growing concern with "an intriguing, though speculative, potential for capital gains." Graze predicted that International Controls earnings would triple in 1968 to $1 a share, when in fact the company ended up posting a net loss of $1.07 a share.

"The most impressive quality about International Controls is its management. For a growing and still small company, the knowledgeable and financially sophisticated expertise of its youthful key people is most striking. . . . While not without some risks, the profit opportunities presented by a sound, fast growing, and well managed company such as

International Controls are considerable," the Graze report concluded, earning its author Vesco's undying admiration in the process.

Now, four years later, Graze was to become one of the principal mechanics in the looting of the IOS funds.

Vesco first unveiled his long-considered plans for looting the IOS funds in early 1972 when he suggested the incorporation of ABC N.V., a planned Dutch Antilles company into which he intended rolling the four open-end investment companies, Fund of Funds, IIT, Venture International, and IOS Growth Fund.

This ABC N.V. was totally different in concept from the ABC Corporation he originally planned to use, then discarded, for the Restructuring of IOS. ABC N.V.—also known under the codename LPI—was to "engage in investment banking activities throughout the world" with the moneys it looted from the four IOS funds. At one of the meetings he held in Fairfield to discuss the locking up of the fund moneys, Vesco drew a diagram on a large flip sheet showing the flow of money into a central box, which he had labeled "LPI." When asked what LPI stood for, he replied with a thin smile, "Looting & Plundering, Inc." To avoid confusion with the first ABC Corporation, this later product of Vesco's imagination, ABC N.V., will be referred to mainly under its other *nom de guerre,* LPI.

At a January 27, 1972, strategy session with Dick Clay, James D. McMenamin from Coopers & Lybrand, and counsel from New York and Toronto for the dollar funds, Vesco instructed the American and Canadian attorneys "to consider the legalities of what might be involved in the creation of ABC N.V.," the looting and plundering vehicle.

"Notification would go out to all fundholders and also in leading publications around the world telling the fundholders that on such and such a date, which was not fixed at the meeting, the directors of the funds intended to invest all of the money in ABC N.V. Anyone who did not redeem and who was still a fundholder at this unstipulated date would at that point receive securities of ABC N.V. for his investment in the fund," McMenamin said Vesco explained at that meeting.[2]

At the end of this close-ending process it was estimated that $150 million in "hot money" would remain unclaimed in the four funds and therefore would be available for transfer to LPI. Then, at the next IOS annual general shareholder meeting scheduled for June 30, 1972, in Saint John, New Brunswick, the plan called for an announcement that, due to rising costs, IOS was going out of the mutual fund business and would henceforth concentrate on "investment banking" activities with the locked-in client cash.

[2] SEC post-trial memorandum, June 8, 1973, p. 13.

Following the January 1972 Fairfield meeting Vesco expected to receive the first legal drafts of the LPI plan from the dollar fund attorneys, but instead he received a top-secret memorandum explaining why the plan was a poor risk.

The memo pointed out the LPI "may be regarded as a scheme designed (i) to frustrate the redemption rights of the fundholders, and (ii) avoid the fund directors' obligation to insure that fund assets are invested in reasonably marketable securities." [3]

The LPI plan was thus stalled until a better way could be found to get the scheme rolling again. Vesco now realized he first had to remove himself from a position of evident control within IOS, then to dismantle and disperse the pieces of the former IOS empire so that he could bring them all together again in a new collection of receptacles without visible lines of attachment. These receptacles were to be used for looting the various mutual funds, investment trusts, and other components of the IOS group.

This he prepared to do in several steps. First he would sell IOS to a shell company in the Bahamas. In phase two he would set up "independent" custodians for the fund assets that were really not independent at all but part of the old IOS empire. In phase three he would sell control of the two "dividend companies"—International Bancorp Limited and Value Capital Limited—to Global Holdings Limited, which became the official name for LPI. These phases completed, the stage was set for the in-depth plundering of the IOS client moneys.

Using as a pretext continuing pressure to sever International Controls from its IOS holdings, Vesco promptly resigned from the hot seat in Geneva, thereby creating the illusion of having relinquished control of IOS and removing himself, he hoped, from the SEC's continuing gaze and concern.

To further this illusion, on April Fools' Day, 1972, International Controls announced that it had sold its 38 per cent interest in IOS Ltd. to Kilmorey Investments Limited. The four owners of Kilmorey turned out to be none other than four close Vesco associates in IOS management, Meissner, Strickler, LeBlanc, and Graze, the new IOS fund manager. Their new company, Kilmorey, was capitalized at only $2,000. But in purchasing the 23.6 million IOS common and preferred shares held by two International Controls subsidiaries, ICC Investments Limited and Hemispheres Financial Services, Kilmorey ostensibly paid $2.8 million in cash and promissory notes.

The purchase price, however, was never substantiated. The cash involved in the demonstrably non-arm's-length transaction was only

[3] *Ibid.*, p. 14.

$200,000, and even this was advanced to Kilmorey by Bahamas Commonwealth Bank.

True to Vesco's accounting principles, International Controls immediately claimed a pre-tax gain of $950,000 on the transaction. In addition, the Fairfield combine retained its dominating interest in the two dividend companies, International Bancorp and Value Capital, which still contained the most valuable assets of the by then denuded IOS (see chart 4).

The press release announcing the Kilmorey sale stated that International Controls officers had resigned "all positions with IOS and its subsidiaries"—another deliberately misleading affirmation. Vesco, Clay, and Beatty continued to serve as directors of Global Natural Resources Properties Limited, the Fund of Funds offshoot formed by interim management in August 1970 to take over FOF's illiquid natural resources investments. Clay and Beatty also remained on the boards of Investment Properties International (IPI) and Property Resources Limited (PRL), a company that was formed for the purpose of misappropriating the assets of IPI and Global Natural Resources.

The Kilmorey deal was an important intermediate step in restructuring the LPI plan in more palatable terms. With the replacement four months before of Credit Suisse as cash receiver for the dollar funds, it fitted a discernable pattern. Under the new cash receiver arrangement, Overseas Development Bank in Luxembourg collected all moneys remitted by the clients for investment in their ongoing IOS accounts before transferring them through a floating account to Credit Suisse in Zurich. But now Credit Suisse notified Bank of New York, the custodian of securities for the funds, that it could no longer function as the cash custodian.

Immediately the Bank of New York became a major stumbling block in Vesco's over-all plan by objecting to the appointment of ODB Lux as the replacement custodian for Credit Suisse and ignoring instructions to transfer to the Luxembourg bank proceeds from the sale of portfolio securities. Bank of New York officials insisted that as prudent bankers they could not entrust the funds' cash to a little-known and thinly-capitalized outfit that was, in spite of representations to the contrary, affiliated with IOS.

According to IOS, however, "independence" had come to ODB Lux's board when Dick Clay, the former merchant seaman who became Vesco's real estate expert and now international banker, was elected the bank's chairman, replacing Meissner, and Gil Straub—"the last person in the world to trust in a fiduciary capacity"—was elected vice-chairman. Clay, at this point, was vice-president, office of the chairman, and a director of International Controls. Straub resigned in April 1972 as director of European services for International Controls but, like Clay, was a director of Bahamas Commonwealth Bank and International Bancorp Limited, respectively an affiliate and parent of the Luxembourg bank.

The Bank of New York definitely was not impressed and certainly had good reason to be cautious. ODB Lux was understaffed for the job of cash custodian. In fact, in June 1971 two of the bank's employees were among four persons arrested by the Luxembourg authorities as members of an international ring of fake and stolen securities traffickers. On the bank's books was a loan for $140,000 collateralized with counterfeit IBM stock and stolen Anheuser-Busch bonds. A total of $7 million worth of bogus or stolen securities, supplied by a Mafia-backed organization headed by the son of a British peer and intended to be sluffed off on ODB Lux in later loan transactions, were uncovered by the Luxembourg police when they arrested the ring members.

To convince Bank of New York that their Luxembourg bucket shop was indeed a worthy institution, Vesco and LeBlanc entered into a classic bootstrapping operation to increase its capital from $1,250,000 to $5 million. ODB Lux was so short of disposable funds that even insiders scoffingly referred to it as the "Overdraft & Debt Bank." And so, to prop it up, the boys in Nassau manufactured a series of intergroup book entries that baffled even SEC investigators.

The group as a whole was so critically short of working capital that the only way they could produce the necessary liquidity was by dipping into the client money. Investment Properties International (IPI), IOS's $100 million real estate unit, was selected as the victim. The operation worked as follows.

In early March 1972, IPI was caused to deposit $4.5 million with Bahamas Commonwealth Bank in Nassau. This gave Bahamas Commonwealth Bank sufficient liquidity to lend its parent, International Bancorp Limited, $4.3 million. Although treated as a deposit with International Bancorp, the money was remitted directly to ODB Lux to permit it to increase its capital. Now, in order to get a part of the money back into Bahamas Commonwealth Bank to cover the gap this had left, ODB Lux redeposited $2.5 million with International Bancorp. A similar amount was transferred in turn to Bahamas Commonwealth Bank.

The net result of this feat of bookkeeping legerdemain was that Vesco was then in a position to demonstrate to Bank of New York that his "Overdraft & Debit Bank" had acquired greater reserves, which were in fact illusory. Next LeBlanc attempted to "discipline" the BoNY people by threatening legal action against them for allegedly interfering with IOS fund management decisions (by refusing to remit the cash received from the sale of portfolio securities in the funds to ODB Lux). This gave Vesco a pretext for the confrontation he was seeking with senior BoNY officials. On April 26, 1972, he stormed into the New York offices of vice-president Joseph L. McElroy and, after some blunt conversation, announced that the bank's function as custodian of securities was terminated.

With little more ceremony, and certainly no disclosure to IOS fundholders, the custodianship of securities was moved from the irreproachable Bank of New York to a bank one-fifth its size. That bank was American National in Morristown.

"The choice of American National as securities custodian for the dollar funds was curious indeed," the SEC commented. "American National's qualifications to act as securities custodian for the dollar funds were somewhat obscure, for the only mutual fund it served in a similar capacity was the Doll Fund, with assets $200,000, roughly equal to .05 per cent of the dollar funds' assets." [4] But the appointment of American National was a necessary step to appointing Bahamas Commonwealth Bank as subcustodian. This Nassau bank was to be a conduit in the looting scheme through which some $280 million from the doomed dollar funds could be siphoned out of client reach.

With his fund-looting props in place, Vesco was now ready to proceed anew with this most delicate but personally fruitful task. After being told by counsel that his first LPI scheme was too crude, at another meeting in Fairfield on May 24, 1972, he unwrapped his new play for closing the funds, with a view to locking up a potential total of close to $400 million in client moneys for his personal investments and self-aggrandizement. LPI was reincarnated in the form of Global Holdings Limited, an empty shell incorporated by the Flying Bishop, IOS lawyer Michael Rogers, in Nassau two months before.

Vesco indicated a certain impatience at the May 24 meeting; one week later the Global Holding scheme was set in motion. The mechanism was subtle, and the timetable complicated.

International Controls still held a 22 per cent interest in International Bancorp Limited and 38 per cent in Value Capital Limited. A quick barometer reading by Vesco's Washington lawyers showed that storm warnings were flying higher than ever at the SEC, so a board meeting of International Controls was called in Fairfield on June 2, 1972.

At this meeting Vesco proposed that International Controls sell its interest in the two dividend companies, International Bancorp and Value Capital Limited, to Global Financial Limited, the operating arm of

[4] *Ibid.*, p. 37.

Global Holdings Limited, for $7.35 million, payable in 5 per cent promissory notes over five years. And Global Holdings, Vesco disclosed, was owned by Nasty Norman the Burble.

Vesco claimed the proposed cashless transaction, if approved by the Fairfield directors, would result in a net profit of $5.3 million, the total gain to International Controls on its seventeen-month association with IOS.

The previous day Norman LeBlanc began a series of financial gyrations as directed by Vesco that set the stage for his leap into the big time as an international swindler. As part of LeBlanc's warmup for this multimillion dollar jump to financial notoriety, he resigned from IOS and announced that he had sold his interest in Kilmorey Investments Limited "at a profit" to Ulrich Strickler, the Swiss "management consultant" brought into IOS by Vesco. LeBlanc then proceeded to acquire, for a cash outlay of $2,000 and the issuing of five IOU's, a controlling interest in the most valuable pieces of the former IOS empire—which three years previously had a book value of close to $100 million—without assuming any of the liabilities. The liabilities were left behind in the old IOS shell.

By reposing voting control of the ex-IOS banking, real estate, and insurance properties in LeBlanc's Global Holdings Limited, Vesco inserted yet another layer of paper between the IOS shareholders and their offshore assets. Now Global Holdings and Global Financial, purchased by LeBlanc for $1,000 each, would evolve as the pivotal entities in a loosely connected network of banks, dummy companies, trusts, and other concerns, all the products of an IOS ripoff, christened by a few jaundiced insiders as "Super Group."

Vesco assured the International Controls board that LeBlanc's offer was fair, that LeBlanc would honor his obligations to pay the $7.35 million in notes as they fell due, and that there was absolutely no connection between LeBlanc and himself. Vesco further informed the directors that the deal as it was proposed carried a unique acceleration clause. "All the notes would become immediately due and payable in the event that 50 per cent or more of the outstanding shares of any class of stock of Global Holdings should cease to be owned by Mr. LeBlanc," he announced.

The International Controls board, explained director Stanley Hiller, Jr., had little choice but to accept the "LeBlanc offer." No other purchaser of the dividend companies was on the horizon, and the Fairfield directors thought they needed to be rid of the IOS remnants in order to get the SEC off their backs.

"By June [1972] International Controls was becoming a basket case. So much time and talent had been drained off [by the SEC investigation] that the basic operation of the company was in an impossible situation," Hiller told the SEC.

"In considering the sale, weighing more heavily than anything else was the question of saving the basic company. . . . I made my decision and voted for this on the basis that I believed this company would have gone down the drain had not the sale been made, and the sale being made as fast as possible," Hiller said.[5]

"It must be realized," Hiller added, "that there's a company called International Controls that is known in the trade as International Disaster."

With LeBlanc working for the moment on a further watering down of the shareholders' interests in the two dividend companies, Vesco briefly concentrated his attention on shoring up his Fairfield flier, which had been pretty well grounded by its offshore entanglements.

Indeed, the company had fallen into a pitiable state. One of its three front-line subsidiaries, Datron Systems Incorporated, had incurred a $2.7 million deficit through what was feared to be "fraudulent" reporting, and the problem of diminishing cash flow in general needed urgent resolution. The board therefore decided to undo the reorganization work begun by Vesco the year before, as it had not proved conceptually sound, and was considering erasing the name of International Controls and its dissonant overtones of offshore dealings from the corporate rolls altogether by merging it into its subsidiary, All American Industries, which had a separate listing on the American Stock Exchange.

Although hardly consistent with the fact that International Controls had its back to the wall, schemer Vesco continued to spend considerable time planning a superb new "world headquarters" for his ramshackle empire, which undoubtedly he would construct with money invested by the IOS clients whose interests he said were so close to his heart. Thus in the spring of 1972 the cashless Fairfield flier's newest subsidiary, Montville Development Corporation, was formed to acquire a piece of prime real estate in neighboring Montville Township. A Trenton firm of development consultants was engaged to draw up plans for a ten-story office building with penthouse suite for the chairman and adjoining motel to be operated by "one of the leading American motel chains."

Vesco's ideas for the Montville complex, which included a communications center, a five-star restaurant, a bar, a private club, and a high-class recreational facility, could only be described as gross. Any need for a "world headquarters" on American soil was dumped, however, with the launching of the SEC civil fraud action at the end of the year, causing Vesco to transfer his plans for such a development to a less regulated offshore location.

[5] Hiller's SEC testimony, San Francisco, October 19, 1972, pp. 152–54.

LeBlanc, meanwhile, had increased the authorized capital of the two Globals. He insisted that he had subscribed for all the voting stock himself by putting $1,015,000 of his own money into the treasury. When asked how a onetime accountant had amassed such a considerable fortune in so short a career, the chain-smoking, puffy-faced LeBlanc merely shrugged and responded vaguely that he and his wife Alice had made some timely investments. The image of Nasty Norman the Burble as an Instant Tycoon was thus consummated.

LeBlanc's next step, he said, was to return to his friends at IOS (specifically Stanley Graze, the ace analyst) and ask them to invest in his marvelous new Global combine. "I said, 'Why don't you guys invest in this company? Here's what I'm going to do with it.' They studied it, and looked at it, and they liked it."

All in all, the "IOS analysts" looked at LeBlanc's two Globals for sixteen days before putting $20 million of Venture International's money into them—$10 million in nonvoting Class B stock of Global Holdings, and $10 million in an unsecured fifteen-year debenture in Global Financial bearing a 7 per cent "prime rate" of interest, which was anything but prime, with a six-month interest-free ride that cost Venture International fund-holders an extra $350,000.

Forty-five per cent of the fund's assets were thus locked up in Global Holdings, a high-risk enterprise whose shares were unmarketable, with no operations and no track record in the financial field, whose only management appeared to be the onetime Montreal accountant previously involved in one of the largest financial scandals in Canada.

And so Global Holdings Limited, with Nasty Norman the Burble at the helm, was unveiled as Vesco's long-planned LPI, and Venture International was selected as its first victim, because the Curaçao-incorporated fund with total assets of $51 million was experiencing the heaviest client redemption rate of the four dollar funds.

The immediate recipient of Venture International's huge "investment" was none other than International Controls, Vesco's cash-tight Fairfield conglomerate. On June 30, 1972, the Global notes were fully prepaid with the Venture money. This injection of $7.35 million in hot cash brought a rush of color back into the pallid International Controls balance sheet, which otherwise would have shown a half-million-dollar loss for the first half of 1972.

Flush with the proceeds of the Global notes, International Controls diverted $2.2 million to repurchase, at a 50 per cent discount on the principal amount, the remaining Eurobonds first sold to IIT fund by Vesco in 1968. This further reduction of International Controls's long-term debt at IOS fund-holders' expense enabled the Fairfield concern to chalk up an additional non-cash gain of about $2 million, for the moment pulling the firm out of the red.

In spite of efforts to gloss over the IOS interlude as financially beneficial for the shareholders of International Controls, by late summer of 1972 a split had developed in the boardroom at Fairfield, with one faction demanding Vesco's retirement. In a last attempt "to clear his skirts with the SEC," Vesco opted to resign from the board of International Controls. But three weeks later, at the end of September, he was reappointed as a director, and it was agreed that he would remain a consultant with the same $120,000 salary and liberal expense account as before.

Vesco's growing isolation inside International Controls produced one consolation. It permitted him to focus his attention on the final phase of his two-year-old scheme of looting the IOS funds.

Work had already started as early as April 1972, when new IOS fund manager Stanley Graze gave orders to begin liquidating the U.S. securities held by the four dollar funds and transferring the proceeds to the new cash depository, Overseas Development Bank, Luxembourg. The tempo increased after the Bank of New York was replaced as custodian of securities, and over the next eight months no less than $224 million worth of essentially blue-chip American stocks were sold on the open market, principally through three low-profile brokerage firms—Ross, Low, Bull, Incorporated in New York; Lynch, Jones & Ryan, of which ex-FOF adviser Dean Melosis was a partner; and Dahlgren, Richardson & Company, a nonmember "third market" specialist, which then had close Vesco ties.

The route down to the Bahamas for the misappropriated cash was greased in mid-October 1972, when Dick Clay informed the "Overdraft & Debit Bank" board of directors that the dollar funds had requested ODB Lux to enter into a subdepository agreement with that pillar of independent financial institutions, Bahamas Commonwealth Bank. He produced a telex from Meissner in his capacity as president of IIT Management Company, Venture International, Funds of Funds, and IOS Growth Fund, which proposed that ODB Lux appoint its Bahamian sister bank as subcustodian of cash. A similar request had already been made to American National, the custodian of securities, to make the same Nassau bank a subcustodian of securities.

Vesco's grand looting scheme was now running like clockwork, and he had every intention of making Global Holdings Limited the queen of spades in his revamped LPI plan by pumping into it other fund moneys as well. The intention, of course, was to set up Global Holdings as his desired closed-end investment banking combine by fattening it with assets totaling $150 million or more plundered from the IOS funds.

Vesco's discovery of Costa Rica as a most tolerant investment haven caused yet another modification in the looting plans. This came about in mid-August 1972 with the second great rip-off from the funds, a $60 million "investment" by The Fund of Funds in a brand new creation known as Inter-American Capital S.A.

Howard Cerny had been hard at work for almost a month putting together Inter-American's corporate shell. For local assistance, since Inter-American was to be a Costa Rican company, he used the prominent San Jose law firm of Facio, Fournier & Canas. The senior partner of the firm, Gonzalo Facio, just happened to be the Foreign Minister of Costa Rica.

How did The Fund of Funds come to invest $60 million in the Sham of Shams? In July 1972 Vesco convened a large number of people in Amsterdam to discuss the "reorganization" of the funds. Among the invited guests were Meissner, LeBlanc, Strickler, Colonel Howkins, and John Schuyler, secretary of the four dollar funds. During a recess in the meeting Schuyler left the conference room in search of the men's room. He was informed by Meissner the following month that while he was out of the room Meissner, Strickler, and Howkins had convened a board meeting of FOF to consider and authorize the $60 million investment in Inter-American.

The "investment" purportedly was made on the basis of a flimsy five-page "first offering prospectus" dated August 1, 1972, some days after the FOF "board meeting." The prospectus listed a five-man board of directors headed by Dr. Alberto Inocente Alvarez, a wealthy Cuban refugee living in Costa Rica.

The prospectus contained a declaration that Inter-American would operate as "an aggressive 'venture capital' investment company" that would seek investment opportunities in "developing countries of the world," would have no investment restrictions at all, and should be viewed by fund-holders as a long-term investment. The prospectus further indicated that only the common shares had voting rights, but nowhere did it identify the owners of the common stock. FOF, as might be imagined, was purchasing the preferred (nonvoting) capital stock.

What the InterAmerican prospectus didn't contain was enough to fill a small book. There were no audited or even unaudited financial statements; no detailed statement regarding the use of the proceeds to be received from the "first offering": no description of the company's organization structure, including remuneration of officers and directors, the number of employees (if any), the place of business (if any), the experience and background of management (if any), the market place of the company's securities (if any), and the pricing mechanism for those securities.

Under the heading "Investment Philosophy" it stated that "inasmuch as the company has just commenced operations, it is contemplated that a significant part of the proceeds from this offering will be invested in one or more closed-end investment companies incorporated under the laws of Panama."

This statement was a dead giveaway for the next phase of the operation: the passage of $57.5 million of the $60 million received by Inter-American to Phoenix Financial Limited, a Panamanian corporation brought into the Super Group fold by Cerny the month before. From there the $57.5 million kept on traveling. Most of it was funneled clear through Phoenix into an account at Trident Bank in Nassau, owned by Vector Limited, which in turn was nominally owned by Norman LeBlanc.

What remained in Inter-American, therefore, was $1.18 million in cash, $804,000 in Costa Rican government bonds, a loan receivable of $117,000, a further sum of $112,500 in organization expenses, and $237,104 in "other investments."

Phoenix's balance sheet was more interesting. It showed $4.8 million invested in Costa Rican government bonds, $991,225 in "miscellaneous receivables," and $2.65 million listed as "investment in land"—period. No details. An additional $49.2 million was in cash and time deposits, of which $2 million had been channeled into an anonymous numbered account at the Union Bank of Switzerland.

The $60 million was committed for the purchase of 6 million preferred shares of Inter-American based upon a one-page letter of agreement. Delivery of the stock certificates was promised within thirty days. They arrived nine months later, and even then, according to an SEC memorandum, there was no way of knowing whether the stock certificates were the originals or duplicates.

When FOF's auditors, Coopets & Lybrand, attempted to obtain documentation attesting to the nature of the Inter-American investment, the information was withheld. This, and LeBlanc's refusal to sign a letter of transmittal for the 1971 International Bancorp Limited audit—which he had previously said he would do—led to the resignation of Coopets & Lybrand as auditors for International Controls, IOS, and the Super Group family of companies in November 1972.

The third major assault on the assets of the funds occurred in early October 1972, when American National Bank & Trust of Morristown was instructed to transmit $15 million from its IIT account to Bahamas Commonwealth Bank for placement with a company called Gulf Stream (Bahamas) Limited. That company, formed the month before and listing five Super Group typists as its charter shareholders, was incorporated by Cerny at the request of Vesco lieutenant Gil Straub. Gulf Stream was to acquire from Resorts International Incorporated the gambling casino on Paradise Island, opposite Nassau, and certain other assets, including the Paradise Island Bridge Company.

The purchase price for the Paradise Island casino and bridge was to have been $20 million in cash and $5 million in notes. The $15 million transferred from the Morristown bank was intended as a first payment. However, once the SEC filed its looting complaint against Vesco and his associates, negotiations for the purchase of the casino came to a "grinding halt." Although the deal collapsed, the money was never returned to IIT and remained on deposit at Bahamas Commonwealth Bank.

A curious investment in September 1972 by two IOS funds in EHG Enterprises Incorporated, a real estate development corporation formed under the laws of Puerto Rico, provided another glaring example of fund moneys being looted for the benefit of Super Group. The owners, two Cuban Americans, Henry and Ariel Gutierrez, as fate would have it, were nephews of Alberto Alvarez, the erstwhile chairman of Inter-American Capital.

Although EHG Enterprises was seeking only $6 million in financing, Vesco, Meissner, and LeBlanc offered the Gutierrez brothers $12 million —$9.5 million in EHG subordinated debentures to be purchased by IIT, and $2.5 million from Venture International for EHG convertible preferred shares. The extra $6 million was immediately put in Bahamas Commonwealth Bank in a six-month certificate of deposit (C/D) bearing a miserable 4 per cent interest rate, less than half the going rate. Dr. Alvarez received a $290,000 finder's fee on the transaction. In a secret side contract, the Gutierrez brothers agreed that their $6 million deposit at Bahamas Commonwealth could be used to purchase debentures of a real estate company in formation by "clients" of the bank.

These four "investments" by the dollar funds totaled $107 million, but five others of more modest proportions existed, involving an additional $11.65 million. This meant that in all a grand total of $118.65 million had been diverted from the funds into highly dubious situations where Vesco and his associates were on both sides of the deal. Furthermore, in October and November 1972 the four dollar funds, from the proceeds of their U.S. securities' sell-off, placed $161 million more on deposit in Bahamas Commonwealth Bank. The looting total was increased thereby to $280 million, and not the $224 million first alleged in the SEC complaint of November 27, 1972.

Other minor fiddles that the SEC investigators were able to trace included:

(1) a $1 million loan by Fund of Funds to Dominion Guarantee S.A., a venture capital firm incorporated in Panama by veteran IOS director

Robert Sutner and onetime IOS fund manager Marty Solomon. Both men supported Vesco in the 1971 proxy contest with the dissidents.

(2) a $1 million loan from FOF Proprietary Funds Limited to Conservative Capital Limited, a dummy corporation incorporated in the Bahamas and headed by the breezy New York promoter Richard Chadwick Pistell, a former chairman of General Host Corporation. Pistell was himself sued by the SEC for fraud in connection with General Host's unsuccessful 1969 attempt to take over Armour & Company, the Chicago meat packers. Conservative's sole asset was an abandoned Quebec copper mine whose shares were listed for trading in Canada under the name Chibex Limited. Since the mine was flooded and hadn't been worked since 1960, public trading in Chibex was very sporadic. But Pistell, who had a sharp eye for stock promotions, planned to use FOF's cash to pump the mine dry and begin working it for marginal gold deposits.

(3) another newly-formed Pistell company, Vencap Limited, obtained a $3 million placement from IIT fund. Pistell said he was a co-owner of Bahamian-incorporated Vencap with French author Henri de Riencourt. "He's one of the world's famous historians and a top-notch economist," Pistell assured the SEC. Pistell added that he had used Reincourt for the past twenty years as a "sounding board" for his various investment schemes around the world. But all of this was of little help to IIT investors. As of late 1973, the only deal entered into by Vancap —whose only asset was the $3 million IIT cash—was a $590,000 loan to Pistell.[6]

In addition to these "investments," in July 1972 Transglobal Financial Services, the holder of the management contracts for the four IOS dollar funds, entered into a rapacious "management" subcontract with the important-sounding International Capital Investments Limited (Incap), a Bahamian corporation, which, it later transpired, was 4 per cent owned by Stanley Graze and 96 per cent owned, at least in name, by LeBlanc. Under the contract Incap agreed to provide statistical and research services for the funds, advise, and make portfolio recommendations. For its services, Incap received a fixed retainer plus 40 per cent of the total management fees paid by the funds to Transglobal Financial Services,

---

[6] In June 1974, the Luxembourg liquidators of IIT filed suit in New York accusing Pistell of wasting some of the $3 million on exorbitant salary and living expenses. Snapped Pistell, "The liquidators don't know what the hell they're talking about. I'm taking $60,000 a year in salary. Is that a lot? I'm working seven days a week. I've made some wonderful deals for the company." Judge Charles Stewart, Jr., responded by granting a restraining order to prevent a further wasting of assets while the liquidators sought recovery of the $3 million as well as punitive damages.

a fraudulent transaction that should have netted the Super Group bandits an average of $180,000 a month, representing a major portion of the old IOS group's remaining income.

Incap's statistical and research services were performed from expensive offices in London. The company was run by Stanley Graze, who announced it represented "a new and deeper concept" in professional portfolio management. Incap received its fees for the first two months, but in an early revolt by middle management over some of the more blatant atrocities of their superiors, who had by then moved their headquarters to Nassau, further payments to Incap were stopped. Though ignored, the Incap contract continued in force until Transglobal's final liquidation.

The looting of the IOS funds undoubtedly would have continued until the remaining $120 million then under management was securely locked up in Vesco's newly styled investment contraptions had not the SEC stepped in with its detailed fraud complaint filed three weeks after the November 1972 U.S. Presidential elections. While until that point there was concern about Vesco's actions and designs over the use of client moneys, few people in the financial world would have believed that such extensive plundering could have been carried out at all, and carried out so quickly.

As imperfect and partial as the internal system of checks and balances built into the unregulated IOS funds might have been, including the custodianships, authorized bank signatories, and a supposedly fail-safe approval function for investment decisions, nevertheless they had to be dismantled before the massive shifting of assets could begin.

But more important, the IOS funds had reputable men on their boards —men of supposed stature like Jimmy Roosevelt, Allan Conwill, and Wilson W. Wyatt. Their very presence as directors played no little role in giving investors confidence that their money was being prudently and honestly managed.

Wilson Wyatt, a Louisville lawyer and veteran politician, resigned from The Fund of Funds board in June 1972, after the hanky-panky started, but apparently didn't think to draw anyone's attention to the first manifestations of foul play. So did Conwill resign. But Conwill, a former SEC division director in charge of mutual fund regulation, continued to act as counsel for the funds and, according to the SEC complaint, helped draw up the contracts for many of the dubious transactions, thereby betraying "the interests of the dollar funds and their public shareholders and lent [his] skills to facilitating and executing Vesco's scheme to mulct the funds." [7]

Roosevelt had an altogether different attitude. He elected to stay on

[7] SEC Complaint, SEC *v.* Robert Vesco *et al.,* p. 28.

the various fund boards until the bitter end. He had a $150,000 loan outstanding from Bahamas Commonwealth Bank and another for $120,000 from a former IOS banking subsidiary, with provisions that payment on the loans be made from fees due to him as a director.

When interviewed by the SEC staff about his role in Vesco's grand looting scheme, Roosevelt had trouble remembering on just which boards he served. Nor did he remember who his fellow directors were. Then, when asked what he knew about one or two of the more blatant self-dealing investments, he replied, "not a blessed thing."

Roosevelt, named as one of the forty-two defendants in the SEC action, found himself in the uncomfortable position of being sued by an agency that his father had created. And to make matters worse, he wasn't being sued as a participant in just any stock fraud but the largest ever investigated by the SEC in its forty-year history.

Rather than go through long and drawn-out court proceedings, in early 1973 Roosevelt elected to sign a consent order and, without admitting or denying the SEC charges, was permanently enjoined from committing further violations of the securities laws.

In a pathetic four-page statement accompanying the final judgment, Roosevelt claimed that his confidence in Vesco's management team had been sadly misplaced and that their corporate conduct required his "prompt" resignation from the boards of IOS and three of the dollar funds—dated February 6, 1973, well after the horse had left the barn.

18

PRL

The creation of a Plunder, Rape & Loot machine allows Vesco to cultivate a new hobby: control of gambling operations in the Bahamas and the Middle East — The emergence of a shadowy combine which insiders snidely refer to as "Super Group" to replace the ruined IOS complex, and how Vesco uses it to dominate the Bahamian economy

> *Expulsis Piratis Restituta Commercia*
> Motto of the Crown Colony
> of the Bahamas

While busily looting $280 million from the IOS dollar funds, Vesco was working on a second scheme to divert $100 million from another IOS entity, Investment Properties International Limited (IPI), a closed-end real estate investment company that owned a Spanish resort development, a luxury condominium complex on Florida's Gold Coast, a Manhattan office building, and $50 million in unrestricted cash.

"Even if everything else failed and we ended up controlling only IPI, our whole involvement with IOS would have been worth it," LeBlanc was said to have remarked. He was echoing a notion close to Vesco's heart: that the $50 million in cash held by Investment Properties International made it the single richest plum to be pulled from the wreckage of IOS. IPI's other $50 million, invested for the most part in prime income-producing properties, was merely incidental. And unlike the IOS mutual funds, which were supposed upon demand to buy back their shares from the public at the current net asset value per share, as a closed-end investment company IPI's assets were not subject to the constant attrition of redemption requests from clients that had afflicted the other IOS products since the eruption of the 1970 crisis.

The vehicle Vesco designed for the looting of Investment Properties

International was Property Resources Limited (PRL), an assetless shell company incorporated in Nassau in March 1972. The founding share-holders of PRL were listed as the local IOS telephonist, two clerks, a bookkeeper, and the IPI accountant.

Vesco had big plans for Property Resources Limited. It was to become the centerpiece of a new gambling, travel, investment banking, and re-sort empire stretching from California to North Africa and the Middle East, and descending even into the more torrid regions of the Persian Gulf oil emirates. And the operations base for this fabulous combine was to be the quaint Caribbean tax and tourist haven of Nassau.

The Bahama Islands, once a freebooters' haven, were taken over by the British in the early eighteenth century and remained a Crown Colony until independence in July 1973. The tiny nation's population was by then 170,000, 85 per cent black, somewhat indolent and eco-nomically backward despite the awesome statistic of 350 banks and bank-like institutions—one for every 485 inhabitants.

The Bahamas bore the heavy cross of a one-crop economy—tourism. The islands' 1.5 million visitors per year generated 70 per cent of the gross national product and 50 per cent of government revenue. But when Robert Vesco started shifting operations there, the Bahamas were faced with a veritable tourist famine and the yield on those tourists who kept coming was less and less.

Vesco, therefore, arrived on Bay Street, Nassau's main business thoroughfare, at a critical time in the sleepy Commonwealth of the Bahama Islands' history. He had spent considerable time in the Bahamas and was known as a high roller at the craps table in the Paradise Island Casino long before asserting his control over IOS. In 1971 he first dis-cussed some of IOS's early relocation plans with Carlton E. Francis, the Finance Minister. Francis introduced him to the then Immigration Minister, Arthur D. Hanna, the second most powerful man in the local government, and finally Vesco walked into the offices of the Prime Minister, Lynden Oscar Pindling, and announced that he was there to help pull the country out of the economic doldrums.

It was Dick Pistell, the brassy venture capital artist whose chief asset was that he knew everybody worth knowing almost anywhere in the world where a fast-rising buccaneer like Vesco might want to conduct business, who first interested Vesco in making a bid for the Paradise Island gambling complex across the oil-slicked harbor from Nassau. Short and stocky Pistell was to become Vesco's most important con-tact man over the next year or so, introducing him to heads of state and prominent government ministers in half-dozen small but sovereign lands.

According to the travel brochure blurbs, Paradise has everything: four miles of virgin beaches with "soft warm sand and crystal clear water," fine horses to explore the "wild jungle trails," and a championship 7,000-yard golf course over "green rolling hills," not to forget Café Martinique, a "posh lakeside restaurant" where James Bond dined on breast of duckling in the movie *Thunderball,* top-name entertainment at Le Cabaret Theater "with a stage only slightly smaller than the one at Radio City," and of course the famous Paradise Island Casino, a Monte Carlo of the Americas.

Not only was this cheap veneer copy of the Monaco gaming temple located a mere thirty minutes by jet from Miami and two and a half hours from New York, it was one of the largest casinos in the world, where enthusiasts had a choice of roulette, craps, black jack, baccarat, and big six, in addition to 350 slot machines, each earning a profit of from $10,000 to $12,000 a year.

Once called Hog Island, these 685 acres of sand, scrub pine, and palmetto were bought in 1959 by supermarket millionaire George Huntington Hartford II, who had visions of transforming them into a watering place for the very rich. Hartford sank some $32 million into creating a resort that would be worthy of its newly chosen name: Paradise Island. But such lavish spending was too much for even the A&P foodstore heir, and by 1966 he had run out of cash. Keeping a 25 per cent interest, he unloaded the rest as a losing proposition for a mere $12 million. The purchaser was Mary Carter Paint Company, a Delaware corporation with headquarters in Tampa, Florida.

Founded in 1958, Mary Carter operated more than 1,000 paint stores in the United States and the Caribbean. One of Mary Carter's more prominent stockholders was former Governor Thomas E. Dewey, who in 1952 had placed in nomination the man the GOP ran as Eisenhower's Vice-President, Richard M. Nixon. After eight years as Vice-President, a close defeat for the Presidency in 1960, and an overwhelming defeat for the governorship of California in 1962, Nixon paid his first of several visits to Paradise Island as the guest of Huntington Hartford.

One of the first deals concluded by James M. Crosby, the chairman of Mary Carter Paint, after acquiring Paradise Island in 1967 was the channeling of $750,000 through Sir Stafford Sands, the swarmy last white Bahamian Minister of Finance and Tourism, to receive an elusive gambling permit. Under this "certificate of exemption" Paradise Enterprises Limited gained exclusive gaming privileges for all adjacent islands and cays within a ten-mile radius of Nassau until December 1977.

By January 1968, a $15 million hotel-casino was completed, as was a $2 million Paradise Island toll bridge connecting the Nassau waterfront and the southern shore of Paradise Island.

Among the long list of celebrities that attended the gala opening of the hotel and casino was Richard Nixon, six years out of the political limelight, and a strong contender for the Republican Presidential candidacy later that year. Nixon apparently struck up a fast relationship with the top brass at Mary Carter, which by then had moved its headquarters to Miami to be nearer its major property. In fact, Nixon enjoyed Paradise Island so much that he wanted to return in November 1968 as President-elect to rest in the sunshine after a hard-fought Presidential campaign, but the Secret Service vetoed the idea, as a gambling resort was thought to be an inappropriate vacationing site for a future occupant of the White House.

Manager of Paradise Island Casino at its 1968 opening was Eddie Cellini, who once ran the Tropicana Club, a famous Mafia gambling joint in Newport, Kentucky. Eddie's elder brother Dino roamed far and wide in the services of master Mafia figure Meyer Lansky, working at the Riviera Casino in Havana, then briefly at casinos in Port-au-Prince, Freeport, London, and Estoril in Portugal.

Deported from the Bahamas in the mid-'sixties, Dino next ran the school for croupiers in London until he became marked in Britain as an undesirable alien. Back in Miami briefly, he took charge of organizing gambling junkets to the Bahamas and Europe. For a $1,500 round-trip airfare, the high rollers were taken to Lisbon and London for nine days and given free hotels, free dining chits, and $1,500 in chips.

To keep Paradise Island's image clean, Crosby employed the services of a former ace troubleshooter for the U.S. Justice Department, Robert "the Needle" Peloquin. Peloquin's security men were to ensure that there was no evidence, at least overtly, of Mob presence around the casino. A year later, "regretfully" some officials said, Eddie Cellini was stop-listed and, like his brother Dino, deported from the Bahamas.

Mary Carter subsequent to the purchase of Paradise Island sold off its paint division and renamed itself Resorts International Incorporated, becoming a hotly traded number on the American Stock Exchange.[1] In 1969 Resorts was very much in the news with a precocious attempt to capture control of Pan American World Airways, a company with revenues almost forty times greater than the Bahamian casino operator. The bid failed in the face of bitter Pan Am resistance, but the action seemed to fit a pattern. The powers that control international gambling were seeking to ring in a captive airline for their round-the-world gambling junkets.

In spite of Resorts International's heavy financial support over the years for the ruling Progressive Liberal Party in the Bahamas, Resorts chairman James Crosby had never enjoyed good personal relations

---

[1] In 1968 The Fund of Funds became a large shareholder in Resorts International by acquiring 283,300 shares of Class A stock, representing about 7 per cent of the outstanding shares of that class.

with Lynden Pindling's black government and was concerned that after independence a move would be made to increase gambling taxes and impose greater controls on casino operations. Therefore, he was only too pleased to negotiate with Vesco a $60 million package deal for the sale of the casino, two hotels, and certain other Paradise properties. Also included in the package was the toll bridge, which was owned privately by a company in which Crosby said he had a 59 per cent interest. Crosby declined to identify his partners in the bridge, although he indicated that they included two "well known, established banks." [2]

Principally involved in the Paradise Island negotiations were Vesco's two lieutenants, Straub and Clay, with New York attorney Howard Cerny acting as legal counsel. Straub called two IOS security men down to Nassau to check the security systems on the island. One of the first things Vesco planned to do if the deal went through was to dispense with the $350,000-per-annum services of Intertel—Peloquin's International Intelligence Incorporated—which handled all security matters on the island. Vesco didn't trust Peloquin, who also handled some of Howard Hughes's security arrangements, and wanted his own security men on the job.

Cerny and Straub were particularly interested in the skimming procedures whereby, it was discovered, millions of dollars were diverted from the cash receipts allegedly without appearing in the books of Paradise Enterprises Limited, operator of the casino. The skimming system implied the continued presence of a Mafia credit man inside the casino. According to one of Vesco's Super Group lawyers, the system centered upon the acceptance of IOU notes from known creditworthy players. The IOUs would not be cleared through the casino's accounting department but would be placed aside and taken to Miami, where they were discounted for cash with a Mob-connected collection agency or bank.

Straub also assumed the task of ingratiating himself with Arthur Hanna the Deputy Prime Minister. Mr. Fixit, as Gil Straub was known by Super Group insiders, apparently worked so diligently that soon LeBlanc was able to boast on the local cocktail circuit that "we have Hanna in our pocket."

Dick Pistell claimed there was only one other serious bidder for Paradise Island, and that was Howard Hughes. Hughes had spent fifteen months as a resident at the Britannia Beach Hotel on Paradise, taking over most of the hotel's ninth floor. Still according to Pistell, when it seemed likely that the very private billionaire might steal away the prize, Mr. Fixit worked his influence with Hanna to get Hughes thrown off the island.

[2] *Wall Street Journal,* November 29, 1972.

Accordingly, in mid-February 1972 a high-ranking immigration official demanded to see the eccentric recluse in his ninth-floor suite but was stopped at the door in an angry confrontation with Hughes's aides. Bahamian regulations stipulate that no visitor can stay more than eight months without obtaining a residence visa—a procedure that requires, among other things, a recent photograph.

When the immigration official returned, accompanied by a small assault force of other immigration officers, Hughes had already departed. Although, according to Pistell, he had undergone plastic surgery only weeks before to patch up the effects of an earlier operation and was still swathed in bandages, dressed as a casual tourist he hired a small boat that took him to Florida, leaving his staff to pack up his belongings (including hospital bed and barbells) for shipment to Managua, the capital of Nicaragua. There he turned up a few days later and barricaded himself in the penthouse suite of the Managua Intercontinental Hotel.[3]

Concurrently with the Paradise Island negotiations Vesco was attempting to refloat a shipwrecked Middle Eastern financial complex, Intra Bank, that otherwise was facing dismemberment under the liquidator's hammer. Vesco badly wanted control of the Beirut-based banking group because of its bargain-priced holdings in a lavish casino operation, a major airline, and other prized assets that he felt would marry well with his projected Caribbean interests.

Founded in 1951 by a Palestinian refugee, in fifteen years Intra Bank had become one of the largest banking networks in the Middle East and Africa, with operations spread through fifteen countries and total assets of 1 billion Lebanese pounds. A spectacular run on Intra's deposits, however, had forced the bank to close its door in October 1966. Although the bank was illiquid, Intra Investment Company S.A.L., the key holding company in the complex, was so rich in assets, Vesco confided to one of his aides, that it offered more scope for profitable rip-offs than even the Golden Goose, IOS.

The affairs of this troubled combine were managed by the trustee corporation, Intra Investment Company, formed by Intra Bank's principal creditors. Its prime holdings included a large shipyard in the south of France, some expensive real estate on the Champs Elysées in Paris, a 75 per cent interest in Middle East Airlines, a long-

[3] In December 1973 Hughes returned to the Bahamas, taking over the top floor of the Xanadu Princess Hotel in Freeport, owned by D. K. Ludwig, a shipping magnate whose wealth rivals that of Hughes. A few months later Hughes purchased the hotel for $15 million, indicating he intended a lengthy stay. This time Vesco was pleased. He announced that Hughes was joining *him* as a fellow exile in the Bahamas.

distance scheduled air carrier, and a 90 per cent interest in the Casino du Liban, largest gambling palace in the world.

The stockholders of Intra Investment Company were the Republic of Lebanon with 45 per cent, the state of Kuwait with 35 per cent, the emirate of Qatar with 13 per cent, and the Commodity Credit Corporation of the U.S. Department of Agriculture with 7 per cent.

Kuwait and Qatar had the largest deposits in Intra when the bank collapsed. The Lebanese Government advanced £150 million to pay off small depositors, and the Commodity Credit Corporation had loaned the Intra group $22 million to finance U.S. wheat shipments to the Middle East. The chairman of the board of Intra Investment Company was Lucien Dahdah, nephew of the President of Lebanon.

To assist him in the Intra Bank negotiations, Vesco formed a support operation in Beirut called Comptrol International, which became the Middle Eastern representative of Super Group's International Bancorp Limited. A friend of Gil Straub, Harold A. Neill, a former CIA station chief in Iraq, was hired as Comptrol's president. Comptrol, it was said, was 70 per cent owned by International Bancorp and 30 per cent by certain undisclosed "distinguished Arabs."

The Beirut negotiations for control of Intra were interrupted by Vesco's untimely arrest in Geneva. But his proposal—a $20 million debenture package for about 40 per cent of Intra's equity—was placed in limbo anyway. It had confounded the Intra Investment Company directors to such an extent that they had requested the Beirut office of Kidder Peabody & Company Limited, their investment banking advisers, to analyze it in depth.

The Kidder Peabody vice-president in the Middle East, Roger Tamraz, studied the Vesco proposal for quite some time before concluding, in the words of one of his colleagues, "It doesn't make much sense to me." Nevertheless, Tamraz was impressed with the people around Vesco, who seemed like "sensible, mature, and able young men." He left the door open for further discussions.

By then Vesco was concerned that his night in Saint Antoine Prison had definitely queered the Intra deal. As one of his aides expressed it, "Serious financiers don't spend nights in Swiss jails."

In an effort to have the Vesco image wiped clean, Gil Straub, Harry Sears, and Larry Richardson went to the White House Executive Office Building on December 17, 1971, for a meeting with John Ehrlichman. Straub told Ehrlichman that a first request to intervene on Vesco's behalf with the U.S. Embassy in Lebanon hadn't produced the desired effect and suggested he call Beirut again. Ehrlichman apparently gave the trio the impression that he would, and after chit-chatting about

Don-Don Nixon's activities they left, satisfied that their mission had been productive.

Because of his reputation and his dealings with IOS, the U.S. Commodity Credit Corporation representative in Beirut and the U.S. Embassy there were opposed to Vesco's bid for Intra. The head of the Middle East desk in Washington was cabled to check out Vesco. The word came back, according to a former State Department official with firsthand knowledge of the affair, to watch out: Vesco was suspected of having underworld connections.

The surprise of the U.S. Embassay staff in Beirut was therefore great when, within days of the Ehrlichman meeting, it was learned that Vesco's representatives in Lebanon were claiming U.S. government support. In particular, the name of Ehrlichman was bandied about. When this got back to the White House, the President's chief domestic affairs adviser said he immediately requested the State Department "to inform the U.S. Embassy in Lebanon and any others involved that there was no White House support for, nor interest in, the Vesco activities."

Vesco meanwhile was busy pulling other irons out of the fires of influence he was stoking in Washington. He had Sears persuade Mitchell to cable or telephone the Beirut Embassy, instructing legal affairs attaché Theodore Korontjis to address a memo to the Ambassador, William E. Buffum, that Vesco was an all right guy.

Buffum didn't like this interference in his Embassy's affairs and wrote his Washington superiors asking what the hell was going on. The State Department, unaware of Mitchell's intervention, queried the Attorney General to find out what exactly was taking place. Mitchell suggested that the legal attaché must have misunderstood or exceeded his instructions. The State Department instructed Buffum that Vesco was to receive no special treatment. The next time Vesco came calling at the Embassy, Buffum refused to see him.

Vesco tried desperately to save the Intra deal. On February 3, 1972, he left London aboard N11RV for Beirut. After three days in the Lebanese capital, he flew to Damascus and from there to Kuwait. He returned to Beirut on February 8, then left for Spain and Newark.

During that jaunt Vesco attempted to sweeten Kidder Peabody's disposition by asking Roger Tamraz to undertake a "study and evaluation" of a proposed Property Resources Limited transaction whereby certain property management assets transferred at book value a few months before by IOS to Value Capital Limited (see chart 4) would be passed on to PRL at a value *fifty times* higher in exchange for 22 per cent of PRL's stock.

Why the Lebanese office of Kidder Peabody got involved in reviewing the valuation of largely intangible assets on the other side of the globe is hard to imagine. When questioned in the matter, a Kidder Peabody official described the Value Capital evaluation as a "straight business deal—evaluation work—which had nothing to do with the Intra Bank negotiations."

As a "straight" business deal, it was undeniably profitable. Kidder Peabody was paid $100,000 for its opinion, which filled six paragraphs of a two-page letter. Once again, Vesco proved that money talks.

So flimsy was the Kidder Peabody opinion that Super Group officials steadfastly refused to identify the "independent firm of investment bankers" that produced it or give details of what it purported to state. But the net result was that the assets examined by Tamraz were up-valued from their old carrying value of $500,000 in the books of Value Capital Limited to a new value of $27 million. This was a little too much for the normally tame auditors, who placed a heavy dis-claimer on the transaction by stating it was "not susceptible to sub-stantiation by auditing procedures" in the 1971 Value Capital annual report.

The service Kidder Peabody rendered Super Group set the stage for the biggest single rip-off of Vesco's career—transferring IOS's former real estate assets and property management assets into this new re-ceptacle, Property Resources Limited, in exchange for a bundle of "Chinese" paper.

During Vesco's intricate side-play with PRL, events at the center of the gameboard had come to an annoying impasse. After four months of weighing their decision, the Intra Bank trustees rejected Vesco's proposal to acquire control of the old Intra complex and finally, in March 1972, closed the door on Super Group. It was a bitter blow to Vesco, who had visions of becoming the czar of international gambling with casinos in the Bahamas and the Middle East and his own inter-national air carrier to ferry ardent gaming enthusiasts back and forth on special charter tours—something that Resorts International had tried to do but failed.

Vesco's failure to conclude the Intra Bank deal was a blow to his vanity, particularly since it represented his first effort at elevating his negotiating artistry to the level of international diplomacy, dealing over the heads of ordinary bankers and financiers with statesmen, govern-ment ministers, and even heads of state. Vesco was working very hard at promoting his image as the first of a new breed of professional, a sort of Supertechnocrat for Superdeals. He existed, or at least wished to, not just in a class of his own but in a country of his own, able to deal on a one-to-one basis with other governments and other states.

This was part of the attraction of the Paradise Island transaction. If he closed the deal with Resorts International he intended to govern those 685 acres of sand and scrub pine like a semi-independent state with its own army of croupiers, armada of pleasure craft, the Big Bird for an air force, and a national bank.

To finance the Paradise Island purchase, Vesco planned to tap the cash of Investment Properties International Limited (IPI), by first folding IPI's assets into Property Resources Limited, since PRL in the long run was to be one of the acquirers of the Paradise Island properties. Also, the name of Eddie Cellini came up in discussions as a possible source of alternate financing.

To help make the entry with the Cellini brothers, it was later revealed, PRL paid $50,000 for undisclosed services to Jimmy Neal, described as a close associate of Eddie and Dino. Neal had succeeded the elder Cellini in organizing gambling tours out of Miami. Then, in July 1972, Vesco flew to Rome's Fiumicino airport for a two-hour meeting with Dino, the ranking statesman of Mafia gambling.

What came out of the Fiumicino talks was not known, although Vesco later mentioned to his associates that N11RV picked up an Italian cappuccino coffee machine. However, the Cellini brothers, who had moved to Italy to escape the long arm of the U.S. Justice Department, were busily prospecting the rim of the Mediterranean for new casino locations. It seemed likely that the Fiumicino summit was intended as the Yalta of offshore gambling, dividing certain areas of the World of Chance into spheres of influence, which either party agreed not to transgress.

Nevertheless, Vesco pressed on with the Paradise Island negotiations and, after a quick flight to Las Vegas in June 1972 with Edward Nixon, the President's younger brother, started looking at other gambling possibilities in the Caribbean and Middle East.

Comptrol International, for example, became interested in a Jordanian casino-cum-investment banking project. Supposedly independent of that prospect, a $2 million bank draft drawn from PRL cash left on the Big Bird with Vesco, LeBlanc, Straub, Clay, and Graze for Beirut in early 1973. The whereabouts or use of that money has remained a mystery. However, on that same Beirut trip our happy band of pilgrims opened a joint bank account at the Société Franco-Libanais, for which Vesco held the power of attorney, purportedly as a conduit for a personal investment by the group in a hydroponics venture.

Just as Super Group had begun looking at other casinos, there were other airlines in the world, too, and this perhaps was one reason why Bahamas Commonwealth Bank financed the $3 million purchase of two Boeing 707's for Bahamas World Airways later in 1972. But also not to be forgotten, BWA's chairman, Everette Bannister, was a close friend and political ally of the Bahamian Prime Minister, Lynden Pindling. A nonscheduled carrier, BWA chartered out its new equipment, brightly painted with the insignia of a frolicking dolphin on their tailpieces, to fly groups of Muslim pilgrims from North and East Africa to Mecca while waiting for the gambling junkets to begin.

Meanwhile Vesco had set in motion the machinations by which he intended to fund the treasury of his rip-off state. The month before the Rome meeting, relying on the two-page Kidder Peabody opinion as his justification, he started inflating PRL by vesting it with some doubtful assets. He caused Value Capital Limited to transfer to PRL the shares of IOS Real Estate Holdings, IPI Management Company, Resources Services Limited, and the IPI voting stock in return for 22 per cent of PRL. By this preliminary maneuver he had transformed PRL, a formerly empty shell, into the semblance of an operating concern with assets that had been ballooned in value from $500,000 a few months before to $27 million at the time of the transfer.

The directors of PRL, as it turned out, were Richard Clay (president), Colonel Walter Ashby Howkins, Norman LeBlanc, Frank Beatty, and Kenneth Beaugrand (secretary). The Value Capital Limited board consisted of the same cast of characters, except that "Yogi Bear" Hoffman replaced Colonel Howkins. In all this reshuffling Value Capital at all times held the PRL voting stock.

Later that same week the directors of Investment Properties International decided to call a special meeting of the IPI common shareholders of record in Nassau for June 29, 1972, to approve "the sale by IPI of all of its [approximately $100 million net] assets (except for $500,000 . . . to cover incidental expenses such as audit, legal, and printing costs) in exchange for 10,810,811 shares of Class A stock of PRL." This constituted 78 per cent of the nonvoting stock of PRL.

The public announcement of this meeting neglected to mention that the single IPI common shareholder—the only one entitled to vote—was PRL, and that the majority of directors of IPI were the same as the directors of PRL, which made it a happy and incestuous family. Not surprisingly, this $100 million questionable deal was unanimously adopted.

And so through this charade the assets of Investment Properties International Limited, a company incorporated under the laws of Ontario, were transferred to an unproven paper company based in the Bahamas. Or, seen the other way around, in giving up assets conservatively valued at $21 million (roughly equal to 22 per cent of IPI's total assets), the IPI shareholders acquired properties valued a few months earlier at $390,000 (equal to 78 per cent of PRL's holdings before their revaluation). Hardly a fair exchange, but there it was. IPI's public shareholders had no voting rights, and the deal had been carried through with a semblance—a travesty really—of legal propriety.

The rape of IPI consummated, Vesco pursued his even more audacious scheme: bringing the soon to be independent Bahama Islands under his economic domination. With LeBlanc he cranked up the Bahamas Commonwealth Bank operations in mid-1972, as soon as the dollar fund moneys started flowing south. According to Harry Sears, a member of the Bahamas Commonwealth Bank board of directors, Vesco's concept was to "create a Bahamian banking enterprise for Bahamians."

The idea, Sears said, "was to get Bahamians to realize that mattresses were for sleeping on and not for keeping money in, that checking accounts were good, and that this kind of commercial operation would be good for the Bahamas." He added they hoped "to develop an ongoing relationship with the government by financing government-sponsored projects, such as housing, public works, and utility development."

Super Group's injection of capital into the islands came at a critical moment. Pindling, a British-educated lawyer who often compared himself to Moses, had chosen September 1972 as the moment to call a general election to seek the voters' backing for his July 1973 independence timetable. The Bahamas Commonwealth Bank with its limitless supply of IOS fund moneys was among the few bright spots upon the economic horizon, and the government was grateful for this show of confidence in the country's future. Coincidentally, they were also grateful for at least $200,000 contributed by Super Group to the campaign expenses of Pindling's Progressive Liberal Party.

The bitterly fought September 1972 election campaign was marred by violence not generally known in Bahamian politics. But the people handed Pindling and his Progressive Liberal Party a resounding landslide victory.

"I will have achieved nothing unless more Bahamians move into the economic mainstream," Pindling told the voters. And Vesco adopted this pronouncement as the theme of his personal campaign to win official support in establishing the Bahamas as the first of his two main retrenchment bases in his coming battle with the U.S. government and the Canadian, Luxembourg, and Swiss authorities.

According to the best estimates of insiders, Super Group proceeded to pump more than $30 million into the Bahamian economy in 1972 and 1973, including several million in Out-Island Debentures and renewable ninety-day Bahamian Treasury Bills used by the government to supplement its overstretched finances, the price Vesco was required to pay for obtaining there a temporary haven safe from foreign prosecution.

Suddenly in the great banking hall of Charlotte House, Super Group's headquarters in downtown Nassau, there was a proliferation of black faces—security guards, receptionists, floor sweepers—as the bank did its bit to help the little people of Nassau catch at least a glimpse of the economic mainstream; the really heavy action in the surging tidewaters of Bahamian commerce and finance was after all reserved for the Big Fish in the Progressive Liberal Party structure, and Vesco—an astute political observer—knew this ever so well.

In a country whose major exports were sea salt, crawfish tails, and rum, the economy was perhaps not too difficult to dominate. Bahamas Commonwealth Bank made a specialty of providing 100 per cent financing to groups with Progressive Liberal Party affiliation. One of the deals it pulled out of the hat was the bankrolling of a $3 million takeover by a close friend of the Prime Minister, Garrett "Tiger" Finlayson, of catering facilities at the Nassau and Freeport airports. The thirty-six-year-old Finlayson, not long before Super Group's arrival in the islands, had been a modest tailor with a shop in the less fashionable "over-the-hill" (from Bay Street) district. He was now the owner of Business Systems Limited, a $100,000 Super Group computer services spinoff, and three catering firms; a major stockholder and director of Bahamas World Airways; and the owner of a resort hotel in Pindling's Kemp's Bay, Andros Island, constituency.

Bahamas Commonwealth Bank also financed the $400,000 acquistion of El Toro Restaurant, a chic eatery on Bay Street, by another Progressive Liberal Party supporter. Then there were loans totaling $900,000 for the purchase of two Nassau bottling companies by Andrew ("Dud") Maynard, the party's chairman; the $120,000 purchase of a Bay Street travel agency; and the providing of a $500,000 construction credit for a new wing and nightclub at the Anchorage Hotel, owned by Bahamas World Airways.

Bahamas Commonwealth Bank was the first entirely new major banking operation to be chartered under the Progressive Liberal Party regime. The government, therefore, wanted it to prosper as a showpiece of its supposedly prudent banking policy. A dozen banks had foundered during the past three years in the Bahamas, all of them chartered under the corrupt white rule of the Bay Street Boys that had preceded Pindling's sweep to power. And for a while it was feared that shaky Butlers Bank might add to Nassau's increasing reputation as a sleazy banking center by suddenly collapsing.

For this and other reasons the Pindling government was prepared to be extraordinarily tolerant of the administrative, legal, and fiduciary inconsistencies of Super Group's International Bancorp and its subsidiaries, principally Bahamas Commonwealth Bank. The government's gratitude to Vesco for having prevented any scandal over the demise of Butlers Bank helped shape this attitude. When Super Group finally stepped in, there wasn't even enough cash in the till to meet the payroll.

The Bahamas Monetary Authority held its breath. A belly-up situation at Butlers Bank would have caused embarrassment to a lot of people in Nassau, Vesco included, since the bank had been instrumental in his taking over IOS at virtually no cost to International Controls, and since afterward he had been forced to prop it up with $20 million of IOS client money. The venture that finally capsized the Butlers Bank was an ill-conceived attempt by its Canadian affiliate, Security Capital Corporation, to acquire another Toronto-based corporation, Seaway Multi-Corp, in a $21 million deal that backfired.

There is every indication that Vesco and LeBlanc mushroomed Allan Butler into a situation where suddenly the fair-haired banker had to either sell out to them or go into instant bankruptcy.

Vesco had verbally assured Butler that Super Group would back him in the proposed takeover of Seaway Multi-Corp, a small Canadian conglomerate with interests in sporting goods, warehousing, and auto parts retailing. To support this impression Vesco had one of the IOS funds transfer $5 million—the front money Allan Butler required to close the Seaway deal—to the Bank of Nova Scotia in Toronto. While Butler saw evidence of the money's presence in Toronto, he was unaware that no designation had been placed on it. The money was sitting there as a decoy.

Vesco, in his own words, was playing "another little game with Butlers." In mid-July 1972 the Seaway deal failed to close. Super Group had withdrawn its support at the last moment. The negotiations collapsed. Security Capital forfeited a $976,250 deposit to Seaway for failure to perform and had to write off $1,625,000 in negotiating expenses, causing the company to report a $2.9 million loss for fiscal 1971, followed by an even worse $10.5 million deficit in fiscal 1972. The great corporate hope that supposedly was being groomed for the role of "bringing the Oakes family fortune back home to Toronto" stood in ruins.

Vesco, wallowing in the Ocean Club swimming pool on Paradise Island, advised one of his accountants, "Now we'll make Allan Butler an offer he can't refuse."

As a result, in early August 1972 IOS's IIT fund loaned Security Capital $4.5 million to tide it over its immediate problems. Of that amount, $3 million was transferred back to Bahamas Commonwealth Bank to reduce an overdraft that Security Capital had with cashless Butlers Bank.

Ten days later Norman LeBlanc announced that Fairborn Corporation Limited, a newly formed Bahamian dummy company, had acquired Lewis-Oakes Limited, the holding company that owned both Butlers and Security Capital. No price was announced for the purchase, but it was later disclosed that Fairborn paid $3 million in notes—which Fairborn never honored—for the debt-ridden bank and other Lewis-Oakes holdings, including a Delaware company, Connex Press Incorporated, whose only asset was Butler's Sabreliner with the registration letters N44SB.

In 1974, Allan and Shirley Butler sued Vesco and LeBlanc in the Bahamas for breach of contract, seeking a court order rescinding the Fairborn transaction since by then Super Group cash (viz. IOS client money) had paid off the Butlers Bank creditors. However Vesco and LeBlanc had hidden ownership of all the Lewis-Oakes assets and the only item that remained was the empty shell of Butlers Bank, renamed Who Holdings. One day Vesco asked LeBlanc what had happened to the assetless Butlers Bank shell. "I mean, who the hell owns it?" he wanted to know. And indeed in an administrative oversight the bank that by then existed only on paper had been left out in the corporate cold. So in tying up the ends of a messy affair it was brought back into the fold, provided with a new set of nominee shareholders, dummy directors, and a new name, and placed in a filing cabinet at Charlotte House for possible future use.

LeBlanc and Vesco moved quickly to dissimilate the Lewis-Oakes assets throughout the Super Group empire. "I have some forty shell companies that I keep putting on top of one another to keep people from finding out what's going on. Of course they are only good for so long, then I put another on top," LeBlanc told Harvey Dale, the Butlers' New York lawyer.

Butlers banking operations immediately were rolled into Bahamas Commonwealth Bank. This gave Bahamas Commonwealth Bank a full foreign exchange dealership, which the Bank of England had been reluctant to grant the Vesco group. Secondly, it made the Vesco-LeBlanc combine one of the largest employers in the Bahama Islands by virtue of the holdings it acquired in the deal with Lewis-Oakes. These included a controlling interest in a Bahamian mini-conglomerate, General Bahamian Companies Limited, which owned Bahama Blenders, a local distillery; Cole-Thompson Pharmacies, a drugstore chain with fifteen outlets; Burns House Limited, a six-store liquor chain; and an 80 per cent interest in ABC Motors, the local Ford dealer; 40 per cent of the Sonesta Beach Hotel and country club on Cable Beach, west of Nassau, reported to be losing $200,000 a month, and 20 per cent of the *Nassau Guardian*, a newspaper.

Vesco was pleased with the Fairborn acquisition even though a preliminary investigation of Butlers Bank indicated that the bank's deficit was roughly $12 million. When it was later discovered to be more than $20 million—which Super Group had to make good— Vesco hit the ceiling and started screaming at the top of his voice about all the terrible things that should happen to bankers who borrow short and lend long.

Butlers's largest single creditor was Edward Krock, a former treasurer and director of Fifth Avenue Coach Lines Incorporated, a controversial outfit once controlled by a group that included Krock, Victor Muscat, and Roy Cohn. Krock had $12.5 million in certificates of deposit at Butlers and wanted his money back.

Krock was one of the bank's more illustrious clients, having just been indicted on a $1.4 million income tax fraud in Boston. As could be imagined under the circumstances, he was not eager to return to the United States. Krock, aboard his 150-foot yacht *The Speculator*, and LeBlanc, aboard the *Sarah Lee*, held yacht-to-yacht conferences in the Nassau yacht basin on possible joint business ventures in the Caribbean.

One day LeBlanc hid in his private toilet in his office at Charlotte House when Krock turned up, somehow got past the security obstacles and was roaming through the executive compound looking for his money. One Krock loan of $900,000 advanced to the Butler organization by his company, Great Expectations Limited, was collateralized by the Charlotte House multideck parking garage and bore an effective interest rate, gimmicks included, of 18 per cent. Krock, the self-made Worcester, Massachusetts, millionaire, threatened to bulldoze the parking garage unless he got his money back. LeBlanc paid.

The remarkable feature about Super Group's structure was that the key companies—Global Holdings, Fairborn, Vector, and others—were listed in the name of Norman the Burble. True, in most cases the statutes of incorporation carried a clause whereby if one director resigned he had to offer his shares to another director. Thus Vesco could remark with confidence to one of his young lawyers who was concerned about everything being in LeBlanc's name and asked what would happen if the Instant Tycoon decided to walk away with the goodies, "Aw, Norman wouldn't do that. He knows it would hurt my feelings."

LeBlanc represented one of the key pieces on the Vesco game board. As a Canadian citizen and resident of both the Bahamas and Costa Rica he was immune to SEC subpoenas, unless, of course, he had the misfortune of being hijacked aboard one of his own jets to the United States. This was in fact of some concern to him. He claimed he was followed everywhere he went by U.S. government agents, and he even hired photographers to photograph the people who took pictures of him in hotel lobbies and other public places.

LeBlanc had special security locks put on all doors at Charlotte House and hired uniformed guards equipped with walkie-talkies to patrol the premises around the clock. A closed-circuit television camera scanned visitors in the main reception areas. The camera monitor was on the desk of his secretary, Wendy Kenyon, an attractive young Englishwoman whom Nasty Norman had appointed the honorary consul of Costa Rica in Nassau. Callers whom LeBlanc deigned to see were admitted by means of a buzzer, which tripped the lock on the heavy wooden door at the inner entrance to the senior executive area.

LeBlanc's office phone, the Burble even claimed, was tapped until one of his security experts uncovered "the little bugger," and from then on, as a matter of routine, the phones were regularly checked and the offices electronically swept for hidden eavesdropping devices.

Security manias aside, LeBlanc became a dazzling sight in Nassau social circles, generally in the company of the swish, efficient honorary Costa Rican consul. James Bond's table at the Café Martinique was soon reserved for the Instant Tycoon. He was known to buy champagne by the case at his favorite nightclub, the Show Club, one of Huntington Hartford's last holdings in Nassau, and he had the bill sent to Bahamas Commonwealth Bank.

The Bahamas Monetary Authority's concern was only mildly stirred when it became apparent in April 1973 that Bahamas Commonwealth Bank and its parent, International Bandwagon, had no auditors—and this situation had existed for at least six months. LeBlanc attempted to deny it was the case.

"Why, all banks have to have auditors," he told me when questioned. But, he admitted, he didn't know just who the auditors were.

He didn't know because there weren't any until a month or so later, when the red-faced Monetary Authority intervened and appointed Peat, Marwick, Mitchell & Company, another of accounting's Big Eight firms, to do a detailed investigative audit. At the end of 1973 LeBlanc, in declining favor, resigned as chairman of International Bancorp and as a director of Value Capital. Bancorp's just-released unaudited financials for 1972 (one year late) showed a loss of $1.7 million; no figures were then available for financially more difficult 1973.

One of LeBlanc's last acts before resigning as chairman of International Bancorp was to "untrack" Prime Minister Pindling's $200,000 mortgage held by Bahamas Commonwealth Bank. The mortgage was on a virtually unoccupied office building owned by the Prime Minister in downtown Nassau. The three-story structure was "sold" to a company formed on behalf of Pindling confidant "Tiger" Finlayson by a Super Group affiliate for $500,000, which was about twice the building's estimated worth. Pindling then repaid the loan at Bahamas Commonwealth Bank and used the balance as the down payment on Woodstar, a $450,000 villa at Skyline Heights that had been built for onetime Gramco director Rafael Navarro.

Among the men appointed to the new International Bancorp board were Stanley Graze, the former economics lecturer; S. Paul Palmer, Straub's old crony from Capital Growth Fund, who was now in charge of Super Group's London offices; and Eusebio A. Morales, a former Panamanian Ambassador to the Court of Saint James's in London.

Tony Morales could boast an exceptionally colorful if dubious past in the world of finance. When Ambassador to Britain, he had supplemented his diplomat's wages by selling Panamanian consulships to the needy and the deserving for $7,000 each. Dashing, suave-mannered Morales was in his early sixties when he discovered Vesco, but, being an eternally tanned sporting type, he looked twenty years younger, which irked the huffy-puffy, overfed threesome of Straub, Graze, and Palmer. Morales also had been around in shady financial circles longer than the paunchy trio.

In the late 1950s he had been vice-president of a Panama City finance company, Atlantida S.A., which arranged loans for such upright American businessmen as Roy Cohn of Fifth Avenue Coach and Moe Dalitz, a member of the Cleveland Mob and co-owner of the Desert Inn in Las Vegas until its sale in 1967 to Howard Hughes.

Later he became vice-president of Banco Suizo-Panameo, a subsidiary of Bank Germann of Basel until its owner, a Swiss fringe banker by the name of Walter Germann, committed suicide. Morales was named in the winding-up proceedings of Fifth Avenue Coach as having bagged a small sum of Fifth Avenue Coach money to Switzerland for redeposit with Banco Suizo-Panameo. That money was never recovered by the creditors of Fifth Avenue Coach.

Morales had since gone to work for Vesco, with Bahamas Commonwealth Bank paying the bill, researching the status of extradition treaties between various countries, including Panama and the United States, and in addition to his position on the Bancorp board he assumed various other directorships with Vesco dummy companies that now began to spring up in Panama like mushrooms after a summer rainstorm.

Vesco all this time was scheming to wrap up the Paradise Island acquisition, which had suffered what appeared to be a five-year delay. A final double-barreled package had been agreed upon with Resorts International in November 1972. Gulf Stream (Bahamas) Limited, with Vesco's Mr. Fixit, Gil Straub, as president, was to acquire the casino and the Paradise Island bridge company. The purchase price for this slice of the transaction was $20 million in cash and $5 million in 6 per cent promissory notes.

The bridge company and the casino represented all the cream on Paradise Island, since the gambling produced an annual net cash flow of $4.5 million and the toll bridge, with virtually no overhead, netted a reported $650,000 a year. The Bahamian Government was offered a 50 per cent stake in Gulf Stream, which was to ensure the transfer of the gaming license to the new owners as well as a hoped for increase in the existing gambling equipment limitation.

The rest of the Paradise Island properties included in the deal were the hogs in the poke, and they were relegated to Property Resources Limited. These included the Britannia Beach Hotel, the Beach Inn, thirty acres of undeveloped and overvalued land, the par-72 golf course, the water and sewage works, Café Martinique, a boatyard, a staff apartment building, a laundry service, and other marginal items.

Pruned of the casino and toll bridge revenues, these assets combined produced an estimated negative cash flow of $1 million per annum, and now they were to be foisted upon the public investors. The purchase price PRL was required to pay for them was $35 million, of which $22 million was in cash, $5 million in promissory notes, and $8 million in the assumption of a mortgage.

The total $42 million cash portion resulting from the two segments of the Paradise Island sale would have given Resorts International close to $5 a share—the deal of a lifetime.

Curiously, secrecy shrouded the identity of the minority shareholders in the Paradise Island bridge company. There were three versions as to who they were. In the first, Resorts International chairman James Crosby and associates were said to hold 70 per cent. His associate, since there was only one, was later identified as C. Gerry Goldsmith, chairman of Grand Bahama Development Company, with a 10 per cent personal interest, and the remaining 30 per cent was supposedly held by two "well-known, established banks."

According to Michael Bennett, the controller of International Bancorp Limited, 70 per cent of the bridge company was owned by Crosby and associate and the remaining 30 per cent by Cosmos Overseas Bank, a subsidiary of Cosmos Bank of Zurich. Cosmos, if the deal went through, was to have purchased Overseas Development Bank in Geneva at a discount as consideration for knocking down the price of the bridge company.

The third version of who owned the toll bridge came indirectly from Allan Butler himself. It concurred on the holdings of Crosby and associate but differed on the percentages held by, and the identity of, their banking partners. In this version, confirmed by other sources, the two "well-known, established banks" referred to by Crosby were said to be Cosmos and Roywest Banking Corporation Limited, a Nassau-based consortium of top-drawer institutions including the Royal Bank of Canada, National Westminister Bank of London, Morgan Grenfell, and Morgan Guarantee Finance Corporation. Roywest was reported to hold at least ten per cent of the bridge company shares. Most interesting of all, however, was the assertion that one or the other of the banks, if not both, was acting as nominee for a group of venturers led by Charles G. ("Bebe") Rebozo, who on occasion had described himself as "an old friend of Jim Crosby." In with Rebozo on the deal, according to this version, was Senator George Smathers of Florida and Richard Milhous Nixon. Strangely, a letter I wrote to the President's special counsel at the White House questioning the authenticity of this report remained unanswered. At any rate, the proposed sale of the bridge company never took place.

The Paradise Island deal collapsed when the SEC came out at the end of November 1972 with its civil complaint against Super Group. Crosby was advised by counsel that Resorts International would face big problems if it went ahead with a transaction involving money that the courts might declare stolen or at best illegally diverted from the IOS funds.

Subsequently it appeared as though Vesco would end up with the Paradise Island Casino anyway, along with the casinos on Grand Bahama Island. Their gambling licenses were slated to lapse in 1977, and the Bahamian Government announced shortly after independence plans to nationalize gambling in the Bahamas. The government, it was speculated at Super Group headquarters, probably would decide, then, to lease the casinos to Mr. Fixit's Gulf Stream (Bahamas) Limited as the new operators.

19

A Message from John M. King

In which John King reappears in a fruitless attempt to "Save Global," a multi-million dollar progeny of the ailing Moneycatcher, and with the help of a symphony orchestra conductor of international renown delays Vesco's plans to suck Global into the Plunder, Rape & Loot machine ∼ How the applecart is finally upset at Charlotte House in Nassau, preventing a further $40 million rip-off

When in early 1971 wind of Bob Vesco's intentions of "rescuing" King Resources Company (KRC) from bankruptcy by merging the Denver-based concern with an unnamed offspring of the Restructured IOS group reached John M. King, the gusty founder of King Resources reacted with the clamor of a stampeding bull elephant, an animal that the portly six-foot-four-inch King much admired and even resembled.

King's favorite painting, visitors to his office atop Denver's Security Life Building were informed, was a portrait of a charging bull elephant that hung behind his custom-built desk. When provoked, a bull elephant spreads its ears, screams with rage, and charges. King, too, when provoked was accustomed to bullying and bellowing his way around. He expressed it differently, though. "I like to charge in and get things done," he explained.

To counter Vesco's takeover plans, the ousted chairman of King Resources Company hired the flamboyant West Coast criminal lawyer Melvin Belli and brought a "racketeering" suit against the new overlord at IOS and certain of his associates, alleging that underworld influence and illegal currency manipulations were being used to force King into personal bankruptcy.

But King soon lost interest in the "racketeering" action against Vesco, since he was unable to serve him with the requisite legal papers. Instead King concentrated his efforts on a new counterplan to capture control of the natural resources interests that King Resources Company had sold to Fund of Funds's Natural Resources Fund account during the golden days of 1968 and 1969.

Terrible things had happened to the poor old Moneycatcher since the 1969 revaluation of its controversial Canadian Arctic oil and gas exportation permits. Confronted with a mounting wave of client redemption requests which the cash-tight creature could not long withstand, the FOF directors (minus Cornfeld and Cowett, by then removed from the board) took a fatal decision in August 1970 to carve all of the illiquid assets out of the fund's investment portfolio and place them in a newly created closed-end company, Global Natural Resources Properties Limited.

The FOF assets contributed to Global Natural Resources included not only the Arctic oil and gas exploration permits but also the unmarketable nonvoting stock of Investment Properties International (IPI), the closed-end real estate investment company underwritten by IOS in 1969 with a $100 million public offering. In a large-scale price support operation which followed the underwriting, IOS had caused FOF to purchase 47 per cent of the IPI stock back from the public at levels just over the $10-a-share issuing price. Undoubtedly this stock support operation would have continued indefinitely but for an Arthur Andersen opinion that any further increase in FOF's holdings would require the fund to list IPI as a subsidiary rather than an investment. As it was, FOF fund-holders had paid $50 million for the IPI shares when their actual market value was no more than $10 million.

The spinning out of FOF's illiquid assets, placing them in Global Natural Resources, was brutal surgery. Effectively it amounted to a closed-ending of two-thirds of The Fund of Funds. To their surprise and anger, investors discovered that over the space of a weekend shares of The Fund of Funds lost two-thirds of their value. The difference was made up to the fund-holders by issuing them as a dividend all the outstanding shares of Global Natural Resources, which of course were not redeemable by the fund for cash and could only be sold on the open market assuming a market existed.

Because the Global Natural Resources spin-out was deemed contrary to the basic operating principles of an open-end mutual fund, six weeks later The Fund of Funds was banned from sale in Switzerland. Already excluded from Portugal, Spain, Belgium, Greece, South Africa, Iran, Japan, and all of South America; unregistered for sale in Canada, the United States, and Germany; and under Arab boycott in the Middle

East, the once dazzling Moneycatcher's death warrant irrevocably was signed.

King's counterplan, devised almost two years later, was to capture control of Global Natural Resources from Vesco with a Bahamian dummy corporation specially formed for the occasion and a stealthy pincer attack involving a long-haired musician of world renown. The plan, had it been successful, would have provided King with a sturdy crutch in his comeback campaign—which never got off the ground— to regain management control and save KRC, since he figured Global Natural Resources's part-interest in the Arctic oil and gas permits, originally sold to The Fund of Funds for $12 million, later transferred to Global Natural Resources at a written-up value of $119 million, had a potential "true worth" of $4.5 billion.

King's reasons for wanting to pry Global Natural Resources out of the IOS complex, therefore, were not hard to follow. The Arctic oil and gas exploration permits, after all, covered some 42 per cent of the Sverdrup Basin, a hydrocarbons-rich geological formation that sloped through the Canadian Arctic Islands.

"Hell, we're bound to hit something up there. Everybody else has," was his logic.

But he failed to acknowledge that most of Global's acreage was undersea, which meant it was covered by drifting pack ice almost all year round. At existing technology levels much of the concession area, consequently, was inaccessible to drilling rigs and considered "prime whale pasture" by industry experts, who otherwise gave it little economic value.

It was a fact, nevertheless, that Panarctic Oils Limited, a consortium including the Canadian Government as its major shareholder, had already discovered a natural gas field in the Sverdrup Basin next to the Global acreage, a discovery considered one of the very richest natural gas finds in the world. "There is four times more natural gas up there than in the largest known field. The potential is tremendous," King insisted.

So the nearly bankrupt Denver wheeler-dealer spent $15,000 in July 1972 on an international advertising campaign in prestige publications under the heading "A Message From John M. King." The ad announced a tender offer for Global Natural Resources shares by the Bahamian-incorporated concern called International Dundee Limited. Interested parties were invited to send for an IDL prospectus.

The prospectus in fact was never issued, but King had intended to offer one preferred share of IDL for every three shares tendered of

Global Natural Resources. The IDL preferred stock supposedly would have entitled the holder, among other things, to a $1 per share annual dividend as an added come-on.

Under the heading "Use of Tendered Shares" the prospectus further explained: "Assuming that IDL acquires substantial numbers of Global shares as a result of this offering, IDL intends to exercise its rights as a stockholder to preserve the property values . . . and to maximize their profit realization. . . . If the existing management prove to be unwilling or incapable of adjusting their policies in accordance with such goals, IDL will attempt to substitute management which will be more responsive and more qualified."

While the IDL prospectus was carefully designed to mislead tendering Global Natural Resources shareholders into believing they would receive a $1 per share annual preferential dividend, they were in reality going to get nonvoting common shares of a holding company organized for the purpose of permitting King to exercise control over Global Natural Resources and its management.

Coincidentally, King's and Vesco's attention focused on the Global Natural Resources plum at precisely the same moment. By then Vesco had lost interest in the high-risk takeover of bankrupt King Resources Company and had shifted his thoughts to the emergence of Property Resources Limited as a perfect vehicle for the looting of IOS's natural resources investments.

Vesco for his part hated Global Natural Resources, because it was one of the few companies in the IOS complex that had issued voting stock to its public shareholders. The fact that he maintained voting control at all was because the Global stock dividend was delivered only to those Fund of Funds shareholders who specifically wrote in and requested physical possession of their bearer shares. Most didn't bother, and so their Global stock was retained in "safekeeping" by IOS Investment Program Limited.

Vesco's dominance of Global's management dated back to March 1971, when he replaced the existing board of directors with a tame board headed by himself and including Dick Clay, Anthony M. Pilaro, Walter H. Saunders, and, two months later, James Roche, the new president. The managing director and, as a corporation, a member of the board, was a cute little number called Resources Services Limited, a wholly owned Bahamian subsidiary of Property Resources Limited.

The only director with professional background in natural resources management was James Roche, a petroleum engineer with forty years' experience, but Roche resigned little more than eighteen months later. Walter Saunders was a New York lawyer who had worked for Greek shipping magnate Stavros Niarchos. Anthony Pilaro was president of

A. M. Pilaro & Sons of New York, private investment bankers. He had gained his previous investment banking experience with Butlers Bank in Nassau. Pilaro was a close Vesco crony. Charged a year later with five counts of securities fraud in an unrelated matter, he fled to Hong Kong rather than face the SEC's charges and had to be dropped from the board.

A latecomer to the Global board was International Controls vice-president Frank Beatty, who was also appointed the Global corporate secretary. However, much to Vesco's disgust, Beatty would play a key role more than one year later in protecting the Global assets from further abuse.

One of Vesco's first actions after installing a new board of directors was to replace Arthur Andersen as Global's independent auditors with Coopers & Lybrand. Next he reversed IOS Ltd.'s 1969 decision to raise sevenfold the book value of the Arctic permits, which was a nice piece of accounting gymnastics.

By this Olympian feat Global Natural Resources's declared net assets, allegedly $217 million at the time of the August 1970 dividend from Fund of Funds, were restated at $57 million in the long-delayed 1970 year-end accounts—representing a considerable depreciation after just four months of operation. To be sure, IOS did not refund the $9.7 million it had siphoned out of Fund of Funds as a "performance fee" in 1969 when the original upward revaluation took place. Furthermore, the late-published 1970 and 1971 annual reports showed an aggregate operating deficit of $22.8 million, which was a sure indication that the company was fast running out of working capital.

Vesco had already completed the placing of IPI's $100 million in assets in Property Resources Limited. Then, halfway through the hectic summer of 1972, he decided to similarly lock up the holdings of Global Natural Resources. Vesco's reasoning was that with IPI's plethora of unregulated cash—almost $50 million—the Plunder, Rape & Loot machine, as insiders sneeringly referred to PRL, could finance the expensive ongoing work obligations attached to Global's Arctic oil and gas exploration permits.

Two things now happened. Global Natural Resources directors called a shareholders' meeting in Nassau for mid-August 1972 to approve a motion retiring the Resources Services Limited management contract, which was programmed to cost the shareholders $500,000 a year, in exchange for 950,000 newly issued shares payable to PRL. This 4.5 per cent dilution of Global Natural Resources stock was the device by which Vesco's recast Super Group, through PRL, hoped to maintain voting control.

But for the timely intervention of a Belgian symphony orchestra conductor masquerading as an indignant shareholder of Fund of Funds and its unmarketable progeny Global Natural Resources, Vesco undoubtedly would have been successful in his design to roll Global into PRL. Edouard van Remoortel's appearance on the scene can be traced back to the days when he conducted the Saint Louis Symphony Orchestra in Saint Louis, Missouri. Unknown to the world, John King was a music lover and came to be a leading fan of van Remoortel.

Following publication of a notice by Global Natural Resources management calling the August 1972 shareholders meeting, an advertisement in leading European newspapers apprised the public that a "Save Global" committee had been formed by Edouard van Remoortel, a self-described dissatisfied Global Natural Resources shareholder. Forty-six-year-old van Remoortel, then music counselor to the Monte Carlo Ballet Company, took Global management to court in London and forced them to postpone the Nassau meeting while requiring the reticent directors to make greater disclosure.

As a result a new shareholder meeting was scheduled at the Halcyon Balmoral Beach Hotel in Nassau in September 1972. Shareholders wishing to attend and vote at that meeting were given three weeks to (1) deposit their shares with a recognized depository in Luxembourg, Munich, Geneva, London, or Nassau, then (2) lodge the deposit certificate at Overseas Development Bank in London up to two days before the meeting. For the average shareholder this meant flying halfway around the world just to obtain the right to attend and vote—something that was beyond the means of all but a select few. It also gave management the edge of being able to tally the possible votes against it forty-eight hours before the crucial vote.

In a three-page "disclosure" letter sent out by order of the London High Court of Justice, it became apparent that Resources Services Limited, a company without staff, had been extracting a minimum of $500,000 per annum fee for supposedly recruiting, administering, and overseeing the management of Global Natural Resources—functions it was patently incapable of performing. What's more, the letter failed to state that the directors of Resources Services Limited were none other than Richard Clay and Frank Beatty.

Though van Remoortel maintained he was acting independently, he was in reality "King's pussycat." He was shipped all over the Western world at King's expense rounding up "Save Global" supporters. "He never made a phone call that King didn't pay for," a former King aide affirmed.

A major problem confronting King, however, was the fact that the previous year he and his wife had requested court protection in personal bankruptcy proceedings under Chapter XI, and his family holding company, Colorado Corporation, was subject to another bankruptcy action. There were 300 creditors hammering at his door. For a man who claimed he couldn't live on less than $20,000 a month he was extremely short of cash, and therefore he abandoned the International Dundee scheme, concentrating solely on the van Remoortel "Save Global" approach as the least costly alternative.

Accompanied by a London solicitor, King's undercover agent traveled to Nassau for the Global Natural Resources extraordinary meeting, carrying the proxies of a few dozen earnest shareholders who had joined his "Save Global" committee. No sooner had he arrived in Nassau than he was called away from his hotel to a mysterious rendezvous that never materialized, and his room was searched, but to no avail—van Remoortel had taken his briefcase with him. Refusing to be intimidated at the next day's meeting in the pink Halcyon Balmoral, the Belgian conductor put up stiff opposition to the Vesco-LeBlanc resolution to issue themselves, in effect, 950,000 Global shares for nothing. But in the end he was steamrollered into the ground, and shareholder "approval" to issue this control block of Global stock was voted through.

Van Remoortel returned to New York and conferred with John King at the Plaza Hotel, following which they called a small press conference to announce their "joining forces" to fight the rape of Global. The press conference was held in van Remoortel's suite.

Invited to attend were Robert Cole of the *New York Times*, Scott Schmedel of the *Wall Street Journal*, an Associated Press reporter, and myself. But two other "reporters" also turned up uninvited and produced multicolored laminated "press" cards to attest to their authenticity. The tall one, spiffily dressed in varying tones of brown, identified himself as Hilton Page of Page Publications, and the little one in a shiny blue suit said in a soft Southern drawl that he was "a friend of Mr. Page." Both carried small tape recorders.

Page asked three questions, written on a small piece of paper. "Mr. King, are you contributing to the expenses of the 'Save Global' committee and its actions?" was one of the questions. The other two were in a similar vein. The little man in blue said nothing.

They didn't act like journalists. After noting the replies to his questions, Page fell asleep for most of the remainder of the press conference. Once the meeting was over—during which King declared the withdrawal of his International Dundee tender offer—Scott Schmedel approached Page and asked what publications came under the umbrella of Page Publications. "*International Security Review*," came the reply. Schmedel allowed as he had never heard of it. "Probably," said Page. "The first number has just come out."

Contrary to all expectations, *International Security Review* did exist, and its first number had come out that week. The twenty-page bimonthly carried articles headed "The Polygraph: Boom in Testing Is On," "How to Spot a Phony Bill," and, topically, "Should Politicians Be Polygraphed?" Who hired Page and his friend to cover the Plaza press conference was never disclosed, but the bets were on Cerny and Vesco.

After the Plaza press conference, van Remoortel filed a new writ in London that caused Vesco to slow up his plans for placing Global Natural Resources in PRL. But John King shortly thereafter abandoned his plans to "Save Global," as he became otherwise occupied with a grand jury investigation into the downfall of his King Resources empire as well as a tardy SEC investigation into the sale of the Arctic permits and other natural resources properties to The Fund of Funds and the mutual fun that flowed from this jumble of tricky dealings. King, just to keep the opposition guessing, switched tactics and announced in early 1974 that he was intending to run as an independent candidate for the U.S. Senate in Colorado.

With King out of the way, Vesco might have thought that PRL's takeover of Global Natural Resources had become just a matter of form. However, the Plunder, Rape & Loot applecart finally was upset by a hirsute young Scotsman, David H. Warham. In April 1973 Warham, the controller of PRL, flew to London and filed the first of a series of court affidavits in an entirely new fraud action against Super Group, this one brought by an IOS Shareholders Defense Committee operating out of Germany.

Warham's first affidavit became a key element in the German shareholder action to preserve the IPI assets absorbed by PRL and resulted in an injunction handed down by the Chancery Division of the London High Court freezing all PRL moneys on deposit in the London interbank market pending a hearing of the German shareholders' charges. The tying up of PRL in litigation had the indirect effect of foiling its intended merger with Global Natural Resources.

Warham's sudden defection to the side of the sorely battered investors caused panic at Super Group's Charlotte House headquarters in Nassau. Bahamas Commonwealth Bank, confronted with a welter of court orders blocking bank funds it had out on redeposit elsewhere in the Western world, was again experiencing serious liquidity problems. PRL, on the other hand, was cash-heavy. It had $40 million invested in first-class certificates of deposit with prime banks in London. Vesco, through LeBlanc, started eying this cash to bail Bahamas Commonwealth Bank out of its acute squeeze. A first indication of their intentions came during March 1973, when $4.5 million of PRL's London C/Ds were liquidated prematurely, incurring a $40,000 penalty, and transferred to Columbus Trust Company in Nassau to help purchase $5.7 million in Costa Rican government bonds from Bahamas Commonwealth Bank.

The next indication of the Vesco-LaBlanc intention to dip into the client cash loomed large when on April 9, 1973, Columbus Trust demanded the transfer of $31.7 million from PRL's bank of deposit in London, David Samuel Trust Company, to Nassau.

A small merchant bank in Cork Street off Piccadilly, in the center of London's tailoring district, David Samuel Trust was a two-floor operation with a 1972 net worth of $2.9 million. Run by a couple of nimble go-go bankers, Leslie Lavy and Herbert Towning, David Samuel Trust was about the only bank in London willing to take a new deposit from a Super Group entity. Lavy, the bank's chairman, and Towning were friends of Donald Bruce Aberle, the Australian president of Columbus Trust in Nassau, newly appointed "investment adviser" and custodian of PRL. David Samuel Trust was known as banker to the tailoring trade and had surprisingly little affinity with the far-flung interests of PRL.

Warham's efforts in alerting investors to the latest Vesco-LeBlanc designs ultimately led to the forced liquidation of Investment Properties International and PRL. Once again, a nasty Super Group plot was foiled just in the nick of time. To insulate PRL from outside attack, Vesco and LeBlanc had sought to call a shareholders' meeting in Nassau to place Ontario-incorporated Investment Properties International in voluntary liquidation and transfer its assets—78 per cent of PRL's stock —to a newly formed Bahamian company, IPI Limited. But the appointment of a Canadian liquidator for the real IPI, by order of the Supreme Court of Ontario, days before the Nassau meeting was scheduled to take place abruptly ended this mockery of corporate law.

However, it was indicative of Vesco's latest thinking. In his over-all defense plan for the Super Group dominions he intended making the Bahamas the first line of retrenchment. Since most of the diverted IOS assets had filtered down to the Bahamas through the Bahamas Commonwealth Bank conduit, in dubious transfers to shell companies, or via non-arm's-length transactions with controlled corporations, it meant that whatever decisions were taken in other jurisdictions by such adversaries as the SEC, the Ontario and Quebec securities commissions, the Luxembourg Banking Commission, and the Geneva Attorney General's office ultimately would have to be enforced through the Bahamian courts, whose judiciary, Vesco had every reason to believe, would be more friendly toward him.

Warham, meanwhile, was threatened with reprisal. He quickly left

Nassau, shipping his car and other belongings to Miami. After a lengthy but not unfriendly questioning at U.S. Immigration, he drove off in his Volkswagen to explore America. Stopping by the roadside to rearrange the luggage on the back seat, he noticed hidden there a package carefully wrapped in plastic. He opened it and discovered inside several small envelopes containing what appeared to be marijuana, along with a small amount of Bahamian and American currency.

Concerned about the consequences of reporting his find—he almost was physically ill with fear—Warham buried the package at the roadside and continued on his way.

LeBlanc, through Columbus Trust Company, brought action against Warham in Nassau for conspiring to prevent an English bank from shipping PRL's cash to the Bahamas. In addition he accused the shaggy Scot, and also Michael Bennett, the British controller of International Bancorp, of being SEC spies. Bennett had collected a file of "mementos and memorabilia" documenting some of Super Group's financial "dirty tricks," which he showed to the SEC staff, consenting to become the SEC's star witness in the civil fraud trial in New York when it opened in April 1973.

Both Warham and Bennett carried with them to the mainland knowledge of Vector Limited, an ultra-secret $10 million steal, which they unveiled to the SEC. Vector was perhaps the dirtiest of the self-dealing Vesco-LeBlanc bargains and most illustrative of their intricate shifting-of-assets techniques.

20

Vector: A Ten-Million-Dollar Anagram

The last annual general meeting of insolvent IOS is held in an east-ern Canadian financial backwater ⏤ An almost total absence of shareholder concern encourages the "Boys in Nassau" to pick the carcass clean ⏤ The sale of ILI to a British merchant banking group

IOS Ltd.'s third annual general meeting was held in Saint John, New Brunswick, the out-of-the-way domicile of the company's registered offices, on June 30, 1972. Virtually devoid of assets at the time, a textbook study in insolvency, the afflicted IOS showed a meager net worth of $14.4 million, which was less than the $15.6 million par value of its outstanding shares.

The selection of Saint John, a dreary seaport with a population of 50,000, as site of the 1972 shareholders' meeting was another care-fully considered stratagem in Vesco's grand looting scheme. Weeks in advance, IOS reserved all the rooms at the Saint John Holiday Inn, venue for the final company gathering, in hopes of discouraging other participants from attending. Sparsely served by scheduled airlines, Saint John had only one other first-class hotel, and it was generally full.

The maneuver met with considerable success, since only nine dispirited shareholders and five journalists showed up. The meeting, such as it was, with Bud Meissner presiding, lasted less than half an hour instead of the two days needed for the previous year's effort in Toronto.

The main item of business on the agenda—a reduction of the existing twenty-seven-member board of directors to a handier nine-man board —was accomplished with ease. The remaining dissidents abstained from voting pending a settlement with Vesco, which they anticipated would be closed within the next few weeks. Management therefore controlled 99 per cent of the 26 million shares represented at the meeting.

Although three months previously Vesco had resigned all his positions with IOS, he called Saint John from San José, Costa Rica, to receive a firsthand report from Meissner on how the meeting went. This was not prompted by any innocent feeling of nostalgia on Vesco's part, one member of the IOS party affirmed. Behind the scenes at IOS, the Bootstrap Kid continued to be omnipresent. He still called all the shots.

The extent to which Vesco remained in control was reflected by the agreement IOS negotiated earlier that spring with Credit Suisse to repurchase several blocks of IOS preferred shares pledged as collateral on personal loans which members of former IOS management had contracted with the bank. Credit Suisse originally extended the loans on condition that IOS guaranteed to repurchase the stock if ever the loans were called. The loans were called during the 1970 crisis but IOS, then in the throes of collapse, contested the legality of the guarantees.

After almost two years of haggling with Credit Suisse, Vesco, through one of his Nassau-based companies, took possession of the 960,000 shares held by the Zurich bank against payment to the bank of $368,000 by IOS.

The shares had belonged to key members of the Old Guard dissident group, and their acquisition by a Vesco-controlled entity helped bury the dissidents. Split by constant bickering among themselves, the dissidents had ceased by then to be a force to contend with and, also, were so intent on concluding a multimillion-dollar settlement of their differences with the Vesco camp that they did not even bother to vote against incumbent management at the Saint John meeting.

In the repurchase from Credit Suisse of the 960,000 shares a new Bahamian creation known as Vector Limited raised its ugly head. Though IOS paid Credit Suisse for the stock, it was deposited with ODB (Bahamas) Limited and subsequently became part of a typical LeBlanc "rollback" situation. In a recently concluded but unannounced transaction, ODB (Bahamas) became the property of Vector Limited, which, although never disclosed, was owned by Vesco and LeBlanc.

First mention of Vector Limited appeared in the commercial registry of the Bahamas dated February 1, 1972, when Vesco associate Gil Straub and attorney Howard Cerny were appointed its founding directors. Within a month of Vector's formation, Straub was replaced as a director by LeBlanc.

Nobody paid any attention when, in early 1972, the unknown Vector Limited appeared on the scene and purchased from International Bancorp Limited four little used banking shells that generally were considered to be of slight value but nevertheless retained some cast-off assets. The transaction was considered to be so insignificant that no disclosure of it was ever made to the International Bancorp shareholders. The purchase price was purportedly $1.1 million, the listed book value of the banks, payable in an unsecured promissory note due in 1976.

Only later did it become apparent that the assets contained in the four banking shells—Investors Overseas Bank, Nassau; ODB (Bahamas) Limited; ODB (Sterling) Limited; and ODB (Curaçao) N.V. —had a value of almost $10 million, much of it in cash. Meanwhile, to distance the transaction as far as possible from the subsequent rejiggering of "true worth" later assigned to these assets, LeBlanc "rolled back" the date of the purchase contract to 1971. By a strange coincidence, the $1.1 million promissory note was written down to $500,000 and included in the International Bancorp annual report for 1971 as a receivable due from an affiliate, even though Vector was formed only in 1972.

Among Vector's "worthless" acquisitions were some serior notes from bankrupt Commonwealth United with an assigned *one dollar* write-off value. But one month before the formation of Vector LeBlanc already knew that these same Commonwealth United notes would be worth at least $2.5 million under a reorganization plan for Commonwealth proposed by a New York investment banking house. However, even this $2.5 million estimation proved low. Less than one year later Vector ended up receiving $3.9 million for the Commonwealth notes— for which it paid one dollar.

Another asset acquired by Vector was all the outstanding voting stock of a company called Hallendale Apartment Corporation (HAC), which had been assigned a nominal book value of $1,000 when transferred from IOS Real Estate Holdings through IOS Financial Holdings and out of International Bancorp to Vector. HAC was the nominee owner of more than 1,000 apartments in the IPI/PRL Hemispheres condominium complex in Florida. When Vesco first discovered the existence of HAC he termed it the "Christmas present company," since most people at IOS apparently had forgotten its existence. In other words, HAC was sitting there waiting for someone to pick it up. Vesco wasted no time.

Once the HAC voting shares went to Vector, Vesco and LeBlanc structured a by-play whereby Vector could have parlayed that $1,000 into $910,000 with no trouble at all. They sold the HAC shares from Vector to Value Capital for $600,000 in cash plus warrants to acquire 620,000 shares of Value Capital at 50 cents apiece, knowing that

Value Capital shares would later be subject to a tender offer by another LeBlanc-controlled company at $1 a share, guaranteeing them a neat 50-cent profit on every Value Capital share acquired by Vector.

Vector, which Super Group insiders claimed was intended as an anagram for Robert Vesco, bore his unmistakable signature. It was one of the clearest examples of how written-down assets were looted from the IOS shareholders in three or four carefully planned stages and ended up directly in the pockets of the bandits.

One of Vector's subsidiaries, ODB (Bahamas) Limited, which Vesco and LeBlanc renamed Trident Bank Limited, provided Super Group with an alternate banking channel in the Bahamas, even though Trident Bank had no staff and was little more than a series of accounts at Bahamas Commonwealth Bank.

Of course, when compared to Inter-American Capital, that Sham of Shams product of Vesco's rich imagination, Vector rated as a minor steal. But Vector was soon raking in hot cash as a management adviser and investment banker to a number of Super Group concerns. Not long afterward it became apparent that Bancorp de Costa Rica S.A., Super Group's operating arm in Central America, was a grandson of Vector, being a subsidiary of Trident Bank. This lineal flim-flam occured in spite of International Bancorp's having funded the Costa Rican Bancorp as well as having transferred $100,000 to Vesco's San José lawyers for its incorporation expenses.

Trident Bank became the investment manager of Inter-American and Phoenix Financial of Panama, but Bancorp de Costa Rica, for reasons of internal security best known only to Vesco and LeBlanc, kept the books of all three.

Another series of curious maneuvers surrounded the disposal of IOS's British operations grouped under International Life Insurance Company (U.K.) Limited to the London merchant banking group of Keyser Ullmann Holdings Limited, with 75,000 shares going to newly elected IOS director George Roberts at book value of $4 a share. Roberts, a baggy-looking English solicitor with a mildly eccentric manner, had been at Oxford at the same time as Meissner, although he only came to know the IOS president in 1964 through mutual business contacts. He was elected to the IOS Ltd. board of directors at the Saint John meeting, but Meissner already had appointed him a director of IOS Insurance Holdings Limited, and he had a $100,000-a-year "consulting contract" with Value Capital.

Keyser Ullmann, under the chairmanship of Edward du Cann, a Member of Parliament and former chairman of the Conservative Party, had risen from a second-line merchant bank to Britain's second largest through an ambitious acquisition program that astounded the City of London.

Keyser Ullman Holdings began purchasing the ILI (U.K.) stock in June 1972 and over the next six months acquired 57 per cent of the company for $4.5 million; du Cann personally purchased another 15.5 per cent for $1.2 million, making a total of $5.7 million, which was paid into an escrow account. Then, at an extraordinary general meeting of shareholders in February 1973, Keyser Ullmann changed the name of ILI (U.K.) to Cannon Assurance Limited, thereby hoping to erase from public memory the firm's IOS origins.

Roberts, meanwhile, had paid for his 9 per cent (75,000 shares) by issuing a note collateralized by the shares and at the same time concluding a separate agreement to put the shares back to ILI (U.K.) under new management at $11 a share. This meant that the potential profit to Roberts on this little deal was a cool $525,000.

Prior to its sale to Keyser Ullmann, ownership of ILI (U.K.)— which still claimed 125,000 policyholders, $775 million of insurance in force, and assets of $187 million under management in its Equity and other unit accounts—had been transferred from IOS Ltd. to Value Capital Limited for notes at the ridiculously low book value of $2.5 million. Therefore Value Capital, solidly controlled by LeBlanc's Global Holdings Limited, stood to make a profit of more than $3 million on the sale, which legitimately should have gone to IOS Ltd. shareholders.

While the sale of ILI (U.K.) was one profit that Vector did not pocket, Vector's tally in direct cash rip-offs was nevertheless not too bad. However, the existence of Vector remained hidden from the public investors and the SEC until the defection in early 1973 of both PRL and International Bancorp controllers, Warham and Bennett.

The SEC investigators, for their part, were swamped by a number of other no less startling discoveries concerning Vesco's true intentions, which became the basis of a seven-month court action in New York. Not surprisingly for those who had come to know Vesco, the New York suit once filed was labeled the largest securities fraud case ever brought by the U.S. government agency, and yet it covered only one-half of the greatest looting escapade in history.

21

Costa Rican Hideaway

The conquest of Costa Rica by the Bootstrap Kid, who fancies a future for himself as president of an extraterritorial financial district, while planning an ultimate escape route to the remote pampas of Paraguay

On November 27, 1972, three weeks after the U.S. Presidential elections the Securities and Exchange Commission filed its long-expected civil fraud complaint against Robert L. Vesco and forty-one other defendants:

Norman LeBlanc
Milton F. Meissner
Ulrich J. Strickler
Stanley Graze
Frank G. Beatty
Richard E. Clay
Wilbert Snipes
James Roosevelt
Frederic J. Weymar
Gilbert R. J. Straub
C. Henry Buhl III
Allan C. Butler
Laurence Richardson
John D. Schuyler
Edward Stoltenberg
Howard F. Cerny
Georges Philippe
Allan F. Conwill
Raymond W. Merritt

John S. D'Alimonte
IOS Ltd.
International Controls Corp.
Bahamas Commonwealth Bank
Overseas Development Bank
   Luxembourg S.A.
International Bancorp Ltd.
Value Capital Ltd.
Butlers Bank Ltd.
Transglobal Financial
   Services Ltd.
Kilmorey Investments Ltd.
Global Holdings Ltd.
Global Financial Ltd.
IIT Management Co. S.A.
FOF Management Co., Ltd.
Venture Management Co., Ltd.
IOS Growth Fund Management
   Co., Ltd.

Bank Cantrade Ltd.
Venture Fund (International) N.V.
Funds of Funds Ltd.

IOS Growth Fund Ltd.
IIT, an International Investment Trust
Consulentia Verwaltungs A.G.

The 17,000-word complaint marked the culmination of a twenty-month investigation by a team of eight SEC attorneys. For a legal document it read more like a Hollywood thriller and cut through jurisdictions, exposing a global maze of conversion and deceit.

On the same day the complaint was filed in the U.S. District Court for the Southern District of New York, trading on the American Stock Exchange in International Controls shares was suspended. Quoted at $12.625 when the investigation began, its last trade before the suspension order was at $3 a share, only a slightly less precipitous decline than the stock of IOS, the company that International Controls was supposed to have "rescued."

The SEC sought through its action to enjoin the defendants from further violations of the antifraud and reporting provisions of the federal securities laws; to require International Controls to correct its filings with the Commission and appoint a receiver-manager for the protection of its shareholders; to appoint a receiver for Fund of Funds, IIT, Venture International, and IOS Growth Fund; to require an accounting by Vesco and others of all moneys allegedly misappropriated from the funds; and to appoint a receiver for LeBlanc's International Bancorp and Value Capital.

The lottery system of assigning cases landed the complicated SEC complaint in the lap of Charles E. Stewart, Jr., a new judge who had been appointed to the federal bench by President Nixon on June 30, 1972. For Judge Stewart's first major case, it was a tough assignment. Buried by an immediate avalanche of exhibits, special briefs, and other legal documents, and with a score of the country's highest-priced lawyers acting for the defendants, it would not be unfair to say that the judge got off to a shaky start.

After three unsuccessful attempts to obtain a temporary order restricting new investments by the IOS dollar funds while the case went to trial, the SEC took the unusual step of bringing Commissioner Philip A. Loomis, Jr., up to New York to impress upon Judge Stewart that the SEC considered Vesco was "at the center of one of the largest securities frauds ever perpetrated."

Judge Stewart responded in early December 1972 by issuing an order limiting the funds to investments in publicly traded U.S. securities and bank deposits in the six largest banks respectively in the United States, Canada, Japan, and the nine Common Market countries, as well as the two largest banks respectively in Australia, Brazil, Hong Kong, Mexico, New Zealand, Norway, Portugal, Singapore, and Sweden.

Meissner, then operating out of London, used Stewart's order—the so-called bridge order—as an excuse to suspend redemptions in the funds, effectively close-ending them, which was Vesco's wish for nearly two years.

Vesco appeared briefly in court during the preliminary legal maneuvering. He was accompanied by his civil attorney, Arthur Liman, a partner in the prestigious New York law firm of Paul, Weiss, Rifkind. But Vesco never reappeared in the courtroom and within three months left the country, fully intending never to return unless absolved of any wrongdoing or offered immunity in future criminal proceedings.

A leak at SEC headquarters forewarned IOS's attorneys in New York —Allan Conwill, Ray Merritt, and John D'Alimonte of Willkie Farr Gallagher—that the SEC's complaint was about to be launched. Vesco, once notified, atempted to exert all his influence to have it quashed before it was publicly filed.

Thus, it was later alleged by the U.S. Attorney's Office in New York that:

> In November 1972, defendant Robert L. Vesco could and did attempt to submit a written memorandum to Donald Nixon, the brother of the President of the United States, the purport and tenor of which was to threaten disclosure of the secret cash contribution and other adverse consequences unless the SEC was directed to drop all legal proceedings against Vesco. When the memorandum came to the attention of defendant John N. Mitchell, he turned it over to the defendant Harry L. Sears and concealed its existence and contents from the SEC and other law enforcement agencies who properly should have been made aware of it. [See appendix 2.]

But Vesco's efforts did not stop there. He discussed sending Gil Straub and Dick Clay down to Key Biscayne in the weeks preceeding the filing of the complaint to meet with Bebe Rebozo and plead for his intervention with the President. There is no record of what resulted from this intention, but in the same time period John Dean III contacted William Casey at the SEC and asked that the proceedings be delayed. Casey was informed by his staff that this was not possible, which information Casey testified he passed on to the White House.

The guts of the SEC's charges came in paragraph 62 of the complaint. "Vesco and his group have converted to their personal pursuits over $125,000,000 of the sales proceeds of high grade United States securities which they caused the dollar funds to sell during the period April through October 1972. Additional sales proceeds from United States securities of about $100,000,000 . . . are unaccounted for," it stated.

But it was paragraph 64 that caused most of the later trouble, since it was responsible for unveiling the New York phase of Watergate. In an elliptical reference to the Washington bag, this paragraph noted: "In addition to the above described transactions, other large sums of cash have been transferred among and between Vesco and his group, Bahamas Commonwealth Bank, International Controls, and other parties. The sources, ownership, use of, and accountability for, said moneys are unknown. Defendants Vesco, Richardson, Clay and other persons have refused to testify on this matter, among others."

In fact, direct reference to the $250,000 transferred in April 1972 from Bahamas Commonwealth Bank to the New York branch of Barclays International and suspected at that point—but not definitely proved— to have gone to CREEP, was made in an earlier draft of the complaint, then removed after Brad Cook, the SEC general counsel, had spoken with Maurice Stans. Cook and Stans went on a goose-hunting trip together at Eagle Lake, Texas, two weeks before the complaint was filed, and they discussed the investigation, with Cook bringing up the matter of the $250,000. He received an evasive reply from Stans, which only served to increase his indecision.

Meanwhile, all hell broke loose in the International Controls board-room. Vesco attempted to bully his fellow directors into supporting his courtroom defense. He hired private detectives to accompany him into the Fairfield offices and disrupted board meetings by "yelling, cursing, and threatening, in order to still any minority opposition," Richardson said in an explosive affidavit filed with the court. Finally, in early February 1973, subjected to the most intense pressure, Richardson stepped down as president and filed a motion with Judge Stewart supporting the SEC's request for an equity receiver to prevent a further "misuse and dissipation of corporate assets."

The court appointed a five-man board of directors to replace International Controls's old eight-man board. The new chairman was John Mosler, a fifty-year-old New York businessman and philanthropist. The new president and director was Allen M. Shinn, a retired U.S. Navy vice admiral. The court also appointed David M. Butowsky, a New York lawyer, as special counsel in lieu of an equity receiver, instructing him to conduct an investigation into the alleged misuse of assets and attempt to recover the millions of dollars in missing assets.

The difficult task of reconstruction began. A first decision in the interest of economy was to shift corporate headquarters from Fairfield to Thomaston, Connecticut, the site of the Radiation unit's head offices. Six months later International Controls's three line subsidiaries came out with the depressing results of 1972 operations: All American declared a net deficit of $13.5 million; Radiation International's net loss was $12.7 million; and Datron Systems did the best of the three with a loss of $11.3 million. Most of this catastrophe represented the writing off of $30 million in "good will" picked up in the 1968 Electronic Specialty acquisition.

The IRS, meanwhile, had placed a lien on Vesco's 1 million shares of International Controls stock, claiming they were owed $800,000 in back taxes. The Luxembourg Banking Commission also intervened in the fray, ordering Bahamas Commonwealth Bank to return to the IOS depository bank in the Grand Duchy some $177 million diverted from the four dollar funds.

As a result of the Luxembourg Banking Commission's intervention, the Supreme Court of the Bahamas issued an order freezing $10 million at Algemene Bank Nederland N.V., $105.37 million at the Bank of Montreal in Montreal, $18.05 million at the Bank of Montreal (Bahamas & Caribbean) Limited in Nassau, $7 million with the Union Commerce Bank of Cleveland in Nassau, and $15 million with Bahamas Commonwealth Bank in Nassau. The remaining $21.5 was found deposited with reputable banks in Luxembourg.

The sudden blocking of $177 million severely hampered Super Group's lending activities in the Bahamas. Nevertheless, such events had been anticipated, and Michael Rogers, the Flying Bishop, was dispatched to Panama City with a briefcase full of money in the company of LeBlanc's personal accountant, where he attempted to open five secret numbered accounts at five different Panamanian banks.

The Panama by-pass was at first unsuccessful. Only when veteran diplomat Tony Morales joined Super Group a few weeks later did things begin to roll smoothly in Panama. Several millions of PRL's money filtered down rather quickly and has not been accounted for since, although $1.5 million of PRL deposits in Panama was suspected of having financed the purchase of a 137-foot pleasure yacht, the *Patricia III,* for Vesco's use.

After the SEC's complaint made headlines around the world, both Vesco and LeBlanc adopted a number of sneaky stratagems for defending themselves against what they alleged was the SEC's attempt to try their case in the press. Their first propaganda counterattack suggested that the Commission was really upset with them because the $225 million removed from the U.S. stock markets had been largely reinvested in developing countries.

Later they modified this claim and stated that they had been nailed in the "trade-off" at the SEC between the hard-noses and the politicos. The hard-noses were permitted to uncork the Vesco case provided the politicos received their assistance in covering up the Nixon-related IT&T scandal, was how they nuanced their second propaganda offensive.

This second version pleased the Costa Ricans much less but was more in tune with the times in Washington.

"Geographical employment of capital," Vesco explained piously on Costa Rican television in the first phase of his upright-image campaign, "runs at cross-purposes with the institutional interests in a capitalistic society.

"I believe that the investment direction of the 'seventies should be back into [developing] countries in the form of sound economic investments that also carry a higher degree of sociological benefit and contribute to the well-being of the country and its people," he said.

"For the SEC, this view is almost treated as a crime; it is also treason to the 'financial establishment' and therefore must be stigmatized as a 'fraud,' " he added.

He hastened to note that "my legal advisers and my conscience tell me that I have done the right thing and that the actions instituted against me by the SEC are without merit and have behind them other motives."

Vesco was introduced to Costa Rica by the New York promoter "Pistol Dick" Pistell in the summer of 1972, about the time the Bootstrap Kid and his lieutenants began looking for a haven to relocate their operations.

The inimitable Mr. Fixit—Gil Straub—had come up with a proposition concerning an island off the southern coast of the Dominican Republic. According to Straub, Isla Saone had its territorial sovereignty guaranteed by China and was up for sale. He proposed that Super Group buy it to run as an independent gambling republic. But the idea was too fantastic even for Vesco to consider for long.

"Pistol Dick" had been invited to Costa Rica in July 1972 to attend a ranch party at Clovis McAlpin's Hacienda Chapernal, a few miles southwest of the capital, San José. Pistell got Vesco to join him, and the two of them and their families flew down to San José in the Big Bird.

McAlpin had purchased his 14,000-acre cattle ranch just outside San José for $3 million in cash belonging to Capital Growth Company S.A., the closed-end successor to Capital Growth Fund. In a subsequent currency control fiddle, McAlpin paid $125,000 to import from Texas a prize Charolais bull appropriately named "Amour d'Amerique." Tican pundits coarsely suggested that McAlpin's bullish investment represented "the most expensive balls in America." For his little housewarming at the hacienda, he had invited every friendly politician in town, including the entire Presidential Cabinet.

"We went out to the ranch, and I'd have to say it was out of the movies," Pistell told the SEC.

"You went to a party?" one of the staff investigators asked him.

"At the ranch. Took all the children. They had a thousand cowboys there. They had everything going and everyone in Costa Rica was there. Every [goverment] minister, everything." [1]

With so many Capital Growth graduates on Super Group's payroll, it was only natural that Vesco and McAlpin finally should meet. However, outside of their infatuation with Costa Rica, the original banana republic, as a shelter for hot money, their self-dealing expertise in running offshore mutual funds into the ground, and the interest in their affairs this generated at the SEC headquarters in Washington, where McAlpin was also under investigation, the two men had little in common.

Pistell introduced Vesco to another old friend, somber, sharp-minded Alberto Inocente Alvarez, a Cuban Foreign Minister under Batista. Alvarez was prospering as one of Costa Rica's most influential business-men, serving as economic adviser and close confidant to President José ("Don Pepe") Figueres. He was reputed to have his finger on the economic pulse beat of the republic and obviously was a key man to know.

Pistell also introduced Vesco to Marti Figueres, eldest son of the President. Marti Figueres was the managing director of Sociedad Agricola y Industrial San Cristobal S.A., a small Costa Rican company founded by his father in 1928. San Cristobal produced a variety of items from coffee to sisal rope, burlap, and polypropylene coffee bags. San Cristobal's pre-eminence in its field was such that every bean of coffee exported from Costa Rica went in a San Cristobal sack.

When Vesco first arrived in the country San Cristobal was embarking on a new project, the manufacture of low-cost prefabricated housing, and needed capital to begin production of the first models. Pistell said he went out to the plant near Don Pepe's farm, had a look at the machinery, studied the cash flow projections, and subsequently persuaded Vesco—whom by this time he had introduced to the President—to make a $2,150,000 placement.

Vesco caused IOS's IIT fund to lend San Cristobal the money against an unsecured promissory note at 7 per cent interest per annum, due in 1977. The loan was contrary to IIT's investment restrictions, but that was the least of anyone's worries. IIT also received warrants to purchase 500,000 shares of San Cristobal common stock at $1 per share over a five-year period; Trident Bank, apparently for nothing, received 1 million warrants on the same terms as IIT; and Dick Pistell, the match-maker, received a $150,000 finder's fee. IIT's cash served as Vesco's key money, giving him easy entry to the Presidential palace.

[1] Pistell's SEC testimony, November 1, 1972.

Of no account was the fact that San Cristobal had a long history of managerial problems and financial instability. As such it could hardly be considered a prudent investment for a liquid mutual fund—no market existed for San Cristobal's paper, and available financial information concerning its operations was skimpy and problematic. None of these considerations had deterred Clovis McAlpin, however. In 1968 he had Capital Growth invest $2 million in the company for a large slice of stock. Shortly afterward, McAlpin received a Costa Rican diplomatic passport, which stated that he was an economic adviser to the Costa Rican mission to the European Economic Community in Brussels.

Likewise, after IIT put in its $2.15 million, Vesco was honored with a Costa Rican diplomatic passport stamped "financial adviser to the president."

In mid-1969, according to Clovis McAlpin's older brother, Gordon, it became apparent that "six or seven hundred thousand dollars" had disappeared from San Cristobal. Apparently, according to the elder McAlpin's testimony before the Costa Rican labor court, "somebody" handling black market coffee sales for San Cristobal "which were said to be quite large . . . had not paid the black market coffee money to Marti Figueres as had been scheduled." So San Cristobal appeared to be in the coffee rustling business as well.

The disappearance of the $600,000 or so, Gordon McAlpin told the labor court, "left San Cristobal in a very precarious financial condition." [2]

San Cristobal, with a net worth of $5.5 million and annual sales of $4.5 million, according to its managing director, reported its last surplus year in fiscal 1970, but with IIT's $2.15 million the company hoped to be back in the black in fiscal 1973. The history and development of San Cristobal was very much the history of Pepe Figueres, a national hero although easily the country's most controversial political figure.

Quixotic, diminutive Don Pepe, three times President of the republic, often astounded his fellow countrymen with the unpredictable. At sixty-six years of age, he personally chased and caught a thief in the streets of San José. On another occasion, armed with a sub-machine gun, he rushed a hijacked airliner that had touched down for refueling at San José's Santamaria airport and stunned the skyjackers into surrendering.

In the mid-1920s Don Pepe attended MIT for a while but didn't graduate because of a hot dispute he had with his professor, whom he accused of being inept. In 1928, at twenty-two, he returned to Costa Rica and with $3,000 borrowed from a friend founded San Cristobal.

[2] Third Labor Court transcript, p. 26.

He carved out of the central highland forests a farm for growing natural fibers as the first step to fulfilling a lifelong dream, which was to produce a 100 per cent Costa Rican product from seed to finish.

The farm—two hours' drive from San José but a weeklong journey by oxcart in the 1920s—was given the name *La Lucha Sin Fin* (Struggle Without End) by the farmers who worked with him.

"San Cristobal went through rough times. It was severely hit by the Depression," said Pepe's son Marti. The company diversified, going into timber and the coffee growing field. A second crisis coincided with the outbreak of World War II.

"The Communists were creating trouble in Costa Rica and the government was weak. In 1942 Don Pepe gave a radio speech lambasting the government for corruption, and before the speech was finished a detachment of soldiers had come to the radio station and dragged him out of the broadcasting studio. Next day he was exiled to San Salvador," Marti continued.

After two years in exile he was allowed back into the country. Meanwhile San Cristobal hobbled on without him, producing coffee and natural fibers.

After the war Costa Rica seemed doomed to become the first country in the American hemisphere to fall under Communist domination. In 1948, when the government took steps to suspend the constitution, Don Pepe raised a 700-man guerrilla army and took to the hills. The campaign that followed lasted five weeks. Government troops burned *La Lucha* to the ground, but in the end Don Pepe's ragtag liberation fighters defeated the pro-Communist regime, and he became Provisional President of Costa Rica in May 1948.

Contrary to political tradition in Latin America, Don Pepe did not install himself as President and national benefactor for life. He introduced social and political reforms that gave Costa Rica the third highest standard of living, the highest literacy rate, and one of the lowest birth rates in Latin America.

His first act as President was to abolish the army. Since Costa Rica was a peace-loving country, it had no need of an army, he declared with typical Figuerian logic. Costa Rica, as a result, has no military budget; it does have a strong National Police Force and a presidential guard. Presidents, elected to four-year terms, could not be returned to office for consecutive terms, and could be elected President only three times in a lifetime.

His constitutional reforms complete, he resigned eighteen months later and called a general election. The people loved him for it. The name Don Pepe was adopted by Ticans as a mark of national respect for their foremost statesman.

An accomplished economist, self-taught engineer, and gentleman farmer, he became one of Latin America's outstanding political thinkers. But above all he was an eccentric. As the fiery leader of the National Liberation Party, which he formed after leaving the Presidency, he was twice re-elected head of the republic, finding time in between to accept appointments as visiting professor of Latin American Affairs at Harvard and Rollins College. He was serving his third and final term as head of state when Vesco arrived on the scene.

In early 1973 Don Pepe went on national TV to defend his financial dealings with Vesco. San Cristobal, he said, urgently needed an injection of new capital. He had looked everywhere for potential investors and finally wound up with the fugitive financier as an investor without knowing him very well.

According to evidence amassed by the SEC, Figueres's New York bank account grew by $325,000 soon after Vesco started investing in Costa Rica—some $255,000 of it coming from Bahamas Commonwealth Bank. The President, in his hour-long broadcast, said the SEC had made an error in its figures. His account at the National Bank of North America, he asserted, had grown not by $325,000 but by $436,000.

"That account in New York is the only foreign account I have, and I can tell you that New York is not the place to have a bank account if you are up to no good," Don Pepe told the nation in his folksy TV appearance.

He explained that one item—a $60,000 "gift" from "two music lovers" in the Bahamas later identified as Dick Pistell and Stanley Graze—was a donation to establish a tree farm as part of the endowment for the Costa Rican National Symphony Orchestra. Other sums of money, he said, had been transited through his account by error for San Cristobal S.A., which maintained a checking facility at the same bank.

After four years of research, in early 1974 San Cristobal went into production of its first wooden housing units. The company planned to turn out the one-family units for between $800 and $3,000 apiece. Most of the blueprints for the prefab houses and even the machinery were designed by Don Pepe himself, who had visions of becoming the Henry Ford of low-cost housing.

Judging by the enthusiastic way he described San Cristobal's low-cost housing plans, Marti Figueres, Don Pepe's son, could have been a million-dollar mutual fund salesman.

"When the project's first stage is completed in mid-1974 we expect production of around 3,000 units a year, 50 per cent for the export market. The global demand for low-cost homes in Costa Rica alone is estimated at 200,000 units. At 1,500 houses a year it will take us 130 years to meet demand here. So we're not afraid of the market drying up on us. But selling 1,500 houses a year means setting up five new houses each day, and to handle that kind of volume you need trained personnel."

We were talking and sipping black Costa Rican coffee at the San Cristobal offices, a modest converted cream-colored house in a back street of San José. For a man of thirty, Marti Figueres possessed the confidence of someone who instinctively knew authority. Married with five children, he was part of the local élite known around San José as the Liberation *Argolla*—families of the clique of men who had fought with Don Pepe in the hills and since had come to dominate much of the country's political and economic life.

Marti Figueres was trim and smartly dressed in a tightly tailored suit. He sported a bushy black mustache and dark-rimmed glasses, spoke flawless English, and was witty and polite. He always kept his small first-floor office locked, the keys dangling from his belt.

Our conversation was interrupted by a phone call. Marti answered; the caller presumably spoke in English, since the replies were in English. The conversation was brief and one-sided.

"Yes, I know," he finally said. "But I can't throw him out. He's already in my office."

He apologized but offered no explanation. I felt the long hand of Robert Vesco reaching out.

We continued sipping coffee. Marti explained his father's policy of encouraging offshore mutual fund groups to settle in Costa Rica. These offshore buccaneers, he maintained, had soaked up about $100 million from Costa Rican nationals and exported it for investment abroad. "So why shouldn't the government encourage some of it to come back? Costa Rica is a developing country, and it is up to the government to do everything it can to invert that flow of funds and bring home as much of it as possible," he said.

A few months later, at a meeting in New York, I asked Don Pepe how much of the Costa Rican flight capital he estimated he had recaptured. "Oh, more than 30 per cent so far," he said with a grin. This seemed like a conservative estimate, since Super Group, through its newly formed Bancorp de Costa Rica, had invested an estimated $25 million in Costa Rican projects, and McAlpin's Capital Growth was said to have contributed $11 million more to the buoyant Tican economy.

At least one Costa Rican resident rumored to be a heavy investor in IOS mutual funds was Alberto Alvarez, which perhaps explained his apparent attachment to Vesco. But even so, the number of investment programs listed in IOS client records as belonging to Ticans was not impressive. According to a September 1971 IOS computer printout, the total number of Costa Rican clients was under 1,000, and the maximum sum invested was far less than $10 million.

Costa Rican had never been a major IOS market, but even so Vesco indicated he was keen to pump ten times more fund-holder money back into the country than IOS salesmen had taken out, provided he received a safe haven in return in the form of an international free zone complete with gambling and banking concessions as his new operations base.

Conceptually, the free zone was to have been an autonomous region with extraterritorial privileges—a sort of Tangiers West of the good old days. And so out of his talks with leading government officials came an ambitious plan to transform Costa Rica into the world's newest flight capital haven. Vaguely reminiscent of a project Meyer Lansky, the Mob's "chairman of the board," had considered in the late 1940s for introducing gambling to Costa Rica, and later discarded, Vesco's reworked version assured him of a headquarters for Super Group in an enclave he would govern, which would be beyond the reach of all major regulatory bodies in the world.

Vesco's international free zone, according to an unsigned memorandum circulated among Liberation Party Congressmen, was to consist of a financial district and satellite resort area with a luxury housing development, hotels, recreational facilities, and "tourist development, including gaming." The zone was to be self-governed by a five-member council titularly headed by a governor appointed by the President of Costa Rica, but in reality controlled by a district director, a role Vesco reserved for himself.

The council would be empowered to enact legislation, maintain law and order, keep a registry of corporations and a maritime registry, issue bonds, collect taxes, assure business and banking secrecy, and create its own banking commission to supervise banks and trusts domiciled in the zone. Under the proposed charter, Costa Rican nationals would be excluded from working or residing in the zone except by permission of the council.

Figueres's parliamentary opponents vigorously attacked the plan. They feared that the zone would become a base for financial piracy, a sanctuary for tax evasion that would attract every kind of gangster and speculator.

One of the most outspoken critics, ex-President Mario Echandi Jiménez, called it an attempt by the "international Mafia" to take over Costa Rica. Figueres defended the project, claiming it would bring in healthy new capital and assist in economic and social development.

To back up his assertion, Bahamas Commonwealth Bank purchased $5.7 million worth of Costa Rican government bonds.

Vesco's agents began buying up tracts of land along the superhighway to the airport. But the political furor finally caused Vesco to stop further work on the scheme, and it was shelved until after the February 1974 Presidential elections. As the candidate of the National Liberation Party—Don Pepe's party—triumphed, a second coming of the free zone was not excluded.

Meanwhile, Don Pepe had become Vesco's greatest public relations booster. The Gringo's attempt to buy the tiny Central American republic was resented by the average Tican, as was the presence of N11RV at San José's international airport. After all, said Romolo Facio, the twenty-one-year-old son of the Foreign Minister, people wondered why this American big shot needed a plane larger than the largest LACSA (Costa Rica's national airlines) plane all for himself.

Don Pepe wrote a pamphlet defending offshore mutual funds that was widely distributed. In July 1972 he also wrote President Nixon indicating his concern that adverse publicity emanating from Vesco's "difficulties" with the SEC might damage Costa Rica's position as a "showpiece of democratic development" in the middle of the Western Hemisphere.

So that life wouldn't be too rustic in his newly adopted "American Arcadia," Vesco had planeloads of household effects, including six Amana ovens, flown down to San José. Even the Vesco stable of horses followed. Also as part of the intended relocation, crates of office furniture were shipped in from IOS's unused offices in Geneva, 5,800 miles away.

The goods were brought into the country without clearing customs, which prompted a question in parliament as to why Vesco was permitted to dispense with the usual customs formalities. From across the square at the Presidential Palace, Don Pepe replied with total disdain that the crates—or at least certain of them—contained toys for under-privileged children.

In addition to Vesco, five other Super Group executives and two pilots were accorded resident status in Costa Rica. Clay, LeBlanc, Straub, Strickler, and Graze were also given provisional Costa Rican passports. Bancorp de Costa Rica, with Strickler, the Spanish-speaking Mr. Will-Be-Done, as general manager, rented seven homes in the San José area and placed armed guards around them to keep out unwanted trespassers.

Vesco purchased for $500,000 a fully furnished ranch-style villa with swimming pool in Bello Horizonte, the embassy residential district about ten minutes' drive from downtown San José, and built an eight-foot-high wall around it for added privacy. Armed bodyguards patrolled the perimeter of the large Vesco compound, which was electronically monitored and floodlit from twilight to dawn. Vesco himself, fearing both kidnappers and U.S. government agents often carried a side arm, and wherever he went was followed by a private security detail. He planned to install a helipad and a communications mast for a direct radio-telephone link with Charlotte House in Nassau and for in-flight calls to and from the Big Bird.

His San José law firm of Facio, Fournier & Cañas, in addition to incorporating Inter-American Capital and Bancorp de Costa Rica, set up four other Costa Rican companies for Super Group under the names Bravo S.A., Costa Rica Communications S.A., Inter-American Aircraft S.A., and Inter-American Oil Company S.A. In addition, $2 million was invested in Maderas Quimicas S.A., a local chemical company whose president, Jiménez Veiga, was a former Labor Minister and a member of the Liberation *argolla*.

Pistell and Alvarez had other schemes they thought might interest Vesco. One was the construction of an oil transmission pipeline across the narrowest part of the country "which would have been a perfect tie-in with the Alaska North Slope field," said Pistell. The country was 110 miles across at the point where the pipeline was projected, with deep-water ports on either coast, and an oil refinery was to be built at one of the terminals. "It would have been a helluva deal," said Pistell.

To counteract the scathing attacks in the local press, Vesco hired Romolo Facio as general dogsbody and PR man for the local Super Group incarnate, Bancorp de Costa Rica, and imported J. Raul Espinosa, a Cuban American who had worked under Herb Klein at the White House and was introduced to Vesco by Dangerous Don Nixon.

Espinosa, who called himself Vesco's "special representative in Costa Rica," proved not to be a good communicator, as the Ticans found him *poco simpatico*. He even managed to put up the back of President Figueres with his outlandish antics and declarations to the press. His staff consisted of a secretary and a private detective to trace the source of unfavorable publicity about Super Gringo and Super Group in general.

To still the virulent press criticism, there were reports that Vesco interests were buying into the two largest local newspapers and that Vesco had financed for his friend Don Pepe the founding of a third, the *Excelsior*. He also put money into two radio stations and two TV stations.

Espinosa, in a series of farcical press releases, claimed he had been threatened by anonymous callers for defending Vesco.

"I am embarrassed and ashamed to realize that a supposedly respected agency of the U.S. government has left its jurisdictional bounderies and is using immoral and malicious methods made popular by the CIA to harass Mr. Vesco in a foreign country," one comuniqué stated.

A few weeks later LeBlanc, not to be outdone, issued his own press release from the Super Group offices in the Numar Building charging that "the improper U.S. government actions in the 'Vesco case' far exceed those employed in the Ellsberg case. They include illegal entry, terrorizing children, wiretaps, mail interruption, immigration and Internal Revenue Service harassment, issuance of false statements to foreign governments, receiving stolen documents, and promoting internal spying."

Then LeBlanc and Espinosa called a joint press conference at a luxury hotel in downtown San José. This time Espinosa claimed the CIA was bugging his telephone. He produced a voltage meter that he said Vesco's security men had used to determine the telephone lines were tapped.

LeBlanc, though, stole the show. Slurring his words, at times so agitated that he was barely coherent, he charged that Peter Johnson, the chief political officer at the U.S. Embassy in San José, was in reality a CIA agent trying to "get rid" of him and Vesco.

It was high paranoia.

The U.S. Ambassador, Viron Vaky, rushed to the Presidential Palace the following day and spent two hours protesting to Don Pepe the vilification of his government's institutions by LeBlanc, a defaulting defendant in the SEC action in New York, and Espinosa, the hired hand of a fugitive from justice. If such scenes continued, Vaky informed the President, relations between their countries were bound to be affected.

Figueres hit the ceiling when he learned of the LeBlanc-Espinosa circus, especially a remark by Espinosa alleging that Vesco had "put Costa Rica on the map." Vesco's "special representative" was told, he said, to stop issuing press releases as Don Pepe personally would handle the Gringo's public relations needs until the storm had blown over. The President promptly issued a statement describing as "fantasies" the LeBlanc affirmations that the U.S. Embassy was engaged in illegal activities, and privately the expatriate Canadian was informed of Don Pepe's extreme displeasure.

A few days later Espinosa was "fired" by Vesco for exceeding his instructions, tentatively rehired by PRL, and exiled to the IPI/PRL Playamar resort development in southern Spain, where no one knew what to do with him. He went on two holiday cruises—one to Greece and the other to Yugoslavia—then, when it was made clear that no job existed for him at Playamar, returned to the United States and found new employment with the Republican National Committee in Washington. When reached there for comment, he denied being embittered at having been made Vesco's fall guy.

"They told me to create a diversion in Costa Rica. So that's what I did," Espinosa, his ego bruised by such thankless treatment, had claimed before leaving Playamar.

Effectively there had been good reason for some diversionary sideplay. At the end of April 1973 the Big Bird flew Vesco, Marti Figueres, Mr. Will-Be-Done, and two unknown passengers on the first of several trips down to Asuncion, capital of Paraguay, and then on to Buenos Aires, the Argentine capital, to pave the way for Vesco's ultimate escape route to the distant pampas of South America, where he was resigned to spending his retirement, if necessary, with such illustrious fugitives as Dr. Josef Mengele, the Nazi doctor of death, and other noted criminals.

These top-secret preparations continued throughout Espinosa's "diversionary" period, sometimes involving Clay, sometimes LeBlanc. The authorities in Asuncion were most receptive. But Asuncion, a hot and dusty city situated 600 miles inland on the Paraguay River, was ever so far removed from the world's financial centers. At least Buenos Aires was a busy, modern city of broad boulevards, tall buildings, and a decent-sized stock exchange.

In October 1973 Vesco's lawyers in Argentina obtained a ruling from a federal judge granting the international fugitive immunity from extradition from that country on any charges arising out of Vesco's involvement with IOS, because they were "deemed to be related to Watergate and therefore brought for political purposes." [3]

Following this astonishing court decision, Vesco, accompanied by four bodyguards, Marti Figueres, and Strickler, chartered a Bahamas World Airways Boeing 707—the Big Bird was grounded in West Palm Beach, Florida, by court order—and returned to Buenos Aires. In response to their earlier petition for residence status, Vesco and Strickler received assurance from Interior Minister Benito Llambi that the necessary authorization had been granted and all that remained to be completed was the official paper work. Pleased with the results of seven months of careful preparation, and after inspecting a house Vesco had purchased there, the party returned to San José.

Three weeks later, with Espinosa no longer around to create "diversions," Scott Schmedel of the *Wall Street Journal* found out about Vesco's newest refuge and publicized it on the *Journal's* front page, with the result that Argentine Foreign Minister Alberto Vignes over-

[3] *Wall Street Journal,* November 19, 1973.

ruled the residency permits, withdrawing access to Vesco's penultimate safe haven.

God forbid, but if worse came to worst, it would be back to Asuncion. Or maybe not. Vesco, in May 1973, had acquired an Italian passport on the pretext that his grandfather, when immigrating to America, had not renounced his Italian citizenship.

What limpid-eyed Romolo Facio couldn't understand in the midst of all this bother was that "these people have so much money and yet it doesn't make them happy. They're always so tense, up-tight, and suspicious."

Vesco, when he arrived in San José, spent most of his time working or in conference. "Figures, figures, figures. He only looks at figures," said Romolo.

Vesco was usually accompanied on his flying visits by Don-Don Nixon. The relationship between Big Bobby and Dangerous Don was another anomaly that never ceased to puzzle young Romolo. "He's always yelling at him. Calls him an idiot," Romolo said. Once, Vesco in a rage was heard to scream at Don-Don, "You stupid bastard! You need me more than I need you! And never forget it!"

"Vesco uses Don as an errand boy," Romolo remarked, perplexed. "He once sent him out to buy tomatoes." Vesco would also send Don-Don into town to pick up packages for Pat. It really *was* a very strange relationship.

"They're great people," Don-Don remarked of the Vescos. "Big Bobby's the best friend I have. But it's a heavy trip that we're all on now, I'm afraid."

After President Figueres's letter to Don-Don's uncle in July 1972 the White House could no longer mistake just how heavy a trip it was. And young Don Nixon remained right in the center of it all, one of the key pawns in Vesco's influence game. Then came a startling phone call from Washington six weeks before the U.S. elections. The White House wanted Vesco to send "Junior" back to the States, supposedly to help in his uncle's election campaign.

Vesco smelled a rat. He remembered that Ehrlichman had earlier confided to Straub how Don-Don should be put on a slow boat to China during the election campaign to keep him out of trouble. So it didn't make sense that the White House suddenly wanted him sent to Washington right in the thick of the campaign. Vesco's reaction was brutally to the point.

"Bob spent twenty minutes cursing, screaming, threatening, and finally slammed the phone down," a horrified Vesco aide reported.

Not only was Don-Don a Vesco pawn, but he had become a hostage as well. Over the next few weeks "Vesco and Straub hid Junior [from the White House staff] by keeping him on the move," the aide said.

LeBlanc lived a less visible life in San José, commuting back and forth between Nassau and the Costa Rican capital on weekends in the old Connex Press Sabreliner. In early 1973 Super Group also leased a gleaming white Grumman G-2 Gulfstream from the Teamsters Union for medium-range flights. The twin-jet Grumman with a yellow and black stripe along its side was lower-profile than the Big Bird and cost only $1,500 per hour to fly, as compared to $3,500 for N11RV.

The Grumman bore the markings N711S. Seven and eleven are a crapshooter's winning rolls, and the "S" was said to stand for Frank Sinatra, who reportedly once owned the plane. However, when Super Group acquired it on a basic $40,000-per-month lease, the Grumman was registered under the name of the Teamsters' billion-dollar Central States, Southeast, and Southwest areas pension fund.

Vesco's leasing of the Teamster jet was intended as a show of good faith. Two years previously he attempted to borrow $30 million in Teamster funds to refinance his International Controls corporate debt, but his loan request was turned down. He did, however, hope that he could turn to the Teamsters again with other proposals. But nothing further developed, and the Grumman G-2 was turned back to its owners in early 1974 after a dispute over the correctness of certain billings.

Meanwhile Vesco worked quickly to consolidate and extend his power base in Costa Rica, while keeping other options more or less out of sight. Thus he opened a northern escape route when he, LeBlanc, Strickler, and Straub jointly purchased a large cattle ranch in Guanacaste province, near the Nicaraguan border, as another of their retreats. It was just "a little private investment" that Vesco and the others had made on the side, LeBlanc let slip in an unguarded moment while sipping highballs on the veranda of his modern home.

Obviously Vesco's power-base building was successful. A 1973 U.S. request for his extradition was turned down by a criminal court judge in San José. So that he would be immune to further "frivolous" extradition requests, one of Don Pepe's last acts of legislation before retiring from the Presidency in early 1974 was to pass a controversial reform of the country's extradition law. It indirectly excluded new extradition hearings relating to Vesco due to an abstruse technicality cleverly drafted into the body of the text. Passage of the bill through Congress drew cries of outrage from the opposition and provoked hostile anti-Vesco student demonstrations in San José.

22

Financing the Cuban Counter-Revolution

Vesco stonewalls the SEC investigators — Trying to unload the moribund IOS structure on an improbable mélange of Spanish royalty and scheming Cuban exiles — A patriotic offer from RLV to RMN

Within four months of meeting former Cuban Foreign Minister, Dr. Alberto Inocente Alvarez, Vesco decided that the IOS shell had been picked about as clean as he could get it.

The company included among its stickiest possessions an ever growing number of lawsuits and three remaining assets:

(1) an 80 per cent interest in Transglobal Financial Services Limited, which held the management contracts for twelve IOS mutual funds, a 49 per cent interest in Fonditalia Management Company, and a 50 per cent interest in the Rothschild Expansion SICAV management contract. The four offshore funds—FOF, IIT, Venture International, and IOS Growth Fund—had been emptied of all but $150 million. Fund of Funds Sterling Limited, with assets of $20 million, remained intact, as did the seven onshore Canadian funds with assets of $260 million, but these seven funds would soon declare their independence and cancel their management contracts with Transglobal;

(2) about $2 million worth of attached real estate in Geneva, including Bella Vista and 1 avenue de la Paix, an unfinished office complex, which Cornfeld had intended as the new IOS world headquarters;

(3) the $2.5 million hole in the ground at Ferney-Voltaire— excavations for the foundations of a planned eleven-story IOS administrative complex—plus 16.8 acres of land and a sprawling set of

faded blue prefabricated buildings that were scheduled to be torn down in 1974.

Vesco, now an erstwhile consultant to shrunken IOS, and Meissner, its president, for months had been puzzling over how to dispose of the near-empty shell. They didn't want to place the company in liquidation for fear of running afoul of the Canada Corporations Act, under whose statutes IOS was incorporated.

In their desperation, Vesco and Meissner had even offered to sell the company back to Cornfeld in the summer of 1972 on a no-cash basis. Cornfeld was seriously interested until he learned of the ventilation of certain fund assets by Vesco and LeBlanc, who by then had begun breezing moneys from the funds through a daisy chain of dummy deals for the purpose of siphoning as much cash as possible into their own banks and trusts in the Bahamas, Costa Rica, and Panama. Although Cornfeld had no idea of the full extent of the looting, he gathered sufficient information to doubt the truthfulness of Vesco's representations that everything was perfectly in order and backed away from the offer. The only other person Vesco could think of interesting in a deal was Alvarez.

After several meetings with Alvarez, Vesco talked the former Cuban Foreign Minister into forming a consortium to buy what remained of IOS with the understanding that it could be used for whatever purposes the new group envisaged. By mid-October 1972 Vesco received word that a Cuban-Spanish consortium was in formation. He flew to Madrid for two days of hurried discussions, then departed for Nassau and back to Newark, leaving Ulrich Strickler behind to follow through with the legwork.

At midweek, Wednesday, October 18, 1972, Vesco made his last appearance before the staff of the SEC. All attempts to get the latest SEC subpoena quashed had come to naught.

"There's no way I'm going to testify [before the SEC]—that will blow the lid on this [$200,000 contribution]," Vesco told attorney Harry Sears a few weeks before.

"Nixon may survive some of those other things, but this would be the crusher," Vesco was quoted as saying. He asked Sears to get hold of John Mitchell and see if anything could be done to have the subpoena withdrawn.

"Mr. Mitchell indicated to me he hoped we would get beyond Election Day" without disclosing the existence of the secret $200,000 contribution, Sears later testified.[1]

[1] United States of America *v.* John N. Mitchell *et al.,* Sears testimony, March 8, 1974.

When Vesco realized that his expensive efforts to buy influence were to no avail he flew into one of his rare rages. "It made him damn mad," said International Controls president Larry Richardson. "He was humiliated beyond words."

Beyond words was just about right. Vesco's deposition, taken by SEC associate general counsel Robert Kushner, was an interesting exercise in invoking constitutional rights, real and imagined, against self-incrimination that began as follows:

Examination

By Mr. Kushner:

Q. Mr. Vesco, what is your business address?

The Witness. For reasons set forth by my counsel this morning, upon the advice and instruction of my counsel, I reluctantly and respectfully decline to answer on the grounds that the rights, protections, privileges and immunities granted to me under the Fourth, Fifth and Sixth Amendments of the Constitution of the United States, including, without limitations, that I have been denied the right of counsel and that I decline to be a witness against myself.

[There followed a brief argument between Kushner and Vesco's two lawyers, Sherwin Markman and Arthur Liman, about representation.]

By Mr. Kushner:

Q. Let us proceed. Mr. Vesco, are you a director of any company?

A. Same privileges.

Q. Are you an officer of any companies?

A. Same privileges.

Q. Do you presently hold any office or directorship or consultant's position with IOS?

A. Same privileges.

Vesco responded to more than thirty questions in a like manner. When it was over he immediately contacted Harry Sears to inform him of his latest sacrifice for President Nixon and the Republican Party. "I hope to hell that will make them happy [at CREEP], because this is just like another contribution," Sears said Vesco had remarked.

Sears noted that Mitchell's reaction was, "Please tell Bob that I'm grateful." [2]

Aside from the humiliation of being forced to take the Fifth Amendment, and also invoking the Fourth and Sixth for good measure— humiliation because he was unable to mobilize with accustomed disdain the monumental influence to which he so often alluded—Vesco realized after refusing to answer the SEC's questions that it was only a matter of weeks at most before the Commission staff would come down with a heavily laden charge sheet against him. In his warped optic of the

---

[2] *Ibid.,* Sears's testimony.

situation, then, one of his last hopes was the unloading of IOS onto a foreign group.

So by Sunday night, October 22, 1972, he was back on board the Big Bird, this time accompanied by his wife Pat, Marti Figueres and his wife, the inevitable Howard Cerny, John D'Alimonte, and a second lawyer from Willkie Farr. They arrived in Madrid the next morning and booked into the palatial Villa Magna Hotel.

During the ten-day interval since Vesco's last visit to Madrid, formation of a high-class group to purchase Kilmorey Investments Limited, IOS's controlling shareholder, had been completed. The group went under the name of Interatlantic Development & Investment Corporation and included some impressive grandees. Interatlantic was headed by Dr. Rafael Diaz-Balart, a noted Cuban exile living in Madrid.

Paradoxically, Diaz-Balart, a brother-in-law of Fidel Castro, had been a highly placed government official under Batista. In Madrid he reputedly managed a large part of the ex-dictator's fortune while serving as managing director of Iberica–La Providence Insurance Company, a medium-size operation that enjoyed a good reputation. Diaz-Balart also managed considerable real estate assets and had been tied in with the Gramco efforts in Spain before Gramco's collapse in 1970. To run IOS he had formed Compania Española de Finanzas y Administracion S.A. (CEFASA), becoming its managing director. Interatlantic planned to give CEFASA a service contract to administer the remains of IOS, once they were shifted to Madrid.

Negotiations were conducted in the strictest secrecy; a veritable security mania had overcome the IOS group. Strategy meetings to decide on negotiating postures were held only on brisk walks through parks, never on the telephone or in closed rooms. Vesco, Meissner, Clay, and LeBlanc, who had joined the negotiations, were experimenting with scramblers, miniature tape recorders, and other paranoiac devices left over from the old IOS security stockpile.

Hovering in the background throughout the weeklong drama was an alert, bright-eyed, and ever-smiling gentleman referred to only as "the Colonel." Later identified as José-Maria Sanchiz, the short and stocky commander of a Madrid tank regiment, he was said to be Franco's closest confidant. Colonel Sanchiz was also one of the founding shareholders and vice-chairman of a manufacturer of ready-to-wear apparel, Confecciones Gibraltar S.A. Nicknamed "the Cheshire Colonel" by IOSers, he followed every phase of the negotiations with the greatest interest and attention.

Immediately upon his arrival at the Villa Magna, Cerny was put to work drafting the closing documents. It took him six hours to come up with a watertight purchase agreement and two consulting agreements. Numerous side-contracts followed, which were part of, but not signed concurrently with, the main agreement.

The purchase price finally settled upon was $5.7 million, which almost corresponded to IOS's net loss during the first half of the year. It was to be paid $1 million in cash and the assumption of a $4.7 million obligation that Kilmorey had outstanding with the defunct Butlers Bank, ceded to Bahamas Commonwealth Bank.

Once everything was set for signing, the existing nine-man board of IOS—which in fact had never formally met—was called upon to resign. It was replaced by Diaz-Balart's new Cuban-Spanish board under the chairmanship of Prince Gonzalo de Borbon y Dampierre, a member of the Spanish royal family. Prince Gonzalo and his brother, Alfonso de Borbon y Dampierre, the Duke of Cadiz and married to General Franco's granddaughter, Maria del Carmen, were grandsons of the last Spanish King, Alfonso XIII, and cousins of Prince Juan Carlos, picked by Franco to ascend the throne after the caudillo's death.

A celebrated member of Madrid's café society, Prince Gonzalo was also chairman of Iberica-La Providence Insurance Company, chairman of the Spanish-Costa Rican Chamber of Commerce, and chairman of CEFASA. Another Spanish nobleman, José-Maria Martinez-Bordiu, Baron de Gotor, was named IOS's vice-chairman. An advisor to General Franco and a noted banker besides, Baron de Gotor was a founding board member of Banco de Madrid and Banco Catalan de Desarallo. His niece was the Duchess of Cadiz.

In this round of Spanish musical chairs, Dr. Alberto Alvarez became IOS's executive vice-president, the presidency being reserved for his compatriot, Diaz-Balart. The IOS technicians who flew in from Ferney-Voltaire to assist in plans for a smooth transition of ownership to the Cuban-Spanish group were not half as impressed with Diaz-Balart as they were with his "statuesque, super-sexy secretary," Petruska, who was described as Prince Gonzalo's girlfriend.

In the midst of the Madrid negotiations, Prince Gonzalo accompanied Vesco to the Presidential Palace for a private audience with Generalissimo Franco. The meeting was agreed to by the Generalissimo's staff because of Vesco's association with the brother of Franco's son-in-law, with members of the royal family, and with Costa Rican President José Figueres, witnessed by the presence of Don Pepe's eldest son, Marti, aboard Vesco's Boeing 707. Vesco's reception by the venerable caudillo was later shown on Spanish TV.

Shortly after his audience with Franco, Vesco paid a "courtesy call" on U.S. Ambassador Horacio Rivero to explain details of the IOS sale and "express his faith" in Spain's favorable investment climate. It was a first-class example of impudent posturing by Vesco, for he was in fact thumbing his nose at the SEC.

Public posturing of this nature was important to Vesco, since he played upon it when presenting the pseudo-motives for his maneuvers to an audience that was "over the heads" of his SEC "persecutors" in a manner designed to distort events and cloud the issues.

Thus, in an unsigned November 1972 memo to F. Donald Nixon, father of Don-Don, which he wanted passed on "to the top," Vesco noted: "The Spanish group that purchased control of IOS consist of the 'financial establishment of Spain,' the Royal family and representatives of certain foreign governments. Their objective, in addition to profit motives, is to make available capital from the IOS mutual funds for investment in Central and South American countries to solidify and establish economic bonds with all Spanish-speaking countries. This transaction and the intended goals was personally discussed by RLV at a recent meeting with the Heads of States of Spain and Costa Rica. . . . (President Figueres had previously written President Nixon indicating concern over SEC harassment of RLV and the possible negative impact on Costa Rica—verbal 'say nothing' response given by lower White House echelon disturbs and hardens view of President Figures.) Entire top level of Spanish government, including Franco, prepared to make 'international incident' if SEC harassment of IOS and their shareholders continues!"

Vesco added in that same memo, "It is in the best interest of the U.S.A. to cause the SEC to drop the entire action . . . since RLV can uniquely assist U.S. objectives in Morocco, Spain, Costa Rica, the Bahamas, Dominican Republic, Haiti, and many South American countries. This capability is available for official use by the U.S. on a clandestine basis. . . .

"RLV influence in developing countries originates from the economic impact of RLV business activities in the respective countries and political parties. Purchases of government bonds, being the largest employer and investor and the primary white supporter of the Pindling Bahamian government has resulted in being called upon for advice on steps to be taken after the 1973 independence (which could include the Bahamian view of U.S. installation if appropriate). The personal relationship with President Figueres of Costa Rica and his reliance on RLV views of economic matters are indisputable. . . . These are only highlights of certain conditions and it should be appreciated that since these countries view RLV as an independent international person and not a representative of the U.S. that intimate real views are necessarily disclosed."

Later Vesco modified his approach, claiming it was *because* of his association with the Nixon family that he was being persecuted. "It's very interesting to note that any person who had a relative degree of success and is in some way related or close to the Nixon family has been subject to some sort of SEC attack," became his new tack. He cited San Diego tycoon C. Arnholt Smith, who was sued by the SEC in 1973 for alleged securities fraud in connection with his troubled conglomerate Westgate-California Corporation, and Howard Hughes, both major contributors to the Nixon re-election campaign.

"No one has put together the entire puzzle, but it's right there. There has been not one major business executive or entrepreneur who has been attacked by the SEC that supported the Democratic Party," he told ABC's Margaret Osmer of TV's "The Reasoner Report" in a blatant fabrication à la Vesco of suitable "fact." [3]

The final closing of the IOS sale to the Spanish-Cuban group was scheduled for Nassau on Friday, October 27, 1972. The Big Bird, with twenty-two passengers aboard, left Madrid on October 26, arriving in the Caribbean that same evening.

Once the signing ceremony was concluded at Charlotte House, Meissner announced the sale from Nassau, claiming the purchase price was $5.7 million in cash—which of course was not the case. But it did sound better than explaining that only $1 million was in cash and the rest was paid with never-never IOUs.

An important consideration for Interatlantic's purchase of IOS to receive high-level Spanish government clearance was the sale to Super Group of Confecciones Gibraltar S.A., the Spanish pants manufacturer in Algeciras, for $3.1 million. This was the sum needed to rescue Confecciones from pending bankruptcy, thereby removing from official concern any hint of financial misdealings in what was intended as a national showcase enterprise.

The Spanish pants factory was founded in the late 1960s with the approbation of Franco's Cabinet in expression of a policy decision to create employment for workers displaced by Madrid's boycott of British-held Gibraltar. Formed by a group of well-intentioned private investors believing they would find favor with Franco, the enterprise received a loan of $5 million from the state-owned Banco de Credito Industrial as seed capital. However, Spanish Pants had a checkered history of poor management and undercapitalization and survived mainly on contracts from the Spanish armed forces.

LeBlanc agreed to have International Bancorp take over Confecciones Gibraltar and inject new working capital into the company, thus saving the original backers from the embarrassment of likely

[3] "The Reasoner Report," produced by ABC News, broadcast of January 19, 1974.

bankruptcy proceedings while keeping the firm's 1,300 workers securely employed. In return Vesco and LeBlanc were reported to have received assurances from "persons close to the government" that Spanish passports would be issued to them.

Two weeks after closing the IOS sale to Interatlantic, LeBlanc returned to Madrid and paid the first $1.3 million installment for the purchase of Spanish Pants. The balance was to follow. Alas, two weeks later the SEC unhelpfully came down with its blockbuster—the 17,000-word complaint detailing for the first time as a matter of public record the broad outline of Vesco's master scheme.

Meanwhile, back in Ferney-Voltaire Consigliere Foglia, the head of the IOS legal department, and IOS treasurer Ed Whitcraft had packed the minute books of IOS Ltd. and Transglobal Financial Services and other sensitive corporate files into five crates and loaded them into the back of a gray IOS Mercedes for the long drive to Madrid.

When they pulled up to the Villa Magna two days later it was apparent that the Spanish interregnum had gotten off to an eventful start. Plans were being prepared to shift the entire Ferney processing machine, client files included, to Madrid as well. Working closely with Waldo Diaz-Balart, brother of Rafael, and the ever-smiling "Cheshire Colonel," Strickler had prepared an immense wall-chart of the proposed Madrid processing facility. It showed an operational staff much too light for the processing needs of 250,000 ongoing client accounts. When it was pointed out that a computer would be needed, the Colonel and Strickler scoured Madrid for one, finally turning up an army surplus model in a barracks outside the city.

As it became evident to Whitcraft and other members of IOS middle management that the Cuban-Spanish group was not "real" in terms of business acumen, it occurred to the Ferney brigade that perhaps considerations other than the mere selling of a destitute company were involved in the secrecy-shrouded transaction. Rumors included the "accidental" loss or destruction of client records during the shipment of corporate documents to Madrid. The resulting chaos, it was reasoned, could only benefit the Super Group generals in Nassau.

This became a cause for concern to some of the operating people whose assistance was requested in implementing an "orderly" transition to new management. "What happens to Ferney?" Whitcraft said he asked Norman LeBlanc in Madrid.

"The best thing would be for it to burn to the ground," the Burble allegedly replied. There was a nervous laugh.

LeBlanc's sense of humor was always very special. What about the transfer of the IOS Investment Program files and other corporate papers? he was asked again.

"They'll drive a dozen trucks up to Ferney, load 'em, and lose two on the way back to Spain," LeBlanc was quoted as saying. Whitcraft was not at all certain that the Burble's mention of losing two trucks was meant light-heartedly.

LeBlanc's seriousness, or lack of it, was never put to a test. The shock of the SEC suit and pressure by the Spanish government, which feared the political consequences of an international financial scandal involving persons close to Franco, caused the cancelation of the sale.

Meissner, relaxing in San José when word of the imminent collapse of the Spanish deal came through, immediately called George Roberts in London and pleaded with the British solicitor and his associate, chartered accountant Jack Douglas Shepard, to go back on the IOS board "to save the company." Roberts and Shepard agreed.

Meissner and Strickler, the two largest IOS shareholders through their interest in Kilmorey, rushed back to Madrid on November 29, 1972, in an attempt to pick up the pieces as gracefully as possible. The Big Bird flew in from San José and Nassau with twelve persons aboard. After an all-night meeting at the Villa Magna it was agreed to unwind the sale and refund the $1 million in cash without recourse to legal proceedings against Super Group for fraudulent misrepresentation.

For once the Colonel wasn't smiling, but tensely pacing the floor in measured step, looking a little like a tank maneuvering for position, Whitcraft thought.

With the Spanish interregnum about to close, IOS lawyer Kenny Klein went over to Diaz-Balart's statuesque secretary, Petruska, and in an attempt at casual repartee asked what the Cuban-Spanish group was going to do without IOS to kick around any more.

"We'll continue with our original plan," Klein said she replied.

"What's that?" he wanted to know.

"The invasion of Cuba."

Whether said in jest or somehow vested with a kernel of truth, that remark characterized perfectly the insane atmosphere that had enveloped the Spanish negotiations, ranging in moods from initial giddy euphoria to near hysteria.

The Super Group representatives left Madrid next morning, after loading the five cases of corporate minute books into the Big Bird, and flew back to Nassau. These records and the other sensitive papers that accompanied them never returned to Ferney-Voltaire.

Later I asked LeBlanc whether he got his Spanish passport as a result of the attempt to save Spanish Pants. He was rather sullen on the subject and would only reply, "Do you really think Spanish passports are for sale?"

Confecciones Gibraltar never did get the remaining $1.8 million promised by Super Group, and in April 1973, unable to pay even its electricity bill, the company closed down, throwing out of work its 1,300 employees. Lack of capital was the official excuse.

As the Spanish deal collapsed about their ears, Meissner and his thralls considered issuing a press release explaining in their words why the sale had to be undone. The release was never issued and existed only in draft form, but after reading it anyone who doubted that Meissner was a silver-tongued cynic would have been convinced. It was a remarkable piece of creative fibbing:

> Dr. Meissner announced today that he had been successful in persuading the "Spanish Group" to rescind the transaction under which they purchased control of IOS from Kilmorey Investments Ltd. As a result, Dr. Meissner has been able to reassume the presidency of IOS and its various subsidiaries and affiliates because by mutual agreement with the "Spanish Group" it was felt that those experienced in the IOS situation could more effectively defend the interests of the hundreds of thousands of small savers, who now constitute the great bulk of money in the IOS dollar funds, against the unjustified charges brought earlier this week by the U.S. Securities and Exchange Commission.
>
> Dr. Meissner also pointed out that something approximating a billion dollars of investors' money was in the other IOS, or former IOS, entities and expressed concern that the irresponsible actions of the SEC in bringing unfounded allegations would cause damage to the owners of these funds as well. . . .

Meissner quickly reconstituted a six-member IOS board consisting of himself, Ulrich Strickler, the blimpish London solicitor George Roberts, his sidekick Jack Shepard, and two non-English-speaking Costa Ricans "acknowledged to be only people of straw."

"King" Klein, who was told to transcribe the reconstituted board in the books of the company, was given the names of Munoz and Rodriguez for the Ticans.

"Any first names?" he asked.

"Luis and Pedro," Meissner replied offhandedly.

"Good," said Klein. "Any particular first name with any surname?"

Klein, obliquely succinct as ever, had driven home his point: IOS no longer had even a semblance of management.

The company and its funds no longer had public auditors.

The funds no longer published quarterly, semiannual, or annual reports to shareholders.

And Meissner was stuck with the bag.

All dollar fund redemptions were soon stopped. The Bank of New

York, in the face of the uncertainties raised by the SEC complaint, suspended its function as custodian of fund certificates for the IOS Investment Program (a separate control function not related to the custodian of cash or securities), with the result that fundholders under the program had their liquidation rights frozen. While Meissner announced the suspension of redemptions, the dribble of client money still sent in under ongoing investment programs naturally was not returned. It was placed in a suspense account at the "Overdraft & Debt Bank" in Luxembourg.

Clients who wrote in for information concerning their investments or who, alternately, wanted to liquidate their programs received the following notice from Ferney-Voltaire:

Dear Client:
In response to your recent enquiry we herewith enclose the text of a letter received from Dr. Milton Meissner, President, Transglobal Financial Services Limited:

"Dear IOS Investment Programholder,
TEMPORARY SUSPENSION OF INVESTMENTS
AND LIQUIDATIONS
We are advised by the boards of directors of the Funds sold exclusively under the IOS Investment Program (IIT, FOF, Venture International, IOS Growth Fund) that they have been compelled as a result of certain legal actions taken by the US Securities and Exchange Commission and the Luxembourg Banking Commission, to suspend temporarily both investments and liquidation transactions.
Other funds (Fonditalia, Regent Growth, Investors Funds, Dreyfus Fund, Lexington Research Fund), which have been offered both under the IOS Investment Program and independently . . . , are affected only as to their shareholders whose investments are currently held through the IOS Investment Program.
We regret the widespread concern, inconvenience and hardship which, without doubt, will result from these governmental actions, which we deem to be ill advised and not in the best interests of the fundholders.
At this time we can only offer our assurance that every effort will be made to obtain relief at the earliest moment for all fundholders affected by this temporary suspension. We shall keep all fundholders advised of developments on a regular basis.
(signed)   Milton Meissner
President"

We therefore must return your letter and other documents.
Yours faithfully,
[s] Peter Wood,
Client Service.

23

How Bernie Got Bagged

In which Bernie Cornfeld gets himself arrested in Geneva, and Milton Meissner suffers a similar fate in Luxembourg as Vesco sets in motion "Operation Monkeywrench"

"If you have a robbery at the local grocery store the authorities are very well set up to handle that kind of situation and they'd probably act quickly, so the chances are very good that the perpetrator of the crime would be apprehended.

"Now you have a phenomenon where several hundred thousand people who have invested hundreds of millions of dollars find that they can't get their money back, and the reason they can't . . . is because a lot of things happened to it that they had every reason to expect couldn't happen to it. Now we're talking about a situation that involves many countries and it's very difficult to put this situation in order and see to it that the people who own this money get it back. To a lot of people this is all the money they have. And this is a constantly depressing kind of cloud that hangs over my head and a feeling of personal frustration exists because there is very little I can do about it. There's very little I can do to help."

So spoke Bernie Cornfeld in April 1973, a few weeks before his arrest in Geneva. The bearded financier quite obviously was not his old flamboyant self. The collapse and rape of IOS lay heavy upon his mind.

We were talking in Cornfeld's tapestried office at Gray Hall, the baronial mansion in the Los Angeles suburb of Beverly Hills that had become his retreat from reality. He was tanned and restlessly relaxed, dressed casually in a sports shirt open to the navel, a pendant around his neck, white slacks, bare-footed, and vacant-faced.

"I don't feel responsible. I feel very sad that it's happened. I always

327

thought that there was a sort of built-in continuity with a large institution, and after all IOS was an institution. We're talking about a company that included half a dozen insurance companies, an equal number of banks, twenty mutual funds and two billion dollars under management.

"I thought that if I had been hit by a beer truck nothing very much would have happened to the ultimate growth and development of the company. As a matter of fact I thought that my own involvement with the company was very dispensable. And I discover that everything that's happened in terms of decline and disintegration has happened because I left and was never replaced with adequate leadership."

Judging by the gaudy trappings and his retinue of friends, Cornfeld had tried his best to transform Gray Hall, which he had purchased from movie actor George Hamilton, into a West Coast Villa Elma. He attempted to capture the same throbbing atmosphere that he knew in Geneva, with lots of eager people surrounding the great mutual fund mogul, awaiting decisions that would make markets jump or jitter. But the sparkle was gone, and in spite of the lavish fittings everything seemed depressingly tawdry.

There were lots of people hanging about, though, many of them very beautiful—movie stars, starlets, languid secretaries, urbane freeloaders in overabundance, even a cast-off *Playboy* writer, several film directors looking for either work or talent, or both, and a new decorator to replace the Velvet Boy.

Bernie was in the film business now. He had financed a part of *The Ten Last Days of Hitler* and a Richard Burton film on Tito, and he was planning another on the life of Karl Marx. His three-story copy of a Norman manor house—with gray stone exterior and huge King Arthur ballroom, suits of armor, tattered standards of silk, jousting arms, a medieval fireplace laid with phony logs in front of a wispy gas flame that was never extinguished, a portrait of some implausible ancestor over the high mantelpiece—was pure Hollywood.

It had been built in the infant days of the West Coast motion picture industry, before World War I, for Douglas Fairbanks, Sr. Not far from Hugh Hefner's new Tudor mansion, it rivaled the Western Playboy palace for sheer opulence and number of bedrooms, many done up with mirrored ceilings and acres of traditional Cornfeld velvet.

In the parking lot at the front of the house, set upon a rise overlooking fashionable Carolyn Way, there were fully two dozen vehicles when I arrived. It was always open house at the Cornfeld mansion. Guests—some invited, some not—drifted in and out at any hour of the night or day. Twenty-six for dinner was not uncommon. After dinner most of the seekers trooped downstairs with Bernie for the screening of the evening's movie in his private projection room. Talk of angel dust and the sweet aroma of pot occasionally floated through the air.

Earlier in the afternoon we had rambled through the house together, walking from his office with the high-beamed ceiling through the empty ballroom and down the hallway to the billiard room, across from the oak-paneled dining room.

"A lot of people have said that you were a visionary, that you were a super-salesman, a great motivator of people, but a very poor administrator. Would you agree with that?" I asked him, once seated in two old-fashioned barber chairs in front of the billiard room's saloon bar. There were bulbous draft beer pumps behind the counter and *art nouveau* advertisements for bustles, high-laced boots, and the like on the wall.

"Well, I don't think that I was a terribly bad administrator," he answered slowly. "We had a huge company that was, up until one day in April of 1970, one of the corporate success phenomena of our century. . . .

"I think one of the things that contributed most to its success was, paradoxically, its greatest weakness, and that was the fact that in a large measure IOS was owned by the people who were building it, and where they had been able to weather crises before they were multi-millionaires, once they became millionaires and had something to lose they could no longer handle a crisis and they panicked.

"This was the problem. And they looked outside the company for help, when anything they conceivably needed was at hand inside the company. We had personnel. We had resources. We had talent. We had money. As a matter of fact, we probably had more money at the time of the crisis than we ever had before in our history."

Whoosh-vroom!

The noise of the billiard room was distracting, and it had nothing to do with the championship billiard table standing in the center of the room under double green-shaded lamps. Whoosh-vroom! It was all very camp. Around the walls were various coin-operated games. The woosh-vroom machine, I soon discovered, was the one with a three-dimensional screen that simulated the cockpit of a jet fighter-bomber on a strike mission over Vietnam. The noise was infernal, so we walked through the French doors out onto the flagstone terrace, where we sat and chatted a while longer around the palm-shaded swimming pool.

"If you could point your finger at any one mistake, what would it be?" I finally asked after listening to him describe "the kind of panic that gripped the company when the price of the stock started going down."

Cornfeld had always maintained that the reaction of his directors in 1970 had been out of porportion to the realities of the situation, and he no doubt was justified in this view.

"I suppose it might have made more sense had I been involved more in the everyday activities of the company rather than in special projects. I thought the role of the chairman was to see that responsibility was well delegated. I thought it was well delegated. There were aspects of the operation that I was totally uninvolved with, and some of these areas were key problem areas. But none of the problems were insurmountable other than the problem of pulling together within the company to face any crisis that we had rather than looking to the outside—and what came in from the outside was immeasurably worse than anything that possibly could have existed within the company."

This was the closest Cornfeld would come to admitting that under his permissive management some very glaring errors had been committed at IOS, that he had been irresponsible in neglecting to repair them when they became known to him, and that, humanly enough, he had made the mistake when at the top of the beanhill of believing in his own infallibility.

Yet he was living in a shipwrecked world. Gray Hall was his desert island where an offshore cruise of fifteen years had come to a sorry end. He even kept as a companion a furry, sad-faced, two-foot-high monkey by the name of Sam who squatted to leave his calling card upon every piece of poolside furniture that was within reach of his lengthy tether.

There were also three parrots roaming about. Albert, the stroller, said "Hi!" with a high-pitched screech every time he walked into a room, startling anyone who was not used to his sudden ankle-high appearances. Saul, his rather shady companion, delighted in ordering people to "Fuck off!"—the full extent of his vocabulary. A third bird was mute, and there had been a fourth, Victoria, but she apparently got fed up one night and walked out.

There was considerable activity around Gray Hall during Easter week of 1973. No fewer than three secretaries were preparing the itinerary for Cornfeld's planned around-the-world voyage that was scheduled to begin in a few weeks. The last plane in his small airborne armada—the ancient Convair 240—was being refurbished in Israel on a scale much less extravagant than Vesco's big Boeing 707. Cornfeld was scheduled to take delivery of his twenty-two-seat Convair in late May and fly through Turkey, Iran, Pakistan, India, and Bangladesh, then on to the Far East.

He had sold his $1.2 million Falcon Jet for $700,000 in 1971. His four-year-old Jet Commander was sold for $215,000 in 1972. The BAC

1-11, which was scheduled for delivery in mid-1970 and for which he had made a $600,000 down payment plus $100,000 more for pilot training, was still the subject of a $3.5 million lawsuit brought against him by British Aircraft Corporation.

Three weeks later I saw Cornfeld again while he stopped over at Château de Pelly, his thirteenth-century castle in Haute Savoie, France, about a forty-five-minute drive southwest of Geneva. He had come from London, where he had appeared in court on an attempted rape charge and was fined $1,000. By Cornfeldian standards he was traveling light, with an entourage of one secretary, two groupies—Leslie, an intense Californian in her early twenties who had seen it all and was tired from several years of traveling in the Elvis Presley camp, and Monika, a lissome former court stenographer from Munich—two airline hostesses, his Hollywood decorator Jim Webber, and a basset puppy. The plan was to rest a few days around the swimming pool of the turreted castle before moving on to the Cannes Film Festival, the next scheduled stop.

From Pelly Cornfeld tried unsuccessfully to reach Milton Meissner to find out why IOS was not honoring the agreement reached earlier in the year to settle the claims of some 250 Swiss ex-employees who had bought IOS common stock at the underwriting on a company-assisted purchase plan.

In January 1973 the first batch of former employees were reimbursed $84,000 for their shares under a settlement worked out by Cornfeld's Swiss attorneys. This was money Cornfeld personally put up—and it had been agreed that the company's lawyers would follow through by settling the remainder of the ex-employees' claims. However, IOS continued to renege on its commitments under the indemnification agreement signed in January 1971 at the time of the Linkink transaction.

The suit causing Cornfeld so much concern was a joint criminal action brought in Geneva the year before—originally by sixty-eight former employees but soon joined by two hundred more when the chances of a settlement seemed good—alleging that they had been enticed into speculating beyond their means in the IOS stock, that the company was fraudulently mismanaged, and that the thirty directors and officers named in the underwriting prospectus knew or should have known at the time of the public offering that the company was in dire financial straits.

Named in the suit along with the original triumvirate were some illustrious co-defendants—James Roosevelt, Sir Eric Wyndham White, Erich Mende, and Wilson Wyatt, to cite a few. But a good number of the Old Guard lineup figured in the list as well.

In the months that followed, Cornfeld's attorneys paid out almost $250,000 to the Swiss plaintiffs, four-fifths of it from Cornfeld personally and the remainder from a small number of other defendants —notably Landau and Cantor. Now Cornfeld wanted IOS to reimburse him.

Cornfeld also had run up bills of $65,000 defending himself in the multimillion-dollar gold trading suit that the U.S. government brought against him and IOS in 1971. He was embarrassed, he said, because a $5,000 bill from former U.S. Supreme Court Justice Arthur Goldberg had been left unpaid by IOS for more than a year. Justice Goldberg had indicated his willingness to undertake the case as lead counsel for both IOS and Cornfeld. "He prepared a ten or twelve page informational brief on the case. . . . A meeting between Mr. Vesco and Justice Goldberg was set up [but] postponed and no further efforts were made to involve Justice Goldberg. . . . Although everyone who has been questioned about this has indicated that payment would be made to date . . . the bill is still outstanding," Cornfeld complained in a letter to Meissner.

Meissner, when he could be reached, assured Cornfeld that instructions had been given to transfer the money to his attorneys and advised him to check with Ed Whitcraft.

The young master of the IOS treasury, when he could be reached, claimed that he was still awaiting final confirmation from Meissner or that maybe the Misanthrope, as Meissner was then called by members of his staff, supposedly either in London or Nassau at the time, at any rate wherever Whitcraft was not, had misrouted or misplaced the disbursement directive. It was the eternal merry-go-round.

Meanwhile Meissner, that same month of May, with IOS only weeks away from forced liquidation—and according to a later treasurer's report already insolvent—had instructed Whitcraft to authorize a 10 per cent increase in compensation for himself and IOS's two British directors, Roberts and Shepard, and this retroactively from February 1973. Thus Meissner's fees and expenses were bumped from $126,000 to $138,600 annually.

"Look, if IOS doesn't pay up I'll have writs issued against Meissner and Vesco—I'll have them arrested, do you hear?" Cornfeld was screaming into the vintage-model French telephone to William Metz, Meissner's attorney in New York, as I entered Pelly's first-floor kitchen that second Friday in May.

He was tired of being given the runaround, he said. Enough was enough, he would start proceedings on Monday if he hadn't heard from Meissner by then. He was undoubtedly feeling heady now that he was so close to the seat of his old empire. That trans-Atlantic call, however, set off a chain of events that would lead to his arrest in Geneva three days later.

The angry Cornfeld's next call was to Raymond Nicolet, his Swiss lawyer, to request that Nicolet and Maître Bruno Keppeler meet with him at the castle the following afternoon for the purpose of instigating by whatever means available a criminal fraud complaint against Vesco and Meissner. Keppeler had been ex-IOS sales manager David Tucker's lawyer and so had the distinction of provoking the arrest of Vesco and Meissner once before. Cornfeld was hoping for a repeat performance.

Metz, in New York, while attempting to calm Cornfeld had suggested that IOS's rump president was expected back in Geneva on the weekend. But in Geneva it was said that Meissner had gone to Luxembourg, where he was reportedly discussing a dusted-off variation of the old LPI scheme with the Luxembourg Banking Commissioner. This version of LPI—dubbed the "Meissner Plan"—envisaged amalgamating the funds into a new open-ended investment company under the control of the West German Banking Commission (since 62 per cent of IOS's remaining clients were German) with the assets to be managed under a three-year contract by a major Luxembourg bank.

Cornfeld's Geneva attorneys arrived at Château de Pelly in Keppeler's Porsche the next afternoon. Rather than confer quietly at the castle, the unorthodox Cornfeld insisted that they drive with him down to Lyon, two and a half hours away, where one of his three-year-old thoroughbreds, Harvest Moon, was running in the sixth race of the day. Their conference, Cornfeld suggested, could be held on the way. The only problem was that Cornfeld had none of his big cars at the castle, and so it was decided that the journey would be made in my seven-year-old Volvo, which became Cornfeld's conference room for the afternoon.

The Volvo was cramped—Cornfeld brought Leslie, his California groupie, along—the afternoon was hot for mid-May, and the roads were bumpy and crowded with weekend drivers. The purse for the Prix Louis Saulnier was 15,000 French francs (roughly $4,000), which Keppeler said represented a day-and-a-half's legal fees. By the time we found the Lyon-Parilly Hippodrome, the race was long over. Cornfeld and his lawyers had missed nothing, however, since Harvest Moon came in dead last in a field of eleven.

Over an early dinner at the Lyon airport while waiting for Keppeler's private plane to fly in and take him and Nicolet back to Geneva, plans were discussed (1) to proceed with the settlement of the ex-employees' suit and (2) to redirect the second outstanding piece of litigation, a Swiss fund-holders' suit—also criminal in nature and highly explosive—

against Vesco and Meissner by coming to an arrangement with the opposing counsel, Maître Claude Gautier. The alternative was to find a willing shareholder to initiate separate fraud proceedings against Vesco and his control group. However, both plans were scuttled by later developments.

Before departing that evening, Nicolet once again warned Cornfeld not to come into Switzerland as long as the claims against him remained unsettled.

On Sunday the elusive Dr. Meissner finally was located in Geneva. Reached by telephone, he agreed to be driven out to Château de Pelly that afternoon by Cornfeld's chauffeur, Biaggio, to discuss the indemnification question and the belated implementation of final settlement of the Swiss ex-employee's action. He arrived about 5 P.M. with Corine Luthi, his Swiss secretary, whom he intended to marry, and announced that he could stay only for a brief time as he had another appointment in Geneva that evening. But he delicately and charmingly suggested that Cornfeld could accompany him back in the car if more time were needed to complete their business.

The Pelly reunion went well, but several points predictably remained to be ironed out. Hesitantly Cornfeld agreed to ride back with Meissner to Geneva in order to complete their discussions on the way. The station wagon stopped at Swiss customs on the way back to town and was passed through without problems. Cornfeld was encouraged.

As the clincher to make Cornfeld stay in Geneva overnight, before stepping out of the car Meissner suggested he could have an $80,000 check ready in the morning in part reimbursement of Bernie's legal expenses and that one more session together could settle the rest. Cornfeld said all right. A meeting was fixed for 11 A.M. Monday, and then he had Biaggio drive him to Villa Elma.

Delighted to be back at his Geneva residence, he telephoned out to the castle and told his entourage to follow him in, as the nearness of a complete settlement of his problems with Meissner called for a celebration.

Cornfeld, dressed in one of his mod costumes of old, was seen that night dining and dancing at his favorite haunt, the Griffin's Club. In fact he left the dining table long enough to call his lead Swiss attorney Pierre Sciclounoff to invite him to join the party. Sciclounoff, a society lawyer and host to Edward M. Kennedy whenever the U.S. senator came to town, declined, pleading a previous engagement.

The Monday morning meeting with Meissner was at La Reserve, a modern luxury hotel along the route de Lausanne almost opposite Bella Vista. Cornfeld arrived fifteen minutes late and waited more than an hour for the Misanthrope to show up. As soon as Meissner arrived they took a table on the terrace and ordered lunch. The meeting lasted almost three hours. At the end Cornfeld believed he had Meissner's complete accord on everything—reimbursement of all outstanding legal expenses and a prompt settlement by the IOS lawyers of the Swiss ex-employee's suit. But Meissner still had not produced the $80,000 check.

This time Cornfeld insisted that Whitcraft be summoned into Geneva from Ferney with the $80,000 check. Whitcraft was unavailable until later that afternoon, so a final meeting was scheduled for 5 P.M. at La Reserve. The $100 lunch bill was paid by Meissner, and Cornfeld left the hotel with a deep feeling of satisfaction. Meissner had given in to every one of his demands.

In the meantime the police had been tipped off that Cornfeld was back in Geneva. While he was meeting with Meissner, a pair of "repairmen" in coveralls had attempted to gain entry into Villa Elma "to inspect the heating system," but, as nobody had ordered a repairman for the heating, they were turned away. Cornfeld drove back from La Reserve to Villa Elma, less than a mile away, uneventfully and waited the ninety minutes until his next meeting with Meissner and Whitcraft. Through the shuttered windows of his study he had not noticed the two men lurking in front of the electronically operated twelve-foot-high iron gates that guarded the entrance of his lakeside property.

At the appointed time he got back into his car and drove out through the gates, oblivious of the surprise that was waiting for him. Before swinging onto the main road he was stopped by two detectives, who stepped out from the shadows and placed him under arrest.

He was held in Saint Antoine Prison overnight and brought the next morning before Examining Magistrate Pierre-Christian Weber, who for months had been buried in the voluminous IOS dossiers without making great headway. With no background in finance or accounting, the ambitious young Weber faced a towering assignment—one that had taken an expert team of SEC investigators almost two years to unpuzzle. And Weber was all alone. He had no budget to hire special advisers, and besides he spoke no English, which meant that the key documents—and there was literally a ton of them—had to be translated into French just for starters.

Weber charged Cornfeld with criminal fraud, criminal misrepresentation, qualified mismanagement, and inciting speculation. He was held in custody until his appearance in arraignment court at midweek.

Under Swiss law, if found guilty on any one of the first three charges Cornfeld risked a maximum prison sentence of fifteen years, which was more than if he had actually murdered one of his IOS clients and could claim extenuating circumstances. In Switzerland, tampering with balance sheets or dishonoring the country's reputation as an international banking center was judged more serious under certain conditions than committing a murder.

Meissner meanwhile canceled plans for a dinner party that evening in Geneva and was driven across the border into France. Two days later he was relaxing on the Via Veneto in Rome. Consigliere Foglia, Vesco's eyes and ears in Europe, had delayed his departure from Ferney by a few days when he learned Cornfeld was in the vicinity. But now Foglia also left town precipitously, flying to Nassau, where Vesco was waiting for him.

Vesco had credited Cornfeld with stirring up many of the problems Super Group faced with the SEC and other authorities. Up to a point he was right. After Cornfeld's ouster from IOS in January 1971 he had been in sporadic contact with the SEC and, since the collapse of the dissidents, represented Vesco's only real nongovernmental opposition. With the bearded IOS founder out of circulation Vesco had one less enemy to contend with.

Encouraged by Cornfeld's arrest, Judge Weber issued additional warrants for Vesco, Meissner, Strickler, Buhl, Cowett, and Roosevelt. Sixteen more warrants were prepared, but for reasons known only to Weber they remained in his desk drawer and never were given international distribution.

When Cornfeld appeared in arraignment court two days after his arrest he was attired in his idea of sober business dress: a plum-colored velvet suit, mauve shirt, and floppy pink necktie. He pretended to stagger as he was led into the crowded courtroom, smiled at the people in the public benches, many of them former IOS secretaries curious to see how humbled the once-dazzling master of offshore finance might appear in the prisoner's dock, then turned to face the one woman he had not expected to see: a small, intense lawyer with swept-back hair and pursed mouth. She was the state prosecutor, Mlle. Martine Berthet, by no means unattractive but altogether too hatchet-faced, sharp-voiced, and tweed-suited for Cornfeld's tastes.

After the lawyers had addressed the court, Cornfeld was allowed to say a few words in his own defense. He spoke in halting French, explaining how he had risen from social worker to international financier. At one point he slipped into a subtle sales pitch for mutual funds. The arraignment judge and two assessors listened in waxen-faced disbelief, and once he had finished they asked him but two questions.

What had been his salary when chairman of IOS?

One hundred fifty thousand dollars a year, Cornfeld replied.

How much had he made at the underwriting?

Seven million eight hundred thousand dollars, Cornfeld answered.

After which the court announced that the charges against him were retained.

"Take him away," the judge ordered the two gendarmes who were guarding him in the dock. They looked like militarized clergymen in their dark gray uniforms with heavy holstered revolvers at their sides as they guided him up the steps into the long passageway back to the dull green prison building behind the courthouse.

"It's a real bummer," said Monika afterward. A slender Bavarian beauty, she was emotionally tied up in knots. Bernie's eighty-seven-year-old mother, recovering from a mild stroke in California, flew to Geneva and was the only person, other than his lawyers, permitted to visit him. Monika and Leslie, the two faithful groupies, moved into Villa Elma with Mrs. Cornfeld for the long wait. Gray Hall was closed, and the staff was paid off. And Bernie made a gift of his Convair to the Israeli government during the October 1973 Yom Kippur War.

From prison Cornfeld wrote the first of two letters to Thomson von Stein at the SEC, pleading for help, and another to Bud Meissner, reminding the good doctor of his verbal undertaking to have IOS indemnify Cornfeld against his more than $500,000 in legal expenses.

"Can you please write Judge Weber and simply tell him I am not a defendant in the SEC action?" Bernie requested in his letter to von Stein. In response the SEC sent a copy of its complaint against Vesco and his associates, which of course excluded Cornfeld, to the Geneva magistrate. But the SEC's matter-of-fact response didn't have the same effect as John Mitchell's call to the U.S. Embassy in Berne after Vesco was arrested by the Swiss in 1971.

Meissner never responded to Cornfeld's letter and, of course, IOS never paid Cornfeld's lawyers. By then Meissner was concentrating on his reorganization of IOS in a manner he hoped would be acceptable to the European regulatory authorities.

In late June 1973 Albert Dondelinger, the Luxembourg Banking Commissioner, invited the heads of the Ontario and Quebec securities commissions and the director of enforcement of the Securities and Exchange Commission to join him in a conference in Luxembourg to decide the fate of the four IOS dollar funds, which were estimated by management to have assets of $358.3 million. Meissner requested immunity from arrest to attend that meeting and explain his salvage plan for IOS. Dondelinger replied that he could offer no guarantees but assured Meissner's local attorney that the Banking Commission was not seeking the IOS president's arrest. Against the advice of his Luxembourg counsel, Meissner decided to come anyway in the company of George Roberts, Jack Shepard, and New York attorneys Bill Metz and

Justin Feldman, the latter having represented IOS in the New York trial on the SEC charges.

In addition to amalgamating the funds into a new open-ended investment company, Meissner's plan also called for the repayment under court supervision of the IOS client moneys siphoned from the funds. However, such an action, even when stretched over three years as proposed in the repayment schedule presented by Meissner, implied that a $24 million hole existed in the books of Bahamas Commonwealth Bank and that this money could not be accounted for.

Now Meissner devised an ingenious scheme for getting around this embarrassing detail. In fact the hole was probably much larger, except that one stage of his plan called for the purchase by Transglobal Financial Services of LeBlanc's interest in Global Holdings Limited, including a $20 million "investment" in Global Holdings and its operating subsidiary by Venture Fund International. Before Venture International purchased Global Holdings, however, LeBlanc was to have acquired from International Bancorp Limited, a Global Holdings subsidiary, the shares of Bahamas Commonwealth Bank.

Once this was accomplished, Meissner proposed that Property Resources Limited purchase Bahamas Commonwealth Bank from LeBlanc so that PRL's cash would then be available to cover the $24 million hole at Bahamas Commonwealth Bank. Had the Meissner Plan worked it would have succeeded in turning Super Group upside down by placing PRL at the top of the pyramid and relegating Global to the bottom line.

The purchase of Bahamas Commonwealth Bank by PRL, Meissner explained to IOS director Roberts, "puts all the assets of over $100 million of a Bahamian company behind its 100 per cent owned Bahamian bank and virtually guarantees the Bahamas Commonwealth Bank certificates of deposit."

Fortunately for the IOS clients, on the morning the Luxembourg conference opened Meissner was arrested in the dining room of his hotel while having breakfast. He was charged by the Attorney General's Office of the Grand Duchy with fraud in connection with the management of IIT, a Luxembourg-registered fund, and he was held for nine months without bail.

The governmental group that attended the Luxembourg conference decided to judicially liquidate the IOS funds rather than try and revive them under new management, and it was agreed to form an interagency committee to implement their decision. IOS, always proud of being a pioneer in its field, thus had unwillingly pioneered the drawing together of regulatory agencies from three countries for the purpose of cutting across issues of national sovereignty in cleaning up what possibly could qualify as the largest financial fraud since John Law, the eighteenth-century Scottish financier who had bankrupted the royal bank of France with his Mississippi scheme.

The Luxembourg summit was regarded as perhaps the first important step toward the creation of an international securities commission—a vital necessity in the era of jet-age communications, increasing internationalization of financial markets, and the growing occurrence of white-collar crime. But no one was under any illusions. The multitude of transnational legal tangles involved made the commissioners' liquidation quest one "the like of which the world has never seen."

Within hours of Meissner's arrest Vesco ordered "Operation Monkeywrench" unleashed. The thrust of this plan was to do everything possible to screw up the works while seeming to cooperate with the authorities in a speedy judicial liquidation of IOS and the four dollar funds. Complete anarchy in corporate records became the goal of the day.

At midnight on July 1, 1973, IOS treasurer Whitcraft received a phone call from Bill Metz in Luxembourg warning him that "the boys in Nassau" might be planning to destroy the IOS computer tapes and records that contained all the essential information concerning ownership, amounts invested, beneficiary, insurance, and other investment statistics of each of the 250,000 remaining client accounts.

Whitcraft immediately called Bob Wood, in charge of custodial bookkeeping, and informed him of the threat against the client records. He asked Wood to secure a duplicate set of tapes, thereby ensuring that if the master set and hard-copy client confirmation slips were destroyed a full record of accounts would nevertheless exist.

Wood picked up a set of duplicate tapes in the morning and placed them in a safety deposit box at Banque de Depôts in Geneva for safe-keeping. The safety deposit box number was not difficult to remember: It was No. 13.

Whitcraft received two more warning calls the next day—the first from IOS's New York attorney Justin Feldman, who said he was "concerned with the various interests that seem to be operating," and the second from English director George Roberts inquiring if the tapes had been properly secured.

The skeleton staff at Ferney—about sixty-two back-office people, all relatively young but crisis-tested—were nonetheless dedicated to the task of keeping the IOS processing machine alive so that one day the bilked clients could get at least some of their money back. The Ferney survivors feared the strong "burn, baby, burn" undercurrent from Nassau and believed it was their mission to protect the custodial bookkeeping system from destruction.

A rebellion of sorts already had broken out against the unloved Super Group bosses in Nassau, and Whitcraft, since learning the summer before of the existence of the Incap advisory contracts with the dollar funds, had held back paying some $3 million allegedly due to one or other of the Super Group entities for such things as a $10,000 lease on nonexistent office space in Charlotte House, Nassau, for IOS Insurance Holdings Limited, which by then had no function and was an abandoned shell, and lawyers fees of more than $1 million for Vesco, LeBlanc, Straub, Clay, and Strickler, as well as fees due under various spurious advisory and service agreements. These unpaid bills were the subject of frequent threatening letters from Nassau, such as one received by Whitcraft in late May 1973 from Nasty Norman the Burble in his capacity as president of Global Holdings Limited:

May 25, 1973

Mr. Ed Whitcraft,
Investors Overseas Services
Ferney-Voltaire,
France
Dear Ed:

As you are aware, Investors Overseas Services has outstanding payments to Bahamas Commonwealth Bank, Value Capital Limited, Property Resources Limited, Global Holdings Limited, and INCAP.

You are hereby given thirty (30) days' notice to make payments, after which time, legal action will be initiated against Investors Overseas Services.

Very truly yours,
GLOBAL HOLDINGS LIMITED
[s] Norman P. LeBlanc
President

The threatened legal action did not ensue, nor were the debts extinguished.

It had occurred to Whitcraft in the early spring that Super Group's intentions were heading to new and darker depths after LeBlanc, slightly in his cups following his third lunchtime double martini at El Toro Restaurant on Nassau's Bay Street, offered him $1 million over five years to move down to the Bahamas and administer what remained of the IOS complex from Nassau. Although left unsaid this implied losing most of the corporate and client records in the course of the transfer, Whitcraft later decided.

Troubled by this offer, on his way back to Ferney he stopped off in New York to discuss the matter with his father, an experienced Wall Street broker.

"If they're so stupid as to offer *you* $1 million, what makes you think they're not smart enough to shoot you?" was his father's response.

Whitcraft thanked him for his soothing words.

The next person to show up in Ferney, five days after Meissner's arrest, was Bob Foglia, Vesco's consigliere, head shaking and eyes flashing when he learned that the tapes had been locked up and Whitcraft wouldn't tell him where.

"It's just like the Spanish deal again, isn't it, Bob?" Whitcraft had told Foglia. "Load the stuff into twelve trucks and then lose two of them on the way out."

Foglia was not pleased by this attitude. He and Whitcraft drove that night to Paris, with the consigliere exerting all his charm to lure the last operations overlord of Ferney down to Nassau for "a closing of the ranks" strategy session. But Whitcraft already had made up his mind. Ferney had to be turned over to a government authority to preserve the records. He flew from Paris to New York and, after telling this to the IOS lawyers there, spoke with the SEC and announced that he wanted to hand over the IOS processing machine to a suitable Canadian authority. This was accomplished in late July 1973, formalized by order of the Public Trustee of Ontario, and Whitcraft returned to Ferney to await the arrival of the Canadian liquidators.

Meanwhile, Judge Weber had decided that two of the people he most wanted to question were Whitcraft and Foglia. In fact, Weber was so keen that one day in early August 1973 he drove across the border and, accompanied by a French magistrate and two vans of French gendarmes, raided the IOS "funny farm" in Ferney.

Foglia was nowhere to be found—afraid of arrest, he had not returned to the Geneva-Ferney area after his July 4 attempt to coax Whitcraft into going along with Operation Monkeywrench—but Judge Weber did find Whitcraft. At the behest of the Canadian liquidators, IOS's thirty-two-year-old chief financial officer had just prepared a treasurer's report for an emergency board meeting of IOS Ltd. in Charlotte House, Nassau, that week. The report revealed that IOS Ltd., without any cash flow of its own, had been forced to borrow $200,000 from its subsidiary, Transglobal Financial Services, during July 1973, and that in spite of projected borrowings of a further $300,000 in August 1973 a nil cash position was anticipated at the end of the month.

Whitcraft's draft balance sheet showed IOS to be insolvent in the amount of $7.8 million at December 31, 1972, and the estimated deficit as of June 30, 1973, was in excess of $9 million.

"I submit to the Board that the company is insolvent and unable to meet its ongoing liabilities, and should, therefore, commence bankruptcy proceedings," he informed the directors in a covering letter.

Weber was fascinated by this and invited Whitcraft to visit him at his office in Geneva the following afternoon. But Whitcraft, mindful of how similar invitations had ended for others involved in the IOS saga, left Ferney that same night for Frankfurt where he boarded a flight to New York.

The only Swiss on Judge Weber's wanted list was IOS director Ulrich Strickler, but Mr. Will-Be-Done maintained only telex contact with Ferney from his Bancorp base in Costa Rica, occasionally traveling as far as Nassau for IOS board meetings. In fact, at the meeting in early August, acting out the role assigned to him under Operation Monkeywrench, Strickler suddenly switched his stance from one of seemingly wanting to assist in putting IOS to bed to a new position of adamantly opposing any "hasty" or "ill-conceived" winding-up petition. He further demanded that $60,000 in outstanding honorariums be paid forthwith to IOS's Costa Rican directors. The Tican strawmen were brought into the boardroom at the conclusion of each session and, incapable of understanding English, had the proceedings summarized for them in Spanish by Marti Figueres before being asked to sign the minutes. Needless to say, this particular $60,000 never filtered into the pockets of the silent Ticans.

During his raid on Ferney Judge Weber had seized stacks of company records and transferred them across the border to his office at the Palais de Justice. He also collected the keys to safety deposit box No. 13, placed magistrate's seals on the client microfilm files, and sequestered the entire IOS computer tape library, although he lacked the programs to read the tapes.

As Weber's investigation of the IOS collapse moved at a snail's pace into a tunnel of darkness, the world soon forgot about Cornfeld languishing in Saint Antoine Prison. For the originator of People's Capitalism, who once had controlled billions of dollars, to be arrested because he came into Geneva to fetch an $80,000 check was the crowning ignominy of his career.

However, in two-and-a-half page letter to his friends that was smuggled out of Saint Antoine prison Cornfeld gave no indication that his spirits were flagging.

> I've experienced a great deal in life. I've known poverty and great wealth, fame, public acclaim, public attack, tremendous success and equally tremendous failure. I've had more luxury and more of what many consider the "good life" than most people experience in their cheeriest of fantasies. I've never experienced prison—at least never from the inside. . . .
>
> Again, prison is not nearly as bad as I expected. The food is good, hardly a star in the "Guide Michelin," but then St. Antoine Prison wasn't really set up to attract tourists. Prisoners are well treated. I have a radio and reading material. I read and write and enjoy freedom of mind and spirit. I'm comforted by my conviction that I have dealt with life and with people honestly and that IOS while I headed it was an honest worthwhile operation in spite of its tragic end. . . .
>
> IOS presently is not just a failure, it's a disaster, and I alone am left

to defend its integrity—the integrity of the people who were associated with it and who devoted the better part of their lives to building IOS, as well as my own integrity. There's a certain joy to my lonely crusade. IOS wasn't just a company, it was a part of the lives of the people who built it, and when IOS as we knew it died, something precious died in all of us. My defense is a kind of commemoration to the hard work, the idealism, the creativity, and the integrity of IOS and the thousands of people who were its soul.

After almost eleven months in custody Cornfeld was finally released on $1.5 million bail—the highest bail ever set in Switzerland and possibly anywhere in the world. A large part of the bail money was put up by his friends, including Seymour "the Head" Lazar, International Credit Bank's Tibor Rosenbaum, former ICB economic adviser Sylvain Ferdmann, movie actors Tony Curtis and George Hamilton, and British movie financier John Heymann.

Cornfeld immediately flew to London, where he entered into negotiations with an Arab prince to sell his Villa Elma property in Geneva and the Château de Pelly in France, and began plotting his revenge against Vesco. But Cornfeld, his once fabulous wealth substantially dissipated, saddled with enough legal expenses as it was, and visibly aged by his confrontation with "La Justice Genevoise," was no longer in top fighting form.

Cornfeld's thoughts were saddened, too, by the news that the number-two man in the IOS triumvirate, Ed Cowett, his forty-fourth birthday only three days past, had died of a heart attack.

Cornfeld's Blue Sky expert, who two months previously had slipped into bankruptcy, was flying back to his home in Miami from testifying before a federal grand jury in Denver when he collapsed. The aircraft made an emergency landing, but Cowett was pronounced dead upon arrival at a Fort Worth, Texas, hospital. An enigma to many of his closest associates, Cowett held the keys to a number of unresolved IOS mysteries.

24

"Nail Vesco"

Vesco, his footwork dazzling, is forced to retreat by U.S. pressure for his extradition — Though he remains cocky and aggressive, the heir-apparent to the throne of the greatest offshore empire sees his world shrink to two small havens

Vesco had made a monkey out of the United States.

> Hon. INZER B. WYATT, Federal
> District Judge, U.S. District
> Court, Southern District of
> New York, August 18, 1973

William Saxbe, while still the Republican senator from Ohio, stated in a speech before the United States Senate that Robert Vesco was one of the best living advertisements for the creation of an international securities commission.

"Vesco [has] flaunted the fact that he is exempt from prosecution because securities laws cannot be enforced internationally. He relied on the fact that there is no multinational procedure to protect investors from highly questionable if not illegal diversion of their money," Saxbe told the Senate in March 1973. He continued:

> This is not the first case of questionable management of mutual funds, nor will it be the last unless steps are taken by the international business circles and the world community of governments. We have experienced the struggle for control of Investors Overseas Services and Vesco's financial shenanigans since early 1971. Now he is using fund assets with complete indiscretion and justifying his actions on the grounds that no country can exercise its securities law if he moves fast enough.
>
> For this reason, I applaud the action taken by the Securities and Exchange Commission against Vesco and the numerous other defendants involved in raising money from small investors and funneling

344

it into projects that will provide maximum personal gain for the fund managers. Vesco's actions are a repugnant breach of his fiduciary [responsibilities]. . . .

I am optimistic that other actions will force return of any misappropriated funds. However, international attention must be given to this problem and I ask that my colleagues give serious consideration to the formation of legislation to expand the operation of the Securities and Exchange Commission by setting up ground rules for an international conference or convention to deal with multinational stock and investment fraud.[1]

Seven months later the Saturday Night Purge burst upon the nation: Nixon fired Watergate Special Prosecutor Archibald Cox and forced the resignations of Attorney General Elliot Richardson and his deputy, William Ruckelshaus. The outspoken fifty-seven-year-old Ohio Republican was nominated to replace Richardson, becoming in January 1974 Nixon's fourth Attorney General. Saxbe's appointment did not augur well for Vesco's future comfort and safety from extradition.

Already three times indicted, in early 1974 Vesco was facing a new criminal investigation by the U.S. Attorney's Office in New York stemming from the SEC's 1972 civil fraud complaint.

Three months before the SEC complaint was launched Vesco sent SEC general counsel Brad Cook a five-page letter protesting against the "Nail Vesco!" attitude of the SEC staff. A copy was sent to Chairman Casey, as Vesco further complained that "the problems in this investigation flow primarily from inadequate supervision [by the five-member Commission] of non-objectivity which has developed among the investigators." As an added piece of cheek, the letter was marked "dictated but not read by" the sender.

A summary of the items read as follows:

(1) issuing "invalid subpoenas" that extended far beyond the scope of the original investigation order
(2) apparent staff leaks to the press
(3) staff interference with U.S. embassies abroad by "attempting to stop embassy assistance to myself and others in resolving certain unrelated problems"
(4) the "secret engagement of Interpol to maintain surveillance of myself and others"
(5) the "indiscriminate use" of U.S. Immigration to harass himself and his traveling companions upon entry into the United States
(6) the "leaking" of information to the U.S. Attorney's Office in New York in an "unrelated case"

[1] *Congressional Record* (S4484), March 13, 1973.

(7) suggestions by the investigators that certain witnesses were "liars" or had committed perjury *"and that the staff was determined to 'nail Vesco'"*

(8) alleged improper subpoenaing of lawyers involved in the case

The foregoing, Vesco claimed, demonstrated "the pattern of staff hostility with which we have had to contend. Others who have been exposed to the staff investigation appear to gain the same impression: that this, rather than being an objective investigation, is one which at this stage appears to be endeavoring to find some result which will justify the time and expense already involved."

The process, he concluded, "is apparently endless [and] the damage being created by the staff is irreparable and extends far beyond the bounderies of the United States."

After President Nixon's re-election, William Casey was transplanted from Chairman of the SEC to the new post of Under Secretary of State for Economic Affairs. A few months later, thirty-five-year-old Brad Cook was named Casey's successor at the SEC.

The appointment of Cook as the SEC's youngest-ever Chairman seemed to herald the beginning of a golden age for the underbudgeted police department of the securities industry. Cook was well-liked by the staff, and as an insider he helped structure many of the policy matters still in the pipeline when Casey departed.

Ironically, it was Cook who had gone along with Sporkin's persistence in pushing ahead with the SEC's investigation of Vesco after pressure had come from the Justice Department and the White House to either "wind down" the probe or delay the issuing of new subpoenas.

As a direct result of John Mitchell's call from the CREEP offices to the SEC, Harry Sears met four times with Chairman Casey, who took the rare action of instructing Cook to oversee the staff investigation of Vesco. Cook's entry had a divided effect. It slowed the filing of a suit on Vesco's takeover of IOS from Cornfeld, but Cook supported broadening the investigation, which resulted in uncovering Vesco's looting scheme.

It was the staff's insistence on following all leads that led to the discovery of Vesco's offshore cash in Stan's office safe, used in part to bankroll the Watergate burglary, a fact that did not speak too well for the thoroughness of the FBI's Watergate investigation.

Sporkin's insistence on tracing the $250,000 transferred from Nassau to a small airfield in eastern New Jersey led Cook to discuss the matter with Maurice Stans, a close friend of the family. Stans was evasive about having received a cash contribution from Vesco but said he would look into it. When Cook later voiced his suspicions about the origins of the cash, Stans suggested that the SEC should limit its investigation to the source of the money and not where it ultimately went. When Cook read Stans the paragraph in the SEC's draft complaint relating to the $250,000, he said Stans remarked, "Oh-oh—that gives me a problem." Stans asked if it could be modified. Cook unfortunately heeded Stans's wish and recommended the removal from the complaint of specific reference to the date or amount of money that had gone from New York to Fairfield.

Cook also conceded he mentioned to Stans that he was considering "making a run for the chairmanship" of the Commission when Casey moved to the State Department, and in due course Stans said he "would put in a good word" for Cook at the White House.

Stans did, and Cook got the job.

Charges that Cook bent to pressure to delete the $250,000 from the SEC's complaint inevitably flowed from his indiscretion in discussing the matter with Stans, even though his general support for the investigation was a major factor in its ultimate success.

In a move that caused a feeling of uneasiness on Wall Street, one week after the May 1973 indictment of Mitchell, Stans, Sears, and Vesco the widening web of Watergate intrigue claimed another victim. Subject to increasing suspicion because of his close relationship with Stans and the fact that he admitted lying five times under oath—three times before the federal grand jury that indicted Mitchell and Stans and twice before congressional committees—concerning his secret discussions of the case with Stans, Bradford Cook resigned as SEC Chairman just ten weeks after being appointed to the job.

In his departing statement to the press, Cook strongly denied that external pressures had altered the SEC's attitude toward Vesco. "The SEC's case against Robert Vesco and forty-one other defendants . . . is one of the most important ever brought by this agency. It was directed at the systematic looting of hundreds of millions of dollars in investor money by Vesco. . . .

"My involvement and views as General Counsel on the building of this case are a matter of record and my view was consistent throughout: that Robert Vesco and the activities of those around him represented a menace and a threat to investor confidence everywhere," he said.

Cook's sudden resignation, for which Vesco took much of the credit, was another high point in a year of legal and political battling that on balance started out well for Vesco. He was successful in clouding the issues of the SEC charges against him—"They have not once suggested that one cent of the $224 million [looted from the funds] went into my pocket," he had the audacity to tell interviewers—and he was making progress in promoting himself as a fair-dealer and honest banker to the smaller developing nations.

He and LeBlanc played games with the Boeing 707 that they both loved so well, flying on exotic excursions to the farthest corners of the Third World, buying foreign ministers along the way. During one of the trips in March 1973 the Big Bird, its interior modified to include a secret compartment capable of concealing highly sensitive or valuable papers and other items of little bulk, left Nassau for Rabat, Agadir, Marrakech, and Casablanca in Morocco, where Vesco, LeBlanc, Straub, Clay, and Graze inspected a number of tourist development projects.

The Moroccan interests, go-between Dick Pistell said, represented "a very substantial deal, pertaining to hotel chains, tourism, et cetera . . . with a group of distinguished Moroccan individuals." The distinguished gentlemen included Ahmed Benhima, the Moroccan Minister of Foreign Affairs, "who is one of my close and personal friends," Pistell said.

Although the Moroccan Embassy in Washington was skeptical that Benhima, as a high-ranking government official, would get involved in any private business venture, he did receive a cash transfer of $70,000 from Super Group in 1973—$20,000 to an account at Overseas Development Bank in Luxembourg, and $50,000 more to his account at Chemical Bank New York Trust for "investment purposes."

Vesco was fairly convinced by this time that by hiding everything he owned or controlled in a revolving succession of Bahamian, Panamanian, and Costa Rican shell companies and by operating through, or in the name of, a long series of untraceable dummy corporations, he had made himself virtually prosecution-proof. But it was shortly after returning from one of his North African jaunts that everything started to fall apart.

There were growing signs of a revolt by the skeleton staff at the IOS complex in Ferney-Voltaire; Vesco was hit by a flying subpoena at Brace Ridge Manor, his residence in Nassau, summoning him to New York to testify before a federal grand jury in the Mitchell-Stans investigation; and he was "nailed" with a summons in a new civil suit in New York charging him with fraud, self-dealing, and breach of fiduciary trust for having wasted between $1 million and $20 million in assets belonging to International Controls Corporation. The "wasting of assets" suit was brought by the court-appointed special counsel of International Controls, David M. Butowsky.

The summer was further spoiled by the issuing of three more arrest warrants against him for contempt of court, attempted fraud, and embezzlement of $50,000, all in all eloquently repegging him as an international fugitive from justice and adding to the roster of both sealed and open criminal charges against him in four countries.

The difficult problem of pinning a summons on Vesco was resolved in the "wasting of assets" action by a "fierce partisan of women's lib" who worked in the New York law firm of Shea, Gould, Climenko & Kramer, associated with special counsel Butowsky on the case.

Lois Sylor Yohonn, a former SEC lawyer, flew down to Nassau in June 1973 to discover just how harrowing an experience it can be to cross Bob Vesco. In an affidavit filed in federal court, Ms. Yohonn said that during her first visit to the Vesco residence, two guards and Tony Vesco, the financier's teenage son, refused to accept the papers and threw them back at her.

Ms. Yohonn returned to her hotel and telephoned Judge Stewart in New York, who authorized her to complete service by depositing the papers on the Vesco premises. She took a taxi back out to the house and threw the papers into the garden, took a picture of them lying there, then got back into the taxi and was about to drive off when two guards suddenly appeared from behind the barred gate, one with a section of pipe and the other with a stick, yanked open the taxi door and ordered her to retrieve the papers.

Ms. Yohonn refused to budge and the taxi driver slowly pulled away. But the guards followed in another car. Becoming seriously concerned that they meant her harm, she had the taxi driver deliver her to the wrong hotel and returned safely to New York the following day.

Rather than appear in court in New York and risk being arrested, Vesco claimed the summons had been improperly served and failed to appear. But to no avail. A default judgment was entered against him.

While this action annoyed Vesco he was not immediately concerned; he long since had transferred ownership of the Boonton Township estate to a series of trusts in his children's names and, apart from his International Controls stock which the IRS had blocked, he had no other property in the United States that could be attached against recovery of the "wasted" assets.

But Vesco overestimated his legal cleverness. When his two favorite playthings, the Boeing 707 and the yacht *Patricia III*, were seized by court order to satisfy in part his allegedly outstanding debt at International Controls, his rage knew no limits.

Patricia III, her ownership disguised through Panamanian registry and a charter that bound her into the service of a dummy Bahamian enterprise, confidently chugged into U.S. territorial waters and was promptly seized by U.S. Customs when she berthed in the Miami River for extensive repairs.

The yacht's certificate of ownership showed a company called Andean Credit S.A., incorporated in Panama City and whose sole stockholder was Tony Morales, the flight capital expert. Morales's ownership notwithstanding, Judge Stewart ordered a lien placed on the yacht for the benefit of International Controls. Although Andean Credit said it had purchased the craft from a British property magnate for $1.5 million, the court decided that it seemed probable that the transaction had been financed by Property Resources Limited with IPI client money.

Using the assumed name Robert Sasek (his mother's maiden name) Vesco first arrived aboard *Patricia III* on June 20, 1973, and was presented to Captain Roland L. Boddy as the owner. Now, Vesco's two oldest sons had developed a passion for power-boat racing in the clear blue waters of the Bahamas and persuaded their father, the new Mr. Sasek, to install derricks aboard the *Patricia III* so they could stow their "cigarette class" racers aboard. The installation cost $40,000, and a check to cover that amount was deposited by "Mrs. Sasek," using her maiden name, Patricia J. Melzer.

Vesco was outraged by the yacht's seizure and attempted through New York counsel for Andean Credit S.A. to obtain an emergency Saturday morning court order in New York to gain the yacht's release.

The federal judge on duty that Saturday at the U.S. Court House in Foley Square, Enzer B. Wyatt, was not amused. When informed by counsel that the yacht had nothing to do with Vesco but was owned by a Panama City corporation, Judge Wyatt was unable to ascertain what sort of business Andean Credit engaged in. "I mean, it buys a yacht. I don't know what its business is. It buys a yacht and immediately leases it to Vesco and names it after Vesco's wife. The suggestion is almost forced upon me that it was done to cloak Vesco's ownership. . . . I'd have to be the sorriest person in the world not to conclude that."

When sputtering counsel attempted to point out that a company called MacKinley Limited was the charterer and not Vesco, and that if the charterer didn't get possession of the yacht that weekend it would cancel the $360,000-a-year lease, Judge Wyatt was even more incredulous.

"Why does MacKinley need the yacht in the Bahamas tomorrow? Is Vesco going on a picnic?" he asked.

But Judge Wyatt was just warming up. "In the first place," he said, "it is highly suspicious that these transactions are originating in the Bahamas. That in itself would lead you to believe there is skullduggery afoot."

Wyatt obviously didn't hold the Bahamas in very high esteem as a business and banking center. "Do you mean for perfectly legitimate purposes people are running around and doing business in the Bahamas? I can't believe it."

He clinched his argument for refusing to dissolve the hold order on the yacht with, "Can you imagine if Andean had no connection with

Vesco that Andean would be running around with a yacht named after the wife of a fugitive from justice?"

The yacht remained berthed in the Miami River, permanently guarded by a U.S. marshal while a purchaser was found.

In the meantime the U.S. Attorney's office in New York had unsealed a third indictment of Vesco charging him with defrauding International Controls of $50,000 allegedly used as a down payment in the 1972 purchase of IOS director C. Henry Buhl's preferred shares. Buhl gave two affidavits on the matter. The first supported the government's allegations and became the basis for an extradition request to the Bahamas for Vesco's return. The second substantially contradicted the first on all major points.

When Vesco learned of this new attempt to bring him back to the United States to stand trial, he treated it with contempt. "To charge me with embezzling $50,000 is on the face of it ridiculous. . . . That's like the man in the street embezzling a penny."

In a scene befitting a musical comedy, in November 1973 Vesco was "arrested" at his offices in Charlotte House by two top-ranking officers of the Royal Bahamas constabulary and escorted around the corner to the old Court House in Parliament Street where he was brought before British-trained Nigerian magistrate Emmanuel Enebeli Osabeday for a five-minute hearing. Bail was fixed at $75,000 and instantly posted by Vesco's lawyers, who had the exact amount of cash on hand. Vesco, described in one of the local newspapers the following day in all seriousness as "the financial godfather of the Bahamas," was released pending the commencement of extradition hearings.

When proceedings began a few days after Vesco's thirty-eighth birthday, the 1931 extradition treaty between Britain and the United States was admitted as extending to the newly independent Commonwealth of the Bahama Islands, against which event Vesco had strengthened his defense team by flying out from London the Rt. Hon. Sir Elwyn Jones, Q.C., former Attorney General of England and Wales.

The best indication that the "Vesco case" had become an affair of state was the presence of the Bahamian Government Information Service at the hearings in an almost protocol capacity, issuing press releases, handling accreditations of out-of-town journalists, and arranging seating in the magistrate's tiny Number One Courtroom on the second floor of the quaint colonial court house.

After several days of arguing between counsel acting for the U.S. government and Judge Osabeday, the case was thrown out of court without Vesco's even being called to the stand.

The official mood in Nassau toward the Vesco camp was one of extreme nervousness. On Bay Street Prime Minister Pindling was said to be irked because a $20 million foreign aid grant was rumored to have been blocked by the U.S. State Department, and the funds were only to be released once Vesco was expelled.

But the alternatives were just as gloomy. Any extradition of Vesco stirred fears of a deepening slump in the local economy. Some Bay Streeters went so far as to forewarn of Super Group retaliation, bringing increased unemployment should Bahamas Commonwealth Bank start calling in loans and closing down businesses that had been "Bahamianized" with 100 per cent financing from Super Group Bankers.

Although not directly referring to the rumored State Department embargo, LeBlanc explained what he thought of such ham-handedness when he boasted, "Our philosophy in a country, which is a philosophy the United States doesn't like . . . is that we represent an economic power. There are small countries where the United States could buy their way in for $10 million in economic aid. Well, we can buy—we have the capacity to go in with $50 million." [2]

But for Vesco the real shock came days before Judge Osabeday handed down his final decision in the extradition case with the surfacing in the American press of the Frank Peroff story.

Peroff was a difficult-to-control Drug Enforcement Agency (DEA) informer with a long history of shady financial dealings. But in his previous undercover work he provided information that led to the arrest of eight narcotics traffickers and the seizure of sizable amounts of heroin and counterfeit money.

Peroff claimed that he was forced into hiding to protect his life after telling White House lawyers of a 100-kilogram deal with a "street value" in excess of $10 million involving Bobby Vesco and Norman LeBlanc. Almost one year previously Peroff had been asked by U.S. Customs agents to help penetrate the organization of a Montreal underworld figure, Conrad Bouchard, who was suspected of preparing a major narcotics run from Europe into the United States.

Peroff, a former owner of a small charter airline that flew between Miami and the Bahamas, was brought to New York and supplied with tape recorders, special intelligence material, and a leased Lear Jet to fly around Bouchard and his men. Everything went smoothly until the end of June 1973, when Peroff alleged that Bouchard first mentioned a connection called Vesco who had lots of cash. And in early July 1973 Peroff recorded a number of conversations in which Bouchard allegedly

[2] "The Reasoner Report," produced by ABC News, broadcast of January 19, 1974.

said that Vesco or his friend LeBlanc would supply $300,000 needed
to finance the 100-kilogram transaction.

The plan called for Peroff to fly to San José and get the cash, fly to
Europe and meet Bouchard, pick up the heroin, and fly it back to
Canada, where clandestine entry of the merchandise into the United
States was to be arranged. After Peroff reported the Vesco connection
to the federal agents he said the Drug Enforcement Agency began to
balk. He was suddenly denied use of the plane and forced to make
impossible demands on Bouchard so that the deal collapsed.

Fearful now, Peroff decided to involve another federal agency. On
July 18, 1973, he phoned the White House and got through to one of
the lawyers handling Watergate matters, who simply stalled. After more
than a dozen calls back and forth between himself and the White House,
Peroff finally read out a statement to a member of the staff that took
Watergate-related calls. Four days later he was arrested at his hotel
in New York.

Peroff was released when his control agent intervened and after he
had consented to testify in Canada concerning Bouchard's counterfeit
operations, which, of course, blew his cover as a narcotics agent and
forced him into hiding.

Desperate to get someone to listen to his Vesco story, Peroff finally
contacted investigators for the Senate Permanent Investigations Subcommittee in October 1973. They apparently were able to confirm many
of Peroff's allegations. Peroff's story was subsequently leaked to the
New York Times and the *Washington Post* by "informed sources" at
the end of November 1973. It caused a sensation, and Vesco lost no
time issuing a statement through a Nassau public relations agency claiming it was a "foul and sneaking lie." Vesco, something of an expert on
foul and sneaking lies, charged the U.S. government with launching
the Peroff balloon in an attempt to influence Judge Osabeday's decision
in the extradition hearings.

Vesco used the opportunity to deny that he was a fugitive from
justice despite the four warrants then outstanding against him. He said
he had never been served with a criminal warrant in the United States,
which on the face of it of course was true, that he had not fled the
United States illegally, which also was neither contested nor relevant,
and that he had "answered in court any charge brought against me in
any country in which I reside." Since to all intents and purposes he
owned the powers that governed in the two countries where he did
reside, this piece of misinformation was not contested either.

Moreover, Judge Osabeday's denial of the U.S. extradition request
proved once again the effectiveness of the Bahamas as Vesco's first

line of defense. It no doubt left both Vesco and LeBlanc feeling fairly
cocky.

LeBlanc and his Bahamian corporations had not bothered to defend
themselves against the SEC fraud charges in the New York court action,
and in June 1973 Judge Stewart handed down a default judgment
ordering the compulsory liquidation of Bahamas Commonwealth Bank,
Value Capital Limited, International Bancorp Limited, Global Holdings
Limited and Global Financial Limited.

Judge Stewart's default order named a New York accountant, John K.
Schemmer, as special receiver for the LeBlanc companies and requested
Schemmer to seek the cooperation of the Bahamian courts in initiating
bankruptcy proceeding. But the Bahamas Supreme Court refused to
accept Judge Stewart's default order and denied a motion by Schemmer
to proceed with a forced winding-up of the defaulting defendants. Thus
a reprieve from the liquidator's hammer was handed to the corporate
light cavalry of the Vesco-LeBlanc forces.

Schemmer was stymied. LeBlanc and Vesco were momentarily
triumphant. However, Schemmer bounced back in March 1974 with a
shareholder's petition to place Value Capital in liquidation, which this
time the court accepted.

But at best Super Group's legal maneuverings in the Bahamas represented a rear-guard action. A full-scale criminal investigation into the
IOS debacle had been called for by the Canadian judicial authorities,
and legally appointed Canadian liquidators armed with winding-up
petitions were preparing their assault on Nassau with the intention of
padlocking the doors of Bahamas Commonwealth Bank, dismantling
the dividend companies, and unwinding PRL.

Still a step ahead of his adversaries on the game board, though, Vesco
increasingly turned to Panama City as a center for his financial dealings,
and in late 1973 the flow of Super Group money to Panamanian banks
quickened considerably. Better secrecy provisions made it easier to
hide away cash and assets in Panama, and a properly planned holding
action there could probably stall the liquidators indefinitely. Also it was
closer to San José, Vesco's next to last retreat.

And as far as members of the Costa Rican National Liberation
argolla were concerned, Vesco's presence in their "American Arcadia"
was a welcome development. Just how welcome was best expressed by
Marti Figueres, the managing director of San Cristobal S.A. "We feel,"
said Figueres of Vesco's investments in Costa Rica, "that this is the
beginning of justice for developing nations."

Epilogue

The complex process of liquidating IOS begins, while Vesco and his inner circle of co-conspirators look forward to dividing up the spoils

On November 5, 1973, insolvent IOS Ltd., a federally chartered nonresident Canadian corporation, was ordered into liquidation under the Winding Up Act of Canada by order of Mr. Justice David M. Dickson of the Supreme Court of New Brunswick.

The once-mighty offshore giant was "utterly incapable of continuing any sort of business," noted Judge Dickson in his toughly worded decision that made legal history in Canada, and "no legitimate bank in the world will now permit IOS or its subsidiaries to maintain even a trading account."

Dickson's seven pages of findings detailed how the company had fallen into a state of "complete and irrevocable disarray and impotency." But lest it be felt that further reasons were required to support his ruling in favor of a forced winding-up, Dickson filled six more pages with additional facts:

• While the shareholders of Kilmorey contended that IOS was solvent, in the absence of any concrete evidence in support of this contention Dickson accepted the accounting contained in the August 2, 1973, treasurer's report, which showed the company to be bankrupt; IOS's estimated deficiency as of June 30, 1973, was in excess of $9 million.
• There existed "ample evidence" that the capital of the company was impaired, a prosecutable offense under the Canada Corporations Act.
• No annual meeting was held, or even proposed, during 1973; no audited financial statements were produced since the publication of the December 31, 1971, accounts.

• The company had no income, nor could it find a qualified auditor willing to serve.

• All of the securities and corporate regulatory bodies in the more important jurisdictions had blacklisted the company. "The present applications have been sponsored by a number of governments in a concerted effort to save what can be saved of the remaining assets . . . for those legitimately entitled to them and to destroy the capacity of the company and its dominating interests to continue what could only be considered the same monstrous practices they have conducted in the past."

• During the first six months of 1973 the company was obliged to meet, in ever accelerating demand, legal fees amounting to some $1.4 million. "There can be no suggestion that the trend would be reversed should the company continue in operation."

• There existed "a most dire and urgent necessity" for an immediate investigation of numerous non-arm's-length transactions between certain of the principals or former principals of the company.

• The company failed to produce its minute books and corporate records. These it claimed were impounded in Charlotte House under "a landlord's lien for rent."

• The New Brunswick hearings probably represented "the only occasion in the history of winding up litigation [in Canada] in which a resisting management group has failed to call a single witness of substance to answer the allegations of an applicant and to endeavour to show in some positive and detailed fashion the justification for continuance of a company's operations and the prospect of benefits which might thereby result for the shareholders and the creditors."

Judge Dickson appointed the Clarkson Company Limited, a Canadian firm of chartered accountants specializing in liquidation work, as official agents in the compulsory winding-up of IOS Ltd. Clarkson had already been appointed by the Public Trustee of Ontario as liquidators of Transglobal.

Clarkson put a team of a dozen auditors and five senior partners on the case. They estimated two years of detective work was required to unravel the corporate maze that Cowett created and Vesco refined for the express purpose of baffling international jurists and keeping enforcement agencies in constant confusion.

One of the Clarkson partners, Victor Barnett, reckoned that ten years or more would be needed before the last nails were hammered into the IOS coffin the wrongdoers apprehended, and the final accounts settled. It was, Barnett agreed, easily the most complex liquidation proceeding ever undertaken anywhere in the world. Already laws were being revised in many jurisdictions, and the Canada Corporations Act strengthened, so that another IOS could not arise.

The complexities of IOS also baffled the Swiss, noted for their banking prowess, and illustrated how ill equipped Swiss justice was to cope with transnational financial scandals. Judge Weber resigned from the case in midstream and was appointed to a lower court bench, only to be replaced by a third examining magistrate, Judge Roger Mock, who was not a specialist in securities fraud, had no budget and no staff to help him, and could only devote one day a week to studying the eighty dossiers of evidence inherited from his predecessor.

"It seems clear even now that local legislation on a country-by-country basis will not adequately deal with the problem of transnational securities markets," former SEC chairman William Casey stated at a 1972 International Meeting on Stock Exchanges in Milan, Italy. His statement seemed, in the light of what Vesco would later accomplish, almost prophetic.

"What will be needed will be a larger, more global approach . . . a type of multinational securities commission," Casey said.

The testimony of Philip R. Manuel, a veteran investigator for the U.S. Senate Permanent Subcommittee on Investigations, at the subcommittee's September 1973 hearings, again reflected this thinking. Manuel told the subcommittee that a burgeoning group of international swindlers had become so practiced at their art that they were able to move "with a minimum fear of legal or government restraint despite the fact that most of the individuals so engaged have been cited by various government agencies for their fraudulent activities. This group has conceived and has applied sophisticated corporate principles to the age-old art of swindling. Their forte is that they know 'how to use bad paper' and, in so doing, are limited only by their own ingenuity."

Among the factors that worked to the advantage of this growing breed of white-collar criminal, Manuel cited "the obvious expansion in the internationalization of banking, commerce, and finance, which has brought with it an increasing dependence on the so-called paper credit philosophy"; and the "existence of certain foreign or remote offshore jurisdictions where bank secrecy laws or complete lack of adequate governmental control in the banking, insurance, and brokerage fields makes it difficult, if not impossible, to analyze corporate ownership, structure, and financing."

But the key to the new generation of securities frauds, Manuel emphasized, was "the fact that the swindler is not limited to any boundary. Therefore, the regional, national, and international scope of the operations has precluded any single jurisdiction from effectively detecting and curtailing these crimes.

"With the modern speed and effectiveness of both transportation and communications, the swindlers can, for example, live in Fort Lauderdale, headquarter their companies in the Bahamas, place their assets in Switzerland or Panama, and victimize persons anywhere else in the world."

Vesco feasted upon the internationalization of banking and, despite court orders impounding, sequestering, grounding, or otherwise disposing of his corporate jets, possessed the mobility to exploit the lack of sophistication in smaller nations whose financial markets he could manipulate. While Vesco played the role of financial godfather to puppet presidents or prime ministers, Judge Stewart in New York delayed in handing down a written decision in the SEC civil fraud proceedings.

In September 1973, Judge Stewart announced that the SEC had shown in the preliminary hearings that "there were acts which occurred in this country which were fraudulent in nature." He said he would issue injunctions against Vesco, Meissner, Strickler, Graze, Weymar, and Straub, in addition to LeBlanc and the other defaulting defendants. But almost a year later, by July 1974, Stewart still had not come down with his written findings. He had signed, however, final consent orders against Fund of Funds and IOS Growth Fund. The charters of both investment companies by then had been revoked by the Ontario government, and they were in the process of liquidation. FOF claimed assets of $97 million and IOS Growth another $7 million.

IIT's registration was withdrawn by the Luxembourg Banking Commissioner, and the fund, with assets of $215.8 million, was placed in forced liquidation. A Curaçao court ordered Venture International, with assets of $38.4 million, into liquidation and appointed a Willemstad chartered accountant and lawyer as receivers. Fund of Funds Sterling was likewise put into liquidation.

By mid-1974 the Vesco forces were in full retreat. Investment Properties International was ordered into compulsory liquidation by the Supreme Court of Ontario. Liquidation petitions were filed in the Bahamas and Britain against Value Capital Limited, Property Resources Limited, and Fairborn Corporation, which had taken over the assets of Lewis-Oakes Limited from Allan and Shirley Butler and then reneged on its obligations.

The Canadian liquidators of Fund of Funds brought two civil fraud actions in New York. The first was a $60 million claim against Vesco, Meissner, LeBlanc, Allan Conwill, Conwill's New York law firm of Willkie Farr & Gallagher, and the Bank of New York; the second, a $120 million suit against John King and his former chief executive officer at King Resources Company, Roland Boucher, the estate of Edward

Cowett, Allan Conwill, Willkie Farr & Gallagher, and Bank of New York, for allegedly conspiring to defraud FOF in the purchase of natural resources properties.

Both complaints charged that Conwill, as legal counsel and a director of FOF, had failed to perform his professional functions in good faith, and that Willkie Farr & Gallagher had been negligent in protecting the rights of the investors. These allegations were vehemently denied.

The liquidators also alleged that the Bank of New York had recklessly and knowingly breached its fiduciary obligations by permitting the transfer of fund moneys to Overseas Development Bank in Luxembourg without alerting the authorities to what was going on, and in failing to safeguard the interests of the fundholders. BoNY said the charges were without foundation.

When the Super Group generals belatedly realized they were being outflanked on the legal front, they had LeBlanc flood the clients with public relations material advising of "the dangers inherent in the appointment of a multiplicity of receivers throughout the world," which LeBlanc piously noted "must result in a chaotic tangle of administrative red tape."

Claiming to be "deeply and gravely concerned," which no doubt he was, since without the fund-holders' assets to shift around his livelihood hardly was assured, LeBlanc requested all investors to return-mail a card with their name, address, and program investment number clearly indicated on it, to signify their support of management. The message was clear: IOS fund-holders, place your trust in Norman LeBlanc, and you just might end up owning a tiny part of the Costa Rican water works, without voting rights of course, or share in the benefits of a $600,000 investment in a Dominican hog farm managed by Dangerous Don Nixon and a young relative of President Balaguer.

For the first time in two years, IOS clients must have felt loved. They received a sudden deluge of material from a management that previously scoffed at their existence. Shortly after LeBlanc's notice informing the program-holders how he was "protecting" their investments, a circular letter addressed by computer and mailed from Nassau notified the same program-holders that a newly formed IOS Programholders Association had hired independent counsel, contacted "management" of IOS Investment Program Limited, (an all but forgotten empty corporate shell with a net worth of $2,800), and reviewed favorably LeBlanc's proposal for the appointment of the Program as official receiver for the funds to supersede the unwanted liquidators from Canada, Luxembourg, Britain, the United States, and the Netherlands Antilles.

The IOS Programholders Association, not to be confused with the German Shareholders Defense Association, was supposedly formed by

"Latin American interests" who wanted their investments kept outside their country of residence. In their general mailing to other IOS fund-holders they requested that each client assign his or her rights of representation over to the Programholders Association with the assurance that it would cost not a penny in legal fees. A good Samaritan in that den of thieves just didn't seem likely. Even the Bahamian courts agreed this time.

However, Vesco's greatest disappointment came in June 1974, when the Bahamian Monetary Authority (since renamed The Bahamas Central Bank) closed Bahamas Commonwealth Bank. The decision to revoke BCB's license was taken by Finance Minister Hanna—whom LeBlanc once boasted he had in his pocket—"on grounds that the licensee has been operating in a manner detrimental to the public's interest and to the interests of its depositors and other creditors." It followed the submission to the government of a confidential 160-page report about the bank's tangled affairs by the international accounting firm of Peat Marwick Mitchell & Company.

Earlier in the year a preliminary audit out of Geneva by The Clarkson Company showed that fallen IOS Ltd. had an excess of liabilities over assets of $13 million. This included a $9.7 million liability for repayment of the contested 1970 King Resources Company loan. It also included receivables from Super Group affiliates listed at $11.5 million, of which the liquidators estimated only $17,000 could be realized. All in all it appeared as if the creditors were out of pocket by $6.4 million and shareholders would receive nothing back on their investment.

A zero valuation! Remarkable. Here, then, was the first certified confirmation of the largest securities swindle of the century. And it implicated the old and new orders at IOS. Five years before, the company had placed a market valuation of $550 million on IOS's common and preferred stock, and now the Clarkson Company was saying it wasn't worth anything.

The situation was not quite as bleak for the shareholders of the four IOS dollar funds, but still hardly short of catastrophic. An initial reimbursement of some $200 million was expected by the interagency control committee in late 1974 or early 1975, with subsequent payments as the liquidators were successful in recovering the dispersed assets that lay buried around the world. Depending on when they invested and in which of the four funds, IOS clients could expect to recoup in the liquidation process anywhere between ten and forty cents per dollar invested.

The fund-holders' global losses through diversion of assets, conversion, overcharging, scalping, negligence, downright awful management, and admittedly poor market conditions amounted to another $550 million *grosso modo*. This was over and above what the authorities and the liquidators might have recovered.

The total IOS swindle, therefore, clearly qualified as unprecedented and gigantic: More than $1 billion in unprotected investments had evaporated or been diverted. In cash and hard assets, Vesco and his group accounted for the removal of at least $500 million—although, obviously, no exact accounting existed. Concerted action by the inter-agency committee resulted in three-fifths of the plundered assets being blocked. By all accounts, that left the Vesco group with between $200 million and $300 million secreted in offshore havens, in foreign banks, hidden trusts, and little-known Hong Kong trading companies.

As Super Group and its 254,000 captive clients headed into the second half of 1974, Vesco and his inner circle of associates were under increasingly heavy siege.

LeBlanc's influence, however, diminished after his resignations from the boards of Value Capital and International Bancorp at the end of 1973. Early in 1974 International Bancorp, minus Bahamas Commonwealth Bank, was "sold" on undisclosed terms by its parent, Global Holdings Limited, to Western Bank Corporation Limited, an Isle of Man registered company owned by Irishman John Martin Birrane, a relatively unknown forty-year-old busnessman whose varied interests included the Aphrodite Club, a million-dollar West End London nightspot and Kong Fat Company, a Far East investment concern involved in financing trade deals with Cuba.

Wanted by the Swiss, the object of intense interest at the U.S. Attorney's Office in New York, and also the target of a Royal Canadian Mounted Police investigation, LeBlanc's travel possibilities were fairly well limited to the Caribbean and a few friendly Central and South American republics.

Meissner was released from prison on $50,000 bail in March 1974 for "medical reasons." One of his lawyers procured a medical certificate questioning his sanity, and also he was said to be suffering from cancer. Meissner was served with a New York federal grand jury subpoena before leaving Luxembourg, which he ignored, traveling to Nassau instead. In April 1974 a warrant was issued in the United States for his arrest on a charge of criminal contempt.

Strickler, the subservient Swiss, was managing the Costa Rican end of the empire, an important assignment, since it was Super Group's major retrenchment base after the Bahamas. He and LeBlanc reportedly were constantly fighting. The target of a Swiss arrest warrant,

Strickler was not eager to return home. Nevertheless, he and his wife still looked forward to one day buying a small hotel somewhere peaceful with the money saved up during their travels with Super Group.

Graze's fortunes had risen, placing him in the number two-and-a-half position in the Vesco pecking order as a satellite of Straub. Graze had been elevated to the rank of director of Property Resources Limited but had suffered a minor heart attack in the interim and was concentrating on losing weight.

Beatty, an experienced chartered accountant possessed of an eternally worried countenance, departed from the inner ranks of the Vesco group after several heated disputes concerning LeBlanc's accounting methods. Beatty, who still resided in Smoke Rise, New Jersey, was spared in the first round of SEC litigation. As president of Global Natural Resources, with the assistance of strong counsel, he attempted to isolate the firm's assets from Vesco's rapacious regard. Ironically, Global Natural Resources of all the IOS orphans potentially was the most valuable investment property with its controversial holdings in the Canadian Arctic.

Clay was perhaps the saddest of the Super Group generals. He had had his differences with Vesco but still could not make the final break. Generally a cheerful, easygoing type, Clay was not enjoying life in exile. He was never able to live in his new Bernardsville home, purchased with the proceeds of a Bahamas Commonwealth Bank loan. Wanted for questioning by the U.S. Attorney's Office in New York, he was found in civil contempt of court for failing to heed a subpoena to testify before a Vesco grand jury sitting in New York.

Weymar, the international banker, ended his Super Group association a victim rather than a villain. He resigned as president of International Bancorp in January 1973 after numerous disputes with LeBlanc about the latter's business conduct.

Weymar claimed he was bamboozled by Vesco into believing that the Bank of America and Prudential were behind the Bootstrap Kid when Vesco moved into a control position at IOS. He paid for his 30 per cent stake in International Bancorp with $300,000 realized from the sale of his Butlers Bank stock and two "short-fused" credit notes for $900,000 and $600,000. When the $900,000 note fell due on June 30, 1972, Weymar defaulted. As a result the notes were transformed into demand notes that could be called by Vesco or LeBlanc at any time.

Weymar spent much of 1972 away from Nassau rescuing Bancorp's European operations from the ravages of Vesco's machinations, while back in the Bahamas strange events were occurring that he knew little or nothing about.

When LeBlanc failed to sign the letter of representation for Bancorp's 1971 audit, as he had assured the auditors he would, Weymar naturally refused to sign as well, even though president of the company.

"Norman," he confided, "is awfully quick with a pencil." His refusal to stand in for LeBlanc and opposition to aspects of the Vector contract (which nevertheless he helped execute) provoked LeBlanc into calling the two demand notes.

Weymar defaulted on the notes, resigned, and turned in his Bancorp stock. He accepted a salary settlement on the outstanding portion of his five-year employment contract and sold his Nassau residence, Brace Ridge Manor, to a company financed by Trident Bank.

Weymar, like all other members of the so-called Vesco group (with the exception of Beatty, who appeared on the witness stand but hid behind the Fifth Amendment), refused to testify in his own defense at the SEC trial in New York. Outside of what he said was a "deeply held conviction that the SEC had spent nine years and many millions of dollars to break IOS at the ultimate expense of hundreds of thousands of small investors," Weymar, European by birth (he reverted to German nationality), represented through his attorneys at the New York hearings that he was not in a position to betray the various statutes of the European countries in which International Bancorp owned banks by testifying in a U.S. federal court.

This led the SEC to conclude in its post-trial memorandum that, "although Weymar purportedly severed his ties with International Bancorp and Bahamas Commonwealth Bank in January 1973, well after the commencement of this lawsuit, the bona fides of that purported severence is completely open to question. This is particularly true because Weymar surrendered his thirty per cent stock interest in International Bancorp to the Vesco group when he could have used that control block of securities to halt the misuse by Bahamas Commonwealth Bank of the dollar funds' assets. . . . In short, [Weymar] had the means to put a halt to the dollar fund looting, but instead, even if one credits his own claim, chose the easy course of abject surrender to the Vesco group." [1]

Straub, the last member of the Vesco group, in effect became the first after Big Bobby himself, even though by his own admission he was incapable of reading a balance sheet. His physical appearance was described by an associate as resembling "an overfed ferret," with an underlying menace in his eyes. Straub reveled in his influential friendships—both F. Donald Nixon, father of Don-Don, and Edward C. Nixon were guests at his 1972 marriage in New York to his second

[1] SEC *v.* Robert L. Vesco *et al.,* SEC's Post-Trial Reply Memorandum, July 23, 1973, pp. 56–57.

wife. He joined most of the major Super Group boards in 1973 to keep a watchful eye on Nasty Norman, whose extravagance became a matter of concern to Vesco. Weymar found this last detail lightly amusing. He said it was like "placing the chief madam in New York City in charge of the vice squad to keep the girls off the street."

Straub was known to have one or two extravagances of his own. He recently had moved into the movie-producing business with Super Group's cash and was eagerly looking for clients. The first film boasting "G. Robert Straub" as its executive producer was titled *House of Horrors*.

With N11RV confiscated by court order, the *Patricia III* sequestered, the Connex Press Sabreliner attached in the compulsory winding up of Fairborn Corporation, and the Grumman G-2 repossessed by the Teamsters for nonpayment of charter fees, Vesco's problems had become logistical as well as extraditional. Running against him were four arrest warrants in the United States, one in Switzerland, and an immigration hold order in Canada, limiting his travel possibilities to Italy, perhaps, and a dozen Latin American republics—if he could get there.

For a while, Vesco and LeBlanc thought they had a solution to their logistical hang-ups.

In defiance of a Bahamian court order, LeBlanc had the six-year-old Sabreliner flown to San José, where he thought it would be safe. But six weeks later, in April 1974, the plane was "hijacked" by its own pilot and flown to the United States, where it was placed under protection of the court.

LeBlanc was indignant. "Connex Press," he said, "intends to take all legal steps, civil and criminal, to recover the aircraft." None was taken. The reason, no doubt, was that the year before Fairborn had sold the Sabreliner to LeBlanc at a depreciated book value and LeBlanc three months later sold it for $1 million to Property Resources Limited.

Similarly, in early 1974 Judge Stewart approved the sale of the aging 707 to Air Inter (Sales) Limited, a Bahamian company whose only shareholder appeared to be a Jamaican lawyer based in Nassau. Air Inter paid $400,000 in cash and $1 million in an IOU for the big jet and flew it back to Nassau. Unknown to the New York court, the up-front money on the N11RV repurchase was financed by a Panamanian corporation, Canceleres S.A. When Air Inter defaulted on its obligations to the Panamanian company, Canceleres seized the jet and moved it to Panama, with the intention of leasing it back to a Super Group shell for Vesco's personal use. Who owned Canceleres remained a mystery jealously guarded by Panamanian secrecy laws.

However, the New Jersey receiver of Fairfield General, the original owner of N11RV, now appeared on the scene with a new lien against the jet. In May 1974 the receiver sent Alwyn Eisenhauer with a flight crew down to Panama "to inspect the aircraft." Eisenhauer claimed he was owed $55,000 by Vesco for unpaid services. Acting in his capacity of aviation director for Fairfield General, unknown to Canceleres he provided a written application to the civil aviation authorities in Panama to fly the aircraft to Miami "for maintenance and inspection," paid the parking fees, then filed a "general declaration" for departure and was given clearance for takeoff. Eisenhauer returned the jet to Newark, where once again it was put up for sale.

Now, that stung Vesco deeply. He lashed out in a public statement, condemning the United States for a "complete breakdown" in its respect of international law and the private property rights of individuals. "These events . . . must make any thinking person deeply apprehensive about the level to which observance of the due process of law had descended in some so-called legal sections of the United States," he complained. Naturally, for someone who had bilked investors out of hundreds of millions of dollars, those were fervently spoken words.

"I anticipate that Panama [will] demand proper redress and suitable apologies to the victims of this violation of international law," he added. That Vesco was so irked about the matter suggested he was the principal victim and that therefore the United States government should address its apologies to him in person.

After all, if these acts of international piracy were permitted to continue, where would it all end?

It was Gil Straub who seemed to have the clearest answer. Straub, by then the target of a U.S. bench warrant for failure to appear before a federal grand jury, told one of the financial controllers of Super Group's banking operations, "I can see it all now. It's going to end in a small candle-lit room on a mountaintop in Haiti with the principal partners sitting around a table, knives drawn, dividing up what's left."

Appendixes

I. Reconciliation of IOS, Ltd. Consolidated Cash Flow
October 1, 1969 to December 31, 1969

		$ Millions	
Cash Position, October 1, 1969		$ 2.0	
Public Offering Proceeds:			
Primary Issue (Drexel)	$52.4		
Canadian Issue (Crang & Co.)	$13.8		
Bahamian Issue (I.O. Bank)[a]	$31.1	$ 97.3	
Less payments to tendering stockholders		(50.1)	$ 47.2
Extraordinary Cash Flow			
Cash Inflows:			
ILI (U.K.) partial repayment of loan	$ 1.5		
Cash Outflows:			
Funds for Beta and Foundation Equipment Ass.			
and Handley Page aircraft loans	(6.8)		
Takeover IPI deposits at I.O. Bank[a]			
(for Commonwealth United notes)	(6.5)		
Increase ODB[b] capitalization	(2.3)		
Repayment of loan to ILI (Lux)	(1.0)		
Increase ILI (Lux) capitalization	(0.9)		
IOS France (Ferney-Voltaire) improvements	(0.4)		
Advance to IOS of Canada Ltd.	(0.3)		
IOS Foundation	(0.2)		
Ferney loan—$180,000	(0.2)		
IOS Deutschland GmbH leasehold			
improvements	(0.2)		
Ferney school special contribution	(0.1)	$(17.4)	
Cash Flows from Operations			
IOS Management Limited dividends		$ 2.9	
Net Cash Flow of Gross Commissions Earned			
less Associates Commissions and general			
operating expenses		$(10.5)	
Cash Position December 31, 1969		$ 24.2	

[a] I.O. Bank = Investors Overseas Bank, Nassau.
[b] ODB = Overseas Development Bank, Geneva.
Source: IOS Accounting Department.

367

2. Harry Sears to John Mitchell, May 18, 1971

May 18, 1971

Hon. John N. Mitchell
U.S. Attorney General
Watergate East Apartments
2510 Virginia Avenue N.W.
Washington, D.C. 20037

Dear John:
I am sure I have mentioned in the past my friend Bob Vesco who is
Chairman of the Board of International Controls Corporation which
has taken active control of I.O.S. Ltd and you are probably generally
familiar with the background and some of the past travails of that
organization. Bob and ICC have sued the Securities and Exchange
Commission in the Federal Court here in New Jersey in an effort
to bring certain matters to a head which he feels are critical if justice
is to be done and his efforts to put I.O.S. back on an even keel are
to succeed. The purpose of this latter is not necessarily to ask any
intervention on your part but simply to make you aware of the reasons
why the suit against the SEC became necessary. It is best set forth
in Bob's letter to Mr. William Casey, Chairman of SEC, dated May
15th, a copy of which is enclosed with an explanatory excerpt from
the moving papers in the suit.
Frankly, Bob's concern is that the suit may be viewed out of context
by the administration. Basically he is trying to get past the staff level
to the chairman and apparently has been unable to do so to date. The
suit was kind of a last resort.
Bob is a good friend otherwise I would not trouble you with this information which as I said is for the sole purpose of insuring that there
can be no misunderstanding with regard to his motives and purposes.
For your political album I enclose a picture, one of many taken at the
dinner, which is still being talked about as the best political affair in
New Jersey. All of that is, of course, attributable to you and Martha
and Em joins me in sending you both our very best.

Sincerely,
[s] Harry Sears

3. José Figueres to Richard Nixon, July 22, 1972

July 22, 1972

Your Excellency Richard M. Nixon
President of the United States
The White House
1600 Pennsylvania Avenue
Washington, D.C.
U.S.A.

Dear President Nixon:

This letter is sent to you in the spirit of good relations which exist between our two countries.

Mr. Robert L. Vesco has been visiting Costa Rica with a view to helping us establish some new instruments of finance and economic development.

I am impressed by his ideas, his group of business leaders and the magnitude of the anticipated investments.

He may provide the ingredient that has been lacking in our plans to create, in the middle of the Western Hemisphere, a show piece of democratic development.

Mr. Vesco has had difficulties with the Securities and Exchange Commission, because of his past association with the I.O.S. Ltd. Mr. John Mitchell, your former Attorney General, is familiar with the matter.

I am concerned that any adverse publicity emanating from the S.E.C. against Mr. Vesco might jeopardize the development of my country. . . .

If we are apprised in time, we may take precautions to counter the adverse effects.

This matter is of importance to our two countries.

My son, Marti, recently met your brother, Edward, in New York, through Mr. Vesco. We understand that your brother has friends in San José, and we have extended to him an invitation to visit our country.

My wife, Karen, joins me in sending affectionate regards to Mrs. Nixon and yourself.

Sincerely,
[s] José Figueres

Index